To

From

Date

Streams in the Desert®

366 Daily Devotional Readings

L. B. Cowman

Edited by James Reimann

Requests for information should be addressed to:

Zondervan, 3900 Sparks Dr., SE, Grand Rapids, MI 49546

ISBN 978-0-310-35368-3

Cover design: Koechel Peterson & Associates
Interior design: James Phinney

Printed in the United States

---

21 22 23 / LSC / 23 22 21 20 19 18 17 16 15 14 13 12

Introduction to the Updated Edition

October 24, 1995, is a date I will never forget. I was called out of a business meeting with the terrifying news that my second-born son, Aaron, had just had a massive brain hemorrhage while away at school. After having won a scholarship to college and spending only six weeks there, he had been found in a park near the school, calling out for help. After a number of people ignored him, a "good Samaritan" finally stopped to help. She called 911—saving him from certain death. Aaron had emergency surgery to remove a blood clot that had grown to the size of a tennis ball.

Since then Aaron has undergone months of therapy and has gracefully endured numerous changes in his life. It is continuing to take much time and hard work, but he is determined to regain what he has lost. And when I look back on the past year, I am also reminded of a number of other changes and trials our family has endured. Yet as a result, each of us has seen the sovereign hand of God at work.

Two days after my son's surgery, Zondervan Publishing House tried to contact me to see if I would be interested in writing an updated edition of *Streams in the Desert*. They had no way of knowing that I was still sitting with my son in intensive care, and from the outset I have seen this timing as sovereign—not coincidental. As I have worked on this book God has ministered to me in a mighty way—meeting me at the point of my own personal need.

Streams in the Desert's enduring power is the result of the selections being firmly based on the truth of Scripture. As the editor of the updated edition, I have endeavored to maintain the beauty of the original without altering its meaning, giving it the same care I gave the updated edition of *My Utmost for His Highest*, which I edited several years ago.

For those of you familiar with both *Streams in the Desert* and *My Utmost for His Highest*, you may be interested in knowing something of the tie between these two best-selling daily devotional books of all time. Not only were they originally published during the same time period (*Streams* in 1925, and *My Utmost* in 1927), but L. B. Cowman, who compiled *Streams in the Desert*, and Oswald Chambers had ministered together. They met when Cowman and her husband were missionaries to Japan and Chambers traveled there to preach. Also, both were greatly influenced by Charles Spurgeon, the great English preacher of the late eighteen hundreds. Chambers came to a saving knowledge of Christ through the preaching of Spurgeon, and Cowman selected more of Spurgeon's writings for *Streams in the Desert* than those of any other person.

I trust you will enjoy reading *Streams in the Desert*. As mentioned before, God has ministered to me in a mighty way as I have worked on this book, and I would like to share one very special example.

One morning as I was reading the Scriptures and praying, all of the events of the past several months seemed to be crushing in on me. My family and I were dealing with a number of changes in our lives including the sale of a business we had owned for twenty years, my oldest son leaving home to join the navy, and Aaron leaving for college. All this was then followed by Aaron's brain hemorrhage and surgery. The next month my mother had to have emergency surgery and was hospitalized for thirty days, and my wife and daughter were in a car wreck and suffered whiplash.

As I reflected on all of this, I found myself complaining to the Lord about my circumstances and all of the things that seemed to be afflicting my family and me.

After I finished my prayer time, asking God to remove all my afflictions, I resumed my work on *Streams in the Desert.* To my amazement, especially since I was not in the best frame of mind, the next devotion I worked on was the one for February 19. You may want to turn to that one now to see how providentially it applied to my situation. The message of this devotion was exactly what I needed to hear and was a great encouragement to me that God certainly is not finished with me yet. And I could honestly say after working on that devotion that my heart was reopened to the words of Paul, who said, "I have learned to be content whatever the circumstances" (Philippians 4:11).

My prayer is that God would also minister to you through *Streams in the Desert* in a similar way. I know firsthand the power of Christ that lies within these pages, and the hope, encouragement, comfort, and strength that comes from His Word being applied to our hearts. I trust these insights into God's Word will be like "streams in the desert" to you during the difficult times of your life, for He has said, "Water will gush forth in the wilderness and streams in the desert" (Isaiah 35:6).

James Reimann
Editor

A Personal Word from L. B. Cowman

In the pathway of faith we come to learn that the Lord's thoughts are not our thoughts, nor His ways our ways. Both in the physical and spiritual realm, *great pressure means great power*! Although circumstances may bring us into the place of death, that need not spell disaster—for if we trust in the Lord and wait patiently, that simply provides the occasion for the display of His almighty power. "Remember his marvelous works that he hath done; his wonders, and the judgments of his mouth" (Psalm 105:5 KJV).

JANUARY 1

The land you are . . . to take possession of is a land of mountains and valleys that drinks rain from heaven. It is a land the LORD *your God cares for; the eyes of the* LORD *your God are continually on it from the beginning of the year to its end.*

DEUTERONOMY 11:11–12

TODAY WE STAND AT THE THRESHOLD OF THE UNKNOWN. BEFORE US lies a new year, and we are going forward to take possession of it. Who knows what we will find? What new experiences or changes will come our way? What new needs will arise? In spite of the uncertainty before us, we have a cheerful and comforting message from our heavenly Father: "The LORD your God cares for [it]; the eyes of the LORD . . . are continually on it from the beginning of the year to its end." The Lord is to be our Source of supply. In Him are springs, fountains, and streams that will never be cut off or run dry. To those who are anxious comes the gracious promise of our heavenly Father: if He is the Source of our mercies, mercy will never fail us. No heat or drought can dry the "river whose streams make glad the city of God" (Psalm 46:4). Yet the land we are to possess is a land of valleys and hills. It is not all flat or downhill. If life were always smooth and level, the boring sameness would weigh us down. We need the valleys *and* the hills. The hills collect the rain for hundreds of fruitful valleys. And so it is with us! It is the difficulty encountered on the hills that drives us to the throne of grace and brings the showers of blessing. Yes, it is the hills, the cold and seemingly barren hills of life that we question and complain about, that bring down the showers. How many people have perished in the wilderness valley, buried under its golden sand, who would have thrived in the hills? And how many would have been killed by the cold, destroyed or swept desolate of their fruitfulness by the wind, if not for the hills—stern, hard, rugged, and so steep to climb? God's hills are a gracious protection for His people against their foes! We cannot see what loss, sorrow, and trials are accomplishing. We need only to trust. The Father comes near to take our hand and lead us on our way today. It will be a good and blessed New Year!

He leads us on by paths we did not know;
Upward He leads us, though our steps be slow,
Though oft we faint and falter on the way,
Though storms and darkness oft obscure the day;
Yet when the clouds are gone,
We know He leads us on.

He leads us on through all the unquiet years;
Past all our dreamland hopes, and doubts and fears,
He guides our steps, through all the tangled maze
Of losses, sorrows, and o'er clouded days;
We know His will is done;
And still He leads us on.

NICHOLAUS LUDWIG ZINZENDORF

JANUARY 2

The side rooms all around the temple were wider at each successive level. The structure surrounding the temple was built in ascending stages, so that the rooms widened as one went upward. A stairway went up from the lowest floor to the top floor through the middle floor.

EZEKIEL 41:7

Still upward be your onward course:
For this I pray today;
Still upward as the years go by,
And seasons pass away.

Still upward in this coming year,
Your path is all untried;
Still upward may you journey on,
Close by your Savior's side.

Still upward although sorrow come,
And trials crush your heart;
Still upward may they draw your soul,
With Christ to walk apart.

Still upward till the day shall break,
And shadows all have flown;
Still upward till in Heaven you wake,
And stand before the throne.

We should never be content to rest in the mists of the valley when the summit of Mount Tabor awaits us. How pure is the dew of the hills, how fresh is the mountain air, how rich the food and drink of those who dwell above, whose windows look into the New Jerusalem! Many saints are content to live like people in coal mines, who never see the sun. Tears sadden their faces when they could be anointed with heavenly oil. I am convinced that many believers suffer in a dungeon when they could walk on a palace roof, viewing the lush landscape and Lebanon. Wake up, believers, from your lowly condition! Throw away your laziness, sluggishness, coldness, or whatever is interfering with your pure love for Christ. Make Him the Source, the Center, and the One who encompasses every delight of your soul. Refuse to be satisfied any longer with your meager accomplishments. Aspire to a higher, a nobler, and a fuller life. Upward to heaven! Nearer to God! Charles H. Spurgeon

I want to scale the utmost height,
And catch a gleam of glory bright;

But still I'll pray, till heaven I've found,
Lord, lead me on to higher ground!

Not many of us are living at our best. We linger in the lowlands because we are afraid to climb the mountains. The steepness and ruggedness discourage us, so we stay in the mist of the valleys and never learn the mystery of the hills. We do not know what is lost by our self-indulgence, what glory awaits if we only have the courage to climb, or what blessings we will find if we will only ascend the mountains of God! J. R. M.

Too low they build who build beneath the stars.

JANUARY 3

I [will] move along slowly at the pace of the flocks and herds before me and the pace of the children.
GENESIS 33:14

WHAT A BEAUTIFUL PICTURE OF JACOB'S THOUGHTFULNESS FOR THE cattle and the children! He would not allow them to be driven too hard for even one day. He would not lead them at a pace equal to what a strong man like Esau could keep or expected them to keep, but only one as fast as *they* were able to endure. He knew exactly how far they could go in a day, and he made that his only consideration in planning their travel. He had taken the same wilderness journey years before and knew from personal experience its roughness, heat, and distance. And so he said, "I will move along slowly, since you have never been this way before" (Joshua 3:4).

We "have never been this way before," but the Lord Jesus has. It is all untraveled and unknown ground to us, but He knows it all through personal experience. He knows the steep places that take our breath away, the rocky paths that make our feet ache, the hot and shadeless stretches that bring us to exhaustion, and the rushing rivers that we have to cross—Jesus has gone through it all before us. As John 4:6 shows, "Jesus, tired as he was from the journey, sat down." He was battered by every possible torrent, but all the floodwaters coming against Him never quenched His love. Jesus was made a perfect leader by the things He suffered. "He knows how we are formed, *he remembers that we are dust*" (Psalm 103:14). Think of that when you are tempted to question the gentleness of His leading. He *remembers* all the time and will never make you take even one step beyond what your feet are able to endure. Never mind if you think you are unable to take another step, for either He will strengthen you to make you able, or He will call a sudden halt, and you will not have to take it at all. Frances Ridley Havergal

In "pastures green"? Not always; sometimes He
Who knowest best, in kindness leadeth me
In weary ways, where heavy shadows be.
So, whether on the hilltops high and fair
I dwell, or in the sunless valleys, where
The shadows lie, what matter? He is there.

Barry

JANUARY 4

"Go," Jesus replied, "your son will live." The man took Jesus at his word and departed.

John 4:50

"Whatever you ask for in prayer, believe."

Mark 11:24

When you are confronted with a matter that requires immediate prayer, pray until you believe God—until with wholehearted sincerity you can thank Him for the answer. If you do not see the external answer immediately, do not pray for it in such a way that it is evident you are not definitely believing God for it. This type of prayer will be a hindrance instead of a help to you. And when you are finished praying, you will find that your faith has been weakened or has entirely gone. The urgency you felt to offer this kind of prayer is clearly from self and Satan. It may not be wrong to mention the matter to the Lord again, if He is keeping you waiting for His answer, but be sure to do so in a way that shows your faith.

Never pray in a way that diminishes your faith. You may tell Him you are waiting, still believing and therefore praising Him for the answer. There is nothing that so fully solidifies faith as being so sure of the answer that you can thank God for it. Prayers that empty us of faith deny both God's promises from His Word and the "Yes" that He whispered to our hearts. Such prayers are only the expression of the unrest of our hearts, and unrest implies unbelief that our prayers will be answered. "Now we who have believed enter that rest" (Hebrews 4:3).

The type of prayer that empties us of faith frequently arises from focusing our thoughts on the difficulty rather than on God's promise. Abraham, "without weakening in his faith . . . faced the fact that his body was as good as dead. . . . Yet he did not waver through unbelief regarding the promise of God, but was strengthened in his faith and gave glory to God" (Romans 4:19–20). May we "watch and pray so that [we] will not fall into [the] temptation" (Matthew 26:41) of praying faith-diminishing prayers. C. H. P.

Faith is not a sense, nor sight, nor reason, but simply taking God at His word. CHRISTMAS EVANS

The beginning of anxiety is the end of faith, and the beginning of true faith is the end of anxiety. GEORGE MUELLER

You will never learn faith in comfortable surroundings. God gives us His promises in a quiet hour, seals our covenants with great and gracious words, and then steps back, waiting to see how much we believe. He then allows the Tempter to come, and the ensuing test seems to contradict all that He has spoken. This is when faith wins its crown. This is the time to look up through the storm, and among the trembling, frightened sailors declare, "I have faith in God that it will happen just as he told me" (Acts 27:25).

Believe and trust; through stars and suns,
Through life and death, through soul and sense,
His wise, paternal purpose runs;
The darkness of His Providence
Is starlit with Divine intents.

JANUARY 5

Then Asa . . . said, "Lord, there is no one like you
to help the powerless against the mighty."
2 Chronicles 14:11

Remind God of His exclusive responsibility: "There is no one like you to help." The odds against Asa's men were enormous. "Zerah the Cushite marched out against them with an army of thousands upon thousands and three hundred chariots" (v. 9). It seemed impossible for Asa to hold his own against that vast multitude. There were no allies who would come to his defense. Therefore his only hope was in God.

It may be that your difficulties have come to such an alarming level that you may be compelled to refuse all human help. In lesser trials, you may have had that recourse, but now you must cast yourself on your almighty Friend. *Put God between yourself and the enemy.*

Asa, realizing his lack of strength, saw Jehovah as standing between the might of Zerah and himself. And he was not mistaken. We are told that the Cushites "were crushed before the Lord *and his forces*" (v. 13), as though heavenly warriors threw themselves against the enemy on Israel's behalf. God's forces so overwhelmed the vast army of the enemy that they fled. Then all Israel had to do was follow up and gather the plunder. Our

God is "the Lord of hosts" (Isaiah 10:16 KJV), who can summon unexpected reinforcements at any moment to help His people. Believe that He is between you and your difficulty, and what troubles you will flee before Him, as clouds in the wind. F. B. MEYER

When nothing on which to lean remains,
When strongholds crumble to dust;
When nothing is sure but that God still reigns,
That is just the time to trust.

It's better to walk by faith than sight,
In this path of yours and mine;
And the darkest night, when there's no outer light
Is the time for faith to shine.

"Abraham believed God" (Romans 4:3), and said to his eyes, "Stand back!" and to the laws of nature, "Hold your peace!" and to an unbelieving heart, "Silence, you lying tempter!" He simply "*believed* God." JOSEPH PARKER

JANUARY 6

"When you pass through the waters . . . they will not sweep over you."

ISAIAH 43:2

GOD DOES NOT OPEN PATHS FOR US BEFORE WE COME TO THEM, OR provide help before help is needed. He does not remove obstacles out of our way before we reach them. Yet when we are at our point of need, God's hand is outstretched.

Many people forget this truth and continually worry about difficulties they envision in the future. They expect God to open and clear many miles of road before them, but He promises to do it step by step, only as their need arises. You must be in the floodwaters before you can claim God's promise. Many people dread death and are distressed that they do not have "dying grace." Of course, they will never have the grace for death when they are in good health. Why should they have it while in the midst of life's duties, with death still far away? Living grace is what is needed for life's work and calling, and then dying grace when it is time to die. J. R. M.

"When you pass through the waters"
Deep the waves may be and cold,
But Jehovah is our refuge,
And His promise is our hold;
For the Lord Himself has said it,
He, the faithful God and true:
"When you come to the waters
You will not go down, but through."

Seas of sorrow, seas of trial,
Bitter anguish, fiercest pain,
Rolling surges of temptation
Sweeping over heart and brain—
They will never overflow us
For we know His word is true;
All His waves and all His billows
He will lead us safely through.

Threatening breakers of destruction,
Doubt's insidious undertow,
Will not sink us, will not drag us
Out to ocean depths of woe;
For His promise will sustain us,
Praise the Lord, whose Word is true!
We will not go down, or under,

For He says, "You will pass through."

Annie Johnson Flint

JANUARY 7

I have learned to be content whatever the circumstances.

Philippians 4:11

Paul, while being denied every comfort, wrote the above words from a dark prison cell.

A story is told of a king who went to his garden one morning, only to find everything withered and dying. He asked the oak tree that stood near the gate what the trouble was. The oak said it was tired of life and determined to die because it was not tall and beautiful like the pine tree. The pine was troubled because it could not bear grapes like the grapevine. The grapevine was determined to throw its life away because it could not stand erect and produce fruit as large as peaches. The geranium was fretting because it was not tall and fragrant like the lilac.

And so it went throughout the garden. Yet coming to a violet, the king found its face as bright and happy as ever and said, "Well, violet, I'm glad to find one brave little flower in the midst of this discouragement. You don't seem to be the least disheartened." The violet responded, "No, I'm not. I know I'm small, yet I thought if you wanted an oak or a pine or a peach tree or even a lilac, you would have planted one. Since I knew you wanted a violet, I'm determined to be the best little violet I can be."

Others may do a greater work,
But you have your part to do;
And no one in all God's family
Can do it as well as you.

People who are God's without reservation "have learned to be content whatever the circumstances." His will becomes their will, and they desire to do for Him whatever He desires them to do. They strip themselves of everything, and in their nakedness find everything restored a hundredfold.

JANUARY 8

"I will send down showers in season; there will be showers of blessing."
EZEKIEL 34:26

WHAT IS YOUR *season* TODAY? ARE YOU EXPERIENCING A SEASON OF drought? If so, then it is the season for showers. Are you going through a season of great heaviness with dark clouds? Then that too is the season for showers. "Your strength will equal your days" (Deuteronomy 33:25). "I will send . . . *showers* of blessing." Notice that the word *showers* is plural.

God will send all kinds of blessings. And all His blessings go together like links in a golden chain. If He gives you saving grace, He will also give you comforting grace. God will send "*showers* of blessings." Look up today, you who are dried and withered plants. Open your leaves and flowers and receive God's heavenly watering. CHARLES H. SPURGEON

Let but your heart become a valley low,
And God will rain on it till it will overflow.

You, O Lord, can transform my thorn into a flower. And I *do* want my thorn transformed into a flower. Job received sunshine after the rain, but was the rain all wasted? Job wants to know, and I want to know, if the rain is related to the sunshine. Only You can tell me—Your cross can tell me. You have crowned Your sorrow. Let this be my crown, O Lord. I will only triumph in You once I have learned the radiance of the rain. GEORGE MATHESON

The fruitful life seeks rain as well as sunshine.
The landscape, brown and dry beneath the sun,
Needs but the cloud to lift it into life;
The dews may dampen the tree and flower,
But it requires the cloud-distilled shower
To bring rich greenness to the lifeless life.
Ah, how like this, the landscape of a life:
Dews of trial fall like incense, rich and sweet;
But meaning little in the crystal tray—
Like moths of night, dews lift at break of day
And fleeting impressions leave, like lips that meet.
But clouds of trials, bearing burdens rare,
Leave in the soul, a moisture settled deep:
Life stirs by the powerful law of God;
And where before the thirsty camel trod,
There richest beauties to life's landscape leap.
Then read you in each cloud that comes to you
The words of Paul, in letters large and clear:
So will those clouds your soul with blessing feed,
And with a constant trust as you do read,
All things together work for good. Fret not, nor fear!

JANUARY 9

I consider that our present sufferings are not worth comparing with the glory that will be revealed in us.

Romans 8:18

I once kept a bottle-shaped cocoon of an emperor moth for nearly one year. The cocoon was very strange in its construction. The neck of the "bottle" had a narrow opening through which the mature insect forces its way. Therefore the abandoned cocoon is as perfect as one still inhabited, with no tearing of the interwoven fibers having taken place. The great disparity between the size of the opening and the size of the imprisoned insect makes a person wonder how the moth ever exits at all. Of course, it is never accomplished without great labor and difficulty. It is believed the pressure to which the moth's body is subjected when passing through such a narrow opening is nature's way of forcing fluids into the wings, since they are less developed at the time of emerging from the cocoon than in other insects.

I happened to witness the first efforts of my imprisoned moth to escape from its long confinement. All morning I watched it patiently striving and struggling to be free. It never seemed able to get beyond a certain point, and at last my patience was exhausted. The confining fibers were probably drier and less elastic than if the cocoon had been left all winter in its native habitat, as nature meant it to be. In any case, I thought I was wiser and more compassionate than its Maker, so I resolved to give it a helping hand. With the point of my scissors, I snipped the confining threads to make the exit just a little easier. Immediately and with perfect ease, my moth crawled out, dragging a huge swollen body and little shriveled wings! I watched in vain to see the marvelous process of expansion in which these wings would silently and swiftly develop before my eyes. As I examined the delicately beautiful spots and markings of various colors that were all there in miniature, I longed to see them assume their ultimate size. I looked for my moth, one of the loveliest of its kind, to appear in all its perfect beauty. But I looked in vain. My misplaced tenderness had proved to be its ruin. The moth suffered an aborted life, crawling painfully through its brief existence instead of flying through the air on rainbow wings.

I have thought of my moth often, especially when watching with tearful eyes those who were struggling with sorrow, suffering, and distress. My tendency would be to quickly alleviate the discipline and bring deliverance. O shortsighted person that I am! How do I know that one of these pains or groans should be relieved? The farsighted, perfect love that seeks the perfection of its object does not weakly shrink away from present, momentary suffering. Our Father's love is too steadfast to be weak. Because He loves His children, He "disciplines us . . . that we may share in his holiness" (Hebrews 12:10). With this glorious purpose in sight, He does not relieve our crying. Made perfect through suffering, as our Elder Brother was, we children of God are disciplined to make us obedient, and brought to glory through much tribulation. FROM A TRACT

JANUARY 10

Paul and his companions . . . [were] kept by the Holy Spirit from preaching the word in the province of Asia.

ACTS 16:6

IT IS INTERESTING TO STUDY THE WAY GOD EXTENDED HIS GUIDANCE TO these early messengers of the Cross. It consisted mainly in prohibiting their movement when they attempted to take a course other than the right one. When they wanted to turn to the left, toward Asia, He stopped them. When they sought to turn to the right, toward Bithynia in Asia Minor, He stopped them again. In his later years, Paul would do some of his greatest work in that very region, yet now the door was closed before him by the Holy Spirit. The time was not yet ripe for the attack on these apparently impregnable bastions of the kingdom of Satan. Apollos needed to go there first to lay the groundwork. Paul and Barnabas were needed more urgently elsewhere and required further training before undertaking this responsible task.

Beloved, whenever you are in doubt as to which way to turn, submit your judgment absolutely to the Spirit of God, asking Him to shut every door but the right one. Say to Him, "Blessed Spirit, I give to You the entire responsibility of closing every road and stopping every step that is not of God. Let me hear Your voice behind me whenever I 'turn aside to the right or to the left' [Deuteronomy 5:32]."

In the meantime, continue along the path you have already been traveling. Persist in your calling until you are clearly told to do something else. O traveler, the Spirit of Jesus is waiting to be to you what He was to Paul. Just be careful to obey even His smallest nudging or warning. Then after you have prayed the prayer of faith and there are no apparent hindrances, go forward with a confident heart. Do not be surprised if your answer comes in doors closing before you. But when doors are shut to the right and left, an open road is sure to lead to Troas. Luke waits for you there, and visions will point the way to where vast opportunities remain open, and faithful friends are waiting. F. B. MEYER

Is there some problem in your life to solve,
Some passage seeming full of mystery?
God knows, who brings the hidden things to light.
He keeps the key.

Is there some door closed by the Father's hand
Which widely opened you had hoped to see?
Trust God and wait—for when He shuts the door
He keeps the key.

Is there some earnest prayer unanswered yet,
Or answered not as you had thought 'twould be?
God will make clear His purpose by and by.
He keeps the key.

Have patience with your God, your patient God,
All wise, all knowing, no long lingerer He,
And of the door of all your future life
He keeps the key.

Unfailing comfort, sweet and blessed rest,
To know of every door He keeps the key.

That He at last when just he sees is best,
Will give it thee.
ANONYMOUS

JANUARY 11

Comfort, comfort my people, says your God.
ISAIAH 40:1

STORE UP COMFORT. THIS WAS THE PROPHET ISAIAH'S MISSION. THE world is full of hurting and comfortless hearts. But before you will be competent for this lofty ministry, you must be trained. And your training is extremely costly, for to make it complete, you too must endure the same afflictions that are wringing countless hearts of tears and blood. Consequently, your own life becomes the hospital ward where you are taught the divine art of comfort. You will be wounded so that in the binding up of your wounds by the Great Physician, you may learn how to render first aid to the wounded everywhere. Do you wonder why you are having to experience some great sorrow? Over the next ten years you will find many others afflicted in the same way. You will tell them how you suffered and were comforted. As the story unfolds, God will apply the anesthetic He once used on you to them. Then in the eager look followed by the gleam of hope that chases the shadow of despair from the soul, *you will know why* you were afflicted. And you will bless God for the discipline that filled your life with such a treasure of experience and helpfulness. SELECTED

God comforts us not to make us comfortable but to make us *comforters.* JOHN HENRY JOWETT

They tell me I must bruise
The rose's leaf,
Ere I can keep and use

Its fragrance brief.

They tell me I must break
The skylark's heart,
Ere her cage song will make
The silence start.

They tell me love must bleed,
And friendship weep,
Ere in my deepest need
I touch that deep.

Must it be always so
With precious things?
Must they be bruised and go
With beaten wings?

Ah, yes! by crushing days,
By caging nights, by scar
Of thorn and stony ways,
These blessings are!

JANUARY 12

Reckon it nothing but joy . . . whenever you find yourselves hedged in by the various trials. Be assured that the testing of your faith leads to power of endurance.

JAMES 1:2–3 WNT

GOD HEDGES IN HIS OWN IN ORDER TO PROTECT THEM. YET OFTEN they only see the wrong side of the hedge and therefore misunderstand His actions. And so it was with Job when he asked, "Why is life given to a man whose way is hidden, whom God has hedged in?" (Job 3:23). Ah, but Satan knew the value of that hedge! He challenged the Lord by saying, "Have you not put a hedge around [Job] and his household and everything he has?" (Job 1:10).

Onto the pages of every trial there are narrow shafts of light that shine. Thorns will not prick you until you lean against them, and not one will touch you without God knowing. The words that hurt you, the letter that caused you pain, the cruelty of your closest friend, your financial need—they are all known to Him. He sympathizes as no one else can and watches to see if, through it all, you will dare to trust Him completely.

The hawthorn hedge that keeps us from intruding,
Looks very fierce and bare
When stripped by winter, every branch protruding
Its thorns that would wound and tear.

But springtime comes; and like the rod that budded,
Each twig breaks out in green;
And cushions soft of tender leaves are studded,
Where spines alone were seen.

The sorrows, that to us seem so perplexing,
Are mercies kindly sent
To guard our wayward souls from sadder vexing,
And greater ills prevent.

To save us from the pit, no screen of roses
Would serve for our defense,
The hindrance that completely interposes
Stings back like thorny fence.

At first when smarting from the shock, complaining
Of wounds that freely bleed,

God's hedges of severity us paining,
May seem severe indeed.

But afterwards, God's blessed springtime cometh,
And bitter murmurs cease;
The sharp severity that pierced us bloometh,
And yields the fruits of peace.

Then let us sing, our guarded way thus wending
Life's hidden snares among,
Of mercy and of judgment sweetly blending;
Earth's sad, but lovely song.

JANUARY 13

In all these things we are more than conquerors
through him who loved us.
Romans 8:37

This is more than victory. This is a triumph so complete that we not only have escaped defeat and destruction but also have destroyed our enemies and won plunder so rich and valuable that we can actually thank God for the battle. How can we be "more than conquerors"? We can receive from the conflict a spiritual discipline that will greatly strengthen our faith and establish our spiritual character. Temptation is necessary to establish and ground us in our spiritual life. It is like the fierce winds that cause the mighty cedars on the mountainside to sink their roots more deeply into the soil. Our spiritual conflicts are among our most wonderful blessings, and the Adversary is used to train us for his own ultimate defeat. The ancient Phrygians of Asia Minor had a legend that every time they conquered an enemy, they absorbed the physical strength of their victims and added to their own strength and bravery. And in truth, meeting temptation victoriously doubles our spiritual strength and weaponry. Therefore it is possible not only to defeat our enemy but also to capture him and make him fight in our ranks.

The prophet Isaiah tells of "fly[ing] upon the shoulders of the Philistines" (Isaiah 11:14 KJV). These Philistines were their deadly foes, but this passage suggests that they would be able not only to conquer the Philistines but also to ride on their backs to further triumphs. Just as a skilled sailor can use a head wind to carry him forward, by using its impelling power to follow a zigzag course, it is possible for us in our spiritual life, through the victorious grace of God, to turn completely around the things that seem most unfriendly and unfavorable. Then we will be able to say continually, "What has happened to me has actually served to advance the gospel" (Philippians 1:12). LIFE MORE ABUNDANTLY

Early sailors believed the coral-building animals instinctively built up the great reefs of the Atoll Islands in order to protect themselves in the inner waterway. He has shown these organisms can only live and thrive facing the open ocean in the highly oxygenated foam of the combative waves. It is commonly thought that a protected and easy life is the best way to live. Yet the lives of all the noblest and strongest people prove exactly the opposite and that the endurance of hardship is the making of the person. It is the factor that distinguishes between merely existing and living a vigorous life. Hardship builds character. SELECTED

But thanks be to God, who always leads us in triumphal procession in Christ and through us spreads everywhere the fragrance of the knowledge of him (2 Corinthians 2:14).

JANUARY 14

When he has brought out all his own, he goes on ahead of them.

JOHN 10:4

This is intensely difficult work for Him and us—it is difficult for us to go, but equally difficult for Him to cause us pain. Yet it must be done. It would not be in our best interest to always remain in one happy and comfortable location. Therefore He moves us forward. The shepherd leaves the fold so the sheep will move on to the vitalizing mountain slopes. In the same way, laborers must be driven out into the harvest, or else the golden grain would spoil.

But take heart! It could never be better to stay once He determines otherwise; if the loving hand of our Lord moves us forward, it must be best. Forward, in His name, to green pastures, quiet waters, and mountain heights! (Psalm 23:2). *"He goes on ahead of [us]."* So whatever awaits us is encountered first by Him, and the eye of faith can always discern His majestic presence out in front. When His presence cannot be seen, it is dangerous to move ahead. Comfort your heart with the fact that the Savior has Himself experienced all the trials He asks you to endure; He would not ask you to pass through them unless he was sure that the paths were not too difficult or strenuous for you.

This is the blessed life—not anxious to see far down the road nor overly concerned about the next step, not eager to choose the path nor weighted down with the heavy responsibilities of the future, but quietly following the Shepherd, *one step at a time.*

Dark is the sky! and veiled the unknown morrow!
Dark is life's way, for night is not yet o'er;
The longed-for glimpse I may not meanwhile borrow;
But, this I know and trust, he goes before.

Dangers are near! and fears my mind are shaking;
Heart seems to dread what life may hold in store;
But I am His—He knows the way I'm taking,
More blessed even still—he goes before.

Doubts cast their weird, unwelcome shadows o'er me,
Doubts that life's best—life's choicest things are o'er;
What but His Word can strengthen, can restore me,
And this blest fact; that still he goes before.

He goes before! Be this my consolation!
He goes before! On this my heart would dwell!
He goes before! This guarantees salvation!
He goes before! And therefore all is well.

J. Danson Smith

The oriental shepherd always walked *ahead* of his sheep. He was always *out in front*. Any attack upon the sheep had to take him into account first. Now God is out in front. He is in our tomorrows, and it is tomorrow that fills people with fear. *Yet God is already there.* All the tomorrows of our life have to pass through Him before they can get to us. F. B. Meyer

God is in every tomorrow,
Therefore I live for today,
Certain of finding at sunrise,
Guidance and strength for my way;
Power for each moment of weakness,
Hope for each moment of pain,
Comfort for every sorrow,
Sunshine and joy after rain.

JANUARY 15

That night the Lord appeared to [Isaac].

Genesis 26:24

It was the same night Isaac went to Beersheba. Do you think this revelation from God was an accident? Do you think the *time* of it was an accident? Do you believe it could have happened any other night as well as this one? If so, you are grievously mistaken. Why did it come to Isaac the night he reached Beersheba? Because that was the night he reached *rest*. In his old land he had been tormented. There had been a whole series of petty quarrels over the ownership of insignificant wells. There is nothing like *little* worries, particularly when there are many of them. Because of these little worries, even after the strife was over, the place held bad memories for Isaac. Therefore he was determined to leave and seek a change of scenery. He pitched his tent far away from the place of his former strife. That very night the revelation came. God spoke to him when there was no inner storm. He could not speak to Isaac when his mind was troubled. God's voice demands the silence of the soul. Only in the *quiet* of the spirit could Isaac hear the garments of his God brush by him. His *still* night became his *shining* night.

My soul, have you pondered these words: "Be still, and know" (Psalm 46:10)? In the hour of distress, you cannot hear the answer to your prayers. How often has the answer seemed to come much later! The heart heard no reply during the moment of its crying, its thunder, its earthquake, and its fire. But once the crying stopped, once the stillness came, once your hand refrained from knocking on the iron gate, and once concern for *other* lives broke through the tragedy of your own life, the long-awaited reply appeared. You must rest, O soul, to receive your heart's desire. Slow the beating of your heart over concerns for your personal care. Place the storm of your individual troubles on God's altar of everyday trials, and the same night, the Lord will appear to you. His rainbow will extend across the subsiding flood, and in your stillness you will hear the everlasting music.
George Matheson

Tread in solitude your pathway,
Quiet heart and undismayed.

You will know things strange, mysterious,
Which to you no voice has said.

While the crowd of petty hustlers
Grasps at vain and meager things,
You will see a great world rising
Where soft sacred music rings.

Leave the dusty road to others,
Spotless keep your soul and bright,
As the radiant ocean's surface
When the sun is taking flight.

From the German of V. Schoffel

JANUARY 16

A furious squall came up.
Mark 4:37

Some of life's storms—a great sorrow, a bitter disappointment, a crushing defeat—*suddenly* come upon us. Others may come *slowly*, appearing on the uneven edge of the horizon no larger than a person's hand. But trouble that seems so insignificant spreads until it covers the sky and overwhelms us.

Yet it is in the storm that God equips us for service. When God wants an oak tree, He plants it where the storms will shake it and the rains will beat down upon it. It is in the midnight battle with the elements that the oak develops its rugged fiber and becomes the king of the forest.

When God wants to make a person, He puts him into some storm. The history of humankind has always been rough and rugged. No one is complete until he has been out into the surge of the storm and has found the glorious fulfillment of the prayer "O God, take me, break me, make me."

A Frenchman painted a picture of universal genius. In his painting stand famous orators, philosophers, and martyrs, all of whom have achieved preeminence in various aspects of life. The remarkable fact about the picture is this: every person who is preeminent for his ability was first preeminent for suffering. In the foreground stands the figure of the man who was denied the Promised Land: Moses. Beside him, feeling his way, is blind Homer. Milton is there, blind and heartbroken. Then there is the form of One who towers above them all. What is His characteristic? His face is marred more than any other. The artist might have titled that great picture *The Storm*.

The beauties of nature come after the storm. The rugged beauty of the mountain is born in a storm, and the heroes of life are the storm-swept and battle-scarred.

You have been in the storms and swept by the raging winds. Have they left you broken, weary, and beaten in the valley, or have they lifted you to the sunlit summits of a richer, deeper, more abiding manhood or womanhood? Have they left you with more sympathy for the storm-swept and the battle-scarred? SELECTED

The wind that blows can never kill
The tree God plants;
It blows toward east, and then toward west,
The tender leaves have little rest,
But any wind that blows is best.
The tree that God plants

Strikes deeper root, grows higher still,
Spreads greater limbs, for God's good will
Meets all its wants.

There is no storm has power to blast
The tree God knows;
No thunderbolt, nor beating rain,

Nor lightning flash, nor hurricane;
When they are spent, it does remain,
The tree God knows,
Through every storm it still stands fast,
And from its first day to its last
Still fairer grows.
SELECTED

JANUARY 17

Daniel, servant of the living God, has your God, whom you serve continually, been able to rescue you?
DANIEL 6:20

WE FIND THE EXPRESSION "*the living God*" MANY TIMES IN THE Scriptures, and yet it is the very thing we are so prone to forget. We know it is written "*the living God,*" but in our daily life there is almost nothing we lose sight of as often as the fact that God is *the living God*. We forget that He is now exactly what He was three or four thousand years ago, that He has the same sovereign power, and that He extends the same gracious love toward those who love and serve Him. We overlook the fact that He will do for us now what He did thousands of years ago for others, simply because He is the unchanging, *living God*. What a great reason to confide in Him, and in our darkest moments to never lose sight of the fact that He *is* still, and ever will be, *the living God*!

Be assured, if you walk with Him, look to Him, and expect help from Him, He will never fail you. An older believer who has known the Lord for forty-four years wrote the following as an encouragement to you: "God has never failed me. Even in my greatest difficulties, heaviest trials, and deepest poverty and need, He has never failed me. Because I was enabled by God's grace to trust Him, He has always come to my aid. I delight in speaking well of His name." GEORGE MUELLER

Martin Luther, deep in thought and needing to grasp hidden strength during a time of danger and fear in his life, was seen tracing on the table with his finger the words, "He lives! He lives!" This is our hope for ourselves, His truth, and humankind. People come and go. Leaders, teachers, and philosophers speak and work for a season and then fall silent and powerless. He abides. They die but He lives. They are lights that glow yet are ultimately extinguished. But He is the true Light from which they draw their brightness, and He shines forevermore. ALEXANDER MACLAREN

"One day I came to know Dr. John Douglas Adam," wrote Charles Gallaudet Trumbull. "I learned he considered his greatest spiritual asset to be his *unwavering awareness of the actual presence of Jesus.* Nothing sustained him as much, he said, as the realization that Jesus was *always* actually present with him. This realization was totally independent of his own feelings, his worthiness, and his perceptions as to how Jesus would demonstrate His presence.

"Furthermore, he said Christ was the center of his thoughts. Whenever his mind was free from other matters, it would turn to Christ. Whenever he was alone, and no matter where he was, he would talk aloud to Christ as easily and as naturally as to any human friend. That is how very real Jesus' *actual presence* was to him."

JANUARY 18

Thanks be to God, who always leads us as captives in Christ's triumphal procession.

2 CORINTHIANS 2:14

GOD WINS HIS GREATEST VICTORIES THROUGH APPARENT DEFEATS. Very often the enemy seems to triumph for a season, and God allows it. But then He comes in and upsets the work of the enemy, overthrows the apparent victory, and as the Bible says, "frustrates the ways of the wicked" (Psalm 146:9). Consequently, He gives us a much greater victory than we would have known had He not allowed the enemy seemingly to triumph in the first place.

The story of the three Hebrew young men who were thrown into the fiery furnace is a familiar one. There was an apparent victory for the enemy. It *looked* as if the servants of the living God were going to suffer a terrible defeat. We have all been in situations where it seemed as though we were defeated, and the enemy rejoiced. We can only imagine what a complete defeat this appeared to be for Daniel's friends. They were thrown into the terrible flames while their enemies watched to see them burn. Yet the enemy was greatly astonished to see them walking around in the fire, enjoying themselves. Then King Nebuchadnezzar told them to come out of the fire. The enemy "crowded around them. They saw that the fire had not harmed their bodies, nor was a hair of their heads singed; their robes were not scorched, and there was no smell of fire on them . . . for no other god can save in this way" (Daniel 3:27, 29).

This apparent defeat resulted in a miraculous victory.

Suppose these three men had lost their faith and courage and had complained, saying, "*Why* didn't God keep us out of the furnace?" They would have been burned, and God would not have been glorified. If there is a great trial in your life today, do not acknowledge it as a *defeat*. Instead, continue by faith to claim the victory through Him who is able to make you "more than conquerors" (Romans 8:37), and a glorious victory will soon be apparent. May we learn that in all the difficult places God takes us, He is giving us opportunities to exercise our faith in Him that will bring about blessed results and greatly glorify His name. LIFE OF PRAISE

Defeat may serve as well as victory
To shake the soul and let the glory out.
When the great oak is straining in the wind,
The limbs drink in new beauty, and the trunk
Sends down a deeper root on the windward side.
Only the soul that knows the mighty grief
Can know the mighty rapture. Sorrows come
To stretch out spaces in the heart for joy.

JANUARY 19

Then Jesus told his disciples . . . that they should always pray and not give up.

LUKE 18:1

"OBSERVE THE ANT," THE GREAT ORIENTAL CONQUEROR TAMERLANE told his friends. In relating a story from his early life, he said, "I once was forced to take shelter from my enemies in a dilapidated building, where I sat alone for many hours. Wishing to divert my mind from my hopeless situation, I fixed my eyes on an ant carrying a kernel of corn larger than itself up a high wall. I counted its attempts to accomplish this feat. The corn fell sixty-nine times to the ground, but the insect *persevered.* The seventieth time it reached the top. The ant's accomplishment gave me courage for the moment, and I never forgot the lesson." THE KING'S BUSINESS

Prayer that uses previously unanswered prayers as an excuse for laziness has already ceased to be a prayer of faith. To someone who prays in faith, unanswered prayers are simply the evidence that the answer is *much closer.* From beginning to end, our Lord's lessons and examples teach us that prayer that is not steadfast and persistent, nor revived and refreshed, and does not gather strength from previous prayers is not the prayer that will triumph. WILLIAM ARTHUR

Arthur Rubinstein, the great pianist, once said, "If I neglect practicing one day, I notice; two days, my friends notice; three days, the public notices." It is the old principle "*Practice makes perfect.*" We must continue believing, praying, and doing His will. In any of the arts, when the artist ceases to practice, we know the result. If we would only use the same level of common sense in our faith that we use in our everyday life, we would be moving on toward perfection.

David Livingstone's motto was, "I resolved never to stop until I had come to the goal and achieved my purpose." He was victorious through unwavering persistence and faith in God.

JANUARY 20

Frustration is better than laughter, because
a sad face is good for the heart.
ECCLESIASTES 7:3

SORROW, UNDER THE POWER OF DIVINE GRACE, PERFORMS VARIOUS ministries in our lives. Sorrow reveals unknown depths of the soul, and unknown capacities for suffering and service. Lighthearted, frivolous people are always shallow and are never aware of their own meagerness or lack of depth. Sorrow is God's tool to plow the depths of the soul, that it may yield richer harvests. If humankind were still in a glorified state, having never fallen, then the strong floods of divine joy would be the force God would use to reveal our souls' capacities. But in a fallen world, sorrow, yet with despair removed, is the power chosen to reveal us to ourselves. Accordingly, it is sorrow that causes us to take the time to think deeply and seriously.

Sorrow makes us move more slowly and considerately and examine our motives and attitudes. It opens within us the capacities of the heavenly life, and it makes us willing to set our capacities afloat on a limitless sea of service for God and for others.

Imagine a village of lazy people living at the foot of a great mountain range, yet who have never ventured out to explore the valleys and canyons back in the mountains. One day a great thunderstorm goes careening through the mountains, turning the hidden valleys into echoing trumpets and revealing their inner recesses, like the twisted shapes of a giant seashell. The villagers at the foot of the hills are astonished at the labyrinths and the unexplored recesses of a region so nearby and yet so unknown. And so it is with many people who casually live on the outer edge of their own souls until great thunderstorms of sorrow reveal hidden depths within, which were never before known or suspected.

God never uses anyone to a great degree until He breaks the person completely. Joseph experienced more sorrow than the other sons of Jacob, and it led him into a ministry of food for all the nations. For this reason, the Holy Spirit said of him, "Joseph is a fruitful vine . . . near a spring, whose branches climb over a wall" (Genesis 49:22). It takes sorrow to expand and deepen the soul. THE HEAVENLY LIFE

The dark brown soil is turned
By the sharp-pointed plow;
And I've a lesson learned.

My life is but a field,
Stretched out beneath God's sky,
Some harvest rich to yield.

Where grows the golden grain?
Where faith? Where sympathy?
In a furrow cut by pain.
MALTBIE D. BABCOCK

Every person and every nation must endure lessons in God's school of adversity. In the same way we say, "Blessed is the night, for it reveals the stars to us," we can say, "Blessed is sorrow, for it reveals God's comfort." A flood once washed away a poor man's home and mill, taking with it everything he owned in the world. He stood at the scene of his great loss, brokenhearted and discouraged. Yet after the waters had subsided, he saw something shining in the riverbanks that the flood had washed bare. "It looks like gold," he said. And it was gold. The storm that had impoverished him made him rich. So it is oftentimes in life. HENRY CLAY TRUMBULL

JANUARY 21

I consider my life worth nothing to me; my only aim is to finish the race and complete the task the Lord Jesus has given me.
ACTS 20:24

We read in 2 Samuel 5:17, "When the Philistines heard that David had been anointed king over Israel, they went up in full force to search for him." The moment we receive anything from the Lord worth fighting for, the Devil comes seeking to destroy us.

When the Enemy confronts us at the threshold of any great work for God, we should accept it as evidence of our salvation, and claim double the blessing, victory, and power. Power is developed through resistance. The force and the amount of damage created by an exploding artillery shell appear to be greater because of the resistance at the point of impact. A power plant produces additional electricity by using the friction of the rotating turbines. And one day, we too will understand that even Satan has been used as one of God's instruments of blessing. Days of Heaven upon Earth

A hero is not fed on sweets,
Daily his own heart he eats;
Chambers of the great are jails,
And head winds right for royal sails.
Ralph Waldo Emerson

Tribulation is the door to triumph. The valley leads to the open highway, and tribulation's imprint is on every great accomplishment. *Crowns are cast in crucibles*, and the chains of character found at the feet of God are forged in earthly flames. No one wins the greatest victory until he has walked the winepress of woe. With deep furrows of anguish on His brow, the "man of sorrows" (Isaiah 53:3 NASB) said, "In this world you will have trouble" (John 16:33). But immediately comes the psalm of promise, "Take heart! I have overcome the world."

The footprints are visible everywhere. The steps that lead to thrones are stained with spattered blood, and scars are the price for scepters. We will wrestle our crowns from the giants we conquer. It is no secret that grief has always fallen to people of greatness.

The mark of rank in nature
Is capacity for pain;
And the anguish of the singer
Makes the sweetest of the strain.

Tribulation has always marked the trail of the true reformer. It was true in the story of Paul, Luther, Savonarola, Knox, Wesley, and the rest of God's mighty army. They came through great tribulation to their point of power.

Every great book has been written with the author's blood. "These are they who have come out of the great tribulation" (Revelation 7:14). In spite of his blindness, wasn't Homer the unparalleled poet of the Greeks? And who wrote the timeless dream of *Pilgrim's Progress*? Was it a prince in royal robes seated on a couch of comfort and ease? No! The lingering splendor of John Bunyan's vision gilded the dingy walls of an old English jail in Bedford, while he, a princely prisoner and a glorious genius, made a faithful transcript of the scene.

Great is the easy conqueror;
Yet the one who is wounded sore,
Breathless, all covered o'er with blood and sweat,
Sinks fainting, but fighting evermore—
Is greater yet.

SELECTED

JANUARY 22

He withdrew . . . to a solitary place.

MATTHEW 14:13

THERE IS NO MUSIC DURING A MUSICAL REST, BUT THE REST IS PART OF the making of the music. In the melody of our life, the music is separated here and there by rests. During those rests, we foolishly believe we have come to the end of the song. God sends us times of forced leisure by allowing sickness, disappointed plans, and frustrated efforts. He brings a sudden pause in the choral hymn of our lives, and we lament that our voices must be silent. We grieve that our part is missing in the music that continually rises to the ear of our Creator. Yet how does a musician read the rest? He counts the break with unwavering precision and plays his next note with confidence, as if no pause were ever there.

God does not write the music of our lives without a plan. Our part is to learn the tune and not be discouraged during the rests. They are not to be slurred over or omitted, nor used to destroy the melody or to change the key. If we will only look up, God Himself will count the time for us. With our eyes on Him, our next note will be full and clear. If we sorrowfully say to ourselves, "There is no music in a rest," let us not forget that the rest is part of the making of the music. The process is often slow and painful in this life, yet how patiently God works to teach us! And how long He waits for us to learn the lesson! John Ruskin

Called aside—
From the glad working of your busy life,
From the world's ceaseless stir of care and strife,
Into the shade and stillness by your Heavenly Guide
For a brief time you have been called aside.
Called aside—
Perhaps into a desert garden dim;
And yet not alone, when you have been with Him,
And heard His voice in sweetest accents say:
"Child, will you not with Me this still hour stay?"
Called aside—
In hidden paths with Christ your Lord to tread,
Deeper to drink at the sweet Fountainhead,
Closer in fellowship with Him to roam,

Nearer, perhaps, to feel your Heavenly Home.
Called aside—
Oh, knowledge deeper grows with Him alone;
In secret oft His deeper love is shown,
And learned in many an hour of dark distress
Some rare, sweet lesson of His tenderness.
Called aside—
We thank You for the stillness and the shade;
We thank You for the hidden paths Your love has made,
And, so that we have wept and watched with Thee,
We thank You for our dark Gethsemane.
Called aside—
O restful thought—He doeth all things well;
O blessed sense, with Christ alone to dwell;
So in the shadow of Your cross to hide,
We thank You, Lord, to have been called aside.

JANUARY 23

Why, Lord, do you stand far off?
Psalm 10:1

"God is . . . an ever-present help in trouble" (Psalm 46:1). But He allows trouble to pursue us, as though He were indifferent to its overwhelming pressure, so we may be brought to the end of ourselves. Through the trial, we are led to discover the treasure of darkness and the immeasurable wealth of tribulation.

We may be sure that He who allows the suffering is with us throughout it. It may be that we will only see Him once the ordeal is nearly passed, but we must dare to believe that He never leaves our trial. Our eyes are blinded so we cannot see the One our soul loves. The darkness and our bandages blind us so that we cannot see the form of our High

Priest. Yet He is there and is deeply touched. Let us not rely on our feelings but trust in His unswerving faithfulness. And though we cannot see Him, let us talk to Him. Although His presence is veiled, once we begin to speak to Jesus as if He were literally present, an answering voice comes to show us He is in the shadow, keeping watch over His own. Your Father is as close to you when you journey through the darkest tunnel as He is when you are under the open heaven! Daily Devotional Commentary

Although the path be all unknown?
Although the way be drear?
Its shades I travel not alone
When steps of Yours are near.

JANUARY 24

But the dove could find no place to set its feet . . . so it returned to Noah in the ark. . . . He waited seven more days and again sent out the dove from the ark. When the dove returned to him in the evening, there in its beak was a freshly plucked olive leaf!
Genesis 8:9–11 WNT

God knows exactly when to withhold or to grant us any visible sign of encouragement. How wonderful it is when we will trust Him in either case! Yet it is better when all visible evidence that He is remembering us is withheld. He wants us to realize that His Word—His promise of remembering us—is more real and dependable than any evidence our senses may reveal. It is good when He sends the visible evidence, but we appreciate it even more after we have trusted Him without it. And those who are the most inclined to trust God without any evidence except His Word always receive the greatest amount of visible evidence of His love. Charles Gallaudet Trumbull

Believing Him; if storm clouds gather darkly 'round,
And even if the heavens seem hushed, without a sound?
He hears each prayer and even notes the sparrow's fall.

And praising Him; when sorrow, grief, and pain are near,
And even when we lose the thing that seems most dear?
Our loss is gain. Praise Him; in Him we have our All.

Our hand in His; e'en though the path seems long and drear
We scarcely see a step ahead, and almost fear?
He guides us right—this way and that, to keep us near.

And satisfied; when every path is blocked and bare,
And worldly things are gone and dead which were so fair?
Believe and rest and trust in Him, He comes to stay.

Delayed answers to prayers are not refusals. Many prayers are received and recorded, yet underneath are the words, "My time has not yet come." God has a fixed time and an ordained purpose, and He who controls the limits of our lives also determines the time of our deliverance. SELECTED

JANUARY 25

Your rod and your staff, they comfort me.
PSALM 23:4

AT MY FATHER'S HOUSE IN THE COUNTRY, THERE IS A LITTLE CLOSET near the chimney, where we keep the canes, or walking sticks, of several generations of our family. During my visits to the old house, as my father and I are going out for a walk, we often go to the cane closet and pick out our sticks to suit the occasion. As we have done this, I have frequently been reminded that the Word of God is a staff.

During the war, when we were experiencing a time of discouragement and impending danger, the verse "He will have no fear of bad news; his heart is steadfast, trusting in the LORD" (Psalm 112:7 WNT) was a staff to walk with on many dark days.

When our child died and we were left nearly brokenhearted, I found another staff in the promise: "Weeping may remain for a night, but rejoicing comes in the morning" (Psalm 30:5 WNT).

When I was forced to be away from home for a year due to poor health, not knowing if God would ever allow me to return to my home and work again, I chose this staff, which has never failed: "For I know the plans I have for you, . . . plans to prosper you and not to harm you, plans to give you hope and a future" (Jeremiah 29:11).

In times of impending danger or doubt, when human judgment seems to be of no value, I have found it easy to go forward with this staff: "In quietness and trust is your strength" (Isaiah 30:15). And in emergencies, when there has been no time for deliberation or for action, this staff has never failed me: "He that believeth shall not make haste" (Isaiah 28:16 KJV). BENJAMIN VAUGHAN ABBOTT

Martin Luther's wife said, "I would never have known the meaning of various psalms, come to appreciate certain difficulties, or known the inner workings of the soul; I would never have understood the practice of the Christian life and work, if God had never brought afflictions to my life." It is quite true that God's rod is like a schoolteacher's pointer to a child, pointing out a letter so the child will notice it. In this same way, God points out many valuable lessons to us that we otherwise would never have learned. SELECTED

God always sends His staff with His rod.

"Thy shoes shall be iron and brass; and as thy days, so shall thy strength be" (Deuteronomy 33:25 KJV).

Each of us may be sure that if God sends us over rocky paths, He will provide us with sturdy shoes. He will never send us on any journey without equipping us well. ALEXANDER MACLAREN

JANUARY 26

"I have begun to deliver. . . . Now begin to conquer and possess."

DEUTERONOMY 2:31

THE BIBLE HAS A GREAT DEAL TO SAY ABOUT WAITING FOR GOD, AND the teaching cannot be too strongly emphasized. We so easily become impatient with God's delays. Yet much of our trouble in life is the result of our restless, and sometimes reckless, haste.

We cannot *wait* for the fruit to ripen, but insist on picking it while it is still green. We cannot *wait* for the answers to our prayers, although it may take many years for the things we pray for to be prepared for us. We are encouraged to walk with God, but often God walks very slowly. Yet there is also another side to this teaching: *God often waits for us.*

Quite often we fail to receive the blessing He has ready for us because we are not moving forward with Him. While it is true we miss many blessings by not waiting for God, we also lose numerous blessings by *over-waiting.* There are times when it takes strength simply to sit still, but there are also times when we are to move forward with a confident step.

Many of God's promises are conditional, requiring some initial action on our part. Once we begin to obey, He will begin to bless us. Great things were promised to Abraham, but not one of them could have been obtained had he waited in Chaldea. He had to leave his home, friends, and country, travel unfamiliar paths, and press on in unwavering obedience in order to receive the promises. The ten lepers Jesus healed were told to show themselves to the priest, and "*as they went, they were cleansed*" (Luke 17:14). If they had waited to *see the cleansing* come to their bodies before leaving, they would never have seen it. God was waiting to heal them, and the moment their faith began to work, the blessing came.

When the Israelites were entrapped by Pharaoh's pursuing army at the Red Sea, they were commanded to "go forward" (Exodus 14:15 KJV). No longer was it their duty to wait, but to rise up from bended knees and "go forward" with heroic faith. Years later the Israelites were commanded to show their faith again by beginning their march over the Jordan while the river was at its highest point. They held the key to unlock the gate into the Land of Promise in their own hands, and the gate would not begin to turn on its hinges until they had approached and unlocked it. The key was faith.

We are destined to fight certain battles, and we think we can never be victorious and conquer our enemies. Yet as we enter the conflict, *One* comes who fights by our side. Through Him we are "more than conquerors" (Romans 8:37). If we had waited in fear and trembling for our Helper to come before we would enter the battle, we would have waited in vain. This would have been the *overwaiting* of unbelief. God is waiting to pour out His richest blessings on you. "Go forward" with bold confidence and take what is yours. "I have begun to deliver. . . . Now begin to conquer and possess." J. R. MILLER

JANUARY 27

Make you strong, firm and steadfast.

1 PETER 5:10

BEFORE WE CAN ESTABLISH A NEW AND DEEPER RELATIONSHIP WITH Christ, we must first acquire enough intellectual light to satisfy our mind that we have been given the right to stand in this new relationship. Even the shadow of a doubt here will destroy our confidence. Then, having seen the light, we must advance.

We must make our choice, commit to it, and take our rightful place as confidently as a tree is planted in the ground. As a bride entrusts herself to the groom at the marriage altar, our commitment to Christ must be once and for all, without reservation or reversal.

Then there follows a time of establishing and testing, during which we must stand still until the new relationship becomes so ingrained in us that it becomes a permanent habit. It is comparable to a surgeon setting a broken arm by splinting it to keep it from moving. God too has His spiritual splints He wants to put on His children to keep them quiet and still until they pass the first stage of faith. Sometimes the trial will be difficult, but "the God of all grace, who called you to his eternal glory in Christ, after you have suffered a little while, will himself restore you and make you strong, firm and steadfast" (1 Peter 5:10). A. B. SIMPSON

There is a natural law at work in sin and in sickness, and if we just drift along following the flow of our circumstances, we will sink under the power of the Tempter. But there is another law of spiritual and physical life in Christ Jesus to which we can rise, and through which we can counterbalance and overcome the natural law that weighs us down.

Doing this, however, requires real spiritual energy, a determined purpose, a sure stance, and the habit of faith. It is the same principle as a factory that uses electricity to run its machinery. The switch must be turned on and left in that position. The power is always available, but the proper connection must be made. And as long as that connection is intact, the power will enable all the machinery to stay in operation.

There is a spiritual law of choosing, believing, abiding, and remaining steadfast in our walk with God. This law is essential to the working of the Holy Spirit in our sanctification and in our healing. DAYS OF HEAVEN UPON EARTH

JANUARY 28

I am jealous for you with a godly jealousy.

2 CORINTHIANS 11:2

OH, HOW THE OLD HARPIST LOVES HIS HARP! HE CUDDLES AND caresses it, as if it were a child resting on his lap. His life is consumed with it. But watch how he tunes it. He grasps it firmly, striking a chord with a sharp, quick blow. While it quivers as if in pain, he leans forward, intently listening to catch the first note rising from it. Just as he feared, the note is distorted and shrill. He strains the string, turning the torturing thumbscrew, and though it seems ready to snap with the tension, he strikes it again. Then he leans forward again, carefully listening, until at last a smile appears on his face as the first melodic sound arises.

Perhaps this is how God is dealing with you. Loving you more than any harpist loves his harp, He finds you nothing but harsh, discordant sounds. He plucks your heartstrings with torturing anguish. Tenderly leaning over you, he strikes the strings and listens. Hearing only a harsh murmur, He strikes you again. His heart bleeds for you while He anxiously waits to hear the strain "Not my will, but yours be done" (Luke 22:42)—a melody as sweet to His ears as angels' songs. And He will never cease from striking the strings of your heart until your humbled and disciplined soul blends with all the pure and eternal harmonies of His own being. SELECTED

Oh, the sweetness that dwells in a harp of many strings,
While each, all vocal with love in a tuneful harmony rings!
But, oh, the wail and the discord, when one and another is rent,
Tensionless, broken and lost, from the cherished instrument.

For rapture of love is linked with the pain or fear of loss,
And the hand that takes the crown, must ache with many a cross;
Yet he who has never a conflict, wins never a victor's palm,
And only the toilers know the sweetness of rest and calm.

Only between the storms can the Alpine traveler know
Transcendent glory of clearness, marvels of gleam and glow;
Had he the brightness unbroken of cloudless summer days,
This had been dimmed by the dust and the veil of a brooding haze.

Who would dare the choice, neither or both to know,
The finest quiver of joy or the agony thrill of woe!
Never the exquisite pain, then never the exquisite bliss,
For the heart that is dull to that can never be strung to this.

JANUARY 29

God is in the midst of her, she will not be moved;
God will help her when morning dawns.
PSALM 46:5 NASB

"WILL NOT BE MOVED"—WHAT AN INSPIRING DECLARATION! IS IT possible for us who are so easily moved by earthly things to come to a point where nothing can upset us or disturb our peace? The answer is yes, and the apostle Paul knew it. When he was on his way to Jerusalem, the Holy Spirit warned him that "prison and hardships" (Acts 20:23) awaited him. Yet he could triumphantly say, "But none of these things move me" (Acts 20:24 KJV).

Everything in Paul's life and experience that could be disturbed had already been shaken, and he no longer considered his life or any of his possessions as having any earthly value. And if we will only let God have His way with us, we can come to the same point. Then, like Paul, neither the stress and strain of little things nor the great and heavy trials of life will have enough power to move us from "the peace of God, which transcends all understanding" (Philippians 4:7). God declares this peace to be the inheritance of those who have learned to rest only on Him.

"The one who is victorious I will make a pillar in the temple of my God. Never again will they leave it" (Revelation 3:12). Becoming as immovable as a pillar in the house of God is such a worthy objective that we would gladly endure all the necessary trials that take us there! HANNAH WHITALL SMITH

When God is the center of a kingdom or a city, He makes it strong "like Mount Zion, which cannot be shaken" (Psalm 125:1). And when God is the center of a soul, although disasters may crowd in on all sides and roar like the waves of the sea, there is a constant calm within. The world can neither give nor take away this kind of peace. What is it that causes people to shake like leaves today at the first hint of danger? It is simply the lack of God living in their soul, and having the world in their hearts instead. R. LEIGHTON

"*Those who trust in the* LORD *are like Mount Zion, which cannot be shaken but endures forever*" (Psalm 125:1). There is an old Scottish version of this psalm that strengthens our blood like iron:

Who clings to God in constant trust
As Zion's mount he stands full just,
And who moves not, nor yet does reel,
But stands forever strong as steel!

JANUARY 30

"I will be like the dew to Israel."
HOSEA 14:5

THE DEW IS A SOURCE OF FRESHNESS. IT IS NATURE'S PROVISION FOR renewing the face of the earth. It falls at night, and without it vegetation would die. It is this great renewal value of the dew that is so often recognized in the Scriptures and used as a symbol of spiritual refreshment. Just as nature is bathed in dew, the Lord renews His people. In Titus 3:5 the same thought of spiritual refreshment is connected with the ministry of the Holy Spirit and referred to as "renewal by the Holy Spirit."

Many Christian workers do not recognize the importance of the heavenly dew in their lives, and as a result lack freshness and energy. Their spirits are withered and droopy for lack of dew.

Beloved fellow worker, you recognize the folly of a laborer attempting to work all day without eating, but do you recognize the folly of a servant of God attempting to minister without eating of the heavenly manna? Neither is it sufficient to have spiritual nourishment only occasionally. Every day you must receive the "renewal by the Holy Spirit." You know the difference between your whole being pulsating with the energy and freshness of God's divine life or feeling worn-out and weary. Quietness and stillness bring the dew. At night when the leaves and grass are still, the plants' pores are open to receive the refreshing and invigorating bath. And

spiritual dew comes from quietly lingering in the Master's presence. Get still before Him, for haste will prevent you from receiving the dew. Wait before God until you feel saturated with His presence. Then move on to your next duty with the awareness of the freshness and energy of Christ.
DR. PARDINGTON

Dew will never appear while there is either heat or wind. The temperature must fall, the wind cease, and the air come to a point of coolness and rest—absolute rest—before the invisible particles of moisture will become dew to dampen any plant or flower. And the grace of God does not come forth to bring rest and renewal to our soul until we completely reach the *point of stillness* before Him.

Drop Your still dews of quietness,
Till all our strivings cease:
Take from our souls the strain and stress;
And let our ordered lives confess
The beauty of Your peace.
Breathe through the pulses of desire
Your coolness and Your balm;
Let sense be mum, its beats expire:
Speak through the earthquake, wind and fire,
O still small voice of calm!

JANUARY 31

He giveth quietness.
JOB 34:29 KJV

HE GIVES QUIETNESS IN THE MIDST OF THE RAGING STORM. AS WE SAIL the lake with Him, reaching deep water and far from land, suddenly, under the midnight sky, a mighty storm sweeps down. Earth and hell seem mobilized against us, and each wave threatens to overwhelm our boat. Then He rises from His sleep and rebukes the wind and the waves. He waves His hand, signaling the end of the raging tempest and the beginning of the restful calm. His voice is heard above the screaming of the wind through the ropes and rigging, and over the thrashing of the waves.

"Quiet! Be still!" (Mark 4:39). Can you not hear it? And instantly there is a great calm. "He giveth quietness"—*quietness even in the midst of losing our inner strength and comforts.* Sometimes He removes these because we make too much of them. We are tempted to look at our joys, pleasures, passions, or our dreams, with too much self-satisfaction. Then through His gracious love He withdraws them, leading us to distinguish between them and Himself. He draws near and whispers the assurance of His presence, bringing an infinite calm to keep our hearts and minds. "He giveth quietness."

"He giveth quietness." O Elder Brother,
Whose homeless feet have pressed our path of pain,
Whose hands have borne the burden of our sorrow,
That in our losses we might find our gain.

Of all Your gifts and infinite consolings,
I ask but this: in every troubled hour
To hear Your voice through all the tumults stealing,
And rest serene beneath its tranquil power.

Cares cannot fret me if my soul be dwelling
In the still air of faith's untroubled day;
Grief cannot shake me if I walk beside you,
My hand in Yours along the darkening way.

Content to know there comes a radiant morning
When from all shadows I will find release;
Serene to wait the rapture of its dawning—
Who can make trouble when You send me peace?

FEBRUARY 1

This is my doing.

1 Kings 12:24

The disappointments of life are simply the hidden appointments of love. C. A. Fox

My child, I have a message for you today. Let me whisper it in your ear so any storm clouds that may arise will shine with glory, and the rough places you may have to walk will be made smooth. It is only four words, but let them sink into your inner being, and use them as a pillow to rest your weary head. "*This is* my *doing.*"

Have you ever realized that whatever concerns you concerns Me too? "For whoever touches you touches the apple of [my] eye" (Zechariah 2:8). "You are precious and honored in my sight" (Isaiah 43:4). Therefore it is My special delight to teach you.

I want you to learn when temptations attack you, and the Enemy comes in "like a pent-up flood" (Isaiah 59:19), that "*this is* my *doing*" and that your weakness needs My strength, and your safety lies in letting Me fight for you.

Are you in difficult circumstances, surrounded by people who do not understand you, never ask your opinion, and always push you aside? "*This is* my *doing.*" I am the God of circumstances. You did not come to this place by accident—you are exactly where I meant for you to be.

Have you not asked Me to make you humble? Then see that I have placed you in the perfect school where this lesson is taught. Your circumstances and the people around you are only being used to accomplish My will.

Are you having problems with money, finding it hard to make ends meet? "*This is* my *doing,*" for I am the One who keeps your finances, and I want you to learn to depend upon Me. My supply is limitless and I "will meet all your needs" (Philippians 4:19). I want you to prove My promises so no one may say, "You did not trust in the Lord your God" (Deuteronomy 1:32).

Are you experiencing a time of sorrow? "*This is* my *doing*." I am "a man of suffering, and familiar with pain" (Isaiah 53:3). I have allowed your earthly comforters to fail you, so that by turning to Me you may receive "eternal encouragement and good hope" (2 Thessalonians 2:16). Have you longed to do some great work for Me but instead have been set aside on a bed of sickness and pain? "*This is* my *doing*." You were so busy I could not get your attention, and I wanted to teach you some of My deepest truths. "They also serve who only stand and wait." In fact, some of My greatest workers are those physically unable to serve, but who have learned to wield the powerful weapon of prayer.

Today I place a cup of holy oil in your hands. Use it freely, My child. Anoint with it every new circumstance, every word that hurts you, every interruption that makes you impatient, and every weakness you have. The pain will leave as you learn to see Me in all things. LAURA A. BARTER SNOW

"This is from Me," the Savior said,
As bending low He kissed my brow,
"For One who loves you thus has led.
Just rest in Me, be patient now,
Your Father knows you have need of this,
Though, why perhaps you cannot see—
Grieve not for things you've seemed to miss.
The thing I send is best for thee."

Then, looking through my tears, I plead,
"Dear Lord, forgive, I did not know,
It will not be hard since You do tread,
Each path before me here below."
And for my good this thing must be,
His grace sufficient for each test.
So still I'll sing, "Whatever be
God's way for me is always best."

FEBRUARY 2

In the shadow of his hand he hid me; he made me into a polished arrow and concealed me in his quiver.
ISAIAH 49:2

"IN THE SHADOW"—EACH OF US MUST GO THERE SOMETIMES. THE glare of the sunlight is too bright, and our eyes become injured. Soon they are unable to discern the subtle shades of color or appreciate neutral tints, such as the shadowed sickroom, the shadowed house of grief, or the shadowed life where the sunlight has departed.

But fear not! It is the shadow of God's hand. He is leading you, and there are lessons that can be learned only where He leads.

The photograph of His face can only be developed in the dark room. But do not assume that He has pushed you aside.

You are still "in his quiver." He has not thrown you away as something worthless.

He is only keeping you nearby till the moment comes when He can send you quickly and confidently on some mission that will bring Him glory. O shadowed, isolated one, remember how closely the quiver is tied to the warrior. It is always within easy reach of his hand and jealously protected. F. B. MEYER

In some realms of nature, shadows or darkness are the places of greatest growth. The beautiful Indian corn never grows more rapidly than in the darkness of a warm summer night. The sun withers and curls the leaves in the scorching light of noon, but once a cloud hides the sun, they quickly unfold. The shadows provide a service that the sunlight does not. The starry beauty of the sky cannot be seen at its peak until the shadows of night slip over the sky. Lands with fog, clouds, and shade are lush with greenery. And there are beautiful flowers that bloom in the shade that will never bloom in the sun. Florists now have their evening primrose as well as their morning glory. The evening primrose will not open in the noonday sun but only reveals its beauty as the shadows of the evening grow longer.

If all of life were sunshine,
Our face would long to gain
And feel once more upon it
The cooling splash of rain.
HENRY JACKSON VAN DYKE

FEBRUARY 3

At once the Spirit sent him out into the wilderness.
MARK 1:12

THIS SEEMED A STRANGE WAY FOR GOD TO PROVE HIS FAVOR. "AT once"—after what? After heaven was opened and the Spirit descended "like a dove" (v. 10), and the Father voiced His blessing, "You are my Son, whom I love; with you I am well pleased" (v. 11). Yet it is not an abnormal experience.

You, my soul, have also experienced it. Aren't your times of deepest depression the moments that immediately follow your loftiest highs? Just yesterday you were soaring high in the heavens and singing in the radiance of the morning. Today, however, your wings are folded and your song is silent. At noon you were basking in the sunshine of the Father's smile, but by evening you were saying from the wilderness, "My way is hidden from the LORD" (Isaiah 40:27).

No, my soul, the actual suddenness of the change is proof that it is not abnormal. Have you considered the comfort of the words "at once," and why the change comes so soon after the blessing? Simply to show that it is the sequel to the blessing. God shines His light on you to make you fit for life's deserts, Gethsemanes, and Calvaries. He lifts you to new heights to strengthen you so that you may go deeper still. He illuminates you so He may send you into the night, making you a help to the helpless.

You are not always worthy of the wilderness—you are only worthy of the wilderness after the splendor of the Jordan River experience. Nothing but the Son's vision can equip you to carry the Spirit's burden, and only the glory of the baptism can withstand the hunger of the desert. George Matheson

After blessings comes the battle.

The time of testing that distinguishes and greatly enriches a person's spiritual career is not an ordinary one but a period when it seems as if all hell were set loose. It is a time when we realize our soul is caught in a net, and we know God is allowing us to be gripped by the Devil's hand. Yet it is a period that always ends in certain triumph for those who have committed the keeping of their souls to God. And the testing "later on . . . produces a harvest of righteousness and peace" (Hebrews 12:11) and paves the way for the thirtyfold to one hundredfold increase that is promised to follow (Matthew 13:23). Aphra White

FEBRUARY 4

"I will cause you to ride in triumph on the heights of the land."

Isaiah 58:14

One of the first rules of aerodynamics is that flying into the wind quickly increases altitude. The wings of the airplane create more lift by flying against the wind. How was this lesson learned? It was learned by watching birds fly. If a bird is simply flying for pleasure, it flies with the wind. But if it senses danger, it turns into the wind to gain altitude, and flies up toward the sun.

The sufferings of life are God's winds. Sometimes they blow against us and are very strong. They are His hurricanes, taking our lives to higher levels, toward His heavens.

Do you remember a summer day when the heat and humidity were so oppressive, you could hardly breathe? But a dark cloud appeared on the horizon, growing larger and larger, until it suddenly brought a rich blessing to your world. The storm raged, lightning flashed, and thunder rumbled. The storm covered your sky, the atmosphere was cleansed, new life was in the air, and your world was changed.

Human life works exactly on the same principle. When the storms of life appear, the atmosphere is changed, purified, filled with new life, and part of heaven is brought down to earth. SELECTED

Facing obstacles should make us sing. The wind finds its voice not when rushing across an open sea but when it is hindered by the outstretched limbs of a pine tree or broken by the strings of an aeolian wind harp. Only then does the harp have songs of power and beauty. Send your soul, which has been set free, sweeping across the obstacles of life. Send it through the relentless forests of pain and against even the smallest hindrances and worries of life, and it too will find a voice with which to sing. SELECTED

Be like a bird that, halting in its flight,
Rests on a limb too slight.
And feeling it give way beneath him sings,
Knowing he has wings.

FEBRUARY 5

You will not leave in haste.

ISAIAH 52:12

I DO NOT BELIEVE WE HAVE EVEN BEGUN TO UNDERSTAND THE WONderful power there is in being still. We are in such a hurry, always doing, that we are in danger of not allowing God the opportunity to work. You may be sure that God will never say to us, "Stand still," "Sit still," or "Be still," unless *He* is going to do something. This is our problem regarding the Christian life: *we* want to do something to be Christians, instead of allowing *Him* to work in us.

Think of how still you stand when your picture is being taken, as the photographer captures your likeness on film. God has one eternal purpose for us: that we should be "conformed to the image of his Son" (Romans 8:29 KJV). But in order for that to happen, we must stand still. We hear so much today about being active, but maybe we need to learn what it means to be quiet. CRUMBS

Sit still, my children! Just sit calmly still!
Nor deem these days—these waiting days—as ill!
The One who loves you best, who plans your way,
Has not forgotten your great need today!
And, if He waits, it's sure He waits to prove
To you, His tender child, His heart's deep love.

Sit still, my children! Just sit calmly still!
You greatly long to know your dear Lord's will!
While anxious thoughts would almost steal their way
Corrodingly within, because of His delay—
Persuade yourself in simple faith to rest
That He, who knows and loves, will do the best.

Sit still, my children! Just sit calmly still!
Nor move one step, not even one, until
His way has opened. Then, ah then, how sweet!
How glad your heart, and then how swift your feet,
Your inner being then, ah then, how strong!
And waiting days not counted then too long.

Sit still, my daughter! Just sit calmly still!
What higher service could you for Him fill?
It's hard! ah yes! But choicest things must cost!
For lack of losing all how much is lost!
It's hard, it's true! But then—He gives you grace
To count the hardest spot the sweetest place.

J. DANSON SMITH

FEBRUARY 6

He turned the sea into dry land, they passed through the waters on foot—come, let us rejoice in him.

PSALM 66:6

IT IS A PROFOUND STATEMENT THAT "THROUGH *the waters*," THE VERY place where we might have expected nothing but trembling, terror, anguish, and dismay, the children of Israel stopped to "rejoice in him"!

How many of us can relate to this experience? Who of us, right in the midst of our time of distress and sadness, have been able to triumph and rejoice, as the Israelites did?

How close God is to us through His promises, and how brightly those promises shine! Yet during times of prosperity, we lose sight of their brilliance. In the way the sun at noon hides the stars from sight, His promises become indiscernible. But when night falls—the deep, dark night of sorrow—a host of stars begins to shine, bringing forth God's blessed constellations of hope, and promises of comfort from His Word.

Just as Jacob experienced at Jabbok, it is only once the sun sets that the Angel of the Lord comes, wrestles with us, and we can overcome. It was at night, "at twilight" (Exodus 30:8), that Aaron lit the sanctuary lamps. And it is often during nights of trouble that the brightest lamps of believers are set ablaze.

It was during a dark time of loneliness and exile that John had the glorious vision of his Redeemer. Many of us today have our "Isle of Patmos," which produces the brightest memories of God's enduring presence, uplifting grace, and love in spite of solitude and sadness.

How many travelers today, still passing through their Red Seas and Jordan Rivers of earthly affliction, will be able to look back from eternity, filled with memories of God's great goodness, and say, "We 'passed through the waters on foot.' And yet, even in these dark experiences, with waves surging all around, we stopped and said, 'Let us rejoice in him'!"

J. R. MACDUFF

"*There* I will give her back her vineyards, and will make the Valley of Achor a door of hope. There she will [sing]" (Hosea 2:15).

FEBRUARY 7

Why, my soul, are you downcast?
PSALM 43:5

IS THERE EVER ANY REASON TO BE DOWNCAST? ACTUALLY, THERE ARE two reasons, but only two. If we were still unbelievers, we would have a reason to be downcast; or if we have been converted but continue to live in sin, we are downcast as a consequence.

Except for these two conditions, there is never a reason to be downcast, for everything else may be brought to God "by prayer and petition, with thanksgiving" (Philippians 4:6). And through all our times of need, difficulty, and trials, we may exercise faith in the power and love of God.

"*Put your hope in God*" (Psalm 43:5). Please remember there is never a time when we cannot hope in God, whatever our need or however great our difficulty may be. Even when our situation appears to be impossible, our work is to "hope in God."

Our hope will not be in vain, and in the Lord's own timing help will come.

Oh, the hundreds, even the thousands, of times I have found this to be true in the past seventy years and four months of my life! When it seemed impossible for help to come, it did come, for God has His own unlimited resources. In ten thousand different ways, and at ten thousand different times, God's help may come to us.

Our work is to lay our petitions before the Lord, and in childlike simplicity to pour out our hearts before Him, saying, "I do not deserve that You should hear me and answer my requests, but for the sake of my precious Lord Jesus; for His sake, answer my prayer. And give me grace to wait patiently until it pleases You to grant my petition. For I believe You will do it in Your own time and way."

"*For I will yet praise him*" (Psalm 43:5). More prayer, more exercising of our faith, and more patient waiting leads to blessings—abundant blessings. I have found it to be true many hundreds of times, and therefore I continually say to myself, "Put your hope in God." GEORGE MUELLER

FEBRUARY 8

"Surely I am with you always."
MATTHEW 28:20

NEVER LOOK AHEAD TO THE CHANGES AND CHALLENGES OF THIS LIFE in fear. Instead, as they arise look at them with the full assurance that God, whose you are, will deliver you out of them. Hasn't He kept you safe up to now? So hold His loving hand tightly, and He will lead you safely through all things. And when you cannot stand, He will carry you in His arms.

Do not look ahead to what *may* happen tomorrow. The same everlasting Father who cares for you today will take care of you tomorrow and every day. Either He will shield you from suffering or He will give you His unwavering strength that you may bear it. Be at peace, then, and set aside all anxious thoughts and worries. FRANCIS DE SALES

"The LORD is my shepherd" (Psalm 23:1).

Not *was*, not *may be*, nor *will be*. "The LORD *is* my shepherd." He *is* on Sunday, on Monday, and through every day of the week. He *is* in January, in December, and every month of the year. He *is* when I'm at home and in China. He *is* during peace or war, and in times of abundance or poverty. J. HUDSON TAYLOR

He will silently plan for you,
His object of omniscient care;
God Himself undertakes to be
Your Pilot through each subtle snare.

He will silently plan for you,
So certainly, He cannot fail!
Rest on the faithfulness of God,
In Him you surely will prevail.

He will silently plan for you
Some wonderful surprise of love.
No eye has seen, no ear has heard,
But it is kept for you above.

He will silently plan for you,
His purposes will all unfold;
Your tangled life will shine at last,
A masterpiece of skill untold.

He will silently plan for you,
Happy child of a Father's care,
As if no other claimed His love,
But you alone to Him were dear.

E. Mary Grimes

Whatever our faith says God is, He will be.

FEBRUARY 9

Jesus did not answer a word.

Matthew 15:23

He will quiet you with his love.

Zephaniah 3:17

Are you reading these verses as a child of God who is experiencing a crushing sorrow, a bitter disappointment, or a heartbreaking blow from a totally unexpected place? Are you longing to hear your Master's voice calling you, saying, "Take courage! It is I. Don't be afraid" (Matthew 14:27)? Yet only silence, the unknown, and misery confront you—"Jesus did not answer a word."

God's tender heart must often ache listening to our sad, complaining cries. Our weak, impatient hearts cry out because we fail to see through our tear-blinded, shortsighted eyes that it is for our own sakes that He does not answer at all or that He answers in a way we believe is less than the best. In fact, the silences of Jesus are as eloquent as His words and may be a sign not of His disapproval but of His approval and His way of providing a deeper blessing for you.

"Why, my soul, are you downcast . . . I will yet praise him" (Psalm 43:5). Yes, praise Him even for His silence. Let me relate a beautiful old story of how one Christian dreamed she saw three other women in prayer.

When they knelt the Master drew near to them. As He approached the first of the three, He bent over her with tenderness and grace. He smiled with radiant love and spoke to her in tones of pure, sweet music. Upon leaving her, He came to the next but only placed His hand upon her bowed head and gave her one look of loving approval. He passed the third woman almost abruptly, without stopping for a word or a glance.

The woman having the dream said to herself, "How greatly He must love the first woman. The second gained His approval but did not experience the special demonstrations of love He gave the first. But the third woman must have grieved Him deeply, for He gave her no word at all, nor even a passing look."

She wondered what the third woman must have done to have been treated so differently. As she tried to account for the actions of her Lord, He Himself came and stood beside her. He said to her, "O woman! How wrongly you have interpreted Me! The first kneeling woman needs the full measure of My tenderness and care to keep her feet on My narrow way. She needs My love, thoughts, and help every moment of the day, for without them she would stumble into failure.

"The second woman has stronger faith and deeper love than the first, and I can count on her to trust Me no matter how things may go or whatever people may do. Yet the third woman, whom I seemed not to notice, and even to neglect, has faith and love of the purest quality. I am training her through quick and drastic ways for the highest and holiest service.

"She knows Me so intimately, and trusts Me so completely, that she no longer depends on My voice, loving glances, or other outward signs to know of My approval. She is not dismayed or discouraged by any circumstances I arrange for her to encounter. She trusts Me when common sense, reason, and even every subtle instinct of the natural heart would rebel, knowing that I am preparing her for eternity, and realizing that the understanding of what I do will come later.

"My love is silent because I love beyond the power of words to express it and beyond the understanding of the human heart. Also, it is silent for your sakes—that you may learn to love and trust Me with pure, Spirit-taught, spontaneous responses. I desire for your response to My love to be without the prompting of anything external."

He "will do wonders never before done" (Exodus 34:10) if you will learn the mystery of His silence and praise Him every time He withdraws His gifts from you. Through this you will better know and love the Giver.
SELECTED

FEBRUARY 10

Do not take revenge, my dear friends.

ROMANS 12:19

THERE ARE TIMES WHEN DOING NOTHING DEMANDS MUCH GREATER strength than taking action. Maintaining composure is often the best evidence of power. Even to the vilest and deadliest of charges, Jesus responded with deep, unbroken silence. His silence was so profound, it caused His accusers and spectators to wonder in awe. To the greatest insults, the most violent treatment, and to mockery that would bring righteous indignation to the feeblest of hearts, He responded with voiceless, confident calmness. Those who are unjustly accused, and mistreated without cause, know the tremendous strength that is necessary to keep silent and to leave revenge to God.

Men may misjudge your aim,
Think they have cause to blame,
Say, you are wrong;
Keep on your quiet way,
Christ is the Judge, not they,
Fear not, be strong.

The apostle Paul said, "None of these things *move* me" (Acts 20:24 KJV). He did not say, "None of these things *hurt* me." It is one thing to be hurt, and quite another to be moved. Paul had a very tender heart, for we do not read of any other apostle who cried as he did. It takes a strong man to cry. "Jesus wept" (John 11:35), and He was the strongest man that ever lived.

Therefore it does not say, "None of these things hurt me." The apostle Paul had determined not to move from what he believed was right. He did not value things as we are prone to do. He never looked for the easy way, and placed no value on his mortal life. He only cared about one thing, and that was his loyalty to Christ—to gain Christ's smile. To Paul, more than to any other man, doing Christ's work was his earthly pay, but gaining Christ's smile was heaven. MARGARET BOTTOME

FEBRUARY 11

As soon as the priests . . . set foot in the Jordan, its waters . . . will be cut off.

JOSHUA 3:13

The Israelites were not to wait in the camp until the Jordan was opened but to "walk by faith" (2 Corinthians 5:7 KJV). They were to break camp, pack up their belongings, form a marching line, and actually step into the river before it would be opened.

If they had come down to the riverbank and then stopped, waiting for the water to divide before stepping into it, they would have waited in vain. They were told to "set foot in the Jordan" before "its waters . . . will be cut off."

We must learn to take God at His word and walk straight ahead in obedience, even when we can see no way to go forward. The reason we are so often sidetracked by difficulties is that we expect to see barriers removed before we even try to pass through them.

If we would only move straight ahead in faith, the path would be opened for us. But we stand still, waiting for the obstacle to be removed, when we ought to go forward as if there were no obstacles at all. Evening Thoughts

What a lesson Christopher Columbus taught the world—a lesson of perseverance in the face of tremendous difficulties!

Behind him lay the gray Azores,
Behind the gates of Hercules;
Before him not the ghost of shores,
Before him only shoreless seas.
The good Mate said: "Now we must pray,
For lo! the very stars are gone.
Brave Admiral, speak, what shall I say?"
"Why, say, 'Sail on! sail on! and on!'"

"My men grow mutinous day by day;
My men grow ghastly pale and weak!"
The strong Mate thought of home; a spray
Of salt wave washed his sunburned cheek.

"What shall I say, brave Admiral, say,
If we sight only seas at dawn?"
"Why, you shall say at break of day,
'Sail on! sail on! sail on! and on!'"

They sailed. They sailed. Then spoke the Mate:
"This mad sea shows its teeth tonight.
He curls his lip, he lies in wait,
With lifted teeth, as if to bite!
Brave Admiral, say but one good word;
What shall we do when hope is gone?"
The words leapt like a leaping sword:
"Sail on! sail on! sail on! and on!"

Then, pale and worn, he kept his deck
And peered through darkness. Ah! that night
Of all dark nights! And then a speck—
A light! A light! A light! A light!
It grew, a starlit flag unfurled!
It grew to be Time's burst of dawn.
He gained a world; he gave that world
Its grandest lesson: "On! sail on!"

J. R. Miller

Faith that goes forward triumphs.

FEBRUARY 12

"Your heavenly Father knows."

Matthew 6:32

A VISITOR AT A SCHOOL FOR THE DEAF WAS WRITING QUESTIONS ON the board for the children. Soon he wrote this sentence: "Why has God made me able to hear and speak, and made you deaf?" The shocking sentence hit the children like a cruel slap on the face. They sat paralyzed, pondering the dreadful word "Why?" And then a little girl arose.

With her lip trembling and her eyes swimming with tears, she walked straight to the board. Picking up the chalk, she wrote with a steady hand these precious words: "*Yes, Father, for this is what you were pleased to do*" (Matthew 11:26). What a reply! It reaches up and claims an eternal truth upon which the most mature believer, and even the youngest child of God, may securely rest—the truth that God is your Father.

Can you state that truth with full assurance and faith? Once you do, your dove of faith will no longer wander the skies in restless flight but will settle forever in its eternal resting place of peace: your Father!

I still believe that a day of understanding will come for each of us, however far away it may be. We will understand as we see the tragedies that today darken and dampen the presence of heaven for us take their proper place in God's great plan—a plan so overwhelming, magnificent, and joyful, we will laugh with wonder and delight. ARTHUR CHRISTOPHER BACON

Chance has not brought this ill to me;
It's God's own hand, so let it be,
For He sees what I cannot see.
There is a purpose for each pain,
And He one day will make it plain
That earthly loss is heavenly gain.
Like as a piece of tapestry
Viewed from the back appears to be
Only threads tangled hopelessly;
But in the front a picture fair
Rewards the worker for his care,
Proving his skill and patience rare.

You are the Workman, I the frame.
Lord, for the glory of Your Name,
Perfect Your image on the same.
Selected

FEBRUARY 13

The forested hill country . . . will be yours.
Joshua 17:18

There is always room higher in the hills. When the valleys are full of Canaanites, whose mighty iron chariots are slowing your progress, go up to the hills and occupy the higher land. If you find you can no longer do work for God, pray for those who can. You may not be able to move things on earth with your words, but you may move heaven. If it seems that your continued growth is impossible on the lower slopes due to limited areas of service, the constraints of maintaining the day-to-day necessities, or other hindrances, allow your life to burst forth, reaching toward the unseen, the eternal, and the heavenly.

Your faith can level forests. Even if the tribes of Israel had realized what treasures awaited them in the hills above, they would never have dreamed it would be possible to actually harvest the thick forests. But as God instructed them to clear the forests, He also reminded them of the sufficient power they possessed. The sight of seemingly impossible tasks, like leveling these forest-covered hills, are not sent to discourage us. They come to motivate us to attempt spiritual feats that would be impossible except for the great strength God has placed within us through His indwelling Holy Spirit.

Difficulties are sent in order to reveal what God can do in answer to faith that prays and works. Are you being squeezed from all sides in the valley? Then "ride on the heights of the land" and be "nourished . . . with honey from the rock" (Deuteronomy 32:13). Gain wealth from the terraced slopes that are now hidden by the forests. Daily Devotional Commentary

Got any rivers they say are uncrossable,
Got any mountains they say "can't tunnel through"?
We specialize in the wholly impossible,
Doing the things they say you can't do.
Song of the Panama Canal Builders

FEBRUARY 14

Rejoice in the Lord always. I will say it again: Rejoice!
Philippians 4:4

It is a good thing to "rejoice in the Lord." Perhaps you have tried it but seemed to fail at first. Don't give it a second thought, and forge ahead. Even when you cannot *feel* any joy, there is no spring in your step, nor any comfort or encouragement in your life, continue to rejoice and "*consider it pure joy*" (James 1:2). "Whenever you face trials of many kinds" (James 1:2), regard it as joy, delight in it, and God will reward your faith. Do you believe that your heavenly Father will let you carry the banner of His victory and joy to the very front of the battle, only to calmly withdraw to see you captured or beaten back by the enemy? Never! His Holy Spirit will sustain you in your bold advance and fill your heart with gladness and praise. You will find that your heart is exhilarated and refreshed by the fullness within.

Lord, teach me to rejoice in You—to "be always joyful" (1 Thessalonians 5:16 wnt). Selected

The weakest saint may Satan rout,
Who meets him with a praiseful shout.

"Be filled with the Spirit. . . . Sing and make music from your heart to the Lord" (Ephesians 5:18–19).

In these verses, the apostle Paul urges us to use singing as inspiration in our spiritual life. He warns his readers to seek motivation not through the body but through the spirit, not by stimulating the flesh but by exalting the soul.

Sometimes a light surprises
The Christian while he sings.

Let us sing even when we do not feel like it, for in this way we give wings to heavy feet and turn weariness into strength. John Henry Jowett

"About midnight Paul and Silas were praying and singing hymns to God, and the other prisoners were listening to them" (Acts 16:25).

O Paul, what a wonderful example you are to us! You gloried in the fact that you "bear on [your] body the marks of Jesus" (Galatians 6:17). You bore the marks from nearly being stoned to death, from three times being "beaten with rods" (2 Corinthians 11:25), from receiving 195 lashes from the Jews, and from being bloodily beaten in the Philippian jail. Surely the grace that enabled you to sing praises while enduring such suffering is sufficient for us. J. Roach

Oh, let us rejoice in the Lord, evermore,
When darts of the Tempter are flying,
For Satan still dreads, as he oft did before,
Our singing much more than our crying.

FEBRUARY 15

Do not fret because of those who are evil or
be envious of those who do wrong.

Psalm 37:1

Never become extremely upset over your circumstances. If worry were ever justified, it would have been during the circumstances surrounding the writing of this psalm. Evil men were "dressed in purple and fine linen and lived in luxury every day" (Luke 16:19). "Those who do wrong" were ascending to the highest places of power and were tyrannizing their brothers who were less fortunate. Sinful men and women strutted through the land with arrogant pride and basked in the light of great prosperity, while good people became fearful and worried.

"Do not fret." Never get unduly upset! Stay cool! Even for a good reason, worrying will not help you. It only heats up the bearings but does not generate any steam. It does not help the locomotive for its axles to become hot; their heat is only a hindrance. The axles become heated because of unnecessary friction.

Dry surfaces are grinding against each other instead of working in smooth cooperation, aided by a thin cushion of oil.

Isn't it interesting how similar the words "fret" and "friction" are? Friction caused by fretting is an indication of the absence of the anointing oil of the grace of God. When we worry, a little bit of sand gets into the bearings. It may be some slight disappointment, ungratefulness, or discourtesy we have experienced—suddenly our life is no longer running smoothly. Friction leads to heat, and heat can lead to very dangerous conditions.

Do not allow your bearings to become heated. Let the oil of the Lord keep you cool so that an unholy heat will not cause you to be regarded as one of the evil men. The Silver Lining

Dear restless heart, be still; don't fret and worry so;
God has a thousand ways His love and help to show;
Just trust, and trust, and trust, until His will you know.

Dear restless heart, be still, for peace is God's own smile,
His love can every wrong and sorrow reconcile;
Just love, and love, and love, and calmly wait awhile.

Dear restless heart, be brave; don't moan and sorrow so,
He has a meaning kind in chilly winds that blow;
Just hope, and hope, and hope, until you braver grow.

Dear restless heart, recline upon His breast this hour,
His grace is strength and life, His love is bloom and flower;
Just rest, and rest, and rest, within His tender power.

Dear restless heart, be still! Don't struggle to be free;
God's life is in your life, from Him you may not flee;
Just pray, and pray, and pray, till you have faith to see.

EDITH WILLIS LINN

FEBRUARY 16

"Although I have afflicted you . . . I will afflict you no more."

NAHUM 1:12

THERE IS A LIMIT TO OUR AFFLICTION. GOD SENDS IT AND THEN removes it. Do you complain, saying, "When will this end?" May we quietly wait and patiently endure the will of the Lord till He comes. Our Father takes away the rod when His purpose in using it is fully accomplished.

If the affliction is sent to test us so that our words would glorify God, it will only end once He has caused us to testify to His praise and honor. In fact, we would not want the difficulty to depart until God has removed from us all the honor we can yield to Him.

Today things may become "completely calm" (Matthew 8:26). Who knows how soon these raging waves will give way to a sea of glass with seagulls sitting on the gentle swells?

After a long ordeal, the threshing tool is on its hook, and the wheat has been gathered into the barn. Before much time has passed, we may be just as happy as we are sorrowful now.

It is not difficult for the Lord to turn night into day. He who sends the clouds can just as easily clear the skies. Let us be encouraged—things are better down the road. *Let us sing God's praises in anticipation of things to come.* CHARLES H. SPURGEON

"The Lord of the harvest" (Luke 10:2) is not always threshing us. His trials are only for a season, and the showers soon pass. "Weeping may stay for a, but rejoicing comes in the morning" (Psalm 30:5). "Our light and momentary troubles are achieving for us an eternal glory that far outweighs them all" (2 Corinthians 4:17). Trials do serve their purpose.

Even the fact that we face a trial proves there is something very precious to our Lord in us, or else He would not spend so much time and energy on us. Christ would not test us if He did not see the precious metal of faith mingled with the rocky core of our nature, and it is to refine us into purity and beauty that He forces us through the fiery ordeal.

Be patient, O sufferer! The result of the Refiner's fire will more than compensate for our trials, once we see the "eternal glory that far outweighs them all." Just to hear His commendation, "Well done" (Matthew 25:21); to be honored before the holy angels; to be glorified in Christ, so that I may reflect His glory back to Him—ah! that will be more than enough reward for all my trials. TRIED BY FIRE

Just as the weights of a grandfather clock, or the stabilizers in a ship, are necessary for them to work properly, so are troubles to the soul. The sweetest perfumes are obtained only through tremendous pressure, the fairest flowers grow on the most isolated and snowy peaks, the most beautiful gems are those that have suffered the longest at the jeweler's wheel, and the most magnificent statues have endured the most blows from the chisel. All of these, however, are subject to God's law. Nothing happens that has not been *appointed* with consummate care and foresight. DAILY DEVOTIONAL COMMENTARY

FEBRUARY 17

"The land which I do give to them, even to the children of Israel."

JOSHUA 1:2 KJV

God is speaking about something immediate in this verse. It is not something He is *going* to do but something He *does* do, at this very moment. As faith continues to speak, God continues to give. He meets you today in the present and tests your faith. As long as you are waiting, hoping, or looking, you are not believing. You may have hope or an earnest desire, but that is not faith, for "faith is confidence in what we hope for and assurance about what we do not see" (Hebrews 11:1). The command regarding believing prayer is: "Whatever you ask for in prayer, believe that you have received it, and it will be yours" (Mark 11:24). We are to believe that we have received—this present moment. Have we come to the point where we have met God in His everlasting now? A. B. Simpson, Joshua

True faith relies on God and believes before seeing. Naturally, we want some evidence that our petition is granted before we believe, but when we "live by faith" (2 Corinthians 5:7), we need no evidence other than God's Word. He has spoken, and in harmony with our faith it will be done. We will see because we have believed, and true faith sustains us in the most trying of times, even when everything around us seems to contradict God's Word.

The psalmist said, "I remain confident of this: *I will see* the goodness of the Lord in the land of the living" (Psalm 27:13). He had not yet seen the Lord's answer to his prayers, but he was confident he would see, and his confidence sustained him.

Faith that believes it will see, will keep us from becoming discouraged. We will laugh at seemingly impossible situations while we watch with delight to see how God is going to open a path through our Red Sea. It is in these places of severe testing, with no human way out of our difficulty, that our faith grows and is strengthened.

Dear troubled one, have you been waiting for God to work during long nights and weary days, fearing you have been forgotten? Lift up your head and begin praising Him right now for the deliverance that is on its way to you. Life of Praise

FEBRUARY 18

"Whatever you ask for in prayer, believe that you have received it, and it will be yours."
MARK 11:24

WHEN MY LITTLE SON WAS ABOUT TEN YEARS OLD, HIS GRANDMOTHER promised him a stamp collecting album for Christmas. Christmas came and went with no stamp album and no word from Grandma. The matter, however, was not mentioned, until his friends came to see his Christmas presents. I was astonished, after he had listed all the gifts he had received, to hear him add, "And a stamp album from my grandmother."

After hearing this several times, I called my son to me and said, "But, George, you didn't get a stamp album from Grandma. Why did you say you did?"

With a puzzled look on his face, as if I had asked a very strange question, he replied, "Well, Mom, Grandma *said*, and that is the same *as*." Not a word from me would sway his faith.

A month passed and nothing else was said about the album. Finally one day, to test his faith and because I wondered in my own heart why the album had not been sent, I said, "George, I think Grandma has forgotten her promise."

"Oh no, Mom," he quickly and firmly responded. "She hasn't." I watched his sweet, trusting face, which for a while looked very serious, as if he were debating the possibility I had suggested. Soon his face brightened as he said, "Do you think it would do any good for me to write Grandma, *thanking* her for the album?"

"I don't know," I said, "but you might try it." A rich spiritual truth then began to dawn on me.

In a few minutes a letter was written and mailed, as George went off whistling his confidence in his grandma. Soon a letter from Grandma arrived with this message:

My dear George,

I have not forgotten my promise to you for a stamp album. I could not find the one you wanted here, so I ordered one from New York. It did not arrive until after Christmas, and it was not the right one. I then ordered another, but it still has not arrived. I have decided to send you thirty dollars instead so that you may buy the one you want in Chicago.

Your loving Grandma.

As he read the letter, his face was the face of a victor. From the depths of a heart that never doubted came the words, "Now, Mom, didn't I tell you?" George "against all hope . . . in hope believed" (Romans 4:18) that the stamp album would come. And while he was trusting, Grandma was working, and in due time faith became sight.

It is only human to want to see before we step out on the promises of God. Yet our Savior said to Thomas and to a long list of doubters who have followed, "Blessed are those who have not seen and yet have believed" (John 20:29). MRS. ROUNDS

FEBRUARY 19

"Every branch that does bear fruit he prunes so that it will be even more fruitful."

JOHN 15:2

A CHILD OF GOD WAS ONCE OVERWHELMED BY THE NUMBER OF AFFLICtions that seemed to target her. As she walked past a vineyard during the rich glow of autumn, she noticed its untrimmed appearance and the abundance of leaves still on the vines. The ground had been overtaken by a tangle of weeds and grass, and the entire place appeared totally unkempt. While she pondered the sight, the heavenly Gardener whispered such a precious message to her that she could not help but share it.

The message was this: "My dear child, are you questioning the number of trials in your life? Remember the vineyard and learn from it. The gardener stops pruning and trimming the vine or weeding the soil only when he expects nothing more from the vine during that season. He leaves it alone, because its fruitfulness is gone and further effort now would yield no profit. In the same way, freedom from suffering leads to uselessness. Do you now want me to stop pruning your life? Shall I leave you alone?"

Then her comforted heart cried, "No!" HOMERA HOMER-DIXON

It is the branch that bears the fruit,
That feels the knife,
To prune it for a larger growth,
A fuller life.

Though every budding twig be trimmed,
And every grace
Of swaying tendril, springing leaf,
May lose its place.

O you whose life of joy seems left,
With beauty shorn;
Whose aspirations lie in dust,
All bruised and torn,

Rejoice, though each desire, each dream,
Each hope of thine
Will fall and fade; it is the hand
Of Love Divine

That holds the knife, that cuts and breaks
With tenderest touch,
That you, whose life has borne some fruit,
Might now bear much.

ANNIE JOHNSON FLINT

FEBRUARY 20

"Nothing will be impossible for you."
MATTHEW 17:20

It is possible FOR BELIEVERS WHO ARE COMPLETELY WILLING TO TRUST the power of the Lord for their safekeeping and victory to lead a life of readily taking His promises exactly as they are and finding them to be true.

It is possible to daily "cast all your anxiety on him" (1 Peter 5:7) and experience deep peace in the process.

It is possible to have our thoughts and the desires of our hearts purified in the deepest sense of the word.

It is possible to see God's will in every circumstance and to accept it with singing instead of complaining.

It is possible to become strong through and through by completely taking refuge in the power of God and by realizing that our greatest weakness and the things that upset our determination to be patient, pure, or humble provide an opportunity to make sin powerless over us. This opportunity comes through Him who loves us and who works to bring us into agreement with His will, and thereby supplies a blessed sense of His presence and His power.

All these are divine possibilities. Because they are His work, actually experiencing them will always humble us, causing us to bow at His feet and teaching us to hunger and thirst for more.

We will never be satisfied with anything less—each day, each hour, or each moment in Christ, through the power of the Holy Spirit—than walking with God. H. C. G. MOULE

We are able to have as much of God as we want. Christ puts the key to His treasure chest in our hands and invites us to take all we desire. If someone is allowed into a bank vault, told to help himself to the money, and leaves without one cent, whose fault is it if he remains poor? And whose fault is it that Christians usually have such meager portions of the free riches of God? ALEXANDER MACLAREN

FEBRUARY 21

Be still before the L*ORD* *and wait patiently for him.*

PSALM 37:7

HAVE YOU PRAYED AND PRAYED, AND WAITED AND WAITED, AND STILL you see no evidence of an answer? Are you tired of seeing no movement? Are you at the point of giving up? Then perhaps you have not waited in the right way, which removes you from the right place—the place where the Lord can meet you.

"*Wait for it patiently*" (Romans 8:25). Patience eliminates worry. The Lord said He would come, and His promise is equal to His presence. Patience eliminates weeping. Why feel sad and discouraged? He knows your needs better than you do, and His purpose in waiting is to receive more glory through it. Patience eliminates self-works. "The work of God is this: to believe" (John 6:29), and once you believe, you may know all is well. Patience eliminates all *want*. Perhaps your desire to receive what you want is stronger than your desire for the will of God to be fulfilled.

Patience eliminates all *weakness*. Instead of thinking of waiting as being wasted time, realize that God is preparing His resources and strengthening you as well. Patience eliminates all *wobbling*. "He touched me and raised me to my feet" (Daniel 8:18). God's foundations are steady, and when we have His patience within, we are steady while we wait. Patience yields *worship*. Sometimes the best part of praiseful waiting is experiencing "great endurance and patience . . . giving joyful thanks" (Colossians 1:11–12). While you wait, "let [all these aspects of] patience have her perfect work" (James 1:4 KJV), and you will be greatly enriched. C. H. P.

Hold steady when the fires burn,
When inner lessons come to learn,
And from this path there seems no turn—
"Let patience have her perfect work."

L. S. P.

FEBRUARY 22

"If you can? . . . Everything is possible for one who believes."
MARK 9:23

I SELDOM HAVE HEARD A BETTER DEFINITION OF FAITH THAN THAT given in one of our meetings, by a sweet, elderly black woman, as she answered a young man who asked, *"How do I obtain the Lord's help for my needs?"*

In her characteristic way, pointing her finger toward him, she said with great insistence, "You just have to believe that He's done it and it's done." The greatest problem with most of us is, after asking Him to do it, we do not believe it is done. Instead, we keep trying to help Him, get others to help Him, and anxiously wait to see how He is going to work.

Faith adds its "Amen" to God's "Yes" and then takes its hands off, leaving God to finish His work. The language of faith is, "Commit your way to the LORD; trust in him and he will do this" (Psalm 37:5). DAYS OF HEAVEN UPON EARTH

I simply take Him at His word,
I praise Him that my prayer is heard,
And claim my answer from the Lord;
I take, He undertakes.

Active faith gives thanks for a promise even though it is not yet performed, knowing that God's contracts are as good as cash. MATTHEW HENRY

Passive faith accepts the Word as true—
But never moves.
Active faith begins the work to do,
And thereby proves.

Passive faith says, "I believe it! every word of God is true.
Well I know He has not spoken what He cannot, will not, do.
He has instructed me, 'Go forward!' but a closed-up way I see,
When the waters are divided, soon in Canaan's land I'll be.
Lo! I hear His voice commanding, 'Rise and walk: take up your bed';
And, 'Stretch to Me your withered hand!' which for so long has been dead.
When I am a little stronger, then, I know I'll surely stand:
When there comes a thrill of healing, I will use with ease my reclaimed hand.
Yes, I know that 'God is able' and full willing all to do:
I believe that every promise, sometime, will to me come true."
Active faith says, "I believe it! and the promise now I take,
Knowing well, as I receive it, God, each promise,
real will make.
So I step into the waters, finding there an open way;
Onward press, the land possessing; nothing can my progress stay.
Yes, I rise at His commanding, walking straight, and joyfully:
This, my hand so sadly shriveled, as I reach, restored will be.
What beyond His faithful promise, would I wish or do I need?
Looking not for 'signs or wonders,' I'll no contradiction heed.
Well I know that 'God is able,' and full willing all to do:
I believe that every promise, at this moment can come true."
Passive faith but praises in the light,
When sun does shine.
Active faith will praise in darkest night—
Which faith is thine?

SELECTED

FEBRUARY 23

And there came a lion.

1 SAMUEL 17:34 KJV

It is a source of inspiration and strength to us to remember how the youthful David trusted God. Through his faith in the Lord, he defeated a lion and a bear and later overthrew the mighty Goliath. When the lion came to destroy his flock, it came as a wonderful *opportunity* for David. If he had faltered and failed, he would have missed God's opportunity for him and probably would never have been the Lord's chosen king of Israel.

"*And there came a lion.*" Normally we think of a lion not as a special blessing from the Lord but only as a reason for alarm. Yet the lion was God's opportunity in disguise. Every difficulty and every temptation that comes our way, if we receive it correctly, is God's opportunity.

When a "lion" comes to your life, recognize it as an opportunity from the Lord, no matter how fierce it may outwardly seem. Even the tabernacle of God was covered with badger skins and goat hair. No one would think there would be any glory there, yet the Shekinah glory of God was very evident underneath the covering. May the Lord open our eyes to see Him, even in temptations, trials, dangers, and misfortunes. C. H. P.

FEBRUARY 24

Though John never performed a sign, all that
John said about this man was true.

John 10:41

Perhaps you are very dissatisfied with yourself. You are not a genius, have no distinctive gifts, and are inconspicuous when it comes to having any special abilities. Mediocrity seems to be the measure of your existence. None of your days are note-worthy, except for their sameness and lack of zest. Yet in spite of this you may live a great life.

John the Baptist never performed a miracle, but Jesus said of him, "Among those born of women there is no one greater" (Luke 7:28). His mission was to be "a witness to the light" (John 1:8), and that may be your mission and mine. John was content to be only a voice, if it caused people to think of Christ.

Be willing to be only a voice that is heard but not seen, or a mirror whose glass the eye cannot see because it is reflecting the brilliant glory of the Son. Be willing to be a breeze that arises just before daylight, saying, "The dawn! The dawn!" and then fades away.

Do the most everyday and insignificant tasks knowing that God can see. If you live with difficult people, win them over through love. If you once made a great mistake in life, do not allow it to cloud the rest of your life, but by locking it secretly in your heart, make it yield strength and character.

We are doing more good than we know. The things we do today—sowing seeds or sharing simple truths of Christ—people will someday refer to as the first things that prompted them to think of Him. For my part, I will be satisfied not to have some great tombstone over my grave but just to know that common people will gather there once I am gone and say, "He was a good man. He never performed any miracles, but he told me about Christ, which led me to know Him for myself." GEORGE MATHESON

THY HIDDEN ONES

Thick green leaves from the soft brown earth,
Happy springtime has called them forth;
First faint promise of summer bloom
Breathes from the fragrant, sweet perfume,
Under the leaves.

Lift them! what marvelous beauty lies
Hidden beneath, from our thoughtless eyes!
Mayflowers, rosy or purest white,
Lift their cups to the sudden light,
Under the leaves.

Are there no lives whose holy deeds—
Seen by no eye save His who reads
Motive and action—in silence grow
Into rare beauty, and bud and blow
Under the leaves?

Fair white flowers of faith and trust,
Springing from spirits bruised and crushed;
Blossoms of love, rose-tinted and bright,
Touched and painted with Heaven's own light
Under the leaves.

Full fresh clusters of duty borne,
Fairest of all in that shadow grown;
Wondrous the fragrance that sweet and rare
Comes from the flower-cups hidden there
Under the leaves.

Though unseen by our vision dim,
Bud and blossom are known to Him;
Wait we content for His heavenly ray—
Wait till our Master Himself one day
Lifts up the leaves.

God calls many of His most valued workers from the unknown multitude (Luke 14:23).

FEBRUARY 25

"I will give you every place where you set your foot, as I promised."
Joshua 1:3

Besides the literal ground still unoccupied for Christ, there is before us the unclaimed and unwalked territory of *God's promises*. What did God say to Joshua? "I will give you *every place* where you set your foot, *as I promised*." Then He set the boundaries of the Land of Promise—all theirs on one condition: *they must march across its length and breadth*, measuring it off with their own feet.

Yet they never marched across more than one-third of the land, and as a consequence, they never *possessed* more than that one-third. They possessed only what they measured off and no more.

In 2 Peter 1:4 we read, "He has given us his very great and precious promises." The land of God's promises is open before us, and it is His will for us to possess it. We must measure off the territory with the feet of obedient faith and faithful obedience, thereby claiming and appropriating it as our own.

How many of us have ever taken possession of the promises of God in the name of Christ? The land of His promises is a magnificent territory for faith to claim by marching across its length and breadth, but faith has yet to do it.

Let us enter into and claim our total inheritance. Let us lift our eyes to the north, south, east, and west and hear God say, "All the land that you see I will give to you" (Genesis 13:15). Arthur Tappan Pierson

Wherever the tribe of Judah set their feet would be theirs, and wherever the tribe of Benjamin set their feet would be theirs, and so on. Each tribe would receive their inheritance by setting foot upon it. Don't you imagine that as each tribe set foot upon a given territory, they instantly and instinctively felt, "This is ours"? An elderly man who had a wonderful testimony of grace was once asked, "Daniel, how is it that you exhibit such peace and joy in your faith?" "Oh, sir!" he replied. "I just fall flat on God's 'very great and precious promises,' and I have all that is in them. Glory! Glory!" One who falls flat on God's promises knows that all the riches abiding in them are his. Faith Papers

The Marquis of Salisbury, an English statesman and diplomat, upon being criticized for his colonial policies, replied, "Gentlemen, get larger maps."

FEBRUARY 26

My grace is sufficient for you.

2 Corinthians 12:9

The other day I was riding home after a hard day's work. I was very tired and deeply depressed, when quickly, and as suddenly as a lightning bolt, the verse came to me: "My grace is sufficient for you." When I arrived home I looked it up in the Word, and it finally came to me this way: "*My grace is sufficient for you.*" My response was to say, "Yes, Lord, I should think it is!" Then I burst out laughing.

Until that time, I had never understood what the holy laughter of Abraham was. This verse seemed to make unbelief totally absurd. I pictured a thirsty little fish who was concerned about drinking the river dry, with Father River saying, "Drink away, little fish; my stream is sufficient for you." I also envisioned a mouse afraid of starving after seven years of plenty, when Joseph says to him, "Cheer up, little mouse; my granaries are sufficient for you." Again, I imagined a man high on a mountain peak, saying to himself, "I breathe so many cubic feet of air every year, I am afraid I will deplete all the oxygen in the atmosphere." But the earth says to him, "Breathe away, filling your lungs forever; my atmosphere is sufficient for you."

O people of God, be great believers! Little faith will bring your souls to heaven, but great faith will bring heaven to your souls. Charles H. Spurgeon

His grace is great enough to meet the great things—
The crashing waves that overwhelm the soul,
The roaring winds that leave us stunned and breathless,
The sudden storms beyond our life's control.

His grace is great enough to meet the small things—
The little pinprick troubles that annoy,
The insect worries, buzzing and persistent,
The squeaking wheels that grate upon our joy.

ANNIE JOHNSON FLINT

There is always a large balance credited to our account in the bank of heaven. It is waiting for us to exercise our faith to draw upon it. Draw heavily on God's resources.

FEBRUARY 27

So Jacob was left alone, and a man wrestled with him till daybreak.

GENESIS 32:24

"LEFT ALONE!" WHAT DIFFERENT EMOTIONS THESE WORDS BRING TO mind for each of us! To some they mean loneliness and grief, but to others they may mean rest and quiet. To be left alone *without* God would be too horrible for words, while being left alone *with* Him is a taste of heaven! And if His followers spent more time alone with Him, we would have spiritual giants again.

Our Master set an example for us. Remember how often He went to be *alone with* God? And there was a powerful purpose behind His command, "When you pray, go into your room, close the door and pray" (Matthew 6:6).

The greatest miracles of Elijah and Elisha took place when they were alone with God. Jacob was alone with God when he became a prince (Genesis 32:28). In the same way, we too may become royalty and people who are "wondered at" (Zechariah 3:8 KJV). Joshua was alone when the Lord came to him (Joshua 1:1). Gideon and Jephthah were by themselves when commissioned to save Israel (Judges 6:11; 11:29). Moses was by himself at the burning bush (Exodus 3:1–5). Cornelius was praying by himself when the Angel of God came to him (Acts 10:1–4). No one was with Peter on the housetop when he was instructed to go to the Gentiles (Acts 10:9–28). John the Baptist was alone in the wilderness (Luke 1:80), and John the Beloved was alone on the island of Patmos when he was the closest to God (Revelation 1:9).

Earnestly desire to get alone with God. If we neglect to do so, we not only rob ourselves of a blessing but rob others as well, since we will have no blessing to pass on to them. It may mean that we do less outward, visible work, but the work we do will have more depth and power. Another wonderful result will be that people will see "no one except Jesus" (Matthew 17:8) in our lives.

The impact of being alone with God in prayer cannot be overemphasized.

If chosen men had never been alone,
In deepest silence open-doored to God,
No greatness would ever have been dreamed or done.

FEBRUARY 28

Let us continually offer to God a sacrifice of praise.
HEBREWS 13:15

AN INNER-CITY MISSIONARY, STUMBLING THROUGH THE TRASH OF A dark apartment doorway, heard someone say, "Who's there, Honey?" Lighting a match, he caught sight of earthly needs and suffering, amid saintly trust and peace. Calm, appealing eyes, etched in ebony, were set within the wrinkles of a weathered black face. On a bitterly cold night in February, she lay on a tattered bed, with no fire, no heat, and no light. Having had no breakfast, lunch, or dinner, she seemed to have nothing at all, except arthritis and faith in God. No one could have been further removed from comfortable circumstances, yet this favorite song of the dear lady played in the background:

Nobody knows the trouble I see,
Nobody knows but Jesus;
Nobody knows the trouble I see—
Sing Glory Hallelu!

Sometimes I'm up, sometimes I'm down,
Sometimes I'm level on the groun',
Sometimes the glory shines aroun'—
Sing Glory Hallelu!

And so it continued: "Nobody knows the work I do, Nobody knows the griefs I have," the constant refrain being, "*Glory Hallelu!*" until the last verse rose:

Nobody knows the joys I have,
Nobody knows but Jesus!

"We are hard pressed on every side, but not crushed; perplexed, but not in despair; persecuted, but not abandoned; struck down, but not destroyed" (2 Corinthians 4:8–9). It takes these great Bible words to explain the joy of this elderly black woman.

Do you remember the words of Martin Luther as he lay on his deathbed? Between groans he preached, "These pains and troubles here are like the type that printers set. When we look at them, we see them backwards, and they seem to make no sense and have no meaning. But up there, when the Lord God prints out our life to come, we will find they make splendid reading." Yet we do not have to wait until then. The apostle Paul, walking the deck of a ship on a raging sea, encouraged the frightened sailors, "Be of good cheer" (Acts 27:22 KJV).

Paul, Martin Luther, and the dear black woman were all human sunflowers, seeking and seeing the Light in a world of darkness. WILLIAM C. GARNETT

MARCH 1

Consider what God has done: Who can straighten what he has made crooked?
ECCLESIASTES 7:13

GOD OFTEN SEEMS TO PLACE HIS CHILDREN IN PLACES OF DEEP DIFficulty, leading them into a corner from which there is no escape. He creates situations that human judgment, even if consulted, would never allow. Yet the cloudiness of the circumstance itself is used by Him to guide us to the other side. Perhaps this is where you find yourself even now.

Your situation is filled with uncertainty and is very serious, but it is perfectly right. The reason behind it will more than justify Him who brought you here, for it is a platform from which God will display His almighty grace and power.

He not only will deliver you but in doing so will impart a lesson that you will never forget. And in days to come, you will return to the truth of it through singing. You will be unable to ever thank God enough for doing exactly what He has done. SELECTED

We may wait till He explains,
Because we know that Jesus reigns.

It puzzles me; but, Lord, You understandest,
And will one day explain this crooked thing.
Meanwhile, I know that it has worked out Your best—
Its very crookedness taught me to cling.

You have fenced up my ways, made my paths crooked,
To keep my wand'ring eyes fixed on You,
To make me what I was not, humble, patient;
To draw my heart from earthly love to You.

So I will thank and praise You for this puzzle,
And trust where I cannot understand.
Rejoicing You do hold me worth such testing,
I cling the closer to Your guiding hand.

F. E. M. I.

MARCH 2

"Be ready in the morning, and then come up. . . . Present yourself to me there on top of the mountain. No one is to come with you."

Exodus 34:2–3

The morning is a critically important time of day. You must never face the day until you have faced God, nor look into the face of others until you have looked into His. You cannot expect to be victorious, if you begin your day in your own strength alone.

Begin the work of every day after having been influenced by a few reflective, quiet moments between your heart and God. Do not meet with others, even the members of your own family, until you have first met with the great Guest and honored Companion of your life—Jesus Christ.

Meet with Him alone and regularly, having His Book of counsel open before you. Then face the ordinary, and the unique, responsibilities of each day with the renewed influence and control of His character over all your actions.

Begin the day with God!
He is your Sun and Day!
His is the radiance of your dawn;
To Him address your day.

Sing a new song at morn!
Join the glad woods and hills;

Join the fresh winds and seas and plains,
Join the bright flowers and rills.

Sing your first song to God!
Not to your fellow men;
Not to the creatures of His hand,
But to the glorious One.

Take your first walk with God!
Let Him go forth with thee;
By stream, or sea, or mountain path,
Seek still His company.

Your first transaction be
With God Himself above;
So will your business prosper well,
All the day be love.

Horatius Bonar

Those who have accomplished the most for God in this world are those who have been found on their knees early in the morning. For example, Matthew Henry would spend from four to eight o'clock each morning in his study. Then, after breakfast and a time of family prayer, he would return to his study until noon. After lunch, he would write till four p.m. and then spend the remainder of the day visiting friends.

Philip Doddridge referred to his *Family Expositor* as an example of the difference of rising at five o'clock, as opposed to seven. He realized that increasing his workday by twenty-five percent was the equivalent of adding ten work years to his life over a period of forty years.

Adam Clarke's Commentary on the Bible was penned primarily in the early morning hours. *Barnes' Notes*, a popular and useful commentary by

Albert Barnes, was also the fruit of the early morning. And Charles Simeon's *Sketches* were mostly written between four and eight a.m.

MARCH 3

The spirit shrieked, convulsed him violently and came out.

MARK 9:26

EVIL NEVER SURRENDERS ITS GRASP WITHOUT A TREMENDOUS FIGHT. We never arrive at any spiritual inheritance through the enjoyment of a picnic but always through the fierce conflicts of the battlefield. And it is the same in the deep recesses of the soul. Every human capacity that wins its spiritual freedom does so at the cost of blood. Satan is not put to flight by our courteous request. He completely blocks our way, and our progress must be recorded in blood and tears. We need to remember this, or else we will be held responsible for the arrogance of misinterpretation. When we are born again, it is not into a soft and protected nursery but into the open countryside, where we actually draw our strength from the distress of the storm. "We must go through many hardships to enter the kingdom of God" (Acts 14:22). JOHN HENRY JOWETT

Faith of our Fathers! living still,
In spite of dungeon, fire and sword:
Oh, how our hearts beat high with joy
Whene'er we hear that glorious word.
Faith of our Fathers! Holy Faith!
We will be true to Thee till death!
Our fathers, chained in prisons dark,
Were still in heart of conscience free;
How sweet would be their children's fate,
If they, like them, could die for Thee!

MARCH 4

Imitate those who through faith and patience
inherit what has been promised.
HEBREWS 6:12

THE BIBLICAL HEROES OF FAITH CALL TO US FROM THE HEIGHTS THEY have won, encouraging us that what man once did, man can do again. They remind us not only of the necessity of faith but also of the patience required for faith's work to be perfected. May we fear attempting to remove ourselves from the hands of our heavenly Guide, or missing even one lesson of His loving discipline due to our discouragement or doubt.

An old village blacksmith once said, "There is only one thing I fear: being thrown onto the scrap heap. You see, in order to strengthen a piece of steel, I must first temper it. I heat it, hammer it, and then quickly plunge it into a bucket of cold water. Very soon I know whether it will accept the tempering process or simply fall to pieces. If, after one or two tests, I see it will not allow itself to be tempered, I throw it onto the scrap heap, only to later sell it to the junkman for a few cents per pound.

"I realize the Lord tests me in the same way: through fire, water, and heavy blows of His hammer. If I am unwilling to withstand the test, or prove to be unfit for His tempering process, I am afraid He may throw me onto the scrap heap." When the fire in your life is the hottest, stand still, for "*later on* . . . it produces a harvest" (Hebrews 12:11) of blessings. Then we will be able to say with Job, "When he has tested me, I will come forth as gold" (Job 23:10). SELECTED

Sainthood finds its source in suffering. Remember, it requires eleven tons of pressure on a piano's strings for it to be tuned. And God will tune you to perfect harmony with heaven's theme if you will withstand the strain.

Things that hurt and things that mar
Shape the man for perfect praise;

Shock and strain and ruin are
Friendlier than the smiling days.

MARCH 5

We have come to share in Christ if indeed we hold
our original conviction firmly till the very end.
HEBREWS 3:14

OFTEN THE LAST STEP IS THE WINNING STEP. IN *Pilgrim's Progress* THE greatest number of dangers were lurking in the area closest to the gates of the Celestial City. It was in that region the Doubting Castle stood. And it was there the enchanted ground lured the tired traveler to fatal slumber. It is when heaven's heights are in full view that the gates of hell are the most persistent and full of deadly peril. "Let us not become weary in doing good, for at the proper time we will reap a harvest *if we do not give up*" (Galatians 6:9). "Run in such a way as to get the prize" (1 Corinthians 9:24).

In the bitter waves of woe
Beaten and tossed about
By the sullen winds that blow
From the desolate shores of doubt,
Where the anchors that faith has cast
Are dragging in the gale,
I am quietly holding fast
To the things that cannot fail.

And fierce though the fiends may fight,
And long though the angels hide,
I know that truth and right
Have the universe on their side;
And that somewhere beyond the stars

Is a love that is better than fate.
When the night unlocks her bars
I will see Him—and I will wait.
WASHINGTON GLADDEN

The greatest challenge in receiving great things from God is holding on for the last half hour. SELECTED

MARCH 6

We had hoped.
LUKE 24:21

I HAVE ALWAYS BEEN SO SORRY THAT THE TWO DISCIPLES WALKING with Jesus on the road to Emmaus did not say to Him, "We *still* hope" instead of "We *had* hoped." The situation is very sad, because in their minds it is over.

Oh, if only they had said, "Everything has come against our hope, and it looks as if our trust were in vain. Yet we will not give up, because we believe we will see Him again." Instead, they walked by His side, declaring their shattered faith. Jesus had to say to them, "How foolish you are, and how slow to believe!" (Luke 24:25).

Are we not in danger of having these same words said to us? We can afford to lose every possession we have, except our faith in the God of truth and love. May we never express our faith, as these disciples did, in the past tense—"*We had hoped.*" Yet may we always say, "*I have hope.*" CRUMBS

The soft, sweet summer was warm and glowing,
Bright were the blossoms on every bough:
I trusted Him when the roses were blooming;
I trust Him now. . . .

Small was my faith should it weakly falter
Now that the roses have ceased to blow;
Frail was the trust that now should alter,
Doubting His love when storm clouds grow.
THE SONG OF A BIRD IN A WINTER STORM

MARCH 7

We were harassed at every turn.
2 CORINTHIANS 7:5

WHY IS IT THAT GOD LEADS US IN THIS WAY, ALLOWING SUCH STRONG and constant pressure on us? One of His purposes is to show us His all-sufficient strength and grace more effectively than if we were free from difficulties and trials. "We have this treasure in jars of clay to show that this all-surpassing power is from God and not from us" (2 Corinthians 4:7).

Another purpose is to bring us a greater awareness of our dependence upon Him. God is constantly trying to teach us how dependent we are on Him—that we are held completely by His hand and reliant on His care alone.

This is exactly where Jesus Himself stood and where He desires us to stand. We must stand not with self-made strength but always leaning upon Him. And our stand must exhibit a trust that would never dare to take even one step alone. This will teach us to trust Him more.

There is no way to learn of faith except through trials. They are God's school of faith, and it is much better for us to learn to trust Him than to live a life of enjoyment. And once the lesson of faith has been learned, it is an everlasting possession and an eternal fortune gained. Yet without trust in God, even great riches will leave us in poverty. DAYS OF HEAVEN UPON EARTH

Why must I weep when others sing?
"To test the deeps of suffering."

Why must I work while others rest?
"To spend my strength at God's request."
Why must I lose while others gain?
"To understand defeat's sharp pain."
Why must this lot of life be mine
When that which fairer seems is thine?
"Because God knows what plans for me
Will blossom in eternity."

MARCH 8

Do as you promised . . . that your name will be great forever.
1 CHRONICLES 17:23–24

THIS IS ONE OF THE MOST BLESSED ASPECTS OF GENUINE PRAYER. Often we ask for things that God has not specifically promised. Therefore we are not sure if our petitions are in line with His purpose, until we have persevered for some time in prayer. Yet on some occasions, and this was one in the life of David, we are fully persuaded that what we are asking is in accordance with God's will. We feel led to select and plead a promise from the pages of Scripture, having been specially impressed that it contains a message for us. At these times, we may say with confident faith, "Do as you promised."

Hardly any stance could be more completely beautiful, strong, or safe than that of putting your finger on a promise of God's divine Word and then claiming it. Doing so requires no anguish, struggle, or wrestling but simply presenting the check and asking for cash. It is as simple as producing the promise and claiming its fulfillment. Nor will there be any doubt or cloudiness about the request. If all requests were this definitive, there would be much more interest in prayer. It is much better to claim a few specific things than to make twenty vague requests. F. B. MEYER

Every promise of Scripture is a letter from God, which we may plead before Him with this reasonable request: "*Do as you promised.*" Our Creator will never cheat those of us of His creation who depend upon His truth. And even more, our heavenly Father will never break His word to His own child.

"*Remember your word to your servant, for you have given me hope*" (Psalm 119:49). This is a very common plea and is a double argument, for it is "your word." Will You not keep it? Why have You spoken it, if You will not make it good? "You have given me hope." Will You now disappoint the hope that You Yourself have brought forth within me? CHARLES H. SPURGEON

"Being fully persuaded that God had power to do what he had promised" (Romans 4:21).

It is the everlasting faithfulness of God that makes a Bible promise "very great and precious" (2 Peter 1:4). Human promises are often worthless, and many broken promises have left broken hearts. But since the creation of the world, God has never broken a single promise to one of His trusting children.

Oh, how sad it is for a poor Christian to stand at the very door of a promise during a dark night of affliction, being afraid to turn the knob and thereby come boldly into the shelter as a child entering his Father's house! GURNAL

Every promise of God's is built on four pillars. The first two are His justice and holiness, which will never allow Him to deceive us. The third is His grace or goodness, which will not allow Him to forget. And the fourth is His truth, which will not allow Him to change, which enables Him to accomplish what He has promised. SELECTED

MARCH 9

Descend from the crest.

SONG OF SONGS 4:8

Bearing the burden of crushing weight actually gives Christians wings. This may sound like a contradiction in terms, but it is a blessed truth. While enduring a severe trial, David cried, "Oh, that I had the wings of a dove! I would fly away and be at rest" (Psalm 55:6). Yet before he finished his meditation, he seems to have realized that his wish for wings was attainable, for then he said, "Cast your cares on the Lord and he will sustain you" (Psalm 55:22).

The word "burden" is described in my Bible commentary as being "what Jehovah has given you." The saints' burdens are God-given, leading us to wait upon Him. And once we have done so, the burden is transformed into a pair of wings through the miracle of trust, and the one who was weighted down "will soar on wings like eagles" (Isaiah 40:31).
Sunday School Times

One day when walking down the street,
On business bent, while thinking hard
About the "hundred cares" which seemed
Like thunderclouds about to break
In torrents, Self-pity said to me:
"You poor, poor thing, you have too much
To do. Your life is far too hard.
This heavy load will crush you soon."
A swift response of sympathy
Welled up within. The burning sun
Seemed more intense. The dust and noise
Of puffing motors flying past
With rasping blast of blowing horn
Incensed still more the whining nerves,
The fabled last back-breaking straw
To weary, troubled, fretting mind.

"Ah yes, it will break and crush my life;
I cannot bear this constant strain
Of endless, aggravating cares;
They are too great for such as I."
So thus my heart consoled itself,
"Enjoying misery," when lo!
A "still small voice" distinctly said,
"'Twas sent to lift you—not to crush."
I saw at once my great mistake.
My place was not beneath the load
But on the top! God meant it not
That I should carry it. He sent
It here to carry me. Full well
He knew my incapacity
Before the plan was made. He saw
A child of His in need of grace
And power to serve; a puny twig
Requiring sun and rain to grow;
An undeveloped chrysalis;
A weak soul lacking faith in God.
He could not help but see all this
And more. And then, with tender thought
He placed it where it had to grow—
Or die. To lie and cringe beneath
One's load means death, but life and power
Await all those who dare to rise above.
Our burdens are our wings; on them
We soar to higher realms of grace;
Without them we must ever roam
On plains of undeveloped faith,
(For faith grows but by exercise
In circumstance impossible).

O paradox of Heaven. The load
We think will crush was sent to lift us
Up to God! Then, soul of mine,
Climb up! Nothing can e'er be crushed
Save what is underneath the weight.
How may we climb! By what ascent
Will we crest the critical cares
Of life! Within His word is found
The key which opens His secret stairs;
Alone with Christ, secluded there,
We mount our loads, and rest in Him.

Mary Butterfield

MARCH 10

My righteous one will live by faith.

Hebrews 10:38

Often our feelings and emotions are mistakenly substituted for faith. Pleasurable emotions and deep, satisfying experiences are part of the Christian life, but they are not the essence of it. Trials, conflicts, battles, and testings lie along the way and are to be counted not as misfortunes but rather as part of our necessary discipline.

In all of these various experiences, we are to rely on the indwelling of Christ in our hearts, regardless of our feelings, as we walk obediently before Him. And this is where many Christians get into trouble. They try to walk by feelings rather than by faith.

A believer once related that it seemed as if God had totally withdrawn Himself from her. His mercy *seemed* completely gone. Her loneliness lasted for six weeks, until the heavenly Lover seemed to say to her, "You have looked for Me in the outside world of emotions, yet all the while I have been waiting inside for you. Meet Me now in the inner chamber of your spirit, *for I am there*."

Be sure to distinguish between the fact of God's presence and the *feeling* of the fact. It is actually a wonderful thing when our soul feels lonely and deserted, as long as our faith can say, "I do not see You, Lord, nor do I feel Your presence, but I know for certain You are graciously here—exactly where I am and aware of my circumstances." Remind yourself again and again with these words: "Lord, You are here. And though the bush before me does not seem to burn, it *does* burn. I will take the shoes from my feet, 'for the place where [I am] standing is holy ground'" (Exodus 3:5). London Christian

Trust God's Word and His power more than you trust your own feelings and experiences. Remember, your Rock is Christ, and it is the sea that ebbs and flows with the tides, not Him. Samuel Rutherford

Keep your eyes firmly fixed on the infinite greatness of Christ's finished work and His righteousness. Look to Jesus and believe—look to Jesus and live! In fact, as you look to Him, unfurl your sails and bravely face the raging storms on the sea of life. Do not exhibit your distrust by staying in the security of the calm harbor or by sleeping comfortably through your life of ease. Do not allow your life and emotions to be tossed back and forth against each other like ships idly moored at port. The Christian life is not one of listless brooding over our emotions or slowly drifting our keel of faith through shallow water. Nor is it one of dragging our anchor of hope through the settling mud of the bay, as if we were afraid of encountering a healthy breeze.

Sail away! Spread your sail toward the storm and trust in Him who rules the raging seas. A brightly colored bird is safest when in flight. If its nest is near the ground or if it flies too low, it exposes itself to the hunter's net or trap. In the same way, if we cower in the lowlands of feelings and emotions, we will find ourselves entangled in a thousand nets of doubt, despair, temptation, and unbelief. "How useless to spread a net where every bird can see it!" (Proverbs 1:17). "Put your hope in God" (Psalm 42:5). J. R. MACDUFF

When I cannot *feel* the faith of assurance, I live by the *fact* of God's faithfulness. MATTHEW HENRY

MARCH 11

After the death of Moses the servant of the LORD, the LORD said to Joshua son of Nun, Moses' aide: "Moses my servant is dead. Now then, you and all these people, get ready to cross the Jordan River."

JOSHUA 1:1–2

YESTERDAY YOU EXPERIENCED A GREAT SORROW, AND NOW YOUR HOME seems empty. Your first impulse is to give up and to sit down in despair amid your dashed hopes. Yet you must defy that temptation, for you are at the front line of the battle, and the crisis is at hand. Faltering even one moment would put God's interest at risk. Other lives will be harmed by your hesitation, and His work will suffer if you simply fold your hands. You must not linger at this point, even to indulge your grief.

A famous general once related this sorrowful story from his own wartime experience. His son was the lieutenant of an artillery unit, and an assault was in progress. As the father led his division in a charge, pressing on across the battlefield, suddenly his eye caught sight of a dead artillery officer lying right before him. Just a glance told him it was his son. The general's fatherly impulse was to kneel by the body of his beloved son and express his grief, but the duty of the moment demanded he press on with his charge. So after quickly kissing his dead son, he hurried away, leading his command in the assault.

Weeping inconsolably beside a grave will never bring back the treasure of a lost love, nor can any blessing come from such great sadness. Sorrow causes deep scars, and indelibly writes its story on the suffering heart. We never completely recover from our greatest griefs and are never exactly the same after having passed through them. Yet sorrow that is endured in the right spirit impacts our growth favorably and brings us a greater sense of compassion for others. Indeed, those who have no scars of sorrow or suffering upon them are poor. "The joy set before" (Hebrews 12:2) us should shine on our griefs just as the sun shines through the clouds, making them radiant. God has ordained our truest and richest comfort to be found by pressing on toward the goal. Sitting down and brooding over our sorrow deepens the darkness surrounding us, allowing it to creep into our hearts. And soon our strength has changed to weakness. But if we will turn from the gloom and remain faithful to the calling of God, the light will shine again and we will grow stronger. J. R. Miller

Lord, You know that through our tears
Of hasty, selfish weeping
Comes surer sin, and for our petty fears
Of loss You have in keeping
A greater gain than all of which we dreamed;
You knowest that in grasping
The bright possessions which so precious seemed
We lose them; but if, clasping
Your faithful hand, we tread with steadfast feet
The path of Your appointing,
There waits for us a treasury of sweet
Delight, royal anointing
With oil of gladness and of strength.

Helen Hunt Jackson

MARCH 12

The Lord made an east wind blow across the land all that day and all that night. By morning the wind had brought

the locusts. . . . Pharaoh quickly summoned Moses and Aaron. . . . And the LORD *changed the wind to a very strong west wind, which caught up the locusts and carried them into the Red Sea. Not a locust was left anywhere in Egypt.*

EXODUS 10:13, 16, 19

IN THESE VERSES WE SEE HOW IN ANCIENT TIMES, WHEN THE LORD fought for Israel against the cruel Pharaoh, it was *stormy winds* that won their deliverance. And again later, in the greatest display of His power, God struck the final blow to the proud defiance of Egypt with *stormy winds.* Yet at first it seemed that a strange and almost cruel thing was happening to Israel. They were hemmed in by a multitude of dangers: in front, a raging sea defied them; on either side, mountains cut off any hope of escape; and above them, a hurricane seemed to blow. It was as if the first deliverance had come only to hand them over to a more certain death. "The Israelites looked up, and there were the Egyptians, marching after them. They were terrified and cried out to the LORD" (Exodus 14:10).

Only when it seemed they were trapped for the enemy did the glorious triumph come. The *stormy wind* blew forward, beating back the waves. The vast multitude of Israelites marched ahead along the path of the deep sea floor—a path covered with God's protecting love. On either side were crystal walls of water, glowing in the light of the glory of the Lord, and high above them roared the thunder of the storm. And so it continued on through the night, until at dawn the next day, as the last of the Israelites set foot on shore, the work of the *stormy wind* was done.

Then Israel sang a song to the Lord of how the *stormy wind* fulfilled His word: "The enemy boasted, 'I will pursue, I will overtake them. I will divide the spoils. . . .' But you blew with your breath, and the sea covered them. They sank like lead in the mighty waters" (Exodus 15:9–10).

Someday, through His great mercy, we too will stand on "a sea of glass," holding "harps given [to us] by God." Then we will sing "the song of God's servant Moses and of the Lamb: 'Great and marvelous are your deeds, Lord God Almighty. Just and true are your ways, King of the nations'" (Revelation 15:2–3). Then we will know how the *stormy winds* have won our deliverance.

Today, only questions surround your great sorrow, but then you will see how the threatening enemy was actually swept away during your stormy night of fear and grief.

Today you see only your loss, but then you will see how God used it to break the evil chains that had begun to restrain you.

Today you cower at the howling wind and the roaring thunder, but then you will see how they beat back the waves of destruction and opened your way to the peaceful Land of Promise. MARK GUY PEARSE

Though winds are wild,
And the gale unleashed,
My trusting heart still sings:
I know that they mean
No harm to me,
He rides upon their wings.

MARCH 13

Just and true are your ways, King of the nations.
REVELATION 15:3

THE FOLLOWING STORY WAS RELATED BY MRS. CHARLES H. SPURGEON, who suffered greatly with poor health for more than twenty-five years: "At the end of a dull and dreary day, I lay resting on my couch as the night grew darker. Although my room was bright and cozy, some of the darkness outside seemed to have entered my soul and obscured its spiritual vision. In vain I tried to see the sovereign hand that I knew held mine and that guided my fog-surrounded feet along a steep and slippery path of suffering.

"With a sorrowful heart I asked, 'Why does the Lord deal with a child of His in this way? Why does He so often send such sharp and bitter pain to visit me? Why does He allow this lingering weakness to hinder the sweet service I long to render to His poor servants?'

"These impatient questions were quickly answered through a very strange language. Yet no interpreter was needed except the mindful whisper of my heart. For a while silence reigned in the little room, being broken only by the crackling of an oak log burning in the fireplace. Suddenly I heard a sweet, soft sound: a faint, yet clear, musical note, like the tender trill of a robin beneath my window.

"I asked aloud, 'What can that be? Surely no bird can be singing outside at this time of year or night.' But again came the faint, mournful notes, so sweet and melodious, yet mysterious enough to cause us to wonder. Then my friend exclaimed, 'It's coming from the log on the fire!' The fire was unshackling the imprisoned music from deep within the old oak's heart!

"Perhaps the oak had acquired this song during the days when all was well with him—when birds sang merrily on his branches, and while the soft sunlight streaked his tender leaves with gold. But he had grown old and hard since then. Ring after ring of knotty growth had sealed up his long-forgotten melody, until the fiery tongues of the flames consumed his callousness. The intense heat of the fire wrenched from him both a song and a sacrifice at once. Then I realized: when the fires of affliction draw songs of praise from us, we are indeed purified, and our God is glorified!

"Maybe some of us are like this old oak log: cold, hard, unfeeling, and never singing any melodious sounds. It is the fires burning around us that release notes of trust in God and bring cheerful compliance with His will. As I thought of this, the fire burned, and my soul found sweet comfort in the parable so strangely revealed before me.

"Yes, singing in the fire! God helping us, sometimes using the only way He can to get harmony from our hard and apathetic hearts. Then, let the furnace be 'heated seven times hotter than usual' [Daniel 3:19]."

MARCH 14

Moses approached the thick darkness where God was.

Exodus 20:21

God still has His secrets—hidden from "the wise and learned" (Luke 10:21). Do not fear these unknown things, but be content to accept the things you cannot understand and to wait patiently. In due time He will reveal the treasures of the unknown to you—the riches of the glory of the mystery. Recognize that the mystery is simply the veil covering God's face.

Do not be afraid to enter the cloud descending on your life, for God is in it. And the other side is radiant with His glory. "Do not be surprised at the fiery ordeal that has come on you to test you as though something strange were happening to you. But rejoice inasmuch as you participate in the sufferings of Christ" (1 Peter 4:12–13). When you feel the most forsaken and lonely, God is near. He is in the darkest cloud. Forge ahead into the darkness without flinching, knowing that under the shelter of the cloud, God is waiting for you. Selected

Have you a cloud?
Something that is dark and full of dread;
A messenger of tempest overhead?
A something that is darkening the sky;
A something growing darker by and by;
A something that you're fearful will burst at last;
A cloud that does a deep, long shadow cast?
God's coming in that cloud.
Have you a cloud?
It is Jehovah's triumph car: in this
He's riding to you, o'er the wide abyss.
It is the robe in which He wraps His form;
For He does dress Him with the flashing storm.
It is the veil in which He hides the light

Of His fair face, too dazzling for your sight.
God's coming in that cloud.
Have you a cloud?
A trial that is terrible to thee?
A dark temptation threatening to see?
A loss of some dear one long your own?
A mist, a veiling, bringing the unknown?
A mystery that insubstantial seems:
A cloud between you and the sun's bright beams?
God's coming in that cloud.
Have you a cloud?
A sickness—weak old age—distress and death?
These clouds will scatter at your last faint breath.
Fear not the clouds that hover o'er your boat,
Making the harbor's entrance woeful to float;
The cloud of death, though misty, chill and cold,
Will yet grow radiant with a fringe of gold.
God's coming in that cloud.

A man once stood on a high peak of the Rocky Mountains watching a raging storm below. As he watched, an eagle came up through the clouds and soared away toward the sun. The water on its wings glistened in the sunlight like diamonds. If not for the storm, the eagle might have remained in the valley. In the same way, the sorrows of life cause us to rise toward God.

MARCH 15

"Do not be afraid, you worm Jacob. . . . I will make you into a threshing sledge, new and sharp, with many teeth."

Isaiah 41:14–15

Could any two things be in greater contrast than a worm and a threshing tool with sharp teeth? A worm is delicate and is easily bruised by a stone or crushed beneath a passing wheel. Yet a threshing tool with sharp teeth can cut through rock and not be broken, leaving its mark upon the rock. And almighty God can convert one into the other. He can take an individual or a nation, who has all the weakness of a worm, and through the energizing work of His own Spirit, endow that person or nation with strength enough to make a profound mark upon the history of their time.

Therefore a "worm" may take heart. Almighty God can make us stronger than our circumstances and can turn each situation to our good. In God's strength we can make them all pay tribute to our soul. We can even take the darkest disappointment, break it open, and discover a precious jewel of grace inside. When God gives us an iron will, we can cut through difficulties just as an iron plowshare cuts through the hardest soil. As He said in the above verse, "I will make you . . ." Will He not do it? John Henry Jowett

Christ is building His kingdom with the broken things of earth. People desire only the strong, successful, victorious, and unbroken things in life to build their kingdoms, but God is the God of the unsuccessful—the God of those who have failed. Heaven is being filled with earth's broken lives, and there is no "bruised reed" (Isaiah 42:3) that Christ cannot take and restore to a glorious place of blessing and beauty. He can take a life crushed by pain or sorrow and make it a harp whose music will be total praise. He can lift earth's saddest failure up to heaven's glory. J. R. Miller

"Follow Me, and I will make you . . ."
Make you speak My words with power,
Make you vessels of My mercy,
Make you helpful every hour.

"Follow Me, and I will make you . . ."
Make you what you cannot be—

Make you loving, trustful, godly,
Make you even just like Me.
L. S. P.

MARCH 16

For our good.
HEBREWS 12:10

IN ONE OF RALPH CONNER'S BOOKS HE TELLS THE STORY OF GWEN. Gwen was an undisciplined and strong-willed girl, always accustomed to having her own way. One day she had a terrible accident that crippled her for life, leading her to become even more rebellious. Once while in a complaining mood, she was visited by a local "sky pilot," or mountaineer missionary. He told her the following parable about the canyon:

"At first there were no canyons but only the vast, open prairie. One day the Master of the prairie, walking across His great grasslands, asked the prairie, 'Where are your flowers?' The prairie responded, 'Master, I have no flower seeds.'

"The Master then spoke to the birds, and they brought seeds of every kind of flower, scattering them far and wide. Soon the prairie bloomed with crocuses, roses, yellow buttercups, wild sunflowers, and red lilies all summer long. When the Master saw the flowers, He was pleased. But He failed to see His favorites and asked the prairie, 'Where are the clematis, columbine, violets, wildflowers, ferns, and the flowering shrubs?'

"So once again He spoke to the birds, and again they brought all the seeds and spread them far and wide. But when the Master arrived, He still could not find the flowers he loved the most, and asked, 'Where are my sweetest flowers?' The prairie cried sorrowfully, 'O Master, I cannot keep the flowers. The winds sweep fiercely across me, and the sun beats down upon my breast, and they simply wither up and blow away.'

"Then the Master spoke to the lightning, and with one swift bolt, the lightning split the prairie through its heart. The prairie reeled and groaned in agony and for many days bitterly complained about its dark, jagged, and gaping wound. But the river poured its water through the chasm, bringing rich, dark soil with it.

"Once again the birds brought seeds and scattered them in the canyon. After a long time the rough rocks were adorned with soft mosses and trailing vines, and all the secluded cliffs were draped with clematis and columbine. Giant elms raised their huge limbs high into the sunlight, while at their feet small cedars and balsam firs clustered together. Everywhere violets, anemones, and maidenhair ferns grew and bloomed, until the canyon became the Master's favorite place for rest, peace, and joy."

Then the "sky pilot" said to her, "'The fruit [or "flowers"] of the Spirit [are] love, joy, peace, patience, kindness, . . . gentleness' [Galatians 5:22–23 NASB], and some of these grow only in the canyon." Gwen softly asked, "Which are the canyon flowers?" The missionary answered, "Patience, kindness, and gentleness. Yet even though love, joy, and peace may bloom in the open spaces, the blossom is never as beautiful, or the perfume as fragrant, as when they are found blooming in the canyon."

Gwen sat very still for quite some time, and then longingly said with trembling lips, "There are no flowers in my canyon—only jagged rocks." The missionary lovingly responded, "Someday they will bloom, dear Gwen. The Master will find them, and we will see them, too."

Beloved, when *you* come to your canyon, remember!

MARCH 17

"Stay there until I tell you."

MATTHEW 2:13

I'll stay where You've put me; I will, dear Lord,
Though I wanted so badly to go;

I was eager to march with the "rank and file,"
Yes, I wanted to lead them, You know.
I planned to keep step to the music loud,
To cheer when the banner unfurled,
To stand in the midst of the fight straight and proud,
But I'll stay where You've put me.
I'll stay where You've put me; I'll work, dear Lord,
Though the field be narrow and small,
And the ground be neglected, and stones lie thick,
And there seems to be no life at all.
The field is Your own, only give me the seed,
I'll sow it with never a fear;
I'll till the dry soil while I wait for the rain,
And rejoice when the green blades appear;
I'll work where You've put me.
I'll stay where You've put me; I will, dear Lord;
I'll bear the day's burden and heat,
Always trusting You fully; when sunset has come
I'll lay stalks of grain at Your feet.
And then, when my earth work is ended and done,
In the light of eternity's glow,
Life's record all closed, I surely will find
It was better to stay than to go; I'll stay where You've put me.

O restless heart—beating against the prison bars of your circumstances and longing for a wider realm of usefulness—allow God to direct all your days. Patience and trust, even in the midst of the monotony of your daily routine, will be the best preparation to courageously handle the stress and strain of a greater opportunity, which God may someday send.

MARCH 18

He answered nothing.

Mark 15:3 KJV

There is no scene in all the Bible more majestic than our Savior remaining silent before the men who were reviling Him. With one quick burst of divine power, or one fiery word of rebuke, He could have caused His accusers to be laid prostrate at His feet. Yet He answered not one word, allowing them to say and do their very worst. He stood in the power of stillness—God's holy silent Lamb.

There is a place of stillness that allows God the opportunity to work for us and gives us peace. It is a stillness that ceases our scheming, self-vindication, and the search for a temporary means to an end through our own wisdom and judgment. Instead, it lets God provide an answer, through His unfailing and faithful love, to the cruel blow we have suffered.

Oh, how often we thwart God's intervention on our behalf by taking up our own cause or by striking a blow in our own defense! May God grant each of us this silent power and submissive spirit. Then once our earthly battles and strife are over, others will remember us as we now remember the morning dew, the soft light of sunrise, a peaceful evening breeze, the Lamb of Calgary, and the gentle and holy heavenly Dove. A. B. Simpson

The day when Jesus stood alone
And felt the hearts of men like stone,
And knew He came but to atone—
That day "He held His peace."

They witnessed falsely to His word,
They bound Him with a cruel cord,
And mockingly proclaimed Him Lord;
"But Jesus held His peace."

They spat upon Him in the face,
They dragged Him on from place to place,
They heaped upon Him all disgrace;
"But Jesus held His peace."

My friend, have you for far much less,
With rage, which you called righteousness,
Resented slights with great distress?
Your Savior "held His peace."

L. S. P.

I remember hearing Bishop Whipple of Minnesota, who was well known as "The Apostle of the Indians," voice these beautiful words: "For the last thirty years, I have looked for the face of Christ in the people with whom I have disagreed."

When this spirit drives us, we will be immediately protected from a feeble tolerance of others, narrow-mindedness, harsh vindictiveness, and everything else that would damage our testimony for Him who came not to destroy lives but to save them. W. H. GRIFFITH-THOMAS

MARCH 19

Dear friends, do not be surprised at the fiery ordeal
that has come on inasmuch as. . . . But rejoice that
you participate in the sufferings of Christ.

1 PETER 4:12–13

MANY HOURS OF WAITING WERE NECESSARY TO ENRICH DAVID'S HARP with song. And hours of waiting in the wilderness will provide us with psalms of "thanksgiving and the sound of singing" (Isaiah 51:3). The hearts of the discouraged here below will be lifted, and joy will be brought to our Father's heavenly home.

What was the preparation for Jesse's son, David, to compose songs unlike any others ever heard before on earth? It was the sinful persecution he endured at the hands of the wicked that brought forth his cries for God's help. Then David's faint hope in God's goodness blossomed into full songs of rejoicing, declaring the Lord's mighty deliverances and multiplied mercies. Every sorrow was yet another note from his harp, and every deliverance another theme of praise.

One stinging sorrow spared would have been one blessing missed and unclaimed. One difficulty or danger escaped—how great would have been our loss! The thrilling psalms where God's people today find expression for their grief or praise might never have been known.

Waiting on God and abiding in His will is to know Him in "the fellowship of his sufferings" (Philippians 3:10 KJV) and "to be conformed to the image of his Son" (Romans 8:29). Therefore if God's desire is to enlarge your capacity for spiritual understanding, do not be frightened by the greater realm of suffering that awaits you. The Lord's capacity for sympathy is greater still, for the breath of the Holy Spirit into His new creation never makes a heart hard and insensitive, but affectionate, tender, and true. Anna Shipton

"I thank Christ Jesus our Lord, who has given me strength, that he considered me faithful, appointing me to his service" (1 Timothy 1:12).

MARCH 20

Sorrowful, yet always rejoicing.

2 Corinthians 6:10

A stoic person despises the shedding of tears, but a Christian is not forbidden to weep. Yet the soul may become silent from excessive grief, just as the quivering sheep may remain quiet beneath the scissors of the shearer. Or, when the heart is at the verge of breaking beneath the waves of a trial, the sufferer may seek relief by crying out with a loud voice. *But there is something even better.*

It is said that springs of sweet, fresh water pool up amid the saltiness of the oceans, that the fairest Alpine flowers bloom in the wildest and most rugged mountain passes, and that the most magnificent psalms arose from the most profound agonies of the soul.

May it continue to be! Therefore, amid a multitude of trials, souls who love God will discover reasons for boundless, leaping joy. Even though "deep calls to deep" (Psalm 42:7), the clear cadence of the Lord's song will be heard. And during the most difficult hour that could ever enter a human life, *it will be possible* to bless the God and Father of our Lord Jesus Christ.

Have you learned this lesson yet? Not simply to endure or to choose God's will but to rejoice in it "with an inexpressible and glorious joy" (1 Peter 1:8). TRIED BY FIRE

I will be still, my bruised heart faintly murmured,
As o'er me rolled a crushing load of woe;
My words, my cries, e'en my low moan was stifled;
I pressed my lips; I barred the teardrop's flow.

I will be still, although I cannot see it,
The love that bares a soul and fans pain's fire;
That takes away the last sweet drop of solace,
Breaks the lone harp string, hides Your precious lyre.

But God is love, so I will stay me, stay me—
We'll doubt not, Soul, we will be very still;
We'll wait till after while, when He will lift us—
Yes, after while, when it will be His will.

And I did listen to my heart's brave promise;
And I did quiver, struggling to be still;
And I did lift my tearless eyes to Heaven,
Repeating ever, "Yes, Christ, have Your will."

But soon my heart spoke up from 'neath our burden,
Rebuked my tight-drawn lips, my face so sad:
"We can do more than this, O Soul," it whispered.
"We can be more than still, we can be glad!"

And now my heart and I are sweetly singing—
Singing without the sound of tuneful strings;
Drinking abundant waters in the desert;
Crushed, and yet soaring as on eagle's wings.
S. P. W.

MARCH 21

"According to your faith let it be done to you."
MATTHEW 9:29

"PRAYING THROUGH" SOMETHING MIGHT BE DEFINED AS FOLLOWS: "Praying your way into full faith; coming to the point of assurance, while still praying, that your prayer has been accepted and heard; and in advance of the event, with confident anticipation, actually becoming aware of having received what you ask."

Let us remember that no earthly circumstances can hinder the fulfillment of God's Word. We must look steadfastly at His immutable Word and not at the uncertainty of this ever-changing world. God desires for us to believe His Word without other evidence, *and then* He is ready to do for us "according to [our] faith."

When once His Word is past,
When He has said, "I will," [Hebrews 13:5]
The thing will come at last;
God keeps His promise still. [2 Corinthians 1:20]

The prayers of the Pentecostal era were prayed with such simple faith that they were like cashing a check. Robert Anderson

"And God said. . . . And it was so" (Genesis 1:9).

MARCH 22

After forty years had passed, an angel appeared to Moses in the flames of a burning bush in the desert near Mount Sinai. . . . Then the Lord said to him, ". . . I have indeed seen the oppression of my people in Egypt. I have heard their groaning and have come down to set them free. Now come, I will send you back to Egypt."

Acts 7:30, 33–34

Forty years was a long time to wait in preparation for a great mission. Yet when God delays, He is not inactive. This is when He prepares His instruments and matures our strength. Then at the appointed time we will rise up and be equal to our task.

Even Jesus of Nazareth had thirty years of privacy, growing in wisdom before He began His work. John Henry Jowett

God is never in a hurry. He spends years preparing those He plans to greatly use, and never thinks of the days of preparation as being too long or boring.

The most difficult ingredient of suffering is often *time*. A short, sharp pain is easily endured, but when a sorrow drags on its long and weary way year after monotonous year, returning day after day with the same dull routine of hopeless agony, the heart loses its strength. Without the grace of God, the heart is sure to sink into dismal despair.

Joseph endured a long trial, and God often has to burn the lessons he learned into the depths of our being, using the fires of prolonged pain. "He will sit as a refiner and purifier of silver" (Malachi 3:3), yet He knows the specific amount of time that will be needed. Like a true goldsmith, God stops the fire the moment He sees His image in the glowing metal.

Today we may be unable to see the final outcome of the beautiful plan that God has hidden "in the shadow of his hand" (Isaiah 49:2). It may be concealed for a very long time, but our faith may rest in the assurance that God is still seated on His throne. Because of this assurance, we can calmly await the time when, in heavenly delight, we will say, "All things [have] work[ed] together for good" (Romans 8:28 KJV).

As Joseph did, we should be more careful to focus on learning all the lessons in the school of sorrow than to focus anxious eyes toward the time of our deliverance. There is a reason behind every lesson, and when we are ready, our deliverance will definitely come. Then we will know we could never have served in our place of higher service without having been taught the very things we learned during our ordeal. God is in the process of educating us for future service and greater blessings. And if we have gained the qualities that make us ready for a throne, nothing will keep us from it once His timing is right.

Don't steal tomorrow from God's hands. Give Him time to speak to you and reveal His will. He is never late—learn to wait. SELECTED

He never shows up late; He knows just what is best;
Fret not yourself in vain; until He comes just rest.

Never run impulsively ahead of the Lord. Learn to await His timing—the second, minute, and hour hand must all point to the precise moment for action.

MARCH 23

Some of the plunder taken in battle they dedicated
for the repair of the temple of the LORD.
1 CHRONICLES 26:27

Great physical force is stored in the depths of the earth, in places such as coal mines. Coal was produced by the tremendous heat that burned the ancient forests. In the same way, spiritual force is stored in the depths of our being and is brought about by the very pain we cannot understand.

Someday we will see that "the plunder taken in battle" from our trials was simply preparing us to become like Great-heart in *Pilgrim's Progress*, so we too could lead our fellow pilgrims triumphantly through trials to the city of the King. But may we never forget that the source of learning to help others must be the experience of victorious suffering. Whining and complaining about our pain never does anyone any good.

Paul never carried the gloom of a cemetery around with him, but a chorus of victorious praise. The more difficult his trial, the more he trusted and rejoiced, shouting from the very altar of sacrifice. He said, "Even if I am being poured out like a drink offering on the sacrifice and service coming from your faith, I am glad and rejoice with all of you" (Philippians 2:17). Lord, help me today to draw strength from everything that comes to me! Days of Heaven upon Earth

He placed me in a little cage,
Away from gardens fair;
But I must sing the sweetest songs
Because He placed me there.
Not beat my wings against the cage
If it's my Maker's will,
But raise my voice to heaven's gate
And sing the louder still!

MARCH 24

Then Jacob prayed, "O God of my father Abraham,
God of my father Isaac, Lord, you who said to me,

'Go back to your country and your relatives, and I will make you prosper, . . . Save me, I pray."

GENESIS 32:9, 11

THERE ARE MANY HEALTHY ASPECTS TO JACOB'S PRAYER. IN SOME respects it could serve as a mold into which we pour our own spirits while we are being melted in the fiery furnace of sorrow.

Jacob began by quoting God's promise twice and by saying, "Who said to me" and "You have said" (v. 12). See how he has God in his grasp! God places Himself within our reach through His promises, and when we can actually say to Him, "You have said," He cannot say no. God must do as He has said.

If Jacob was so careful over his words, what great care will God take over His promises? Therefore while in prayer be sure to stand firmly on a promise of God. By doing so, you will obtain enough power to throw open the gates of heaven and to take it by force. PRACTICAL PORTIONS FOR THE PRAYER-LIFE

Jesus desires that we would be very specific in our requests, asking for something definite. "What do you want me to do for you?" (Matthew 20:32) is the question He asks everyone who comes to Him during trials and affliction. Make your requests earnestly and specifically, if you desire definite answers. It is the aimlessness of prayer that accounts for so many seemingly unanswered prayers. Be specific in your petitions. Fill out your check for something definite, and it will be cashed at the bank of heaven when it is presented in Jesus' name. *Dare to be specific with God.* SELECTED

Frances Ridley Havergal once said, "Every year I live—in fact, nearly every day—I seem to see more clearly how all the peace, happiness, and power of the Christian life hinges on one thing. That one thing is taking God at His word, believing He really means exactly what He says, and accepting the very words that reveal His goodness and grace, without substituting other words or changing the precise moods and tenses He has seen fit to use." Take Christ's Word—His promise—and Christ's sacrifice—His blood—with you to the throne of grace through prayer, and not one of heaven's blessings can be denied you. Adam Clarke

MARCH 25

Without faith it is impossible to please God, because anyone who comes to him must believe that he exists and that he rewards those who earnestly seek him.

Hebrews 11:6

We all need faith for desperate days, and the Bible is filled with accounts of such days. Its story is told with them, its songs are inspired by them, its prophecy deals with them, and its revelation has come through them. Desperate days are the stepping-stones on the path of light. They seem to have been God's opportunity to provide our school of wisdom.

Psalm 107 is filled with stories of God's lavish love. In every story of deliverance, it was humankind coming to the point of desperation that gave God His opportunity to act. Arriving at "their wits' end" (Psalm 107:27) of desperation was the beginning of God's power.

Remember the promise made to a couple "as good as dead," that their descendants would be "as numerous as the stars in the sky and as countless as the sand on the seashore" (Hebrews 11:12). Read once again the story of the Red Sea deliverance, and the story of how "the priests who carried the ark of the covenant of the Lord stood firm on dry ground in the middle of the Jordan" (Joshua 3:17 NASB). Study once more the prayers of Asa, Jehoshaphat, and Hezekiah when they were severely troubled, not knowing what to do. Go over the history of Nehemiah, Daniel, Hosea, and Habakkuk. Stand with awe in the darkness of Gethsemane, and linger by the tomb in Joseph of Arimathea's garden through those difficult days.

Call to account the witnesses of the early church, and ask the apostles to relate the story of their desperate days.

Desperation is better than despair. Remember, our faith did not create our desperate days. Faith's work is to sustain us through those days and to solve them. Yet the only alternative to desperate faith is despair. Faith holds on and prevails.

There is not a more heroic example of desperate faith than the story of the three Hebrew young men Shadrach, Meshach, and Abednego. Their situation was desperate, but they bravely answered, "If we are thrown into the blazing furnace, the God we serve is able to deliver us from it, and he will deliver us from Your Majesty's hand. But even if he does not, we want you to know, Your Majesty, that we will not serve your gods or worship the image of gold you have set up" (Daniel 3:17–18). I especially like the words "But even if he does not"!

Let me briefly mention the Garden of Gethsemane and ask you to ponder its "nevertheless." "If it be possible . . . nevertheless . . ." (Matthew 26:39 KJV). Our Lord's soul was overwhelmed by deep darkness. To trust meant experiencing anguish to the point of blood, and darkness to the very depths of hell—Nevertheless! Nevertheless!

Find a hymnal and sing your favorite hymn of desperate faith. S. CHADWICK

When obstacles and trials seem
Like prison walls to be,
I do the little I can do
And leave the rest to Thee.

And when there seems no chance, no change,
From grief can set me free,
Hope finds its strength in helplessness,
And calmly waits for Thee.

MARCH 26

"Look around from where you are, north and south, to the east and west. All the land that you see I will give to you."

GENESIS 13:14–15

NO DESIRE WILL EVER BE PLACED IN YOU BY THE HOLY SPIRIT UNLESS He intends to fulfill it. So let your faith rise up and soar away to claim all the land you can discover. S. A. KEEN

Everything you can comprehend through faith's vision belongs to you. Look as far as you can, for it is all yours. All you long to be as a Christian, and all you long to do for God, are within the possibilities of faith. Then draw closer to Him, and with your Bible before you, and your soul completely open to the power of the Spirit, allow your entire being to receive the baptism of His presence. As He opens your understanding, enabling you to see His fullness, believe He has it all for you. Accept for yourself all the promises of His Word, all the desires He awakens within you, and all the possibilities of what you could become as a follower of Jesus. All the land you see is given to you.

The provision of His grace, which helps us along the way to the fulfillment of His promise, is actually tied to the inner vision God has given us. He who puts the natural instinct in the heart of a bird to fly across a continent in search of a warmer climate is too good to deceive it. Just as we are confident He placed the instinct within the bird, we can be assured He has also provided balmy breezes and springlike sun to meet it when it arrives.

And He who breathes heavenly hope into our hearts will not deceive or fail us when we press forward toward its realization. SELECTED

"They left and found things just as Jesus had told them" (Luke 22:13).

MARCH 27

I consider that our present sufferings are not worth comparing with the glory that will be revealed in us.

ROMANS 8:18

A REMARKABLE EVENT OCCURRED RECENTLY AT A WEDDING IN England. The bridegroom, a very wealthy young man of high social standing, had been blinded by an accident at the age of ten. In spite of his blindness, he had graduated from the university with honors and had now won the heart of his beautiful bride, although he had never looked upon her face. Shortly before his marriage he underwent a new round of treatments by specialists, and the result was ready to be revealed on the day of his wedding.

The big day arrived, with all the guests and their presents. In attendance were cabinet ministers, generals, bishops, and learned men and women. The groom, dressed for the wedding but with his eyes still covered by bandages, rode to the church with his father. His famous ophthalmologist met them in the vestry of the church.

The bride entered the church on the arm of her white-haired father. She was so moved, she could hardly speak. Would the man she loved finally see her face—a face others admired but he knew only through the touch of his delicate fingertips?

As she neared the altar, while the soft strains of the wedding march floated through the church, she saw an unusual group. There before her stood the groom, his father, and the doctor. The doctor was in the process of cutting away the last bandage.

Once the bandage was removed, the groom took a step forward, yet with the trembling uncertainty of someone who is not completely awake. A beam of rose-colored light from a pane in the window above the altar fell across his face, but he did not seem to see it.

Could he see anything? Yes! Recovering in an instant his steadiness and demeanor, and with a dignity and joy never before seen on his face, he stepped forward to meet his bride. They looked into each other's eyes, and it seemed as if his gaze would never wander from her face.

"At last!" she said. "At last," he echoed solemnly, bowing his head. It was a scene with great dramatic power, as well as one of great joy. Yet as beautiful as this story is, it is but a mere suggestion of what will actually take place in heaven when Christians, who have been walking through this world of trial and sorrow, "shall see [him] face to face" (1 Corinthians 13:12). Selected

Just longing, dear Lord, for you,
Jesus, beloved and true;
Yearning and wondering when
You'll be coming back again,
Under all I say and do,
Just longing, dear Lord, for you.

Some glad day, all watching past,
You will come for me at last;
Then I'll see you, hear your voice,
Be with you, with you rejoice;
How the sweet hope thrills me through,
Sets me longing, dear Lord, for you.

MARCH 28

As soon as the priests who carry the ark of the Lord*—the* Lord *of all the earth—set foot in the Jordan, its waters flowing downstream will be cut off and stand up in a heap.*

Joshua 3:13

Who can help but admire those brave Levites! They carried the ark of the covenant right into the water, for the river was not divided until "their feet touched the water's edge" (v. 15). God had promised nothing else.

God honors faith—stubborn faith—that sees His promise and looks to that alone. We can only imagine how bystanders today, watching these holy men of God march on, would say, "You will never catch me running that risk! The ark will be swept away!" Yet "the priests . . . stood on dry ground" (v. 17). We must not overlook the fact that faith on our part helps God to carry out His plans. Be willing to come to the help of the Lord.

The ark of the covenant was equipped with poles so the priests could raise it to their shoulders. So even the ark of God did not move itself but was carried. When God is the architect, men are the bricklayers and laborers. Faith assists God. It can shut the mouths of lions and quench the most destructive fire. Faith still honors God, and God honors faith. Oh, for the kind of faith that will move ahead, leaving God to fulfill His promise when He sees fit! Fellow Levites, let us shoulder our load, without looking as though we were carrying God's coffin. It is the ark of the living God! Sing as you march toward the flood! Thomas Champness

One of the distinguishing marks of the Holy Spirit in the New Testament church was the spirit of boldness. One of the great essential qualities of the kind of faith that will attempt great things for God and expect great things from God is holy boldness and daring. When dealing with a supernatural Being and taking things from Him that are humanly impossible, it is actually easier for us to take a lot than it is to take a little. And it is easier to stand in a place of bold trust than in a place where we cautiously and timidly cling to the shore.

Like wise sailors living a life of faith, let us launch our ships into the deep. We will find that all things are "possible with God" (Luke 18:27), and "everything is possible for him one believes" (Mark 9:23).

Today let us attempt great things for God, taking His faith to believe great things and taking His strength to accomplish them! Days of Heaven upon Earth

MARCH 29

"See how the flowers of the field grow."

Matthew 6:28

Many years ago there was a monk who needed olive oil, so he planted an olive tree sapling. After he finished planting it, he prayed, "Lord, my tree needs rain so its tender roots may drink and grow. Send gentle showers." And the Lord sent gentle showers. Then the monk prayed, "Lord, my tree needs sun. Please send it sun." And the sun shone, gilding the once-dripping clouds. "Now send frost, dear Lord, to strengthen its branches," cried the monk. And soon the little tree was covered in sparkling frost, but by evening it had died.

Then the monk sought out a brother monk in his cell and told him of his strange experience. After hearing the story, the other monk said, "I also have planted a little tree. See how it is thriving! But I entrust my tree to its God. He who made it knows better than a man like me what it needs. I gave God no constraints or conditions, except to pray, 'Lord, send what it needs—whether that be a storm or sunshine, wind, rain, or frost. You made it, and you know best what it needs.'"

Yes, leave it with Him,
The lilies all do,
And they grow—
They grow in the rain,
And they grow in the dew—
Yes, they grow:
They grow in the darkness, all hid in the night—
They grow in the sunshine, revealed by the light—
Still they grow.
Yes, leave it with Him,
It's more dear to His heart,
You will know,
Than the lilies that bloom,
Or the flowers that start
'Neath the snow:
Whatever you need, if you seek it in prayer,

You can leave it with Him—for you are His care.
You, you know.
SELECTED

MARCH 30

"But now, all you who light fires and provide yourselves with flaming torches, go, walk in the light of your fires and of the torches you have set ablaze. This is what you shall receive from my hand: You will lie down in torment."
ISAIAH 50:11

THIS IS A SOLEMN WARNING TO THOSE WHO WALK IN DARKNESS AND who try to help themselves find the light. They are described as the kindling for a fire that is surrounding itself with sparks. What does this mean?

It means that when we are in darkness, the temptation is to find our own way without trusting in the Lord and relying upon Him. Instead of allowing Him to help us, we try to help ourselves. We seek the light of the natural way and the advice of our friends. We reason out our own conclusions and thereby may be tempted to accept a path of deliverance that would not be of God at all.

The light we see may be the fires from our own kindling, or deceptive beacons leading us toward the danger of the rocks. And God will allow us to walk in the false light of those sparks, but the end will be sorrow.

Beloved, never try to get out of a dark place except in God's timing and in His way. A time of trouble and darkness is meant to teach you lessons you desperately need. Premature deliverance may circumvent God's work of grace in your life. Commit the entire situation to Him, and be willing to abide in darkness, knowing He is present.

Remember, it is better to walk in the dark with God than to walk alone in the light. THE STILL SMALL VOICE

Stop interfering with God's plans and with His will. Touching anything of His mars the work. Moving the hands of a clock to suit you does not change the time. You may be able to rush the unfolding of some aspects of God's will, but you harm His work in the long run. You can force a rosebud open, but you spoil the flower. Leave everything to Him, without exception. "Not what I will, but what you will" (Mark 14:36). Stephen Merritt

His Way

God sent me on when I would stay
('Twas cool within the wood);
I did not know the reason why.
I heard a boulder crashing by
'Cross the path where I had stood.

He had me stay when I would go;
"Your will be done," I said.
They found one day at early dawn,
Across the way I would have gone,
A serpent with a mangled head.

I ask no more the reason why,
Although I may not see
The path ahead, His way I go;
For though I know not, He does know,
And He will choose safe paths for me.

Sunday School Times

MARCH 31

The wind was against it.

Matthew 14:24

The winds of March are often cruel and blustery. And yet they typify the stormy seasons of my life. Indeed, I should be glad to have the opportunity to come to know these seasons. It is better for the rains to descend and the floods to come than to always live in the legendary land of Lotus or the lush Valley of Avalon, where the sun always shines and strong winds never blow. The storms of temptation may appear cruel, but don't they lead to a greater intensity and earnestness in my prayer life? Don't they compel me to cling to God's promises with a tighter grasp? And don't they leave me with character that is more refined?

The storms of sorrow through bereavement are intense, but they are one of the Father's ways of driving me to Himself. His purpose is to softly and tenderly speak to my heart in the secret, hidden place of His presence. There is a certain glory of the Master that can only be seen when the wind is contrary and my ship is being tossed by the waves.

Jesus Christ is not my security *against* the storms of life, but He is my perfect security *in* the storms. He has never promised me an easy passage, only a safe landing.

Oh, set your sail to the heavenly gale,
And then, no matter what winds prevail,
No reef can wreck you, no calm delay;
No mist will hinder, no storm will stay;
Though far you wander and long you roam
Through salt sea sprays and o'er white sea foam,
No wind can blow but that will speed you Home.

Annie Johnson Flint

APRIL 1

Though he slay me, yet will I hope in him.

Job 13:15

Because I know whom I have believed.

2 Timothy 1:12

I will not doubt, though all my ships at sea
Come drifting home with broken masts and sails;
I will believe the Hand that never fails,
From seeming evil works to good for me.
And though I weep because those sails are tattered,
Still will I cry, while my best hopes lie shattered:
"I trust in Thee."

I will not doubt, though all my prayers return
Unanswered from the still, white realm above;
I will believe it is an all-wise love
That has refused these things for which I yearn;
And though at times I cannot keep from grieving,
Yet the pure passion of my fixed believing
Undimmed will burn.

I will not doubt, though sorrows fall like rain,
And troubles swarm like bees about a hive.
I will believe the heights for which I strive
Are only reached by anguish and by pain;
And though I groan and writhe beneath my crosses,
Yet I will see through my severest losses
The greater gain.

I will not doubt. Well anchored is this faith,
Like some staunch ship, my soul braves every gale;
So strong its courage that it will not fail
To face the mighty unknown sea of death.
Oh, may I cry, though body leaves the spirit,

"I do not doubt," so listening worlds may hear it,
With my last breath.

An old seaman once said, "In fierce storms we must do one thing, for there is only one way to survive: we must put the ship in a certain position and keep her there." And this, dear Christian, is what you must do.

Sometimes, like Paul, you cannot see the sun or the stars to help you navigate when the storm is bearing down on you. This is when you can do only one thing, for there is only one way. Reason cannot help you, past experiences will shed no light, and even prayer will bring no consolation. Only one course remains: you must put your soul in one position and keep it there.

You must anchor yourself steadfastly upon the Lord. And then, come what may—whether wind, waves, rough seas, thunder, lightning, jagged rocks, or roaring breakers—you must lash yourself to the helm, firmly holding your confidence in God's faithfulness, His covenant promises, and His everlasting love in Christ Jesus. Richard Fuller

APRIL 2

They looked . . . and there was the glory of
the Lord appearing in the cloud.
Exodus 16:10

You should get into the habit of looking for the silver lining of storm clouds. And once you have found it, continue to focus on it rather than the dark gray of the center. Do not yield to discouragement no matter how severely stressed or surrounded by problems you may be. A discouraged soul is in a helpless state, being neither able to "stand against the devil's schemes" (Ephesians 6:11) himself nor able to prevail in prayer for others. Flee every symptom of the deadly foe of discouragement as you would run from a snake. Never be slow to turn your back on it, unless you desire to eat the dust of bitter defeat.

Search for specific promises of God, saying aloud of each one, "This promise is *mine*." Then if you still experience feelings of doubt and discouragement, pour your heart out to God, asking Him to rebuke the Adversary who is so mercilessly harassing you.

The very instant you wholeheartedly turn away from every symptom of discouragement and lack of trust, the blessed Holy Spirit will reawaken your faith and breathe God's divine strength into your soul. Initially you may be unaware that this is happening, but as you determine to uncompromisingly *shun* every attack of even the tendency toward doubt and depression, you will quickly see the powers of darkness being turned back.

Oh, if only our eyes could see the mighty armies of strength and power that are always behind our turning away from the hosts of darkness toward God, there would be no attention given to the efforts of our cunning Foe to distress, depress, or discourage us! All the miraculous attributes of the Godhead are marshaled on the side of even the weakest believer who, in the name of Christ and in simple, childlike trust, yields himself to God and turns to Him for help and guidance. SELECTED

One day in autumn, while on the open prairie, I saw an eagle mortally wounded by a rifle shot. With his eyes still gleaming like small circles of light, he slowly turned his head, giving one last searching and longing look toward the sky. He had often swept those starry spaces with his wonderful wings. The beautiful sky was the home of his heart. It was the eagle's domain. It was there he had displayed his splendid strength a thousand times. In those lofty heights, he had played with the lightning and raced the wind. And now, far below his home, the eagle lay dying. He faced death because—just once—he forgot and flew too low.

My soul is that eagle. This is not its home. It must never lose its skyward look. I must keep faith, I must keep hope, I must keep courage, I must keep Christ. It would be better to crawl immediately from the battlefield than to not be brave. There is no time for my soul to retreat. Keep your skyward look, my soul; keep your skyward look!

Keep looking up—
The waves that roar around your feet,
Jehovah-Jireh will defeat
When looking up.
Keep looking up—
Though darkness seems to wrap your soul;
The Light of Light will fill your soul
When looking up.
Keep looking up—
When worn, distracted with the fight;
Your Captain gives you conquering might
When you look up.

We can never see the sunrise by looking toward the west. JAPANESE PROVERB

APRIL 3

Glorify ye the LORD in the fires.

ISAIAH 24:15 KJV

NOTICE THE LITTLE WORD "IN"! WE ARE TO HONOR THE LORD *in* THE trial—*in* the very thing that afflicts us. And although there are examples where God did not allow His saints to even feel the fire, usually the fire causes pain.

It is precisely there, in the heat of the fire, we are to glorify Him. We do this by exercising perfect faith in His goodness and love that has permitted this trial to come upon us. Even more, we are to believe that out of the fire will arise something more worthy of praise to Him than had we never experienced it.

To go through some fires will take great faith, for little faith will fail. We must win the victory *in* the furnace. Margaret Bottome

A person has only as much faith as he shows in times of trouble. The three men who were thrown into the fiery furnace came out just as they went in—*except for the ropes* that had bound them. How often God removes our shackles in the furnace of affliction!

These three men walked through the fire unhurt—their skin was not even blistered. Not only had the fire "not harmed their bodies, nor was a hair of their heads singed; their robes were not scorched, and there was no smell of fire on them" (Daniel 3:27).

This is the way Christians should come out of the furnace of fiery trials—liberated from their shackles but untouched by the flames.

Triumphing over them in it (Colossians 2:15 KJV).

This is the real triumph—triumphing over sickness *in it*, triumphing over death *in* dying, and triumphing over other adverse circumstances *in* them. Believe me, there is a power that can make us victors *in* the conflict.

There are heights we can reach where we can look back over the path we have come and sing our song of triumph on this side of heaven. We can cause others to regard us as rich, while we are poor, and make many rich in our poverty. We are to triumph *in it.*

Christ's triumph was *in* His humiliation. And perhaps our triumph will also be revealed through what others see as humiliation. Margaret Bottome

Isn't there something captivating about the sight of a person burdened with many trials, yet who is as lighthearted as the sound of a bell? Isn't there something contagious and valiant in seeing others who are greatly tempted but are "more than conquerors" (Romans 8:37)? Isn't it heartening to see a fellow traveler whose body is broken, yet who retains the splendor of unbroken patience?

What a witness these give to the power of God's gift of grace! John Henry Jowett

When each earthly brace falls under,
And life seems a restless sea,
Are you then a God-held wonder,
Satisfied and calm and free?

APRIL 4

Elisha prayed, "Open his eyes Lord*, so that he may see."*
2 Kings 6:17

This is the prayer we need to pray for ourselves and one another: "Lord, open our eyes so we may see." We are surrounded, just as the prophet Elisha was, by God's "horses and chariots of fire" (2 Kings 6:17), waiting to transport us to places of glorious victory.

Once our eyes are opened by God, we will see all the events of our lives, whether great or small, joyful or sad, as a "chariot" for our souls. Everything that comes to us becomes a chariot the moment we treat it as such. On the other hand, even the smallest trial may become an object crushing everything in its path into misery and despair if we allow it.

The difference then becomes a choice we make. It all depends not on the events themselves but on how we view them. If we simply lie down, allowing them to roll over and crush us, they become an uncontrollable car of destruction. Yet if we climb into them, as riding in a car of victory, they become the chariots of God to triumphantly take us onward and upward.
Hannah Whitall Smith

There is not much the Lord can do with a crushed soul. That is why the Adversary attempts to push God's people toward despair and hopelessness over their condition or the condition of the church. It has often been said that a discouraged army enters a battle with the certainty of defeat. I recently heard a missionary say she had returned home sick and disheartened because her spirit had lost its courage, which led to the consequence of an unhealthy body.

We need to better understand these attacks of the Enemy on our spirit and how to resist them. If he can dislodge us from our proper position, he then seeks to "wear out the saints of the most High" (Daniel 7:25 KJV) through a prolonged siege, until we finally, out of sheer weakness, surrender all hope of victory.

APRIL 5

Go inside and shut the door behind you and your sons.

2 KINGS 4:4

THE WIDOW AND HER TWO SONS WERE TO BE ALONE WITH GOD. THEY were not dealing with the laws of nature, human government, the church, or the priesthood. Nor were they even dealing with God's great prophet, Elisha. They had to be isolated from everyone, separated from human reasoning, and removed from the natural tendencies to prejudge their circumstance. They were to be as if cast into the vast expanse of starry space, depending on God alone—in touch with the Source of miracles.

This is an ingredient in God's plan of dealing with us. We are to enter a secret chamber of isolation in prayer and faith that is very fruitful. At certain times and places, God will build a mysterious wall around us. He will take away all the supports we customarily lean upon, and will remove our ordinary ways of doing things. God will close us off to something divine, completely new and unexpected, and that cannot be understood by examining our previous circumstances. We will be in a place where we do not know what is happening, where God is cutting the cloth of our lives by a new pattern, and thus where He causes us to look to Him.

Most Christians lead a treadmill life—a life in which they can predict almost everything that will come their way. But the souls that God leads into unpredictable and special situations are isolated by Him. All they know is that God is holding them and that He is dealing in their lives. Then their expectations come from Him alone.

Like this widow, we must be detached from *outward* things and *attached inwardly to the Lord alone* in order to see His wonders. *Soul Food*

It is through the most difficult trials that God often brings the sweetest discoveries of Himself. GEMS

God sometimes shuts the door and shuts us in,
That He may speak, perhaps through grief or pain,
And softly, heart to heart, above the din,
May tell some precious thought to us again.

APRIL 6

I will stand at my watch and station myself on the ramparts; I will look to see what he will say to me.
HABAKKUK 2:1

WITHOUT WATCHFUL EXPECTATION ON OUR PART, WHAT IS THE SENSE in waiting on God for help? There will be no help without it. If we ever fail to receive strength and protection from Him, it is because we have not been looking for it. Heavenly help is often offered yet goes right past us. We miss it because we are not standing in the tower, carefully watching the horizon for evidence of its approach, and then are unready to throw the gates of our heart open so it may enter. The person who has no expectations and therefore fails to be on the alert will receive little help. Watch for God in the events of your life.

There is an old saying: "They who watch for the providence of God will never lack the providence of God to watch for." And we could turn the saying around as well and say, "They who never watch for the providence of God will never have the providence of God to watch for." Unless you put the water jars out when it rains, you will never collect the water.

We need to be more businesslike and use common sense with God in claiming His promises. If a man were to go to the bank several times a day, lay his check at the teller's window, and then pick it up and leave without cashing it, it would not be long before the bank would have him ordered from the premises.

People who go to the bank have a purpose in mind. They present their check, receive their cash, and then leave, having transacted real business. They do not lay their check on the counter, discuss the beauty of the signature, and point out the lovely design on it. No, they want to receive money for their check and will not be satisfied without it. These are the people who are always welcome at the bank, unlike those who simply waste the teller's time.

Unfortunately, a great many people also play at praying. They do not expect God to give them an answer, so they simply squander their prayer time. Our heavenly Father desires us to transact real business with Him in our praying. CHARLES H. SPURGEON

"Your hope will not be cut off" (Proverbs 23:18).

APRIL 7

"Their strength is to sit still."

ISAIAH 30:7 KJV

Inner stillness IS AN ABSOLUTE NECESSITY TO TRULY KNOWING GOD. I remember learning this during a time of great crisis in my life. My entire being seemed to throb with anxiety, and the sense of need for immediate and powerful action was overwhelming. Yet the circumstances were such that I could do nothing, and the person who could have helped would not move.

For a time it seemed as if I would fall to pieces due to my inner turmoil. Then suddenly "a still small voice" (1 Kings 19:12 KJV) whispered in the depths of my soul, "Be still, and know that I am God" (Psalm 46:10). The words were spoken with power and I obeyed. I composed myself, bringing my body to complete stillness, and forced my troubled spirit into quietness. Only then, while looking up and waiting, did I know that it was God who had spoken. He was in the midst of my crisis and my helplessness, and I rested in Him.

This was an experience I would not have missed for anything. I would also say it was from the stillness that the power seemed to arise to deal with the crisis, and that very quickly brought it to a successful resolution. It was during this crisis I effectively learned that my "strength is to sit still." HANNAH WHITALL SMITH

There is a perfect passivity that is not laziness. It is a living stillness born of trust. Quiet tension is not trust but simply *compressed anxiety.*

Not in the turmoil of the raging storm,
Not in the earthquake or devouring flame;
But in the hush that could all fear transform,
The still, small whisper to the prophet came.
O Soul, keep silence on the mount of God,
Though cares and needs throb around you like a sea;
From prayers, petitions, and desires unshod,
Be still, and hear what God will say to thee.

All fellowship has interludes of rest,
New strength maturing in each level of power;
The sweetest Alleluias of the blest
Are silent, for the space of half an hour.

O rest, in utter quietude of soul,
Abandon words, leave prayer and praise awhile;
Let your whole being, hushed in His control,
Learn the full meaning of His voice and smile.

Not as an athlete wrestling for a crown,
Not taking Heaven by violence of will;

But with your Father as a child sit down,
And know the bliss that follows His "Be Still!"
MARY ROWLES JARVIS

APRIL 8

That is why, for Christ's sake, I delight in weaknesses,
in insults, in hardships, in persecutions, in difficulties.
For when I am weak, then I am strong.
2 CORINTHIANS 12:10

THE LITERAL TRANSLATION OF THIS VERSE ADDS A STARTLING EMPHASIS to it, allowing it to speak for itself with power we have probably never realized. It is as follows: "Therefore I take pleasure in being without strength, being insulted, experiencing emergencies, and being chased and forced into a corner for Christ's sake; for when I am without strength, I am *dynamite*."

The secret of knowing God's complete sufficiency is in coming to the end of everything in ourselves and our circumstances. Once we reach this point, we will stop seeking sympathy for our difficult situation or ill treatment, because we will recognize these things as the necessary conditions for blessings. We will then turn from our circumstances to God, realizing they are the evidence of Him working in our lives. A. B. SIMPSON

George Matheson, the well-known blind preacher of Scotland, once said, "My dear God, I have never thanked You for my thorns. I have thanked You a thousand times for my roses but not once for my thorns. I have always looked forward to the place where I will be rewarded for my cross, but I have never thought of my cross as a present glory itself.

"Teach me, O Lord, to glory in my cross. Teach me the value of my thorns. Show me how I have climbed to You through the path of pain. Show me it is through my tears I have seen my rainbows."

Alas for him who never sees
The stars shine through the cypress trees.

APRIL 9

Everything is against me!
GENESIS 42:36

All things God works for the good of those who love him.
ROMANS 8:28

MANY PEOPLE ARE LACKING WHEN ITS COMES TO POWER. BUT HOW IS power produced?

The other day, my friend and I were passing by the power plant that produces electricity for the streetcars. We heard the hum and roar of the countless wheels of the turbines, and I asked my friend, "How is the power produced?" He replied, "It simply is generated by the turning of those wheels and the friction they create. The rubbing produces the electric current."

In a similar way, when God desires to create more power in your life, He creates more friction. He uses this pressure to generate spiritual power. Some people cannot handle it, and run from the pressure instead of receiving the power and using it to rise above the painful experience that produced it.

Opposition is essential to maintaining true balance between forces. It is the centripetal and centrifugal forces acting in opposition to each other that keep our planet in the proper orbit. The propelling action coupled with the repelling counteraction keep the earth in orbit around the sun instead of flinging it into space and a path of certain destruction.

God guides our lives in the same way. It is not enough to have only a propelling force. We need an equal repelling force, so He holds us back through the testing ordeals of life. The pressures of temptations and trials and all the things that seem to be against us further our progress and strengthen our foundation.

Let us thank Him for both the weights and the wings He produces. And realizing we are divinely propelled, let us press on with faith and patience in our high and heavenly calling. A. B. Simpson

In a factory building there are wheels and gearings,
There are cranks, pulleys, belts either tight or slack—
Some are whirling swiftly, some are turning slowly,
Some are thrusting forward, some are pulling back;
Some are smooth and silent, some are rough and noisy,
Pounding, rattling, clanking, moving with a jerk;

In a wild confusion in a seeming chaos,
Lifting, pushing, driving—but they do their work.
From the mightiest lever to the smallest cog or gear,
All things move together for the purpose planned;
And behind the working is a mind controlling,
And a force directing, and a guiding hand.

So all things are working for the Lord's beloved;
Some things might be hurtful if alone they stood;
Some might seem to hinder; some might draw us backward;
But they work together, and they work for good,
All the thwarted longings, all the stern denials,
All the contradictions, hard to understand.
And the force that holds them, speeds them and retards them,
Stops and starts and guides them—is our Father's hand.

Annie Johnson Flint

APRIL 10

Tell me what charges you have against me.

Job 10:2

O tested soul, perhaps the Lord is sending you through this trial to develop your gifts. You have some gifts that would never have been discovered if not for trials. Do you not know that your faith never appears as great in the warm summer weather as it does during a cold winter? Your love is all too often like a firefly, showing very little light except when surrounded by darkness. And hope is like the stars—unseen in the sunshine of prosperity and only discovered during a night of adversity. Afflictions are often the dark settings God uses to mount the jewels of His children's gifts, causing them to shine even brighter.

Wasn't it just a short time ago that on your knees you prayed, "Lord, I seem to have no faith. Please show me that I do"? Wasn't your prayer, even though you may not have realized it at the time, actually asking for trials? For how can you know if you have faith, until your faith is exercised? You can depend upon the fact that God often sends trials so our gifts may be discovered and so we may be certain of their existence. And there is more than just discovering our gifts—we experience *real growth in grace* as another result of our trials being sanctified by Him.

God trains His soldiers not in tents of ease and luxury but by causing them to endure lengthy marches and difficult service. He makes them wade across streams, swim through rivers, climb mountains, and walk many tiring miles with heavy backpacks.

Dear Christian, could this not account for the troubles you are now experiencing? Could this not be the reason He is dealing with you?
Charles H. Spurgeon

Being left alone by Satan is not evidence of being blessed.

APRIL 11

"What I tell you in the dark, speak in the daylight; what is whispered in your ear, proclaim from the roofs."
MATTHEW 10:27

OUR LORD IS CONSTANTLY TAKING US INTO THE DARK IN ORDER TO tell us something. It may be the darkness of a home where bereavement has drawn the blinds; the darkness of a lonely and desolate life, in which some illness has cut us off from the light and the activity of life; or the darkness of some crushing sorrow and disappointment.

It is there He tells us His secrets—great and wonderful, eternal and infinite. He causes our eyes, blinded by the glare of things on earth, to behold the heavenly constellations. And our ears suddenly detect even the whisper of His voice, which has been so often drowned out by the turmoil of earth's loud cries.

Yet these revelations always come with a corresponding responsibility: "What I tell you . . . *speak* in the daylight . . . *proclaim* from the roofs." We are not to linger in the darkness or stay in the closet. Soon we will be summoned to take our position in the turmoil and the storms of life. And when that moment comes, we are to *speak* and *proclaim* what we have learned.

This gives new meaning to suffering, the saddest part of which is often the apparent feeling of uselessness it causes. We tend to think, "How useless I am! What am I doing that is making a difference for others? Why is the 'expensive perfume' (John 12:3) of my soul being wasted?" These are the desperate cries of the sufferer, but God has a purpose in all of it. He takes His children to higher levels of fellowship so they may hear Him speaking "face to face, as one speaks to a friend" (Exodus 33:11), and then deliver the message to those at the foot of the mountain. Were the forty days Moses spent on the mountain wasted? What about the time Elijah spent at Mount Horeb or the years Paul spent in Arabia?

There is no shortcut to a life of faith, which is an absolute necessity for a holy and victorious life. We must have periods of lonely meditation and fellowship with God. Our souls must have times of fellowship with Him on the mountain and experience valleys of quiet rest in the shadow of a great rock. We must spend some nights beneath the stars, when darkness has covered the things of earth, silenced the noise of human life, and expanded our view, revealing the infinite and the eternal. All these are as absolutely essential as food is for our bodies.

In this way alone can the sense of God's presence become the unwavering possession of our souls, enabling us to continually say, as the psalmist once wrote, "You are near, LORD" (Psalm 119:151). F. B. MEYER

Some hearts, like evening primroses, open more beautifully in the shadows of life.

APRIL 12

Jesus, full of the Holy Spirit, left the Jordan and was led by the Spirit into the wilderness, where for forty days he was tempted by the devil.

LUKE 4:1–2

JESUS WAS FILLED WITH THE HOLY SPIRIT AND YET WAS TEMPTED. The strongest force of temptation often comes upon a person when he is closest to God. Someone once said, "The Devil aims high." In fact, he caused one disciple to say he did not even know Christ.

Why is it that very few people have had as great a conflict with the Devil as Martin Luther had? It is because Martin Luther was shaking the very kingdom of hell itself. And remember the tremendous struggles John Bunyan had!

When a person has the fullness of the Spirit of God, he will experience great conflicts with the Tempter. God allows temptation because it does for us what storms do for oak trees, rooting us deeper, and it does for us what heat does for paint on porcelain, giving us long-lasting endurance.

You will never fully realize the level of strength of your grasp on

Christ, or His grasp on you, until the Devil uses all his force to attract you to himself. It is then you will feel the tug of Christ's right hand. Selected

Extraordinary afflictions are not always the punishment of extraordinary sins but are sometimes the trials resulting from God's extraordinary gifts. God uses many sharp-cutting instruments, and polishes His jewels with files that are rough. And those saints He especially loves, and desires to make shine the most brilliantly, will often feel His tools upon them. R. Leighton

I willingly bear witness to the fact that I owe more to my Lord's fire, hammer, and file than to anything else in His workshop. Sometimes I wonder if I have ever learned anything except at the end of God's rod. When my classroom is darkest, I see best. Charles H. Spurgeon

APRIL 13

The hand of the Lord was on me there, and he said to me, "Get up and go out to the plain, and there I will speak to you."

Ezekiel 3:22

Have you ever heard of anyone being greatly used by Christ who did not experience a special time of waiting, or a complete upset of his plans at first? From the apostle Paul's being sent into the Arabian wilderness for three years—during which time he must have been overflowing with the Good News—down to the present day, it seems those who will be used will have a time of waiting. Have you been looking forward to *telling* about trusting Jesus, but instead He is asking you to *show* what trust is, by waiting?

My own experience is far less severe than Paul's but reveals the same principle. Once when I thought the door was being thrown open for me to enter the literary field with a great opportunity, it was just as quickly shut. My doctor stepped in and simply said, "Never! You must choose between writing and living, for you cannot do both." The year was 1860, and I did not come out of my shell of isolation with my book *Ministry of Song* until 1869. By then I saw the distinct wisdom of having been kept waiting for nine years in the shade.

God's love is unchangeable, and He is just as loving even when we do not see or feel it. And His love and His sovereignty are equal and universal. Therefore He often withholds our enjoyment and awareness of our progress, because He knows best what will actually ripen and further His work in us. FRANCES RIDLEY HAVERGAL

I laid it down in silence,
This work of mine,
And took what had been sent me—
A resting time.
The Master's voice had called me
To rest apart;
"Apart with Jesus only,"
Echoed my heart.

I took the rest and stillness
From His own hand,
And felt this present illness
Was what He planned.
How often we choose labor,
When He says "Rest"—
Our ways are blind and crooked;
His way is best.

Work He Himself has given,
He will complete.
There may be other errands
For tired feet;
There may be other duties

For tired hands,
The present, is obedience
To His commands.
There is a blessed resting
In lying still,
In letting His hand mold us,
Just as He will.
His work must be completed.
His lesson set;
He is the Master Workman:
Do not forget!

It is not only "working."
We must be trained;
And Jesus "learned" obedience,
Through suffering gained.
For us, His yoke is easy,
His burden light.
His discipline most needful,
And all is right.

We are to be His servants;
We never choose
If this tool or if that one
Our hands will use.
In working or in waiting
May we fulfill
Not ours at all, but only
The Master's will!

SELECTED

God provides resting places as well as working places. So rest and be thankful when He brings you, tired and weary, to streams along the way.

APRIL 14

The Lord himself will come down from heaven, with a loud command, with the voice of the archangel and with the trumpet call of God, and the dead in Christ will rise first. After that, we who are still alive and are left will be caught up together with them in the clouds to meet the Lord in the air. And so we will be with the Lord forever.

1 Thessalonians 4:16–17

It was "very early in the morning" (Luke 24:1), "while it was still dark" (John 20:1), that Jesus rose from the dead. Only the morning star, not the sun, shone down upon His tomb as it opened. Jerusalem's shadows had not yet retreated, and its citizens were still asleep. Yes, it was still night, during the hours of darkness and sleep, when He arose, but His rising did not break the slumbering of the city.

And it will be during the darkness of the early morning, while only the morning star is shining, that Christ's body—His church—will arise. Like Him, His saints will awake while the children of the night and darkness are still sleeping their slumber of death. Upon rising, the saints will disturb no one, and the world will not hear the voice that summons them. As quietly as Jesus has laid them to rest—each in their own silent grave, like children held in the arms of their mothers—He will just as quietly and gently awake them when the hour arrives. To each will come the life-giving words, "let those who dwell in the dust, wake up and shout for joy" (Isaiah 26:19). Into their graves the earliest ray of glory will find its way. The saints will soak up the first light of morning, while the clouds of the eastern sky will give only the faintest hints of the uprising. The gentle fragrance of the morning, along with its soothing stillness, invigorating freshness, sweet loneliness, and quiet purity—all so solemn and yet so full of hope—will be theirs.

Oh, how great the contrast between these blessings and the dark night through which they have just passed! Oh, how great the contrast between

these blessings and the graves from which they have been freed! They will shake off the dirt of earth that once held them, flinging mortality aside, and will rise with glorified bodies "to meet the Lord in the air." The light of "the bright Morning Star" (Revelation 22:16) will guide them upward along a brand-new path. The beams of that Star of the Morning will, like the star of Bethlehem, direct them to the presence of the King. "Weeping may stay for the night, but rejoicing comes in the morning" (Psalm 30:5).
Horatius Bonar

While the hosts cry Hosanna, from heaven descending,
With glorified saints and the angels attending,
With grace on His brow, like a halo of glory,
Will Jesus receive His own.

"'I am coming soon.' Amen. Come, Lord Jesus" (Revelation 22:20).

A soldier once said, "When I die, do not play taps over my grave. Instead, play reveille, the morning call, the summons to arise."

APRIL 15

I trust in your word.
Psalm 119:42

The strength of our faith is in direct proportion to our level of belief that God will do exactly what He has promised. Faith has nothing to do with feelings, impressions, outward appearances, nor the probability or improbability of an event. If we try to couple these things with faith, we are no longer resting on the Word of God, because faith is not dependent on them. *Faith rests on the pure Word of God alone.* And when we take Him at His Word, our hearts are at peace.

God delights in causing us to exercise our faith. He does so to bless us individually, to bless the church at large, and as a witness to unbelievers. Yet we tend to retreat from the exercising of our faith instead of welcoming it. When trials come, our response should be, "My heavenly Father has placed this cup of trials into my hands so I may later have something pleasant."

Trials are the food of faith. Oh, may we leave ourselves in the hands of our heavenly Father! It is the joy of His heart to do good to all His children. Yet trials and difficulties are not the only way faith is exercised and thereby increased. *Reading the Scriptures also acquaints us with God as He has revealed Himself in them.*

Are you able to genuinely say, from your knowledge of God and your relationship with Him, that He is indeed a beautiful Being? If not, let me graciously encourage you to ask God to take you to that point, so you will fully appreciate His gentleness and kindness, so you will be able to say just how good He is, and so you will know what a delight it is to God's heart to do good for His children.

The closer we come to this point in our inner being, the more willing we are to leave ourselves in His hands and the more satisfied we are with all of His dealings with us. Then when trials come, we will say, "I will patiently wait to see the good God will do in my life, with the calm assurance He will do it." In this way, we will bear a worthy testimony to the world and thereby strengthen the lives of others. George Mueller

APRIL 16

By faith Abraham, when called to go to a place he would later receive as his inheritance, obeyed and went, even though he did not know where he was going.

Hebrews 11:8

Abraham "did not know where he was going"—it simply was enough for him to know he went with God. He did not lean as much on the promises as he did on the Promiser. And he did not look at the difficulties of his circumstances but looked to His King—the eternal, limitless, invisible, wise, and only God—who had reached down from His throne to direct his path and who would certainly prove Himself.

O glorious faith! Your works and possibilities are these: contentment to set sail with the orders still sealed, due to unwavering confidence in the wisdom of the Lord High Admiral; and a willingness to get up, leave everything, and follow Christ, because of the joyful assurance that earth's best does not compare with heaven's least. F. B. Meyer

In no way is it enough to set out cheerfully with God on any venture of faith. You must also be willing to take your ideas of what the journey will be like and tear them into tiny pieces, for nothing on the itinerary will happen as you expect.

Your Guide will not keep to any beaten path. He will lead you through ways you would never have dreamed your eyes would see. He knows no fear, and He expects you to fear nothing while He is with you.

The day had gone; alone and weak
I groped my way within a bleak
And sunless land.
The path that led into the light
I could not find! In that dark night
God took my hand.

He led me that I might not stray,
And brought me by a safe, new way
I had not known.
By waters still, through pastures green
I followed Him—the path was clean
Of briar and stone.

The heavy darkness lost its strength,
My waiting eyes beheld at length
The streaking dawn.
On, safely on, through sunrise glow

I walked, my hand in His, and lo,
The night had gone.
ANNIE PORTER JOHNSON

APRIL 17

The hand of the LORD has done this.
JOB 12:9

A NUMBER OF YEARS AGO THE MOST MAGNIFICENT DIAMOND IN THE history of the world was found in an African mine. It was then presented to the king of England to embellish his crown of state. The king sent it to Amsterdam to be cut by an expert stonecutter. Can you imagine what he did with it?

He took this gem of priceless value and cut a notch in it. Then he struck it one hard time with his hammer, and the majestic jewel fell into his hand, broken in two. What recklessness! What wastefulness! What criminal carelessness!

Actually, that is not the case at all. For you see, that one blow with the hammer had been studied and planned for days, and even weeks. Drawings and models had been made of the gem. Its quality, defects, and possible lines along which it would split had all been studied to the smallest detail. And the man to whom it was entrusted was one of the most skilled stonecutters in the world.

Now do you believe that blow was a mistake? No, it was the capstone and the culmination of the stonecutter's skill. When he struck that blow, he did the one thing that would bring that gem to its most perfect shape, radiance, and jeweled splendor. The blow that seemed to be the ruin of the majestic precious stone was actually its perfect redemption, for from the halves were fashioned two magnificent gems. Only the skilled eye of the expert stonecutter could have seen the beauty of two diamonds hidden in the rough, uncut stone as it came from the mine.

Sometimes, in the same way, God lets a stinging blow fall on your life. You bleed, feeling the pain, and your soul cries out in agony. At first you think the blow is an appalling mistake. But it is not, for you are the most precious jewel in the world to God. And He is the most skilled stonecutter in the universe.

Someday you are to be a jewel adorning the crown of the King. As you lie in His hand now, He knows just how to deal with you. Not one blow will be permitted to fall on your apprehensive soul except what the love of God allows. And you may be assured that from the depths of the experience, you will see untold blessings, and spiritual enrichment you have never before imagined. J. H. M.

In one of George MacDonald's books, one of the characters makes this bitter statement: "I wonder why God made me. I certainly don't see any purpose in it!" Another of the characters responds, "Perhaps you don't see any purpose yet, but then, He isn't finished making you. And besides, you are arguing with the process."

If people would only believe they are still in the process of creation, submit to the Maker, allowing Him to handle them as the potter handles clay, and yield themselves in one shining, deliberate action to the turning of His wheel, they would soon find themselves able to welcome every pressure from His hand on them, even if it results in pain. And sometimes they should not only believe but also have God's purpose in sight: "bringing many sons and daughters to glory" (Hebrews 2:10).

Not a single blow can hit,
Till the God of love sees fit.

APRIL 18

He will do this.

PSALM 37:5

I once believed that after I prayed, it was my responsibility to do everything in my power to bring about the answer. Yet God taught me a better way and showed me that self-effort always hinders His work. He also revealed that when I prayed and had confident trust in Him for something, He simply wanted me to wait in an attitude of praise and do only what He told me. Sitting still, doing nothing except trusting in the Lord, causes a feeling of uncertainty, and there is often a tremendous temptation to take the battle into our own hands.

We all know how difficult it is to rescue a drowning person who tries to help his rescuer, and it is equally difficult for the Lord to fight our battles for us when we insist upon trying to fight them ourselves. It is not that God will not but that He cannot, for our interference hinders His work. C. H. P.

Spiritual forces cannot work while we are trusting earthly forces.

Often we fail to give God an opportunity to work, not realizing that it takes time for Him to answer prayer. It takes time for God to color a rose or to grow a great oak tree. And it takes time for Him to make bread from wheat fields. He takes the soil, then grinds and softens it. He enriches it and wets it with rain showers and with dew. Then He brings the warmth of life to the small blade of grass, later grows the stalk and the amber grain, and finally provides bread for the hungry.

All this takes time. Therefore we sow the seed, till the ground, and then wait and trust until God's purpose has been fulfilled. We understand this principle when it comes to planting a field, and we need to learn the same lesson regarding our prayer life. It takes time for God to answer prayer. J. H. M.

APRIL 19

Stand firm and you will see the deliverance
the Lord will bring you today.
Exodus 14:13

THIS VERSE CONTAINS GOD'S COMMAND TO ME AS A BELIEVER FOR those times when I am confronted with dire circumstances and extraordinary difficulties. What am I to do when I cannot retreat or go forward and my way is blocked to the right and to the left?

The Master's word to me is, "Stand firm." And the best thing I can do at these times is to listen only to my Master's word, for others will come to me with their suggestions and evil advice. *Despair* will come, whispering, "Give up—lie down and die." But even in the worst of times, God would have me be cheerful and courageous, rejoicing in His love and faithfulness.

Cowardice will come and say, "You must retreat to the world's ways of acting. It is too difficult for you to continue living the part of a Christian. Abandon your principles." Yet no matter how much Satan may pressure me to follow his course, I cannot, for I am a child of God. The Lord's divine decree has commanded me to go from "strength to strength" (Psalm 84:7). Therefore I will, and neither death nor hell will turn me from my course. And if for a season He calls me to "stand firm," I will acknowledge it as time to renew my strength for greater strides in the future.

Impatience will come, crying, "Get up and do something! To 'stand firm' and wait is sheer idleness." Why is it I think I *must* be doing something right now instead of looking to the Lord? He will not only do *something*—He will do *everything*.

Arrogance will come, boasting, "If the sea is blocking your way, march right into it and expect a miracle." Yet true faith never listens to arrogance, impatience, cowardice, or despair but only hears God saying, "Stand firm." And then it stands as immovable as a rock.

"Stand firm." I must maintain the posture of one who stands, ready for action, expecting further orders, and cheerfully and patiently awaiting the Director's voice. It will not be long until God will say to me, as distinctly as He told Moses to tell the children of Israel, "Move on" (Exodus 14:15). CHARLES H. SPURGEON

Be quiet! Why this anxious heed
About your tangled ways?
God knows them all. He gives you speed
And He allows delays.
It's good for you to walk by faith
And not by sight.
Take it on trust a little while.
Soon will you read the mystery aright
In the full sunshine of His smile.

In times of uncertainty—*wait*. If you have any doubt—*wait*, never forcing yourself into action. If you sense any restraint in your spirit, do not go against it—*wait* until the way is clear.

APRIL 20

"Not by might nor by power, but by my Spirit," says the Lord *Almighty.*
Zechariah 4:6

Once as I walked along the road on a steep hill, I caught sight of a boy on a bicycle near the bottom. He was pedaling uphill against the wind and was obviously working tremendously hard. Just as he was exerting the greatest effort and painfully doing the best he could do, a streetcar, also going up the hill, approached him. It was not traveling too fast for the boy to grab hold of a rail at the rear, and I am sure you can guess the result. He went up the hill as effortlessly as a bird gliding through the sky.

This thought then flashed through my mind: "I am like that boy on the bicycle in my weariness and weakness. I am pedaling uphill against all kinds of opposition and am almost worn out with the task. But nearby there is great power available—the strength of the Lord Jesus. All I must do is get in touch with Him and maintain communication with Him. And even if I grab hold with only one little finger of faith, it will be enough to make His power mine to accomplish the act of service that now overwhelms me."

Seeing this boy on his bicycle helped me to set aside my weariness and to recognize this great truth. THE LIFE OF FULLER PURPOSE

ABANDONED

Utterly abandoned to the Holy Ghost!
Seeking all His fullness, whatever the cost;
Cutting all the moorings, launching in the deep
Of His mighty power—strong to save and keep.

Utterly abandoned to the Holy Ghost!
Oh! The sinking, sinking, until self is lost!
Until the emptied vessel lies broken at His feet;
Waiting till His filling shall make the work complete.

Utterly abandoned to the will of God;
Seeking for no other path than my Master trod;
Leaving ease and pleasure, making Him my choice,
Waiting for His guidance, listening for His voice.

Utterly abandoned! No will of my own;
For time and for eternity, His, and His alone;
All my plans and purposes lost in His sweet will,
Having nothing, yet in Him all things possessing still.

Utterly abandoned! It's so sweet to be
Captive in His bonds of love, yet wondrously free;
Free from sin's entanglements, free from doubt and fear,
Free from every worry, burden, grief, or care.

Utterly abandoned! Oh, the rest is sweet,
As I tarry, waiting, at His blessed feet;
Waiting for the coming of the Guest divine,
Who my inmost being will perfectly refine.

Lo! He comes and fills me, Holy Spirit sweet!
I, in Him, am satisfied! I, in Him, complete!
And the light within my soul will nevermore grow dim
While I keep my covenant—abandoned unto Him!

AUTHOR UNKNOWN

APRIL 21

He did not waver . . . regarding the promise . . . being fully persuaded that God had power to do what he had promised.

ROMANS 4:20–21

SCRIPTURE TELLS US THAT ABRAHAM, "WITHOUT WEAKENING IN HIS faith, . . . faced the fact that his body was as good as dead" (v. 19). He was not discouraged, because he was not looking at himself but at almighty God. "He did not *waver* . . . regarding the promise" but stood straight, not bending beneath the staggering load of God's blessing. Instead of growing weak, his faith grew stronger, exhibiting more power, even as more difficulties became apparent. Abraham glorified God for His complete sufficiency and was "fully persuaded that God had power to do what he had promised."

The literal translation of this passage from the Greek expresses the thought in this way: God is not merely able but abundantly able, bountifully and generously able, with an infinite surplus of resources, and eternally able "to do what he had promised."

He is the God of limitless resources—the only limit comes from us. Our requests, our thoughts, and our prayers are too small, and our expectations are too low. God is trying to raise our vision to a higher level, call us to have greater expectations, and thereby bring us to greater appropriation. Shall we continue living in a way that mocks His will and denies His Word?

There is no limit to what we may ask and expect of our glorious El Shaddai—our almighty God. And there is no way for us to measure His blessing, for He is "able to do immeasurably more than all we ask or imagine, according to his power that is at work within us" (Ephesians 3:20).
A. B. Simpson

The way to find God's treasure-house of blessing is to climb the ladder of His divine promises. Those promises are the key that opens the door to the riches of God's grace and favor.

APRIL 22

He knows the way that I take.
Job 23:10

O believer, what a glorious assurance this verse is! What confidence I have because "the way that I take"—this way of trials and tears, however winding, hidden, or tangled—"He knows"! When the "furnace [is] heated seven times hotter than usual" (Daniel 3:19), I can know He still lights my way. There is an almighty Guide who knows and directs my steps, whether they lead to the bitter water at the well of Marah or to the joy and refreshment of the oasis at Elim (Exodus 15:23, 27).

The way is dark to the Egyptians yet has its own pillar of cloud and fire for God's Israel. The furnace may be hot, but not only can I trust the hand that lights the fire, I can also have the assurance the fire will not consume but only refine. And when the refining process is complete, not a moment too soon or too late, "I will come forth as gold" (Job 23:10).

When I feel God is the farthest away, He is often the nearest to me. "*When* my spirit grows faint within me, it is you who watch over my way" (Psalm 142:3). Do we know of another who shines brighter than the most radiant sunlight, who meets us in our room with the first waking light, who has an infinitely tender and compassionate watchfulness over us throughout our day, and who "knows the way that [we] take"?

The world, during a time of adversity, speaks of "providence" with a total lack of understanding. They dethrone God, who is the living, guiding Sovereign of the universe, to some inanimate, dead abstraction. What they call "providence" they see as occurrences of fate, reducing God from His position as our acting, powerful, and personal Jehovah.

The pain would be removed from many an agonizing trial if only I could see what Job saw during his time of severe affliction, when all earthly hope lay dashed at his feet. He saw nothing but the hand of God—God's hand behind the swords of the Sabeans who attacked his servants and cattle, and behind the devastating lightning; God's hand giving wings to the mighty desert winds, which swept away his children; and God's hand in the dreadful silence of his shattered home.

Thus, seeing God in everything, Job could say, "*The* LORD gave and *the* LORD has taken away; may the name of *the* LORD be praised" (Job 1:21). Yet his faith reached its zenith when this once-powerful prince of the desert "sat among the ashes" (Job 2:8) and still could say, "Though he slay me, yet will I hope in him" (Job 13:15). J. R. MACDUFF

APRIL 23

Though I walk in the midst of trouble, you preserve my life.
PSALM 138:7

THE HEBREW OF THIS VERSE LITERALLY MEANS TO "GO ON IN THE CENTER of trouble." What descriptive words! And once we have called on God during our time of trouble, pleaded His promise of deliverance but not received it, and continued to be oppressed by the enemy until we are in the very thick of the battle—or the "center of trouble"—others may tell us, "Don't bother the teacher anymore" (Luke 8:49).

When Martha said, "Lord, . . . if you had been here, my brother would not have died" (John 11:21), Jesus countered her lack of hope with His greater promise, "Your brother will rise again" (John 11:23). And when we walk "in the center of trouble" and are tempted to think, like Martha, that we are past the point of ever being delivered, our Lord also answers us with a promise from His Word: "Though I walk in the midst of trouble, you preserve my life."

Although His answer seems so long in coming and we continue to "walk in the midst of trouble," "the center of trouble" is the place where He preserves us, not the place where He fails us. The times we continue to walk in seemingly utter hopelessness are the very times He will "stretch out [His] hand against the anger of [our] foes" (Psalm 138:7). He will bring our trouble to completion, causing the enemy's attack to cease and to fail.

In light of this, what reason would there ever be for despair? APHRA WHITE

The Eye of the Storm

Fear not that the whirlwind will carry you hence,
Nor wait for its onslaught in breathless suspense,
Nor shrink from the blight of the terrible hail,
But pass through the edge to the heart of the tale,
For there is a shelter, sunlighted and warm,
And Faith sees her God through the eye of the storm.

The passionate tempest with rush and wild roar
And threatenings of evil may beat on the shore,
The waves may be mountains, the fields battle plains,
And the earth be immersed in a deluge of rains,
Yet, the soul, stayed on God, may sing bravely its psalm,
For the heart of the storm is the center of calm.

Let hope be not quenched in the blackness of night,
Though the cyclone awhile may have blotted the light,
For behind the great darkness the stars ever shine,
And the light of God's heavens, His love will make thine,
Let no gloom dim your eyes, but uplift them on high
To the face of your God and the blue of His sky.

The storm is your shelter from danger and sin,
And God Himself takes you for safety within;
The tempest with Him passes into deep calm,
And the roar of the winds is the sound of a psalm.
Be glad and serene when the tempest clouds form;
God smiles on His child in the eye of the storm.

APRIL 24

Faith is confidence . . . assurance about of what we do not see.

HEBREWS 11:1

GENUINE FAITH PUTS ITS LETTER IN THE MAILBOX AND LETS GO. Distrust, however, holds on to a corner of the envelope and then wonders why the answer never arrives. There are some letters on my desk that I wrote weeks ago, but I have yet to mail them because of my uncertainty over the address or the contents. Those letters have not done any good for me or anyone else at this point. And they never will accomplish anything until I let go of them, trusting them to the postal service.

It is the same with genuine faith. It hands its circumstance over to God, allowing Him to work. Psalm 37:5 is a great confirmation of this: "Commit your way to the LORD; trust in him and he will do this." He will never work until we *commit.* Faith is receiving—or even more, actually appropriating—the gifts God offers us. We may believe in Him, come to Him, commit to Him, and rest in Him, but we will never fully realize all our blessings until we begin to receive from Him and come to Him having the spirit of abiding and appropriating. Days of Heaven upon Earth

Dr. Payson, while still a young man, once wrote to an elderly mother who was extremely worried and burdened over the condition of her son. He wrote,

> You are worrying too much about him. Once you have prayed for him, as you have done, and committed him to God, you should not continue to be anxious. God's command, "Do not be anxious about anything" (Philippians 4:6), is unlimited, and so is the verse, "Cast *all* your anxiety on him" (1 Peter 5:7). If we truly have cast our burdens upon another, can they continue to pressure us? If we carry them with us from the throne of grace, it is obvious we have not left them there. In my own life I test my prayers in this way: after committing something to God, if I can come away, like Hannah did, with no more sadness, pain, or anxiety in my heart, I see it as proof that I have prayed the prayer of faith. But if I pray and then still carry my burden, I conclude my faith was not exercised.

APRIL 25

Mary Magdalene and the other Mary were sitting there opposite the tomb.

Matthew 27:61

Oh, how slow grief is to come to understanding! Grief is ignorant and does not even care to learn. When the grieving women "were sitting there opposite the tomb," did they see the triumph of the next two thousand years? Did they see anything except that Christ was gone?

The Christ you and I know today came from their loss. Countless mourning hearts have since seen resurrection in the midst of their grief, and yet these sorrowing women watched at the beginning of this result and saw nothing. What they regarded as the end of life was actually the preparation for coronation, for Christ remained silent that He might live again with tenfold power.

They did not see it. They mourned, wept, went away, and then came again to the sepulcher, driven by their broken hearts. And still it was only a tomb—unprophetic, voiceless, and drab.

It is the same with us. Each of us sits "opposite the tomb" in our own garden and initially says, "This tragedy is irreparable. I see no benefit in it and will take no comfort in it." And yet right in the midst of our deepest and worst adversities, our Christ is often just lying there, waiting to be resurrected.

Our Savior is where our death seems to be at the end of our hope, we find the brightest beginning of fulfillment. Where darkness seems the deepest, the most radiant light is set to emerge. And once the experience is complete, we find our garden is not disfigured by the tomb.

Our joys are made better when sorrow is in the midst of them. And our sorrows become bright through the joys God has planted around them. At first the flowers of the garden may not appear to be our favorites, but we will learn that they are the flowers of the heart. The flowers planted at the grave deep within the Christian heart are love, hope, faith, joy, and peace.

'Twas by a path of sorrows drear
Christ entered into rest;
And shall I look for roses here,
Or think that earth is blessed?
Heaven's whitest lilies blow
From earth's sharp crown of woe:
Who here his cross can meekly bear,
Shall wear the kingly purple there.

APRIL 26

I consider everything a loss because of the surpassing worth of knowing Christ Jesus my Lord.

PHILIPPIANS 3:8

LIGHT IS ALWAYS COSTLY AND COMES AT THE EXPENSE OF THAT WHICH produces it. An unlit candle does not shine, for burning must come before the light. And we can be of little use to others without a cost to ourselves. Burning suggests suffering, and we try to avoid pain.

We tend to feel we are doing the greatest good in the world when we are strong and fit for active duty and when our hearts and hands are busy with kind acts of service. Therefore when we are set aside to suffer, when we are sick, when we are consumed with pain, and when all our activities have been stopped, we feel we are no longer of any use and are accomplishing nothing.

Yet if we will be patient and submissive, it is almost certain we will be a greater blessing to the world around us during our time of suffering and pain than we were when we thought we were doing our greatest work. Then we are burning, and shining brightly as a result of the fire. EVENING THOUGHTS

The glory of tomorrow is rooted in the drudgery of today.

Many people want the glory without the cross, and the shining light without the burning fire, but crucifixion comes before coronation.

Have you heard the tale of the aloe plant,
Away in the sunny clime?
By humble growth of a hundred years
It reaches its blooming time;
And then a wondrous bud at its crown
Breaks into a thousand flowers;
This floral queen, in its blooming seen,
Is the pride of the tropical bowers,

But the flower to the plant is sacrifice,
For it blooms but once, and it dies.

Have you further heard of the aloe plant,
That grows in the sunny clime;
How every one of its thousand flowers,
As they drop in the blooming time,
Is an infant plant that fastens its roots
In the place where it falls on the ground,
And as fast as they drop from the dying stem,
Grow lively and lovely all 'round?
By dying, it liveth a thousandfold
In the young that spring from the death of the old.

Have you heard the tale of the pelican,
The Arabs' Gimel el Bahr,
That lives in the African solitudes,
Where the birds that live lonely are?
Have you heard how it loves its tender young,
And cares and toils for their good,
It brings them water from mountains far,
And fishes the seas for their food.
In famine it feeds them—what love can devise!
The blood of its bosom—and, feeding them, dies.

Have you heard this tale—the best of them all—
The tale of the Holy and True,
He dies, but His life, in untold souls
Lives on in the world anew;
His seed prevails, and is filling the earth,
As the stars fill the sky above.
He taught us to yield up the love of life,

For the sake of the life of love.
His death is our life, His loss is our gain;
The joy for the tear, the peace for the pain.
SELECTED

APRIL 27

I am the Living One; I was dead, and now
look, I am alive for ever and ever!
REVELATION 1:18

FLOWERS! EASTER LILIES! SPEAK TO ME THIS MORNING THE SAME SWEET lesson of immortality you have been speaking to so many sorrowing souls for years. Wise old Book! Let me read again in your pages the steady assurance that "to die is gain" (Philippians 1:21). Poets! Recite for me your verses that resound the gospel of eternal life in every line. Singers! Break forth once more into hymns of joy—let me hear again my favorite resurrection songs.

Trees, blossoms, and birds; and seas, skies, and winds—whisper it, sound it anew, sing it, echo it, let it beat and resonate through every atom and particle on earth, and let the air be filled with it. Let it be told and retold again and again, until hope rises to become conviction, and conviction becomes the certainty of knowing. Let it be told until, like Paul, even when we face our death, we will go triumphantly, with our faith secure and a peaceful and radiant expression on our face.

O sad-faced mourners, who each day are wending
Through churchyard paths of cypress and of yew,
Leave for today the low graves you are tending,
And lift your eyes to God's eternal blue!

It is no time for bitterness or sadness;
Choose Easter lilies, not pale asphodels;

Let your souls thrill to the caress of gladness,
And answer the sweet chime of Easter bells.

If Christ were still within the grave's low prison,
A captive of the Enemy we dread;
If from that rotting cell He had not risen,
Who then could dry the gloomy tears you shed?

If Christ were dead there would be need to sorrow,
But He has risen and vanquished death today;
Hush, then your sighs, if only till tomorrow,
At Easter give your grief a holiday.

MAY RILEY SMITH

A well-known preacher was once in his study writing an Easter sermon when this thought gripped him: "My Lord is *living*!" With excitement he jumped up, paced the floor, and began repeating to himself, "Christ is alive. His body is warm. He is not the great 'I was' but the great 'I am.'"

Christ is not only a fact but a *living* fact. He is the glorious truth of Easter Day!

Because of that truth, an Easter lily blooms and an angel sits at every believer's grave. We believe in a risen Lord, so do not look to the past to worship only at His tomb. Look above and within to worship the Christ who lives. Because He lives, we live. ABBOTT BENJAMIN VAUGHAN

APRIL 28

When they cried out to the LORD, he raised up for them
a deliverer, Othniel . . . Caleb's younger brother, who
saved them. The Spirit of the LORD came on him.

JUDGES 3:9–10

God is continually preparing His heroes, and when the opportunity is right, He puts them into position in an instant. He works so fast, the world wonders where they came from.

Dear friend, let the Holy Spirit prepare you, through the discipline of life. And when the finishing touch has been made on the sculpture, it will be easy for God to put you on display in the perfect place.

The day is coming when, like Othniel, we will also judge the nations and will rule and reign with Christ on earth during His millennial kingdom. But before that glorious day, we must allow God to prepare us, as He did Othniel at Kiriath Sepher (Judges 1:11–13). We must allow God to work amid our present trials and in the little victories, the future significance of which we can only imagine. Yet we can be sure that if the Holy Spirit has His way with us, the Lord of heaven and earth has also prepared for us a throne. A. B. Simpson

Human strength and human greatness
Spring not from life's sunny side,
Heroes must be more than driftwood
Floating on a waveless tide.

Every highway of life descends into the valley now and then. And everyone must go through the tunnel of tribulation before they can travel on the high road of triumph.

APRIL 29

Elijah was a man just like us. He prayed earnestly.

James 5:17 CEB

Thank God Elijah was "just like us"! He sat under a tree, complained to God, and expressed his unbelief—just as we have often done. Yet this was not the case at all when he was truly in touch with God. "Elijah was a man just like us," *yet* "he prayed earnestly." The literal meaning of this in the Greek is magnificent: instead of saying, "earnestly," it says, "He prayed in prayer." In other words, "He kept on praying." The lesson here is that you must *keep praying.*

Climb to the top of Mount Carmel and see that great story of faith and sight. After Elijah had called down fire from heaven to defeat the prophets of Baal, rain was needed for God's prophecy to be fulfilled. And the man who could command fire from heaven could bring rain using the same methods. We are told, "Elijah . . . bent down to the ground and put his face between his knees" (1 Kings 18:42), shutting out all sights and sounds. He put himself in a position, beneath his robe, to neither see nor hear what was happening.

Elijah then said to his servant, "Go and look toward the sea" (1 Kings 18:43). Upon returning, the servant replied, "There is nothing there." How brief his response must have seemed! *"Nothing!"* Can you imagine what we would do under the same circumstances? We would say, "Just as I expected!" and then would stop praying. But did Elijah give up? No. In fact, six times he told his servant, "Go back." Each time the servant returned saying, "Nothing!"

Yet "the seventh time the servant reported, 'A cloud as small as a man's hand is rising from the sea'" (1 Kings 18:44). What a fitting description, for a man's hand had been raised in prayer to God before the rains came. And the rains came so fast and furiously that Elijah warned Ahab to "go down before the rain stops you."

This is a story of faith and sight—faith cutting itself off from everything except God, with sight that looks and yet sees nothing. Yes, in spite of utterly hopeless reports received from sight, this is a story of faith that continues "praying in prayer."

Do you know how to pray in that way—how to prevail in prayer? Let your sight bring you reports as discouraging as possible, but pay no attention to them. Our heavenly Father lives, and even the delays of answers to our prayers are part of His goodness. ARTHUR TAPPAN PIERSON

Each of three young boys once gave a definition of faith that illustrates the important aspect of tenacity. The first boy defined faith as "taking hold of Christ," the second as "keeping our hold on Him," and the third as "not letting go of Him."

APRIL 30

The cows that were ugly and gaunt ate up the seven sleek, fat cows. . . . The thin heads of grain swallowed up the seven healthy, full heads.

GENESIS 41:4, 7

THESE DREAMS SHOULD BE A WARNING TO EACH OF US. YES, IT *is* POSsible for the best years of our life, the best experiences we have enjoyed, the best victories we have won, and the best service we have rendered, to be swallowed up by times of failure, defeat, dishonor, and uselessness in God's kingdom. Some people whose lives offered exceptional promise and achievement have come to such an end. It is certainly terrible to imagine, but it is true. *Yet it is never necessary.*

Samuel Dickey Gordon once said that the only safe assurance against such a tragedy is to have a "fresh touch with God daily—or even hourly." My blessed, fruitful, and victorious experiences of yesterday have no lingering value to me today. In fact, they can be "swallowed up" or reversed by today's failures, unless I see them as incentives to spur me on to even better and richer experiences today.

Maintaining this "fresh touch with God," by abiding in Christ, will be the only thing to keep the "ugly and gaunt . . . cows" and the "thin heads of grain" from consuming my life. MESSAGES FOR THE MORNING WATCH

MAY 1

God, who does not lie, promised.

TITUS 1:2

FAITH IS NOT CONJURING UP, THROUGH AN ACT OF YOUR WILL, A SENSE of certainty that something is going to happen. No, it is recognizing God's promise as an actual fact, believing it is true, rejoicing in the knowledge of that truth, and then simply resting because God said it.

Faith turns a promise into a prophecy. A promise is contingent upon our cooperation, but when we exercise genuine faith in it, it becomes a prophecy. Then we can move ahead with certainty that it will come to pass, because "God . . . does not lie." DAYS OF HEAVEN UPON EARTH

I often hear people praying for more faith, but when I listen carefully to them and get to the essence of their prayer, I realize it is not more faith they are wanting at all. What they are wanting is their faith to be changed to sight.

Faith does not say, "I see this is good for me; therefore God must have sent it." Instead, faith declares, "God sent it; therefore it must be good for me."

Faith, when walking through the dark with God, only asks Him to hold his hand more tightly. PHILLIPS BROOKS

The Shepherd does not ask of thee
Faith in your faith, but only faith in Him;
And this He meant in saying, "Come to me."
In light or darkness seek to do His will,
And leave the work of faith to Jesus still.

HYMNAL

MAY 2

The LORD has established his throne in heaven,
and his kingdom rules over all.

PSALM 103:19

Some time ago as I went out my door in the early spring, a blast of easterly wind rounded the corner. It seemed defiant and merciless and was fierce and dry, raising a cloud of dust ahead of it. As I removed the key from the door, I quite impatiently began to say, "*I wish the wind would . . .*" What I was about to say was *change*, but my thought was stopped and the sentence was never finished.

As I continued on my way, this incident became a parable for me. I imagined an angel handing me a key and saying, "My Master sends you His love and asked me to give you this." Wondering, I asked, "What is it?" "It is *the key to the winds*," the angel said and then disappeared.

My first thought was, "This indeed will bring me happiness." So I hurried high into the hills to the source of the winds and stood amid the caves. I proclaimed, "I will do away with the terrible east wind—it will never plague us again!" I summoned that unfriendly wind to me, closed the door behind it, and heard it echoing through the hollow caves. As I turned the key, triumphantly locking it in, I said, "There, I am finished with that." Then looking around me, I asked myself, "What should I put in its place?" I thought of the warm southerly wind and how pleasant it must be to newborn lambs and new flowers and plants of all kinds. But as I put the key in the door, it began to burn my hand. I cried aloud, "What am I doing? Who knows what damage I may cause? How do I know what the fields want and need? Ten thousand problems may result from this foolish wish of mine!"

Bewildered and ashamed, I looked up and asked the Lord to send His angel to take away the key. Then I promised I would never ask for it again. To my amazement, the Lord Himself came and stood by me. He stretched out His hand to take the key, and as I placed it there, I saw it touch that sacred scar.

I was filled with remorse as I wondered how I could ever have complained about anything done by Him who bore such sacred signs of His love. Then He took the key and hung it on His belt. I asked, "Do you keep the key to the winds?" "I do, my child," He graciously answered. And as He spoke, I noticed that all the keys to my life were hanging there as well. He saw my look of amazement and asked, *"Did you not know, dear child, that my 'kingdom rules over all'?"*

"If you rule 'over all,'" I questioned, "is it safe to complain about anything?" Then He tenderly laid His hand upon me to say, "My dear child, your only safety comes from loving, trusting, and praising Me through everything." MARK GUY PEARSE

MAY 3

Everyone who calls on the name of the LORD will be saved.

JOEL 2:32

SO WHY DON'T I CALL ON HIS NAME? WHY DO I RUN TO THIS PERSON or that person, when God is so near and will hear my faintest call? Why do I sit down to plot my own course and make my own plans? Why don't I immediately place myself and my burden on the Lord?

Straight ahead is the best way to run, so why don't I run directly to the living God? Instead, I look in vain for deliverance everywhere else, but with God I will find it. With Him I have His royal promise: "[I] *will* be saved." And with Him I never need to ask if I may call on Him or not, for the word "everyone" is all encompassing. It includes me and means anybody and everybody who calls upon His name. Therefore I will trust in this verse and will immediately call on the glorious Lord who has made such a great promise.

My situation is urgent, and I cannot see how I will ever be delivered. Yet this is not my concern, for He who made the promise will find a way to keep it. My part is simply to obey His commands, not to direct His ways. I am His servant, not His advisor. I call upon Him and He will deliver me. CHARLES H. SPURGEON

MAY 4

He wounds, but he also binds up; he
injures, but his hands also heal.
Job 5:18

The ministry of great sorrow!

As we walk beside the hills that have been so violently shaken by a severe earthquake, we realize that times of complete calm follow those of destruction. In fact, pools of clear, still water lie in the valley beneath the fallen rocks of those hills as water lilies reflect their beauty to the sky. The reeds along the streams whisper in the wind, and the village rises once again, forgetting the graves of the past. And the church steeple, still bright after weathering the storm, proclaims a renewed prayer for protection from Him who holds the corners of the earth in His hands and gives strength to the hills. John Ruskin

God plowed one day with an earthquake,
And drove His furrows deep!
The huddled plains upstarted,
The hills were all aleap!

But that is the mountains' secret,
Long hidden in their breast;
"God's peace is everlasting,"
Are the dream words of their rest.

He made them the haunts of beauty,
The home chosen for His grace;
He spreads forth His mornings upon them,
His sunsets light their face.

His winds bring messages to them—
Strong storm-news from the main;
They sing it down the valleys
In the love song of the rain.

They are nurseries for young rivers,
Nests for His flying cloud,
Homesteads for newborn races,
Masterful, free, and proud.

The people of tired cities
Come up to their shrines and pray;
God freshens them within again,
As He passes by all day.

And lo, I have caught their secret!
The beauty deeper than all!
This faith—that life's hard moments,
When the jarring sorrows befall,

Are but God plowing His mountains;
And those mountains yet will be
The source of His grace and freshness,
And His peace everlasting to me.

William C. Garnett

MAY 5

As they began to sing and praise, the Lord set ambushes against the men . . . who were invading Judah, and they were defeated.

2 Chronicles 20:22

OH, IF ONLY WE WOULD WORRY LESS ABOUT OUR PROBLEMS AND SING and praise more! There are thousands of things that shackle us that could be turned into instruments of music, if we just knew how to do it. Think of those people who ponder, meditate, and weigh the affairs of life, and who continually study the mysterious inner workings of God's providence, wondering why they suffer burdens and are opposed and battled on every front. How different their lives would be, and how much more joyful, if they would stop indulging in self-centered and inward thinking and instead would daily lift their experiences to God, praising Him for them.

It is easier to sing your worries away than to reason them away. Why not sing in the morning? Think of the birds—they are the first to sing each day, and they have fewer worries than anything else in creation. And don't forget to sing in the evening, which is what the robins do when they have finished their daily work. Once they have flown their last flight of the day and gathered the last bit of food, they find a treetop from which to sing a song of praise.

Oh, that we might sing morning and evening, offering up song after song of continual praise throughout our day! SELECTED

Don't let the song go out of your life
Although it sometimes will flow
In a minor strain; it will blend again
With the major tone you know.

Although shadows rise to obscure life's skies,
And hide for a time the sun,
The sooner they'll lift and reveal the rift,
If you let the melody run.

Don't let the song go out of your life;
Though the voice may have lost its trill,

Though the quivering note may die in your throat,
Let it sing in your spirit still.

Don't let the song go out of your life;
Let it ring in your soul while here;
And when you go hence, it will follow you thence,
And live on in another sphere.

MAY 6

The secret of the Lord is with them that fear him.

Psalm 25:14 KJV

There are certain secrets of God's providence He allows His children to learn. Often, however, at least on the surface, His dealings with them appear to be harsh and hidden. Yet faith looks deeper and says, "This is God's secret. You are looking only on the outside, but I look deeper and see the hidden meaning."

Remember, diamonds are found in the rough, and their true value cannot be seen. And when the tabernacle was built in the wilderness, there was nothing ornate about its outward appearance. In fact, the outer covering of the thick hides of sea cows gave no hint of the valuable things inside.

Dear friend, God may send you some valuable gifts wrapped in unattractive paper. But do not worry about the wrappings, for you can be sure that inside He has hidden treasures of love, kindness, and wisdom. If we will simply take what He sends *and trust Him* for the blessings inside, we will learn the meaning of the secrets of His providence, even in times of darkness. A. B. Simpson

Not until each loom is silent,
And the crossthreads cease to fly,
Will God unroll the pattern
And explain the reason why

The dark threads are as needful
In the Weaver's skillful hand,
As the threads of gold and silver
For the pattern He has planned.

A person who has Christ as his Master is the master of every circumstance. Are your circumstances pressing in on you? Do not push away, for they are the Potter's handstand. You will learn to master them not by stopping their progress but by enduring their discipline. Your circumstances are not only shaping you into a vessel of beauty and honor but also providing you with resources of great value.

MAY 7

Jesus told his disciples a parable to show them that
they should always pray and not give up.
LUKE 18:1

THE FAILURE TO *persevere* IS THE MOST COMMON PROBLEM IN PRAYER and intercession. We begin to pray for something, raising our petitions for a day, a week, or even a month, but then if we have not received a definite answer, we quickly give up and stop praying for it altogether.

This is a mistake with deadly consequences and is simply a trap where we begin many things but never see them completed. It leads to ruin in every area of life. People who get into the habit of starting without ever finishing form the habit of failure. And those who begin praying about something without ever praying it through to a successful conclusion form the same habit in prayer. Giving up is admitting failure and defeat. Defeat then leads to discouragement and doubt in the power of prayer, and that is fatal to the success of a person's prayer life.

People often ask, "How long should I pray? Shouldn't I come to the place where I stop praying and leave the matter in God's hands?" The only answer is this: *Pray until what you pray for has been accomplished or until you have complete assurance in your heart that it will be.* Only when one of these two conditions has been met is it safe to stop persisting in prayer, for prayer not only is calling upon God but is also a battle with Satan. And because God uses our intercession as a mighty weapon of victory in the conflict, He alone must decide when it is safe to cease from petitioning. Therefore we dare not stop praying until either the answer itself has come or we receive assurance it will come.

In the first instance, we stop because we actually see the answer. In the second, we stop because we believe, and faith in our hearts is as trustworthy as the sight of our eyes, for it is "faith *from* God" (Ephesians 6:23) and the "faith *of* God" (Romans 3:3 KJV) that we have within us.

As we live a life of prayer, we will more and more come to experience and recognize this God-given assurance. We will know when to quietly rest in it or when to continue praying until we receive His answer. THE PRACTICE OF PRAYER

Wait at God's promise until He meets you there, for He always returns by the path of His promises. SELECTED

MAY 8

Walking around in the fire.

DANIEL 3:25

WHEN SHADRACH, MESHACH, AND ABEDNEGO WERE THROWN INTO the furnace, the fire did not stop them from moving, for they were seen "walking around." Actually, the fire was one of the streets they traveled to their destination. The comfort we have from Christ's revealed truth is not that it teaches us freedom *from* sorrow but that it teaches us freedom *through* sorrow.

O dear God, when darkness overshadows me, teach me that I am merely traveling through a tunnel. It will then be enough for me to know that someday it will be all right.

I have been told that someday I will stand at the top of the Mount of Olives and experience the height of resurrection glory. But heavenly Father, I want more—I want Calvary to lead up to it. I want to know that the shadows of darkness are the shade on a road—the road leading to Your heavenly house. Teach me that the reason I must climb the hill is because Your house is there! Knowing this, I will not be hurt by sorrow, if I will only *walk* in the fire. George Matheson

"The road is too rough," I said;
"It is uphill all the way;
No flowers, but thorns instead;
And the skies overhead are gray."
But One took my hand at the entrance dim,
And sweet is the road that I walk with Him.

"The cross is too great," I cried—
"More than the back can bear,
So rough and heavy and wide,
And nobody near to care."
And One stooped softly and touched my hand:
"I know. I care. And I understand."

Then why do we fret and cry;
Cross-bearers all we go:
But the road ends by and by
In the dearest place we know,
And every step in the journey we
May take in the Lord's own company.

MAY 9

Abraham remained standing before the Lord.

Genesis 18:22

In this chapter, Abraham pleaded with God for the lives of others. A friend of God's can do exactly that. But perhaps you see Abraham's level of faith and his friendship with God as something far beyond your own possibilities. Do not be discouraged, however, for Abraham grew in his faith not by giant leaps but step by step. And we can do the same.

The person whose faith has been severely tested yet who has come through the battle victoriously is the person to whom even greater tests will come. The finest jewels are those that are the most carefully cut and polished, and the most precious metals are put through the hottest fires. You can be sure Abraham would never have been called the Father of Faith had he not been tested to the utmost.

Read Genesis 22. In verse 2 God said to Abraham, "Take your son, your only son—whom you love Isaac—and . . . sacrifice him." We then see him climbing Mount Moriah with his heart heavy and yearning yet humbly obedient. He climbed with Isaac, the object of his great love, who was about to be sacrificed at the command of God—the One whom Abraham faithfully loved and served!

What a lesson this should be to us when we question God's dealings in our lives! Rebuke all explanations that try to cast doubt on this staggering scene, for this was an object lesson for all ages! Angels also looked on in awe. Will Abraham's faith not stand forever as a strength and a help to all God's people? Will his trial not be a witness to the fact that unwavering faith will always prove the faithfulness of God?

The answer is a resounding—yes! And once Abraham's faith had victoriously endured its greatest test, the Angel of the Lord—the Lord Jesus, Jehovah, and He in whom the "many promises God has made . . . are 'Yes' . . . [and] 'Amen'" (2 Corinthians 1:20)—spoke to him and said, "Now I know that you fear God" (Genesis 22:12). The Lord said to him, in effect, "Because you have trusted me through this great trial, I will trust you, and you will forever be 'my friend' [Isaiah 41:8]." The Lord promised Abraham, "I will surely bless you . . . and through your offspring all nations on earth will be blessed, because you have obeyed me" (Genesis 22:17–18).

It is true, and always will be, that "*those who rely on faith are blessed along with Abraham, the man of faith*" (Galatians 3:9). SELECTED

Having a friendship with God is no small thing.

MAY 10

I would have despaired unless I had believed that I would see the goodness of the LORD. . . . *Wait for the* LORD; *be strong and let your heart take courage.*

PSALM 27:13–14 NASB

DO NOT DESPAIR!

Oh, how great the temptation is to despair at times! Our soul becomes depressed and disheartened, and our faith staggers under the severe trials and testing that come into our lives, especially during times of bereavement and suffering. We may come to the place where we say, "I cannot bear this any longer. I am close to despair under these circumstances God has allowed. He tells me not to despair, but what am I supposed to do when I am at this point?"

What have you done in the past when you felt weak physically? You could not *do* anything. You *ceased* from doing. In your weakness, you leaned on the shoulder of a strong loved one. You leaned completely on someone else and rested, becoming still, and trusting in another's strength.

It is the same when you are tempted to despair under spiritual afflictions. Once you have come close to the point of despair, God's message is not, "Be strong and courageous" (Joshua 1:6), for He knows that your strength and courage have run away. Instead, He says sweetly, "Be still, and know that I am God" (Psalm 46:10).

Hudson Taylor was so weak and feeble in the last few months of his life that he told a friend, "I am so weak I cannot write. I cannot read my Bible. I cannot even pray. All I can do is lie still in the arms of God as a little child, trusting Him." This wonderful man of God, who had great spiritual power, came to the point of physical suffering and weakness where all he could do was lie still and trust.

That is all God asks of you as His dear child. When you become weak through the fierce fires of affliction, do not try to "*be strong.*" Just "*be still, and know that [He is] God.*" And know that He will sustain you and bring you through the fire.

God reserves His best medicine for our times of deepest despair.

"Be strong and take heart" (Psalm 27:14).

Be strong, He has not failed you
In all the past,
And will He go and leave you
To sink at last?
No, He said He will hide you
Beneath His wing;
And sweetly there in safety
You then may sing.

SELECTED

MAY 11

We went through fire and water, but you brought us to a place of abundance.

PSALM 66:12

IT MAY SEEM PARADOXICAL, BUT THE ONLY PERSON WHO IS AT REST has achieved it through conflict. This peace, born of conflict, is not like the ominous lull before the storm but like the serenity and the quietness following the storm, with its fresh, purified air.

The person who may appear to be blessed, having been untouched by sorrow, is typically not one who is strong and at peace. His qualities have never been tested, and he does not know how he would handle even a mild setback. The safest sailor is certainly not one who has never weathered a storm. He may be right for fair-weather sailing, but when a storm arises, wouldn't you want an experienced sailor at the critical post? Wouldn't you want one at the helm who has fought through a gale and who knows the strength of the ship's hull and rigging, and how the anchor may be used to grasp the rocks of the ocean floor?

Oh, how everything gives way when affliction first comes upon us! The clinging stems of our hopes are quickly snapped, and our heart lies overwhelmed and prostrate, like a vine the windstorm has torn from its trellis. But once the initial shock is over and we are able to look up and say, "It is the Lord" (John 21:7), faith begins to lift our shattered hopes once more and securely binds them to the feet of God. And the final result is confidence, safety, and peace. SELECTED

The adverse winds blew against my life;
My little ship with grief was tossed;
My plans were gone—heart full of strife,
And all my hope seemed to be lost—
"Then He arose"—one word of peace.
"There was a calm"—a sweet release.

A tempest great of doubt and fear
Possessed my mind; no light was there
To guide, or make my vision clear.
Dark night! 'twas more than I could bear—
"Then He arose," I saw His face—
"There was a calm" filled with His grace.

My heart was sinking 'neath the wave
Of deepening test and raging grief;
All seemed as lost, and none could save,
And nothing could bring me relief—

"Then He arose"—and spoke one word,
"There was a calm!" "It is the Lord."

L. S. P.

MAY 12

"Everything is possible for one who believes."

MARK 9:23

THE "EVERYTHING" MENTIONED HERE DOES NOT ALWAYS COME SIMPLY by asking, because God is always seeking to teach you the way of faith. Your training for a life of faith requires many areas of learning, including the trial of faith, the discipline of faith, the patience of faith, and the courage of faith. Often you will pass through many stages before you finally realize the result of faith—namely, the victory of faith.

Genuine moral fiber is developed by enduring the discipline of faith. When you have made your request to God, and the answer still has not come, what are you to do? Keep on believing His Word! Never be swayed from it by what you may see or feel. Then as you stand firm, your power and experience is being developed, strengthened, and deepened. When you remain unswayed from your stance of faith, even in view of supposed contradictions to God's Word, you grow stronger on every front.

God will often purposely delay in giving you His answer, and in fact the delay is just as much an answer to your prayer as is the fulfillment when it comes. He worked this way in the lives of all the great Bible characters. Abraham, Moses, and Elijah were not great in the beginning but made great through the discipline of their faith. Only through that discipline were they then equipped for the work to which God had called them.

Think, for example, of Joseph, whom the Lord was training for the throne of Egypt. Psalm 105:19 (KJV) says, "*The word of the* LORD *tried him.*" It was not the prison life with its hard beds or poor food that "tried him" but "the word of the LORD." The words God spoke into his heart in his early years, concerning his elevated place of honor above his brothers, were the words that were always before him. He remained alone in prison, in spite of his innocence, and watched others being released who were justly incarcerated. Yet he remembered God's words even when every step of his career made fulfillment seem more and more impossible.

These were the times that tried his soul, but they were also the times of his spiritual growth and development. Then when word of his release from prison finally came, he was found ready and equipped for the delicate task of dealing with his wayward brothers. And he was able to do so with a love and a patience only surpassed by God Himself.

No amount of persecution will try you as much as experiences like these—ones in which you are required to wait on God. Once He has spoken His promise to work, it is truly hard to wait as you see the days go by with no fulfillment. Yet it is this discipline of faith that will bring you into a knowledge of God that would otherwise be impossible.

MAY 13

We do not know what we ought to pray for.
ROMANS 8:26

OFTEN IT IS SIMPLY THE ANSWERS TO OUR PRAYERS THAT CAUSE MANY of the difficulties in the Christian life. We pray for patience, and our Father sends demanding people our way who test us to the limit, "because . . . *suffering produces perseverance*" (Romans 5:3). We pray for a submissive spirit, and God sends suffering again, for we learn to be obedient in the same way Christ "*learned obedience from what he suffered*" (Hebrews 5:8).

We pray to be unselfish, and God gives us opportunities to sacrifice by placing other people's needs first and by laying down our lives for other believers. We pray for strength and humility, and "a messenger of Satan" (2 Corinthians 12:7) comes to torment us until we lie on the ground pleading for it to be withdrawn.

We pray to the Lord, as His apostles did, saying, "Increase our faith!" (Luke 17:5). Then our money seems to take wings and fly away; our children become critically ill; an employee becomes careless, slow, and wasteful; or some other new trial comes upon us, requiring more faith than we have ever before experienced.

We pray for a Christlike life that exhibits the humility of a lamb. Then we are asked to perform some lowly task, or we are unjustly accused and given no opportunity to explain, for "he was led like a lamb to the slaughter, and . . . did not open his mouth" (Isaiah 53:7).

We pray for gentleness and quickly face a storm of temptation to be harsh and irritable. We pray for quietness, and suddenly every nerve is stressed to its limit with tremendous tension so that we may learn that when He sends His peace, no one can disturb it.

We pray for love for others, and God sends unique suffering by sending people our way who are difficult to love and who say things that get on our nerves and tear at our hearts. He does this because "love is patient, love is kind. . . . It does not dishonor others . . . it is not easily angered. . . . *It always protects*, always trusts, always hopes, always perseveres. Love never fails" (1 Corinthians 13:4–5, 7–8).

Yes, we pray to be like Jesus, and God's answer is: "I have tested you in the furnace of affliction" (Isaiah 48:10); "Will your courage endure or your hands be strong?" (Ezekiel 22:14); "Can you drink the cup?" (Matthew 20:22).

The way to peace and victory is to accept every circumstance and every trial as being straight from the hand of our loving Father; to live "with him in the heavenly realms" (Ephesians 2:6), above the clouds, in the very presence of His throne; and to look down from glory on our circumstances as being lovingly and divinely appointed. SELECTED

I prayed for strength, and then I lost awhile
All sense of nearness, human and divine;
The love I leaned on failed and pierced my heart,

The hands I clung to loosed themselves from mine;
But while I swayed, weak, trembling, and alone,
The everlasting arms upheld my own.

I prayed for light; the sun went down in clouds,
The moon was darkened by a misty doubt,
The stars of heaven were dimmed by earthly fears,
And all my little candle flames burned out;
But while I sat in shadow, wrapped in night,
The face of Christ made all the darkness bright.

I prayed for peace, and dreamed of restful ease,
A slumber free from pain, a hushed repose;
Above my head the skies were black with storm,
And fiercer grew the onslaught of my foes;
But while the battle raged, and wild winds blew,
I heard His voice and perfect peace I knew.

I thank You, Lord, You were too wise to heed
My feeble prayers, and answer as I sought,
Since these rich gifts Your bounty has bestowed
Have brought me more than all I asked or thought;
Giver of good, so answer each request
With Your own giving, better than my best.

Annie Johnson Flint

MAY 14

On that very day Abraham [did] . . . as God told him.

Genesis 17:23

Instant obedience is the only kind of obedience there is, for *delayed* obedience is disobedience. Each time God calls upon us to do something, He is offering to make a covenant with us. Our part is to obey, and then He will do His part to send a special blessing.

The only way to be obedient is to obey instantly—"*On that very day,*" as Abraham did. I know we often postpone doing what we know to do, and then later do it as well as we can. Certainly this is better than not doing it at all. By then, however, it is at best only a crippled, disfigured, and partial attempt toward obedience. *Postponed obedience can never bring us the full blessing God intended or what it would have brought had we obeyed at the earliest possible moment.*

What a pity it is how we rob ourselves, as well as God and others, by our procrastination! Remember, "On that very day" is the Genesis way of saying, "Do it now!" Messages for the Morning Watch

Martin Luther once said, "A true believer will crucify, or put to death, the question, 'Why?' He will simply obey without questioning." And I refuse to be one of those people who "unless . . . [I] see signs and wonders . . . will never believe" (John 4:48). I will obey without questioning.

Ours not to make reply,
Ours not to reason why,
Ours but to do and die.

Obedience is the fruit of faith; patience is the early blossom on the tree of faith. Christina Rossetti

MAY 15

Men see not the bright light which is in the clouds.

Job 37:21 KJV

Much of the world's beauty is due to clouds. The unchanging blue of a beautiful, sunlit sky still does not compare to the glory of changing clouds. And earth would become a wilderness if not for their ministry to us.

Human life has its clouds as well. They provide us with shade, refresh us, yet sometimes cover us with the darkness of night. But there is never a cloud without its "bright light." God has told us, "I have set my rainbow in the clouds" (Genesis 9:13). If only we could see clouds from above—in all their billowing glory, bathed in reflective light, and as majestic as the Alps—we would be amazed at their shining magnificence.

We see them only from below, so who will describe for us the "bright light" that bathes their summits, searches their valleys, and reflects from every peak of their expanse? Doesn't every drop of rain in them soak up health-giving qualities, which will later fall to earth?

O dear child of God! If only you could see your sorrows and troubles from above instead of seeing them from earth. If you would look down on them from where you are seated "with Christ . . . in the heavenly realms" (Ephesians 2:6), you would know the beauty of the rainbow of colors they reflect to the hosts of heaven. You would also see the "bright light" of Christ's face and would finally be content to see those clouds cast their deep shadows over the mountain slopes of your life.

Remember, clouds are always moving ahead of God's cleansing wind.
Selected

Should rage so fiercely round me in its wrath;
But this I know—God watches all my path,
And I can trust.
I cannot know why suddenly the storm
I may not draw aside the unseen veil
I have no power to look across the tide,
That hides the unknown future from my sight,
Nor know if for me waits the dark or light;

But I can trust.
To see while here the land beyond the river;
But this I know—I will be God's forever;
So I can trust.

MAY 16

"Do not be afraid, Daniel. Since the first day that you set your mind to gain understanding and to humble yourself before your God, your words were heard, and I have come in response to them. But the prince of the Persian kingdom resisted me twenty-one days."

Daniel 10:12–13

This passage is a wonderful teaching on prayer and shows us the direct hindrance Satan can be in our lives. Daniel had fasted and prayed for twenty-one difficult days. As far as we can tell from the biblical account, the difficulty came not because Daniel was not a good person nor because his prayer was not right but because of a special attack from Satan.

The Lord had sent His angelic messenger to tell Daniel that his prayer was answered the moment he began to pray, but the good angel was hindered by an evil angel who met him along the way and wrestled with him. This conflict occurred in the heavens, yet Daniel experienced the same kind of conflict here on earth as he agonized in prayer.

"Our struggle is not against flesh and blood, but against the rulers, against the authorities, . . . and against the spiritual forces of evil in the heavenly realms" (Ephesians 6:12). Satan's attack and the ensuing struggle delayed the answer three full weeks. Daniel was nearly defeated, and Satan would have been glad to kill him, but God would not allow anything to come upon Daniel beyond what he could bear (1 Corinthians 10:13).

Many prayers of believers are hindered by Satan. Yet you do not need to fear when your unanswered prayers are piling up, for soon they will break through like a flood. When that happens, not only will your answers flow through, but they will also be accompanied by new blessings.

Hell works the hardest on God's saints. The most worthy souls will be tested with the most pressure and the highest heat, but heaven will not desert them. William L. Watkinson

MAY 17

After forty years had passed, an angel appeared to
Moses . . . in the desert. . . . Then the Lord said to him,
". . . Now come, I will send you back to Egypt."
Acts 7:30, 33–34

Often the Lord calls us aside from our work for a season and asks us to be still and learn before we go out again to minister. And the hours spent waiting are not lost time.

An ancient knight once realized, as he was fleeing from his enemies, that his horse needed a shoe replaced. The prudent course of action seemed to be to hurry on without delay. Yet higher wisdom told him to stop for a few minutes at the blacksmith's along the road. Although he heard the galloping hooves of the enemies' horses close behind, he waited until his steed was reshod before continuing his escape. Just as the enemy appeared, only a hundred yards away, he jumped into the saddle and dashed away with the swiftness of the wind. Then he knew his stopping had actually hastened his escape.

Quite often God will ask us to wait before we go, so we may fully recover from our last mission before entering the next stage of our journey and work. Days of Heaven upon Earth

Waiting! Yes, patiently waiting!
Till next steps made plain will be;
To hear, with the inner hearing,
The Voice that will call for me.

Waiting! Yes, hopefully waiting!
With hope that need not grow dim;
The Master is pledged to guide me,
And my eyes are unto Him.

Waiting! Expectantly waiting!
Perhaps it may be today
The Master will quickly open
The gate to my future way.

Waiting! Yes, waiting! still waiting!
I know, though I've waited long,
That, while He withholds His purpose,
His waiting cannot be wrong.

Waiting! Yes, waiting! still waiting!
The Master will not be late:
Since He knows that I am waiting
For Him to unlatch the gate.

J. Danson Smith

MAY 18

We were under great pressure, . . . so that we despaired of life itself. . . . But this happened that we might not rely on ourselves but on God, who raises the dead.

2 Corinthians 1:8–9

Pressed beyond measure; yes, pressed to great length;
Pressed so intensely, beyond my own strength;
Pressed in my body and pressed in my soul,
Pressed in my mind till the dark surges roll.

Pressure from foes, and pressure from dear friends.
Pressure on pressure, till life nearly ends.

Pressed into knowing no helper but God;
Pressed into loving His staff and His rod.
Pressed into liberty where nothing clings;
Pressed into faith for impossible things.
Pressed into living my life for the Lord,
Pressed into living a Christ-life outpoured.

The pressure of difficult times makes us value life. Every time our life is spared and given back to us after a trial, it is like a new beginning. We better understand its value and thereby apply ourselves more effectively for God and for humankind. And the pressure we endure helps us to understand the trials of others, equipping us to help them and to sympathize with them.

Some people have a shallowness about them. With their superficial nature, they lightly take hold of a theory or a promise and then carelessly tell of their distrust of those who retreat from every trial. Yet a man or woman who has experienced great suffering will never do this. They are very tender and gentle, and understand what suffering really means. This is what Paul meant when he said, "Death is at work in us" (2 Corinthians 4:12).

Trials and difficult times are needed to press us forward. They work in the way the fire in the hold of a mighty steamship provides the energy that moves the pistons, turns the engine, and propels the great vessel across the sea, even when facing the wind and the waves. A. B. Simpson

MAY 19

Before he had finished praying, Rebekah came out with her jar on her shoulder. . . . Then the man bowed down and

worshiped the L*ORD*, *saying, "Praise be to the* L*ORD*, . . .
who has not abandoned his kindness and faithfulness."

GENESIS 24:15, 26–27

EVERY GODLY PRAYER IS ANSWERED BEFORE THE PRAYER ITSELF IS finished—"*Before* he had finished praying . . ." This is because Christ has pledged in His Word, "My Father will give you whatever you ask in my name" (John 16:23). When you ask in faith and in Christ's name—that is, in oneness with Him and His will—"it will be done for you" (John 15:7).

Since God's Word cannot fail, whenever we meet these simple conditions, the answer to our prayer has already been granted and is complete in heaven *as we pray*, even though it may not be revealed on earth until much later. Therefore it is wise to close every prayer with praise to God for the answer He has already given.

"Praise be to the LORD, . . . who has not abandoned his kindness and faithfulness" (Genesis 24:27). MESSAGES FOR THE MORNING WATCH

When we believe God for a blessing, we must have an attitude of faith and begin to act and pray as if the blessing were already ours. We should respond to God as if He has granted our request. This attitude of trust means leaning upon Him for what we have claimed and simply taking it for granted that He has given us our request and will continue to give it.

When people get married, they immediately have a new perspective and begin to act accordingly. This is how it should be when we take Christ as our Savior, our Sanctifier, our Healer, or our Deliverer. He expects us to have a new perspective, in which we recognize Him in the capacity and the role we have trusted Him for, and in which we allow Him to be everything to us we have claimed by faith. SELECTED

The thing I ask when God leads me to pray,
Begins in that same act to come my way.

MAY 20

"Shall I not drink the cup the Father has given me?"

JOHN 18:11

GOD IS A THOUSAND TIMES MORE METICULOUS WITH US THAN EVEN AN artist is with his canvas. Using many brush strokes of sorrow, and circumstances of various colors, He paints us into the highest and best image He visualizes, if we will only receive His bitter gifts of myrrh in the right spirit.

Yet when our cup of sorrows is taken away and the lessons in it are suppressed or go unheeded, we do more damage to our soul than could ever be repaired. No human heart can imagine the incomparable love God expresses in His gift of myrrh. However, this great gift that our soul should receive is allowed to pass by us because of our sleepy indifference, and ultimately nothing comes of it.

Then, in our barrenness we come and complain, saying, "O Lord, I feel so dry, and there is so much darkness within me!" My advice to you, dear child, is to open your heart to the pain and suffering, and it will accomplish more good than being full of emotion and sincerity. TAULER

The cry of man's anguish went up to God,
"Lord, take away pain:
The shadow that darkens the world You have made,
The close, choking chain
That strangles the heart, the burden that weighs
On the wings that would soar,
Lord, take away pain from the world You have made,
That it love You the more."
Then answered the Lord to the cry of His world:
"Shall I take away pain,
And with it the power of the soul to endure,
Made strong by the strain?
Shall I take away pity, that knits heart to heart

And sacrifice high?
Will you lose all your heroes that lift from the fire
Wisdom toward the sky?
Shall I take away love that redeems with a price
And smiles at the loss?
Can you spare from your lives that would climb unto Me
The Christ on His cross?"

MAY 21

I remembered my songs in the night.

PSALM 77:6

I READ SOMEWHERE OF A LITTLE BIRD THAT WILL NEVER SING THE song its owner desires to hear while its cage is full of light. It may learn a note of this or a measure of that but will never learn an entire song until its cage is covered and the sunlight is shut out.

Many people are the same, never learning to sing until the shadows of darkness fall. We need to remember: the fabled nightingale sings with its breast against a thorn; it was on that Bethlehem night the song of angels was heard; and it was "at midnight the cry rang out: 'Here's the bridegroom! Come out to meet him!'" (Matthew 25:6).

It is indeed extremely doubtful that a person's soul can really know the love of God in its richness and in its comforting, satisfying completeness until the skies are dark and threatening. Light emerges from darkness, and morning is born from the womb of night.

James Creelman once journeyed through the Balkans in search of Natalie, the exiled queen of Serbia. In one of his letters, he described his trip this way:

> During that memorable journey, I learned that the world's supply of rose oil comes from the Balkan Mountains. The thing that interested me most was that the roses had to be gathered during the darkest hours, with the

pickers starting at one o'clock and finishing by two. Initially this practice seemed to me to be a relic of superstition or tradition, but as I investigated further, I learned that actual scientific tests had proved that a full forty percent of the fragrance of the roses disappeared in the light of day.

And it is also a real and unquestionable fact of human life and culture that a person's character is strengthened most during the darkest days. MALCOLM J. MCLEOD

MAY 22

Commit your way to the LORD; trust in him and he will do this.
PSALM 37:5

THE LITERAL MEANING OF THIS VERSE IS: "*Roll* YOUR WAY ONTO *Jehovah* and trust upon Him, and *He works.*" This brings to our attention the immediacy of God's action once we commit, or "roll," burdens of any kind from our hands into His. Whether our burden is a sorrow, difficulty, physical need, or concern over the salvation of a loved one, "*He works.*"

When does He work? "He works" *now.* We act as if God does not immediately accept our trust in Him and thereby delays accomplishing what we ask Him to do. We fail to understand that "He works" *as we commit.* "He works" now! Praise Him for the fact that this is true.

Our expectation that He will work is the very thing enabling the Holy Spirit to accomplish what we have "rolled" onto Him. At that point it is out of our grasp, and we are not to try to do it ourselves. "He works!" Take comfort from this and do not try to pick it up again. What a relief there is in knowing He really is at work on our difficulty!

And when someone says, "But I don't see any results," pay him no attention.

"He works" if you have "rolled" your burdens onto Him and are "looking unto Jesus" (Hebrews 12:2 KJV) to do it. Your faith may be tested, but "He works." His Word is true! V. H. F.

"I cry out to God Most High, to God, who vindicates me" (Psalm 57:2).

One beautiful old translation of this verse says, "He will perform the cause I hold in my hand." That makes it very real to me today. The very thing "I hold in my hand"—my work today, this concern that is beyond my control, this task in which I have greatly overestimated my own abilities—*this* is what I may "cry out" for Him to do "for me," with the calm assurance He will perform it. "The wise and what they do are in God's hands" (Ecclesiastes 9:1). FRANCES RIDLEY HAVERGAL

The Lord will follow through on His covenant promises. Whatever He takes and holds in His hand, He will accomplish. Therefore His past mercies are guarantees for the future, and worthy reasons for continuing to cry out to Him. CHARLES H. SPURGEON

MAY 23

They were at their wits' end. Then they cried out to the LORD *in their trouble, and he brought them out of their distress.*

PSALM 107:27–28

Are you standing at "Wits' End Corner,"
Christian, with troubled brow?
Are you thinking of what is before you,
And all you are bearing now?
Does all the world seem against you,
And you in the battle alone?
Remember—at "Wits' End Corner"
Is just where God's power is shown.

Are you standing at "Wits' End Corner,"
Blinded with wearying pain,
Feeling you cannot endure it,
You cannot bear the strain,
Bruised through the constant suffering,

Dizzy, and dazed, and numb?
Remember—at "Wits' End Corner"
Is where Jesus loves to come.

Are you standing at "Wits' End Corner"?
Your work before you spread,
All lying begun, unfinished,
And pressing on heart and head,
Longing for strength to do it,
Stretching out trembling hands?
Remember—at "Wits' End Corner"
The Burden-Bearer stands.

Are you standing at "Wits' End Corner"?
Then you're just in the very spot
To learn the wondrous resources
Of Him who fails you not:
No doubt to a brighter pathway
Your footsteps will soon be moved,
But only at "Wits' End Corner"
Is the "God who is able" proved.

Antoinette Wilson

Do not get discouraged—it may be the last key on the ring that opens the door. Stansifer

MAY 24

Sarah became pregnant and bore a son to Abraham in his old age, at the very time God had promised him.

Genesis 21:2

"THE PLANS OF THE LORD STAND FIRM FOREVER, THE PURPOSES OF HIS heart through all generations" (Psalm 33:11). But we must be prepared to wait on God's timing. His timing is precise, for He does things "at the very time" He has set. It is not for us to know His timing, and in fact we cannot know it—we must wait for it.

If God had told Abraham while he was in Haran that he would have to wait thirty years before holding his promised child in his arms, his heart might have failed him. So God, as an act of His gracious love, hid from Abraham the number of weary years he would be required to wait. Only as the time was approaching, with but a few months left to wait, did God reveal His promise: "At the appointed time next year . . . Sarah will have a son" (Genesis 18:14). The "appointed time" came at last, and soon the joyous laughter that filled the patriarch's home caused the now elderly couple to forget their long and tiring wait.

So take heart, dear child, when God requires you to wait. The One you wait for will not disappoint you. He will never be even five minutes behind "the appointed time." And soon "your grief will turn to joy" (John 16:20).

Oh, how joyful the soul that God brings to laughter! Then sorrow and crying flee forever, as darkness flees the dawn. SELECTED

As passengers, it is not for us to interfere with the charts and the compass. We should leave the masterful Captain alone to do His own work. ROBERT HALL

Some things cannot be accomplished in a day. Even God does not make a glorious sunset in a moment. For several days He gathers the mist with which to build His beautiful palaces in the western sky.

Some glorious morn—but when? Ah, who will say?
The steepest mountain will become a plain,
And the parched land be satisfied with rain.
The gates of brass all broken; iron bars,
Transfigured, form a ladder to the stars.
Rough places plain, and crooked ways all straight,

For him who with a patient heart can wait.
These things will be on God's appointed day:
It may not be tomorrow—yet it may.

MAY 25

I endure everything for the sake of the elect, that they too may obtain the salvation that is in Christ Jesus, with eternal glory.
2 TIMOTHY 2:10

OH, IF ONLY JOB HAD KNOWN, AS HE SAT IN THE ASHES, TROUBLING HIS heart over the thought of God's providence, that millions down through history would look back on his trials. He might have taken courage in the fact that his experience would be a help to others throughout the world.

No one lives to himself, and Job's story is like yours and mine, only his was written for all to see. The afflictions Job faced and the trials he wrestled with are the very things for which he is remembered, and without them we would probably never have read of him in God's Word.

We never know the trials that await us in the days ahead. We may not be able to see the light through our struggles, but we can believe that those days, as in the life of Job, will be the most significant we are called upon to live. ROBERT COLLYER

Who has not learned that our most sorrowful days are frequently our best? The days when our face is full of smiles and we skip easily through the soft meadow God has adorned with spring flowers, the capacity of our heart is often wasted.

The soul that is always lighthearted and cheerful misses the deepest things of life. Certainly that life has its reward and is fully satisfied, but the depth of its satisfaction is very shallow. Its heart is dwarfed, and its nature, which has the potential of experiencing the highest heights and the deepest depths, remains undeveloped. And the wick of its life burns quickly to the bottom, without ever knowing the richness of profound joy.

Remember, Jesus said, "Blessed are those who mourn" (Matthew 5:4). Stars shine the brightest during the long dark night of winter. And the gentian wildflowers display their fairest blooms among the nearly inaccessible heights of mountain snow and ice.

God seems to use the pressure of pain to trample out the fulfillment of His promises and thereby release the sweetest juice of His winepress. Only those who have known sorrow can fully appreciate the great tenderness of the "man of suffering" (Isaiah 53:3). SELECTED

You may be experiencing little sunshine, but the long periods of gloomy darkness have been wisely designed for you, for perhaps a lengthy stretch of summer weather would have made you like parched land or a barren wilderness. Your Lord knows best, and the clouds and the sun wait for His command. SELECTED

When told, "It's a gray day," an old Scottish cobbler once replied, "Yes, but didn't ya see the patch of blue?"

MAY 26

Spring up, O well! Sing about it.

NUMBERS 21:17

THIS WAS A STRANGE SONG AND A STRANGE WELL. THE CHILDREN OF Israel had been traveling over the desert's barren sands, and they were desperate for water, but there was none in sight. Then God spoke to Moses and said, "Gather the people together and I will give them water" (v. 16).

The people then gathered around with their rods. As they began to dig deeply into the burning sand, they sang, "*Spring up, O well! Sing about it.*" Soon a gurgling sound was heard, and suddenly a rush of water appeared, filling the well and running along the ground. As they had dug the well in the desert, they had tapped the stream that ran below and that had been unseen for a very long time.

What a beautiful picture this is! And it describes for us the river of blessings that flows through our lives. If only we will respond with faith and *praise*, we will find our needs supplied even in the most barren desert.

Again, how did the children of Israel reach the water of this well? It was through *praise*. While standing on the burning sand and digging the well with their staff of promise, they sang a *praise* song of faith.

Our *praise* will bring forth "water . . . in the wilderness and streams in the desert" (Isaiah 35:6), while complaining will only bring judgment. Even prayer by itself may fail to reach the fountain of blessings.

Nothing pleases the Lord as much as *praise*. There is no greater evidence of faith than the virtue of genuine thanksgiving. *Are you praising God enough?* Are you thanking Him for the countless blessings He has bestowed on you? Are you boldly praising Him even for the trials in your life, which are actually blessings in disguise? And have you learned to praise Him in advance for answers yet to come? SELECTED

You're waiting for deliverance!
O soul, you're waiting long!
Believe that your deliverance
Does wait for you in song!
Complain not till deliverance
Your fettered feet does free:
Through songs of glad deliverance
God now surroundeth thee.

MAY 27

"Bring them here to me."
MATTHEW 14:18

DO YOU FIND YOURSELF AT THIS VERY MOMENT SURROUNDED WITH needs, and nearly overwhelmed with difficulties, trials, and emergencies? Each of these is God's way of providing vessels for the Holy Spirit to fill. If you correctly understand their meaning, you will see them as opportunities for receiving new blessings and deliverance you can receive in no other way.

The Lord is saying to you, "Bring them here to me." Firmly hold the vessels before Him, in faith and in prayer. Remain still before Him, and stop your own restless working until He begins to work. Do nothing that He Himself has not commanded you to do. Allow God time to work and He surely will. Then the very trials that threatened to overcome you with discouragement and disaster will become God's opportunity to reveal His grace and glory in your life, in ways you have never known before.

"Bring [your needs] here to me." A. B. SIMPSON

"My God will meet all your needs according to the riches of his glory in Christ Jesus" (Philippians 4:19).

What a source—"God!" What a supply—"his glorious riches!" What a channel—"Christ Jesus!" It is your heavenly privilege to trust "all your needs" to his glorious riches, and to forget your needs in the presence of his . . . riches. In His great love, He has thrown open to you His exhaustive treasury. Go in and draw upon Him in simple childlike faith, and you will never again have the need to rely on anything else. C. H. M.

MY CUP OVERFLOWS (PSALM 23:5)

There is always something "over,"
When we trust our gracious Lord;
Every cup is overflowing,
His great rivers all are broad.
Nothing narrow, nothing sparing,
Ever springing from His store;
To His own He gives full measure,
Overflowing, evermore.

There is always something "over,"
When we, from the Father's hand,

Take our portion with thanksgiving,
Praising for the path He planned.
Satisfaction, full and deepening,
Fills the soul, and lights the eye,
When the heart has trusted Jesus
All its needs to satisfy.

There is always something "over,"
When we tell of all His love;
Unreached depths still lie beneath us,
Unscaled heights rise far above:
Human lips can never utter
All His wondrous tenderness,
We can only praise and wonder,
And His name forever bless.
Margaret E. Barber

"He who did not spare his own Son, but gave him up for us all—how will he not also, along with him, graciously give us all things?" (Romans 8:32).

MAY 28

"I will not let you go unless you bless me." . . .
Then he blessed him there.
Genesis 32:26, 29

Jacob won the victory and the blessing here not by wrestling *but by clinging.* His hip was out of joint and he could struggle no longer, but he would not let go. Unable to wrestle further, he locked his arms around the neck of his mysterious opponent, helplessly resting all his weight upon him, until he won at last.

We too will not win the victory in prayer until we cease our struggling.

We must give up our own will and throw our arms around our Father's neck in clinging faith.

What can our feeble human strength take by force from the hand of omnipotence? Are we able to wrestle blessings from God by force? Strong-willed violence on our part will never prevail with Him. What wins blessings and victories is the strength of clinging faith.

It is not applying pressure or insisting upon our own will that brings victory. It is won when humility and trust unite in saying, "Not my will, but yours be done" (Luke 22:42).

We are strong with God only to the degree that self is conquered and is dead. Blessings come not by wrestling but by clinging to Him in faith.
J. R. Miller

An incident from the prayer life of Charles H. Usher illustrates how "*wrestling prayer*" is actually a hindrance to prevailing prayer. He shared this story: "My little boy, Frank, was very ill, and the doctors held out little hope of his recovery. I used all the prayer knowledge I possessed on his behalf, but he continued to worsen. This went on for several weeks.

"One day as I stood watching him while he lay on his bed, I realized he could not live much longer without a quick turn for the better. I said to the Lord, 'Oh, God, I have spent much time in prayer for my son, and yet he is no better. I will now leave him to You and give myself to prayer for others. If it is Your will to take him, I choose Your will—I surrender him entirely to You.'

"I called in my dear wife and told her what I had done. She shed some tears but also handed him over to God. Two days later a godly man came to visit us. He had been very interested in our son Frank and had prayed often for him. He told us, 'God has given me faith to believe that your son will recover. Do you have that faith?'

"I responded, 'I have surrendered him to God, but I will now go again to Him regarding my son.' I did just that and while in prayer discovered I had faith for his recovery. From that time forward he began to get better. I then realized that it was the '*wrestling*' of my prayers that had hindered

God's answer, and that if I had continued to wrestle, being unwilling to surrender him to God, he would probably not be here today."

O dear child of God, if you want God to answer your prayers, you must be prepared to walk "in the footsteps of the faith that our father Abraham had" (Romans 4:12), even to the mountain of sacrifice.

MAY 29

"I have called you friends."

JOHN 15:15

YEARS AGO THERE WAS AN OLD GERMAN PROFESSOR WHOSE BEAUTIFUL life was a wonder to his students. Some of them were determined to learn the secret of it, so one night they sent someone to hide in the study where the professor spent his evenings.

It was quite late when the teacher finally came. He was very tired but sat down and spent one hour with his Bible. Then he bowed his head in silent prayer, and finally closing the Book of books, he said, "Well, Lord Jesus, we still have the same old relationship."

"To know Christ" (Philippians 3:10) is life's greatest achievement. At all costs, every Christian should strive to "have the same old relationship" with Him.

The reality of knowing Jesus comes as a result of hidden prayer, and personal Bible study that is devotional and consistent in nature. Christ becomes more real to those who persist in cultivating His presence.

Speak unto Him for He hears you,
And Spirit with spirit will meet!
Nearer is He than breathing,
Nearer than hands and feet.

MALTBIE D. BABCOCK

MAY 30

No one could learn the song except the 144,000
who had been redeemed from the earth.
REVELATION 14:3

CERTAIN SONGS CAN ONLY BE LEARNED IN THE VALLEY. NO MUSIC school can teach them, for no theory can cause them to be perfectly sung. Their music is found in the heart. They are songs remembered through personal experience, revealing their burdens through the shadows of the past, and soaring on the wings of yesterday.

In this verse, John tells us that even in heaven there will be a song that will only be sung by those "who had been redeemed from the earth." It is undoubtedly a song of triumph—a hymn of victory to the Christ who set us free. Yet the sense of triumph and freedom will be born from the memory of our past bondage.

No angel, nor even an archangel, will be able to sing the song as beautifully as we will. To do so would require them to pass through our trials, which is something they cannot do. Only the children of the Cross will be equipped to learn the song.

Therefore, dear soul, in this life you are receiving a music lesson from your Father. You are being trained to sing in a choir you cannot yet see, and there will be parts in the chorus that only you can sing. There will be notes too low for the angels to reach, and certain notes so far above the scale that only an angel could reach them. But remember, the deepest notes belong to *you* and will only be reached by you.

Your Father is training you for a part the angels cannot sing, and His conservatory is the school of sorrows. Others have said that He sends sorrow to *test* you, yet this is not the case. He sends sorrow to *educate* you, thereby providing you with the proper training for His heavenly choir.

In the darkest night He is composing your song. In the valley He is tuning your voice. In the storm clouds He is deepening your range. In the rain showers He is sweetening your melody. In the cold He is giving your notes expression. And as you pass at times from hope to fear, He is perfecting the message of your lyrics.

O dear soul, do not despise your school of sorrow. It is bestowing on you a unique part in the heavenly song. George Matheson

Is the midnight closing 'round you?
Are the shadows dark and long?
Ask Him to come close beside you,
And He'll give you a new, sweet song.

He'll give it and sing it with you;
And when weakness slows you down,
He'll take up the broken cadence,
And blend it with His own.

And many a heavenly singer
Among those sons of light,
Will say of His sweetest music,
"I learned it in the night."

And many a lovely anthem,
That fills the Father's home,
Sobbed out its first rehearsal,
In the shade of a darkened room.

MAY 31

You will come to the grave in full vigor,
like sheaves gathered in season.
Job 5:26

A MAN WHO ONCE WROTE ABOUT THE SALVAGING OF OLD SHIPS STATED that it was not the age of the wood from the vessel alone that improved its quality. The straining and the twisting of the ship by the sea, the chemical reaction produced by the bilgewater, and the differing cargoes also had an effect.

Several years ago some boards and veneers cut from an oak beam from an eighty-year-old ship were exhibited at a fashionable furniture store on Broadway in New York City. They attracted attention, because of their elegant coloring and beautiful grain. Equally striking were some mahogany beams taken from a ship that sailed the seas sixty years ago. The years of travel had constricted the pores of the wood and deepened its colors, so that they were as magnificent and bright as those of an antique Chinese vase. The wood has since been used to make a cabinet that sits in a place of honor in the living room of a wealthy New York family.

There is also a great difference between the quality of elderly people who have lived listless, self-indulgent, and useless lives and the quality of those who have sailed through rough seas, carrying cargo and burdens as servants of God, and as helpers of others. In the latter group, not only has the stress and strain of life seeped into their lives but the aroma of the sweetness of their cargo has also been absorbed into the very pores of each fiber of their character. LOUIS ALBERT BANKS

When the sun finally drops below the horizon in the early evening, evidence of its work remains for some time. The skies continue to glow for a full hour after its departure.

In the same way, when a good or a great person's life comes to its final sunset, the skies of this world are illuminated until long after he is out of view. Such a person does not die from this world, for when he departs he leaves much of himself behind—and being dead, he still speaks. HENRY WARD BEECHER

When Victor Hugo was more than eighty years old, he expressed his faith in this beautiful way: "Within my soul I feel the evidence of my future life. I am like a forest that has been cut down more than once, yet the new growth has more life than ever. I am always rising toward the sky, with the sun shining down on my head. The earth provides abundant sap for me, but heaven lights my way to worlds unknown.

"People say the soul is nothing but the effect of our bodily powers at work. If that were true, then why is my soul becoming brighter as my body begins to fail? Winter may be filling my head, but an eternal spring rises from my heart. At this late hour of my life, I smell the fragrance of lilacs, violets, and roses, just as I did when I was twenty. And the closer I come to the end of my journey, the more clearly I hear the immortal symphonies of eternal worlds inviting me to come. It is awe-inspiring yet profoundly simple."

JUNE 1

He said, "This is the resting place, let the weary rest"; and,
"This is the place of repose"—but they would not listen.
Isaiah 28:12

Why do you worry? What possible use does your worrying serve? You are aboard such a large ship that you would be unable to steer even if your Captain placed you at the helm. You would not even be able to adjust the sails, yet you worry as if you were the captain or the helmsman of the vessel. Be quiet, dear soul—God is the Master!

Do you think all the commotion and the uproar of this life is evidence that God has left His throne? He has not! His mighty steeds rush furiously ahead, and His chariots are the storms themselves. But the horses have bridles, and it is God who holds the reins, guiding the chariots as He wills!

Our God Jehovah is still the Master! Believe this and you will have peace. "Don't be afraid" (Matthew 14:27). Charles H. Spurgeon

Tonight, my soul, be still and sleep;
The storms are raging on God's deep—
God's deep, not yours; be still and sleep.

Tonight, my soul, be still and sleep;
God's hands will still the Tempter's sweep—
God's hands, not yours; be still and sleep.

Tonight, my soul, be still and sleep;
God's love is strong while night hours creep—
God's love, not yours; be still and sleep.

Tonight, my soul, be still and sleep;
God's heaven will comfort those who weep—
God's heaven, not yours; be still and sleep.

I implore you to not give in to despair. It is a dangerous temptation, because our Adversary has refined it to the point that it is quite subtle. Hopelessness constricts and withers the heart, rendering it unable to sense God's blessings and grace. It also causes you to exaggerate the adversities of life and makes your burdens seem too heavy for you to bear. Yet God's plans for you, and His ways of bringing about His plans, are infinitely wise. MADAME GUYON

JUNE 2

Against all hope, Abraham in hope believed. . . .
Without weakening in his faith.
ROMANS 4:18–19

I WILL NEVER FORGET THE STATEMENT WHICH THAT GREAT MAN OF faith George Mueller once made to a gentleman who had asked him the best way to have strong faith: "The *only* way to know strong faith is to endure great trials. I have learned my faith by standing firm through severe testings."

How true this is! *You must trust when all else fails.*

Dear soul, you may scarcely realize the value of your present situation. If you are enduring great afflictions right now, you are at the source of the strongest faith. God will teach you during these dark hours to have the most powerful bond to His throne you could ever know, if you will only submit. "Don't be afraid; just believe" (Mark 5:36). But if you ever are afraid, simply look up and say, "When I am afraid, I put my trust in you" (Psalm 56:3). Then you will be able to thank God for His school of sorrow that became for you the school of faith. A. B. Simpson

Great faith must first endure great trials.

God's greatest gifts come through great pain. Can we find anything of value in the spiritual or the natural realm that has come about without tremendous toil and tears? Has there ever been any great reform, any discovery benefiting humankind, or any soul-awakening revival, without the diligence and the shedding of blood of those whose sufferings were actually the pangs of its birth? For the temple of God to be built, David had to bear intense afflictions. And for the gospel of grace to be extricated from Jewish tradition, Paul's life had to be one long agony.

Take heart, O weary, burdened one, bowed down
Beneath your cross;
Remember that your greatest gain may come
Through greatest loss.
Your life is nobler for a sacrifice,
And more divine.
Acres of blooms are crushed to make a drop
Of perfume fine.
Because of storms that lash the ocean waves,
The waters there
Keep purer than if the heavens o'erhead
Were always fair.
The brightest banner of the skies floats not
At noonday warm;

The rainbow follows after thunderclouds,
And after storm.

JUNE 3

"Let us go over to the other side."
MARK 4:35

EVEN THOUGH WE FOLLOW CHRIST'S COMMAND, WE SHOULD NOT expect to escape the storm. In this passage of Scripture, the disciples were obeying His command, yet they encountered the fiercest of storms and were in great danger of being drowned. In their distress, they cried out for Christ's assistance.

Christ may delay coming to us during our times of distress, but it is simply so our faith may be tested and strengthened. His purpose is also that our prayers will be more powerful, our desire for deliverance will be greater, and when deliverance finally comes we will appreciate it more fully.

Gently rebuking His disciples, Christ asked, "Why are you so afraid? Do you still have no faith?" (v. 40). In effect, He was saying, "Why didn't you face the storm victoriously and shout to the raging winds and rolling waves, 'You cannot harm us, for Christ, the mighty Savior, is on board'?"

Of course, it is much easier to trust God when the sun is shining than to trust Him when the storm is raging around us.

Yet we will never know our level of genuine faith until it is tested in a fierce storm, and that is why our Savior is on board.

If you are ever to "be strong in the Lord and in his mighty power" (Ephesians 6:10), your strength will be born during a storm. SELECTED

With Christ in my vessel,
I smile at the storm.

Christ said, "Let us go over to the other side"—not "to the middle of the lake to be drowned." DANIEL CRAWFORD

JUNE 4

All that night the LORD drove the sea back.

EXODUS 14:21

IN THIS VERSE, THERE IS A COMFORTING MESSAGE SHOWING HOW GOD works during darkness. The real work of God for the children of Israel did not happen when they awoke that morning to find they could cross the Red Sea, but it occurred "*all that night*."

There may be a great work occurring in your life when things seems their darkest. You may see no evidence yet, but God is at work. God was just as much at work "all that night" as He was the next day, when the Israelites finally saw the evidence. The next day simply revealed what God had done during the night.

Are you reading this from a place in your life where everything seems dark? Do you have faith to see but are still not seeing? Are you lacking continual victory in your spiritual growth? Is your daily, quiet communion gone, and there is nothing but darkness all around?

"All that night the LORD drove the sea back." Don't forget—it was "*all that night*." God works through the night until the morning light dawns. You may not see it yet, but through the *night* of your life, as you trust Him, He works. C. H. P.

"All that night" the Lord was working,
Working in the tempest blast,
Working with the swelling current,
Flooding, flowing, free and fast.

"All that night" God's children waited—
Hearts, perhaps in agony—

With the enemy behind them,
And, in front, the cruel sea.

"All that night" seemed blacker darkness
Than they ever saw before,
Though the light of God's own presence
Near them was, and sheltered o'er.

"All that night" that weary vigil
Passed; the day at last did break,
And they saw that God was working
"All that night" a path to make.

"All that night," O child of sorrow,
Can you not your heartbreak stay?
Know your God in darkest midnight
Works, as well as in the day.

L. S. P.

JUNE 5

Ask the Lord *your God for a sign, whether in the deepest depths or in the highest heights.*

Isaiah 7:11

Make your petition deep, O heart of mine,
Your God can do much more Than you can ask;
Launch out on the Divine,
Draw from His love-filled store.
Trust Him with everything;
Begin today,
And find the joy that comes
When Jesus has His way!

Selected

We must continue to *pray* and "*wait* for the Lord" (Isaiah 8:17), until we hear the sound of His mighty rain. There is no reason why we should not ask for great things. Without a doubt, we will receive them if we ask in faith, having the courage to wait with patient perseverance for Him and meanwhile doing those things that are within our power to do.

It is not within our power to create the wind or to change its direction, but we can raise our sails to catch it when it comes. We do not create electricity, yet we can tap into it with a wire that will conduct it, allowing it to work. We do not control God's Spirit, but we can place ourselves before the Lord out of obedience to what He has called us to do, and we will come under the influence and power of His mighty breath. Selected

Can't the same great wonders be done today that were done many years ago? Where is the God of Elijah? He is *waiting* for today's Elijah to call on Him.

The greatest Old or New Testament saints who ever lived were on a level that is quite within our reach. The same spiritual force that was available to them, and the energy that enabled them to become our spiritual heroes, are also available to us. If we exhibit the same faith, hope, and love they exhibited, we will achieve miracles as great as theirs. A simple prayer from our mouths will be powerful enough to call down from heaven God's gracious dew or the melting fire of His Spirit, just as the words from Elijah's mouth called down literal rain and fire. All that is required is to speak the words with the same complete assurance of faith with which he spoke. Dr. Goulburn, Former Dean of Norwich

JUNE 6

Watch and pray so that you will not fall into temptation.

Matthew 26:41

Dear friend, never go out into the danger of the world without praying first. There is always a temptation to shorten your time in prayer. After a difficult day of work, when you kneel at night to pray with tired eyes, do not use your drowsiness as an excuse to resign yourself to early rest. Then when the morning breaks and you realize you have overslept, resist the temptation to skip your early devotion or to hurry through it.

Once again, you have not taken the time to "watch and pray." Your alertness has been sacrificed, and I firmly believe there will be irreparable damage. You have failed to pray, and you will suffer as a result.

Temptations are waiting to confront you, and you are not prepared to withstand them. Within your soul you have a sense of guilt, and you seem to be lingering some distance from God. It certainly is no coincidence that you tend to fall short of your responsibilities on those days when you have allowed your weariness to interfere with your prayer life.

When we give in to laziness, moments of prayer that are missed can never be redeemed. We may learn from the experience, but we will miss the rich freshness and strength that would have been imparted during those moments. FREDERICK WILLIAM ROBERTSON

Jesus, the omnipotent Son of God, felt it necessary to rise each morning before dawn to pour out His heart to His Father in prayer. Should we not feel even more compelled to pray to Him who is the giver of "every good and perfect gift" (James 1:17) and who has promised to provide whatever we need?

We do not know all that Jesus gained from His time in prayer, but we do know this—a life without prayer is a powerless life. It may be a life filled with a great deal of activity and noise, but it will be far removed from Him who day and night prayed to God. SELECTED

JUNE 7

Where is God my Maker, who gives songs in the night?

JOB 35:10

Do you ever experience sleepless nights, tossing and turning and simply waiting for the first glimmer of dawn? When that happens, why not ask the Holy Spirit to fix your thoughts on God, your Maker, and believe He can fill those lonely, dreary nights with song?

Is your night one of bereavement? Focusing on God often causes Him to draw near to your grieving heart, bringing you the assurance that He needs the one who has died. The Lord will assure you He has called the eager, enthusiastic spirit of your departed loved one to stand with the invisible yet liberated, living, and radiant multitude. And as this thought enters your mind, along with the knowledge that your loved one is engaged in a great heavenly mission, a song begins in your heart.

Is your night one of discouragement or failure, whether real or imagined? Do you feel as if no one understands you, and your friends have pushed you aside? Take heart: your Maker "will come near to you" (James 4:8) and give you a song—a song of hope, which will be harmonious with the strong, resonant music of His providence. Be ready to sing the song your Maker imparts to you. Selected

What then? Shall we sit idly down and say
The night has come; it is no longer day?
Yet as the evening twilight fades away,
The sky is filled with stars, invisible to day.

The strength of a ship is only fully demonstrated when it faces a hurricane, and the power of the gospel can only be fully exhibited when a Christian is subjected to some fiery trial. We must understand that for God to give "songs in the night," He must first make it night. Nathaniel William Taylor

JUNE 8

Everyone born of God overcomes the world. This is the victory that has overcome the world, even our faith.

1 John 5:4

If a person allows it, he can find something at every turn of the road that will rob him of his victory and his peace of mind. Satan is far from retiring from his work of attempting to deceive and destroy God's children. At each milestone in your life, it is wise to check the temperature of your experience in order to be keenly aware of the surrounding conditions.

If you will do this and firmly exhibit your faith at the precise moment, you can sometimes actually snatch victory from the very jaws of defeat.

Faith can change any situation, no matter how dark or difficult. Lifting your heart to God in a moment of genuine faith in Him can quickly alter your circumstances.

God is still on His throne, and He can turn defeat into victory in a split second, if we will only trust Him.

God is mighty! He is able to deliver;
Faith can victor be in every trying hour;
Fear and care and sin and sorrow be defeated
By our faith in God's almighty, conquering power.

Have faith in God, the sun will shine,
Though dark the clouds may be today;
His heart has planned your path and mine,
Have faith in God, have faith alway.

When you have faith, you need never retreat. You can stop the Enemy wherever you encounter him. Marshal Ferdinand Foch

JUNE 9

Trust in the Lord and do good; dwell in
the land and enjoy safe pasture.
Psalm 37:3

I ONCE MET A POOR WOMAN WHO EARNED A MEAGER LIVING THROUGH hard domestic labor but was a joyful, triumphant Christian. Another Christian lady, who was quite sullen, said to her one day, "Nancy, I understand your happiness today, but I would think your future prospects would sober you. Suppose, for instance, you experience a time of illness and are unable to work. Or suppose your present employers move away, and you cannot find work elsewhere. Or suppose—"

"Stop!" cried Nancy. "I never 'suppose.' 'The LORD is my shepherd, I shall not want' [Psalm 23:1 KJV]. And besides," she added to her gloomy friend, "it's all that 'supposing' that's making you so miserable. You'd better give that up and simply trust the Lord."

The following Scripture is one that will remove all the "supposing" from a believer's life if received and acted on in childlike faith: "Be content with what you have, because God has said, 'Never will I leave you; never will I forsake you.' So we say with confidence, 'The Lord is my helper; I will not be afraid. What can mere mortals do to me?'" (Hebrews 13:5–6).

HANNAH WHITALL SMITH

There's a stream of trouble across my path;
It is dark and deep and wide.
Bitter the hour the future hath
When I cross its swelling tide.
But I smile and sing and say:
"I will hope and trust alway;
I'll bear the sorrow that comes tomorrow,
But I'll borrow none today."

Tomorrow's bridge is a dangerous thing;
I dare not cross it now.
I can see its timbers sway and swing,
And its arches reel and bow.
O heart, you must hope alway;

You must sing and trust and say:
"I'll bear the sorrow that comes tomorrow,
But I'll borrow none today."

The eagle that soars at great altitudes does not worry about how it will cross a river. SELECTED

JUNE 10

We know that in all things God works for the good of those who love him, who have been called according to his purpose.
ROMANS 8:28

WHAT A TREMENDOUS CLAIM PAUL MAKES IN THIS VERSE! HE DOES not say, "We know that in *some* things," "*most* things," or even "*joyful* things" but "ALL things." This promise spans from the very smallest detail of life to the most important, and from the most humbling of daily tasks to God's greatest works of grace performed during a crisis.

Paul states this in the present tense: "God *works.*" He does not say, "*worked*" or "*will work.*" It is a continuing operation.

We also know from Scripture that God's "justice [is] like the great deep" (Psalm 36:6); at this very moment the angels in heaven, as they watch with folded wings the development of God's great plan, are undoubtedly proclaiming, "The LORD is righteous in *all* his ways and faithful in *all* he does" (Psalm 145:17).

Then when God orchestrates "*all things . . . for the good,*" it is a beautiful blending. He requires many different colors, which individually may be quite drab, to weave into the harmonious pattern.

Separate tones, notes, and even discords are required to compose melodious musical anthems; a piece of machinery requires many separate wheels, parts, and connections. One part from a machine may be useless, or one note from an anthem may never be considered beautiful, but *taken together, combined, and completed*, they lead to perfect balance and harmony.

We can learn a lesson of faith from this: "You do not realize now what I am doing, but later you will understand" (John 13:7). J. R. Macduff

In a thousand trials, it is not just five hundred of them that work "for the good" of the believer, but nine hundred and ninety-nine, *plus one.* George Mueller

God Meant It unto Good

"God meant it unto good"—O blest assurance,
Falling like sunshine all across life's way,
Touching with Heaven's gold, earth's darkest storm clouds,
Bringing fresh peace and comfort day by day.

'Twas not by chance the hands of faithless brothers
Sold Joseph captive to a foreign land;
Nor was it chance that, after years of suffering,
Brought him before the pharaoh's throne to stand.

One Eye all-seeing saw the need of thousands,
And planned to meet it through that one lone soul;
And through the weary days of prison bondage
Was working toward the great and glorious goal.

As yet the end was hidden from the captive,
The iron entered even to his soul;
His eye could scan the present path of sorrow,
Not yet his gaze might rest upon the whole.

Faith failed not through those long, dark days of waiting,
His trust in God was reimbursed at last,

The moment came when God led forth his servant
To comfort many, all his sufferings past.

"It was not you but God, that led me to here,"
Witnessed triumphant faith in later days;
"God meant it unto good," no other reason
Mingled their discord with his song of praise.

"God means it unto good" for you, beloved,
The God of Joseph is the same today;
His love permits afflictions strange and bitter,
His hand is guiding through the unknown way.

Your Lord, who sees the end from the beginning,
Has purposes for you of love untold.
Then place your hand in His and follow fearless,
Till you the riches of His grace behold.

There, when you stand firm in the Home of Glory,
And all life's path lies open to your gaze,
Your eyes will see the hand that you're now trusting,
And magnify His love through endless days.

Freda Hanbury Allen

JUNE 11

The servant of the Lord must . . . be gentle.

2 Timothy 2:24 KJV

When God finally conquers us and changes our unyielding nature, we receive deep insights into the Spirit of Jesus. Then, as never before, we see His extraordinary *gentleness of spirit* at work in this dark and unheavenly world. Yet the *gifts* of "the fruit of the Spirit" (Galatians 5:22) do not automatically become evident in our lives. If we are not discerning enough to recognize their availability to us, to desire them, and then to nourish them in our thoughts, they will never become embedded in our nature or behavior. Every further step of spiritual growth in God's grace must be preceded by acknowledging our lack of a godly attribute and then by exhibiting a prayerful determination to obtain it.

However, very few Christians are willing to endure the suffering through which complete gentleness is obtained. We must die to ourselves before we are turned into gentleness, and our crucifixion involves suffering. It will mean experiencing genuine brokenness and a crushing of self, which will be used to afflict the heart and conquer the mind.

Today many people are attempting to use their mental capacity and logical thinking to obtain sanctification, yet this is nothing but a religious fabrication. They believe that if they just mentally put themselves on the altar and believe the altar provides the gift of sanctification, they can then logically conclude they are fully sanctified. Then they go happily on their way, expressing their flippant, theological babble about the "deep" things of God.

Yet the heartstrings of their old nature have not been broken, and their unyielding character, which they inherited from Adam, has not been ground to powder. Their soul has not throbbed with the lonely, gushing groans of Gethsemane. Having no scars from their death on Calvary, they will exhibit nothing of the soft, sweet, gentle, restful, victorious, overflowing, and triumphant life that flows like a spring morning from an empty tomb. G. D. W.

"And abundant grace was upon them all" (Acts 4:33).

JUNE 12

In him you have been enriched in every way.

1 CORINTHIANS 1:5

Have you ever seen people who through some disaster were driven to great times of prayer? And have you noticed that once the disaster was long forgotten, a spiritual sweetness remained that warmed their souls?

It reminds me of a severe storm I once saw in late spring—one in which darkness covered the sky, except where the lightning violently split the clouds with its thundering power. The wind blew and the rain fell, as though heaven had opened its windows.

What devastation there was! The storm uprooted even the strongest of oaks, and not one spiderweb escaped the wind, despite being hidden from view. But soon, after the lightning was gone, the thunder ceased and was silent, and the rain was over; a western wind arose with a sweet and gentle breath, chasing the dark clouds away. I saw the retreating storm throw a scarf of rainbows over her fair shoulders and her glowing neck. She looked back at me, smiled, and then passed from my sight.

For many weeks after the storm, the fields raised their hands, full of heavenly, fragrant flowers, toward the sky. And all summer long the grass was greener, the streams were filled, and the trees, because of their lush foliage, cast a more restful shade.

All this—*because the storm had come.* All this—even though the rest of the earth had long forgotten the storm, its rainbows, and its rain.
Theodore Parker

God may not give us an easy journey to the Promised Land, but He will give us a safe one. Horatius Bonar

It was a storm that led to the discovery of the gold mines in India. Have we not seen storms drive people to the discovery of the priceless mines of the love of God in Christ?

Is it raining, little flower?
Be glad of rain;
Too much sun would wither one;
It will shine again.

The clouds are very dark, it's true;
But just behind them shines the blue.
Are you weary, tender heart?
Be glad of pain:
In sorrow, sweetest virtues grow,
As flowers in rain.
God watches, and you will have sun,
When clouds their perfect work have done.

LUCY LARCOM

JUNE 13

"My peace I give you."

JOHN 14:27

TWO PAINTERS WERE ONCE ASKED TO PAINT A PICTURE ILLUSTRATING his own idea of rest. The first chose for his scene a quiet, lonely lake, nestled among mountains far away. The second, using swift, broad strokes on his canvas, painted a thundering waterfall. Beneath the falls grew a fragile birch tree, bending over the foam. On its branches, nearly wet with the spray from the falls, sat a robin on its nest.

The first painting was simply a picture of *stagnation and inactivity.* The second, however, depicted *rest.*

Outwardly, Christ endured one of the most troubled lives ever lived. Storms and turmoil, turmoil and storms—wave after wave broke over Him until His worn body was laid in the tomb. Yet His inner life was as smooth as a sea of glass, and a great calm was always there.

Anyone could have gone to Him at any time and found rest. Even as the human bloodhounds were dogging Him in the streets of Jerusalem, He turned to His disciples, offering them a final legacy: "My peace."

Rest is not some holy feeling that comes upon us in church. It is a state of calm rising from a heart deeply and firmly established in God. HENRY DRUMMOND

My peace I give in times of deepest grief,
Imparting calm and trust and My relief.

My peace I give when prayer seems lost, unheard;
Know that My promises are ever in My Word.

My peace I give when you are left alone—
The nightingale at night has sweetest tone.

My peace I give in times of utter loss,
The way of glory leads right to the cross.

My peace I give when enemies will blame,
Your fellowship is sweet through cruel shame.

My peace I give in agony and sweat,
For My own brow with bloody drops was wet.

My peace I give when nearest friend betrays—
Peace that is merged in love, and for them prays.

My peace I give when there's but death for thee—
The gateway is the cross to get to Me.

L. S. P.

JUNE 14

I have prayed for you . . . that your faith may not fail.

Luke 22:32

Dear Christian, remember to take good care of your faith, for *faith is the only way to obtain God's blessings.* Prayer alone cannot bring answers down from His throne, because it is the earnest prayer of one who believes that leads to answers.

Faith is the communication link between heaven and earth. It is on this link of faith that God's messages of love travel so quickly that even before we ask, He answers. And while we are still speaking, "he hears us" (1 John 5:14). So when the connection of faith is broken, how will we obtain His promises?

Am I in trouble? I can receive help by expressing faith. Am I being battered by the Enemy? My soul will find refuge by leaning in faith upon God. But without faith, I call to Him in vain, for faith is the only road between my soul and heaven. If the road is blocked, how can I communicate with the great King?

Faith links me to Holy God and clothes me with the power of Jehovah. Faith ensures me that each of His attributes will be used in my defense, helping me to defy the hosts of hell. It causes me to march triumphantly over the necks of my enemies. So without faith, how can I receive anything from the Lord?

Therefore, O Christian, carefully watch your faith. "Everything is possible for one who believes" (Mark 9:23). Charles H. Spurgeon

We as a people take such pride in being so practical that we want something more sure than faith. Yet Paul said, "The promise comes by FAITH, so that it may . . . be GUARANTEED" (Romans 4:16). Daniel Crawford

Faith honors God, and God honors faith.

JUNE 15

God has made me fruitful in the land of my suffering.

Genesis 41:52

A poet stands by the window watching a summer shower. It is a fierce downpour, beating and pounding the earth. But the poet, in his mind's eye, sees more than a rain shower falling. He sees a myriad of lovely flowers raining down, soon breaking forth from the freshly watered earth, and filling it with their matchless beauty and fragrance. And so he sings:

It isn't raining rain to me—it's raining daffodils;
In every dripping drop I see wildflowers upon the hills.
A cloud of gray engulfs the day, and overwhelms the town;
It isn't raining rain to me—it's raining roses down.

Perhaps you are undergoing some trial as God's child, and you are saying to Him, "O God, it is raining very hard on me tonight, and this test seems beyond my power to endure. Disappointments are pouring in, washing away and utterly defeating my chosen plans. My trembling heart is grieved and is cowering at the intensity of my suffering. Surely the rains of affliction are beating down upon my soul."

Dear friend, you are completely mistaken. God is not raining rain on you—*He is raining blessings*. If you will only believe your Father's Word, you will realize that springing up beneath the pounding rain are spiritual flowers. And they are more beautiful and fragrant than those that ever grew before in your stormless and suffering-free life.

You can see the rain, but can you also see the flowers? You are suffering through these tests, but know that God sees sweet flowers of faith springing up in your life beneath these very trials. You try to escape the pain, yet God sees tender compassion for other sufferers finding birth in your soul. Your heart winces at the pain of heavy grief, but God sees the sorrow deepening and enriching your life.

No, my friend, it is not raining afflictions on you. It is raining tenderness, love, compassion, patience, and a thousand other flowers and fruits of the blessed Holy Spirit. And they are bringing to your life spiritual enrichment that all the prosperity and ease of this world could never produce in your innermost being. J. M. M.

Songs Across the Storm

A harp stood in the calm, still air,
Where showers of sunshine washed a thousand fragrant blooms;
A traveler bowed with loads of care
Struggled from morning till the dusk of evening glooms
To strum sweet sounds from the songless strings;
The pilgrim strives in vain with each unanswering chord,
Until the tempest's thunder sings,
And, moving on the storm, the fingers of the Lord
A wondrous melody awakes;
And though the battling winds their soldier deeds perform,
Their trumpet-sound brave music makes
While God's assuring voice sings love across the storm.

JUNE 16

My hope comes from him.
Psalm 62:5

So often we simply neglect to look for the answers to what we have asked, which shows the lack of earnestness in our petitions. A farmer is never content until he reaps a harvest; a marksman observes whether or not his bullet has hit the target; and a physician examines the effect of the medicine he prescribes. Should a Christian be any less careful regarding the effect of his labor in prayer?

Every prayer of the Christian, whether for temporal or spiritual blessings, will be fully answered if it meets certain biblical requirements. It must be prayed in faith and in accordance with God's will. It must rely on God's promise, be offered up in the name of Jesus Christ, and be prayed under the influence of the Holy Spirit.

God always answers the general intent of His people's prayers. He does so not only to reveal His own glory but also to provide for the Christian's spiritual and eternal welfare. Since we see in Scripture that Jesus Christ never rejected even a single petitioner who came to Him, we can believe that no prayer made in His name will be in vain.

The answer to our prayer may be coming, although we may not discern its approach. A seed that is underground during winter, although hidden and seemingly dead and lost, is nevertheless taking root for a later spring and harvest. BICKERSTETH

Delayed answers to prayer are not only trials of faith; they also give us opportunities to honor God through our steadfast confidence in Him even when facing the apparent denial of our request. CHARLES H. SPURGEON

JUNE 17

Then there came a voice from above the vault over their heads as they stood with lowered wings.
EZEKIEL 1:25

WHAT IS THE SIGNIFICANCE OF THESE WORDS: "THEY STOOD WITH lowered wings"? People often ask, "How can I hear the voice of the Lord?" This is the secret: these "living creatures" (v. 5) heard the voice when "they stood with lowered wings."

We have all seen a bird flutter its wings while standing in place. But in this verse, we are told that "there came a voice . . . as they stood with lowered wings."

Do you ever sit, or even kneel, before the Lord and yet are conscious of a fluttering in your spirit? If so, you are not exhibiting a sense of genuine stillness while in His presence.

A dear person told me of this very thing a few days ago. "I prayed about a certain thing," she said, "but I did not wait for the answer to come." She did not get still enough to hear God speak but instead went away and followed her own thinking in the matter. The result proved disastrous, and she was forced to retrace her steps.

Oh, how much energy we waste! How much time we lose by refusing to lower the wings of our spirit and become totally quiet before Him! Imagine the calm, the rest, and the peace that will come as we wait in His presence until we hear from Him!

Then, and only then, we too may speed "back and forth like flashes of lightning" (v. 14), going directly to "wherever the spirit would go" (v. 20).

Be still! Just now be still!
Something your soul has never heard,
Something unknown to any song of bird,
Something unknown to any wind, or wave, or star,
A message from the Father's land afar,
That with sweet joy the homesick soul will thrill,
And comes to you only when you're still.

Be still! Just now be still!
There comes a presence very mild and sweet;
White are the sandals of His noiseless feet.
It is the Comforter whom Jesus sent
To teach you what the words He uttered meant.
The willing, waiting spirit, He does fill.
If you would hear His message,
Dear soul, be still!

JUNE 18

Lift up the hands which hang down, and the feeble knees;
And make straight paths for your feet, lest that which is
lame be turned out of the way; but let it rather be healed.
HEBREWS 12:12–13 KJV

THIS VERSE IS GOD'S WORD OF ENCOURAGEMENT TO US TO LIFT THE hands of faith and to fortify the knees of prayer. All too often our faith becomes tired, weak, and listless, and our prayers lose their power and effectiveness.

The Lord's illustration here is quite compelling. He is pointing out to us that when we become so discouraged and fearful that even one little obstacle depresses and frightens us, we are tempted to walk around it. We would rather take the easy way than face it. Perhaps there is some physical ailment that God is ready to heal, but it requires exertion on our part. The temptation is to find help from someone else or to walk around the obstacle in some other way.

We tend to find many ways of walking around emergencies instead of walking straight through them. So often we are faced with something that frightens or overwhelms us and seek to evade the problem with the excuse: "I'm not quite ready for that now." It may require some sacrifice, or demand our obedience in some area. Perhaps there is some Jericho we are facing, or we are lacking the courage to help someone else and to pray through his concern with him. Perhaps we have a prayer that awaits completion, or a physical problem that is partially healed and we continue to walk around it.

God says, "Lift up the hands which hang down." March straight through the flood, and behold! The waters will divide, the Red Sea will open, the Jordan will part, and the Lord will lead you through to victory.

Do not allow your feet to "be turned out of the way," but let your body "be healed," and your faith strengthened. Go straight ahead, leaving no Jericho unconquered behind you, and no place where Satan can boast of having overwhelmed you. This is a valuable lesson and is extremely practical. How often we find ourselves in this very situation!

Perhaps this is where you find yourself today. A. B. SIMPSON

Pay as little attention to discouragement as possible. Plow ahead like a steamship, which moves forward whether facing rough or smooth seas, and in rain or shine. Remember, the goal is simply to carry the cargo and to make it to port. MALTBIE D. BABCOCK

JUNE 19

Grain must be ground to make bread.

Isaiah 28:28

Many of us cannot be used as food for the world's hunger, because we have yet to be broken in Christ's hands. "Grain must be ground to make bread," and being a blessing of His often requires sorrow on our part. Yet even sorrow is not too high a price to pay for the privilege of touching other lives with Christ's blessings. The things that are most precious to us today have come to us through tears and pain. J. R. Miller

God has made me as bread for His chosen ones, and if it is necessary for me to "be ground" in the teeth of lions in order to feed His children, then blessed be the name of the Lord. Ignatius

To burn brightly our lives must first experience the flame.

In other words, we cease to bless others when we cease to bleed.

Poverty, hardship, and misfortune have propelled many a life to moral heroism and spiritual greatness. Difficulties challenge our energy and our perseverance but bring the strongest qualities of the soul to life. It is the weights on the old grandfather clock that keep it running. And many a sailor has faced a strong head wind yet used it to make it to port. God has chosen opposition as a catalyst to our faith and holy service.

The most prominent characters of the Bible were broken, threshed, and ground into bread for the hungry. Because he stood at the head of the class, enduring affliction while remaining obedient, Abraham's diploma is now inscribed with these words: "The Father of Faith."

Jacob, like wheat, suffered severe threshing and grinding. Joseph was beaten and bruised, and was forced to endure Potiphar's kitchen and Egypt's prison before coming to his throne.

David, hunted like an animal of prey through the mountains, was bruised, weary, and footsore, and thereby ground into bread for a kingdom. Paul could never have been bread for Caesar's household if he had not endured the bruising of being whipped and stoned. He was ground into fine flour for the Roman royal family.

Combat comes before victory. If God has chosen special trials for you to endure, be assured He has kept a very special place in His heart just for you. A badly bruised soul is one who is chosen.

JUNE 20

Whether you turn to the right or to the left, your ears will hear a voice behind you, saying, "This is the way; walk in it."

ISAIAH 30:21

WHEN WE HAVE DOUBTS OR ARE FACING DIFFICULTIES, WHEN OTHERS suggest courses of action that are conflicting, when caution dictates one approach but faith another, we should be still. We should quiet each intruding person, calm ourselves in the sacred stillness of God's presence, study His Word for guidance, and with true devotion focus our attention on Him. We should lift our nature into the pure light radiating from His face, having an eagerness to know only what God our Lord will determine for us. Soon He will reveal by His secret counsel a distinct and unmistakable sense of His direction.

It is unwise for a new believer to depend on this approach alone. He should wait for circumstances to also confirm what God is revealing. Yet Christians who have had many experiences in their walk with Him know the great value of secret fellowship with the Lord as a means of discerning His will.

Are you uncertain about which direction you should go? Take your question to God and receive guidance from either the light of His smile or the cloud of His refusal. You must get alone with Him, where the lights and the darknesses of this world cannot interfere and where the opinions of others cannot reach you. You must also have the courage to wait in silent expectation, even when everyone around you is insisting on an immediate decision or action. If you will do these things, the will of God will become clear to you. And you will have a deeper concept of who He is, having more insight into His nature and His heart of love.

All this will be your unsurpassed gift. It will be a heavenly experience, a precious eternal privilege, and the rich reward for the long hours of waiting. DAVID

"Stand still," my soul, for so your Lord commands:
E'en when your way seems blocked, leave it in His wise hands;
His arm is mighty to divide the wave.
"Stand still," my soul, "stand still" and you will see
How God can work the "impossible" for thee,
For with a great deliverance He does save.

Be not impatient, but in stillness stand,
Even when surrounded on every hand,
In ways your spirit does not comprehend.
God cannot clear your way till you are still,
That He may work in you His blessed will,
And all your heart and will to Him do bend.

"Be still," my soul, for just when you are still,
Can God reveal Himself to you; until
Through you His love and light and life can freely flow;
In stillness God can work through you and reach
The souls around you. He then through you can teach
His lessons, and His power in weakness show.

"Be still"—a deeper step in faith and rest.
"Be still and know" your Father does know best
The way to lead His child to that fair land,
A "summer" land, where quiet waters flow;

Where longing souls are satisfied, and "know
Their God," and praise for all that He has planned.

SELECTED

JUNE 21

The people heard that he had come home.

MARK 2:1

THE ADULT CORAL INVERTEBRATES, KNOWN AS POLYPS, WORK UNDERwater constructing coral reefs. They do so never even imagining they are building the foundation of a new island, which will someday support plants and animals and will be a home where the children of God will be born and equipped for eternal glory as "co-heirs with Christ" (Romans 8:17).

Beloved, if your place in God's army is hidden and secluded, do not grumble and complain. Do not seek to run from His will and the circumstances in which He has placed you. Remember, without the polyps, the coral reefs would never be built, and God calls some people to be spiritual polyps. He is looking for those who are willing to serve in places hidden from the sight of others, yet in full view of heaven, and who are sustained by the Holy Spirit.

A day is coming when Jesus will bestow His rewards. On that day some people may wonder how you came to merit a certain reward, since they have never heard of you. But remember, He makes no mistakes. SELECTED

Just where you stand in the conflict,
There is your place.
Just where you think you are useless,
Hide not your face.
God placed you there for a purpose,
Whate'er it be;

Think He has chosen you for it;
Work loyally.
Put on your armor! Be faithful
At toil or rest!
Whate'er it be, never doubting
God's way is best.
Out in the fight or on lookout,
Stand firm and true;
This is the work that your Master
Gives you to do.

SELECTED

With freedom from danger, we can leave a crowded meeting of believers, an inspiring mountaintop experience, or a helpful fellowship with "righteous [men] made perfect" (Hebrews 12:23), in order to return to our modest and simple Emmaus, to the dreaded home of the Colossians, or even to the mission field of distant Macedonia. We can do so with the calm assurance that wherever God has placed us, and in every detail of our daily lives, He has ordained the land we are to possess to its very borders and has ordained the victory to be won. NORTHCOTE DECK

JUNE 22

Love covers over all wrongs.

PROVERBS 10:12

Follow the way of love.

1 CORINTHIANS 14:1

WHEN YOU ARE TROUBLED, SHARE YOUR PROBLEMS WITH GOD ALONE. Recently I read the personal experience of a precious child of God. It made such an impression on me that I would like to relate it to you here.

"At midnight I found myself completely unable to sleep," she wrote. "Waves of cruel injustice were sweeping over me, and the covering of love seemed to have been unknowingly removed from my heart. In great agony I cried to God for the power to obey His admonition, 'Love covers over all wrongs.'

"Immediately His Spirit began to work the power into me that ultimately brought about forgetfulness. I mentally dug a grave, deliberately throwing the dirt out until the hole was very deep. With sorrow, I lowered the offense that had wounded me into the grave and quickly shoveled the soil over it. Then I carefully covered the hole with green sod, planted beautiful white roses and forget-me-nots on top, and briskly walked away.

"Suddenly restful sleep came to me. And the wound that had seemed so deadly was healed without a scar. God's love has covered so completely that today I cannot remember what caused my grief."

There was a scar on yonder mountainside,
Gashed out where once the cruel storm had trod;
A barren, desolate chasm, reaching wide
Across the soft green sod.

But years crept by beneath the purple pines,
And veiled the scar with grass and moss once more,
And left it fairer now with flowers and vines
Than it had been before.

There was a wound once in a gentle heart,
From which life's sweetness seemed to ebb and die;
And love's confiding changed to bitter smart,
While slow, sad years went by.

Yet as they passed, unseen an angel stole
And laid a balm of healing on the pain,

Till love grew purer in the heart made whole,
And peace came back again.

JUNE 23

Peter got down out of the boat, walked on the water and came toward Jesus. But when he saw the wind, he was afraid and, beginning to sink, cried out, "Lord, save me!"
MATTHEW 14:29–30

JOHN BUNYAN SAID THAT PETER DID HAVE A LITTLE FAITH, EVEN IN the midst of his doubts. In spite of crying out in fear, it was by getting out of the boat and walking that he got to Jesus.

In this passage of Scripture, we see that Peter's sight was actually a hindrance. Once he had stepped out of the boat, the waves were none of his business. His only concern should have been the path of light shining across the darkness from Christ Himself. Even the glow of a kingdom ten times brighter than that of ancient Egypt should not have diverted Peter's eyes.

When the Lord calls you to come across the water, step out with confidence and joy. And never glance away from Him for even a moment. You will not prevail by measuring the waves or grow strong by gauging the wind. Attempting to survey the danger may actually cause you to fall before it. Pausing at the difficulties will result in the waves breaking over your head.

"Lift up [your] eyes to the mountains" (Psalm 121:1) and go forward. There is no other way.

Do you fear to launch away?
Faith lets go to swim!
Never will He let you go;
It's by trusting you will know
Fellowship with Him.

JUNE 24

Concerning the work of my hands command ye me.

ISAIAH 45:11 KJV

THE LORD JESUS TOOK THIS VERY APPROACH WITH GOD WHEN HE SAID, "Father, I want those you have given me to be with me" (John 17:24). Joshua used it during the moment of his greatest victory, when he lifted his spear toward the setting sun and cried aloud, "Sun, stand still" (Joshua 10:12). Elijah employed it when he stopped the rain from heaven and started it again after three and a half years. Martin Luther followed it when, kneeling by his dying colleague, Philipp Melanchthon, he forbid death to take its victim.

This is a wonderful relationship that God invites us to enter. We are certainly familiar with passages of Scripture like the one that follows the above verse: "My own hands stretched out the heavens; I marshaled their starry hosts" (Isaiah 45:12). But knowing that God invites us to command Him to act reveals a surprising change in our normal relationship!

What a distinction there is between this attitude and the hesitancy and uncertainty of our prayers of unbelief, to which we have become so accustomed! The constant repetition of our prayers has also caused them to lose their sharp cutting edge.

Think how often Jesus, during His earthly ministry, put others in a position to command Him. "As Jesus and his disciples were leaving Jericho," Jesus stopped and responded to two blind men who had called out to Him. "What do you want me to do for you?" (Matthew 20:29, 32). It was as though He said, "I am yours to command."

Could we ever forget how Jesus yielded the key to His resources to the Greek woman from Syrian Phoenicia because of her reply to Him? In effect, He told her to help herself to all that she needed (Mark 7:24–30).

What human mind can fully realize the total significance of the lofty position to which God lovingly raises His little children? He seems to be saying, "All my resources are at your command." "*And I will do whatever you ask in my name*" (John 14:13). F. B. MEYER

Say to this mountain, "Go,
Be cast into the sea";
And doubt not in your heart
That it will be to thee.
It will be done, doubt not His Word,
Challenge your mountain in the Lord!

Claim your redemption right,
Purchased by precious blood;
The Trinity unite
To make it true and good.
It will be done, obey the Word,
Challenge your mountain in the Lord!

Self, sickness, sorrow, sin,
The Lord did meet that day
On His beloved One,
And you are freed away.
It has been done, rest on His Word,
Challenge your mountain in the Lord!

Surround the rival's wall
With silent prayer, then raise—
Before its ramparts fall—
The victor's shout of praise.
It will be done, faith rests assured,
Challenge your mountain in the Lord!

The massive gates of brass,
The bars of iron yield,
To let the faithful pass,
Conquerors in every field.

It will be done, the foe ignored,
Challenge your mountain in the Lord!

Take then the faith of God,
Free from the taint of doubt;
The miracle-working rod
That casts all reasoning out.
It will be done, stand on the Word,
Challenge your mountain in the Lord!

SELECTED

JUNE 25

The LORD said to Moses, "... Tell the Israelites to move on. Raise your staff and stretch out your hand over the sea."

EXODUS 14:15–16

DEAR CHILD OF GOD, JUST IMAGINE THAT TRIUMPHAL MARCH! Picture the excited children being constantly hushed and restrained by their parents from their outbursts of wonder. Think how the women must have experienced an uncontrollable excitement as they found themselves suddenly saved from a fate worse than death. Imagine how the men who accompanied them must have felt ashamed and admonished for mistrusting God and for complaining against Moses. And as you envision the Red Sea's mighty walls of water, separated by the outstretched hand of the Eternal in response to the faith of a single man, learn what God will do for His own.

Never dread any consequence resulting from absolute obedience to His command. Never fear the rough waters ahead, which through their proud contempt impede your progress. God is greater than the roar of raging water and the mighty waves of the sea. "The LORD sits enthroned over the flood; the LORD is enthroned as King forever" (Psalm 29:10). A storm is simply the hem of His robe, the sign of His coming, and the evidence of His presence.

Dare to trust Him! Dare to follow Him! Then discover that the forces that blocked your progress and threatened your life become at His command the very materials He uses to build your street of freedom. F. B. Meyer

Have you come to the Red Sea place in your life,
Where, in spite of all you can do,
There is no way out, there is no way back,
There is no other way but through?
Then wait on the Lord with a trust serene
Till the night of your fear is gone;
He will send the wind, He will heap the floods,
When He says to your soul, "Move on."

And His hand will lead you through—clear through—
Ere the watery walls roll down,
No foe can reach you, no wave can touch,
No mightiest sea can drown;
The tossing billows may rear their crests,
Their foam at your feet may break,
But o'er the seabed you will walk dry ground
In the path that your Lord will make.

In the morning watch, 'neath the lifted cloud,
You will see but the Lord alone,
When He leads you on from the place of the sea
To a land that you have not known;
And your fears will pass as your foes have passed,
You will be no more afraid;
You will sing His praise in a better place,
A place that His hand has made.

Annie Johnson Flint

JUNE 26

What if some were unfaithful? Will their unfaithfulness nullify God's faithfulness?
ROMANS 3:3

I SUSPECT THAT THE SOURCE OF EVERY BIT OF SORROW IN MY LIFE CAN be traced to simple unbelief. If I truly believe the past is totally forgiven, the present is supplied with power, and the future is bright with hope, how could I be anything but completely happy?

Yes, the future is bright because of God's faithfulness. His abiding truth does not change with my mood, and He never wavers when I stumble and fall over a promise of His through my unbelief. His faithfulness stands firm and as prominent as mountain peaks of pearl splitting the clouds of eternity. And each base of His hills is rooted at an unfathomable depth on the rock of God.

Mont Blanc does not disappear, becoming a passing vision or a whimsical mist, simply because a climber grows dizzy on its slopes. JAMES SMETHAM

Is it any wonder that we do not receive God's blessing after stumbling over His promise through unbelief? I am not saying that faith merits an answer or that we can work to earn it. But God Himself has made *believing* a condition of receiving, and the Giver has a sovereign right to choose His own terms for His gifts. SAMUEL HART

Unbelief continually asks, "How can this be possible?" It is always full of "hows," yet faith needs only one great answer to even ten thousand "hows." That answer is—GOD! C. H. M.

No one accomplishes *so much* in *so little* time as when he or she is praying. And the following thought certainly aligns well with all that the Lord Jesus Christ taught on prayer: If only one believer with total faith rises up, *the history of the world will be changed.*

Will *you* be that one to rise up, submitting yourself to the sovereignty and guidance of God our Father? A. E. MCADAM

Prayer without faith quickly degenerates into an aimless routine or heartless hypocrisy. However, prayer with faith brings the omnipotence of God to the support of our petitions. It is better not to pray until your entire being responds to, and understands, the power of prayer. When genuine prayer is even whispered, earth and heaven, and the past and future, say, "Amen!"

This is the kind of prayer Christ prayed. P. C. M.

Nothing lies beyond the reach of prayer except those things outside the will of God.

JUNE 27

Summon your power, God; show us your strength.

PSALM 68:28

THE LORD IMPARTS TO ME THE UNDERLYING STRENGTH OF CHARACTER that gives me the necessary energy and decision-making ability to live my life. He strengthens me "with power through his Spirit in [my] inner being" (Ephesians 3:16). And the strength He gives is continuous, for He is a source of power I cannot exhaust.

"Your strength will equal your days" (Deuteronomy 33:25)—my strength of will, affection, judgment, ideals, and achievement will last a lifetime.

"The LORD is my strength" (Exodus 15:2) *to go on*. He gives me the power to walk the long, straight, and level path, even when the monotonous way has no turns or curves offering pleasant surprises and when my spirit is depressed with the terrible drudgery.

"The LORD is my strength" *to go up*. He is my power to climb the straight and narrow path up the Hill of Difficulty, as Christian did in *Pilgrim's Progress*, and not be afraid.

"The LORD is my strength" *to go down*. It is often once I leave the invigorating heights, where the wind and sunlight have surrounded me, and begin to descend to the more confining, humid, and stifling heat of the valley below that my heart grows faint. In fact, I recently heard someone say, referring to his own increasing physical frailty, "It is coming down that tires me most!"

"The Lord is my strength" *to sit still.* And what a difficult accomplishment this is! I often say to others during those times when I am compelled to be still, "If only I could do something!" I feel like the mother who stands by her sick child but is powerless to heal. What a severe test! Yet to do nothing except to sit still and wait requires tremendous strength.

"The Lord is my strength!" "Our competence comes from God" (2 Corinthians 3:5). The Silver Lining

JUNE 28

There before me was a door standing open in heaven.

Revelation 4:1

We should remember that John wrote these words while on the island of Patmos. He was there "because of the word of God and the testimony of Jesus" (Revelation 1:9). He had been banished to this island, which was an isolated, rocky, and inhospitable prison. Yet it was here, under difficult circumstances—separated from all his loved ones in Ephesus, excluded from worshiping with the church, and condemned to only the companionship of unpleasant fellow captives—that he was granted this vision as a special privilege. It was as a prisoner that he saw "a door standing open in heaven."

We should also remember Jacob, who laid down in the desert to sleep after leaving his father's house. "He had a dream in which he saw a stairway resting on the earth, with its top reaching to heaven, and . . . above it stood the Lord" (Genesis 28:12–13).

The doors of heaven have been opened not only for these two men but also for many others. And in the world's estimation, it seems as if their circumstances were utterly unlikely to receive such revelations. Yet how often we have seen "a door standing open in heaven" for those who are prisoners and captives, for those who suffer from a chronic illness and are bound with iron chains of pain to a bed of sickness, for those who wander the earth in lonely isolation, and for those who are kept from the Lord's house by the demands of home and family.

But there are conditions to seeing the open door. We must know what it is to be "in the Spirit" (Revelation 1:10). We must be "pure in heart" (Matthew 5:8) and obedient in faith. We must be willing to "consider everything a loss because of the surpassing worth of knowing Christ Jesus" (Philippians 3:8). Then once God is everything to us, so that "in him we live and move and have our being" (Acts 17:28), the door to heaven will stand open before us as well. DAILY DEVOTIONAL COMMENTARY

God has His mountains bleak and bare,
Where He does bid us rest awhile;
Cliffs where we breathe a purer air,
Lone peaks that catch the day's first smile.

God has His deserts broad and brown—
A solitude—a sea of sand,
Where He does let heaven's curtain down,
Unveiled by His Almighty hand.

JUNE 29

There we saw the giants.

NUMBERS 13:33 KJV

YES, THE ISRAELI SPIES SAW GIANTS, BUT JOSHUA AND CALEB SAW God! Those who doubt still say today, "*We can't attack . . . ; they are stronger than we are*" (v. 31). Yet those who believe say, "*We should go up and take possession . . . for we can certainly do it*" (v. 30).

Giants represent great difficulties, and they stalk us everywhere. They are in our families, our churches, our social life, and even our own hearts. We must overcome them or they will devour us, just as the ancient Israelites, fearing those in Canaan, said, "The land we explored devours those living in it. All the people we saw there are of great size" (v. 32). We should exhibit faith as did Joshua and Caleb, who said, "Do not be afraid . . . , because we will swallow them up" (Numbers 14:9). In effect, they told the others, "We will be stronger by overcoming them than if there had been no giants to defeat."

In fact, unless we have overcoming faith, we will be swallowed up—consumed by the giants who block our path. "With that same spirit of faith" (2 Corinthians 4:13) that Joshua and Caleb had, let us look to God, and He will take care of the difficulties. SELECTED

We encounter giants only when we are *serving* God and *following* Him. It was when Israel was going *forward* that the giants appeared, for when they turned back into the wilderness, they found none.

Many people believe that the power of God in a person's life should keep him from all trials and conflicts. However, the power of God actually brings conflict and struggles. You would think that Paul, during his great missionary journey to Rome, would have been kept by God's sovereignty from the power of violent storms and of his enemies. Yet just the opposite was true. He endured one long, difficult struggle with the Jews who were persecuting him. He faced fierce winds, poisonous snakes, and all the powers of earth and of hell. And finally, he narrowly escaped drowning, by swimming to shore at Malta after a shipwreck nearly sent him to a watery grave.

Does this sound like a God of infinite power? Yes, it is just like Him. And that is why Paul told us that once he took the Lord Jesus Christ as his life in his body, a severe conflict immediately arose. In fact, the conflict never ended. The pressure on Paul was persistent, but from the conflict he always emerged victorious through the strength of Jesus Christ.

Paul described this in quite vivid language: "We are hard pressed on every side, but not crushed; perplexed, but not in despair; persecuted, but not abandoned; struck down, but not destroyed. We always carry around in our body the death of Jesus, so that the life of Jesus may also be revealed in our body" (2 Corinthians 4:8–10).

What a ceaseless and strenuous struggle he related! It is nearly impossible to express in English the impact of the original language. Paul gives us five different images in succession. In the first, he has us picture enemies completely surrounding and pressuring but not crushing him, because the heavenly "police" have protected him and cleared a path just wide enough for him to escape. The literal meaning is, "We are crowded from all sides, but not defeated."

The second image is that of someone whose way is completely blocked or thwarted by the enemy. Yet he has persevered, for there is just enough light for him to see the next step. Paul said, "Perplexed, but not in despair," or as one literal translation put it, "Without a road, but not without a 'side road' of escape."

The third picture, "Persecuted, but not abandoned," is one of the enemy in hot pursuit of him while the divine Defender stands nearby. He is pursued, but not left alone.

The fourth is even more vivid and dramatic. The enemy has overtaken him, struck him, and knocked him down. But it is not a fatal blow—he is able to rise again. He has been "struck down, but not destroyed," or literally, "overthrown, but not overcome." In the fifth and final image, Paul advances the thought still further, giving us a picture that *appears* to be one of death itself: "We always carry around in our body the death of Jesus." Yet he does not die, for "the life of Jesus" comes to his aid, and he lives through Christ's life until his lifework is complete.

The reason so many people fail to experience this divine principle is that they expect to receive it all without a struggle. When conflict comes and the battle rages on, they become discouraged and surrender. God has nothing worth having that is easily gained, for there are no cheap goods on the heavenly market. The cost of our redemption was everything God had to give, and anything worth having is expensive. Difficult times and places are our schools of faith and character. If we are ever to rise above mere human strength, and experience the power of the life of Christ in our mortal bodies, it will be through the process of conflict that could very well be called the "labor pains" of the new life. It is like the story of Moses, who "saw that though the bush was on fire it did not burn up" (Exodus 3:2); although Satan's demons tried to extinguish the flame in Moses' life by continually pouring water on his plans, they could not, because God's angels were ever vigilant, pouring oil on the flame to keep it burning brightly.

Dear child of God, you may be suffering, but you cannot fail if you will only dare to believe, stand firm, and refuse to be overcome. FROM A TRACT

JUNE 30

I heard a hushed voice.

JOB 4:16

SOME TWENTY YEARS AGO A FRIEND GAVE ME A BOOK ENTITLED *True Peace*. It had an old medieval message and this one primary thought—that God was waiting in the depths of my being to speak to me if I would only be still enough to hear His voice.

I assumed this would not be a difficult thing to do, so I tried to be still. No sooner had I begun to do so than complete pandemonium seemed to break loose. Suddenly I heard a thousand voices and sounds from without and within, until I could hear nothing except these incredible noises. Some were my own words, my own questions, and even my own prayers, while others were temptations of the Enemy, and the voices of the world's turmoil.

In every direction I turned, I was pushed, pulled, and confronted with indescribable unrest and overwhelming noises. I seemed compelled to listen to some of them and to respond in some way. But God said, "Be still, and know that I am God" (Psalm 46:10). Then my mind was filled with worries over my responsibilities and plans for tomorrow, and God said again, "Be still."

As I listened and slowly learned to obey, I shut my ears to every other sound. Soon I discovered that once the other voices ceased, or once I ceased to hear them, "a gentle whisper" (1 Kings 19:12) began to speak in the depths of my being. And it spoke to me with an inexpressible tenderness, power, and comfort.

This "gentle whisper" became for me the voice of prayer, wisdom, and service. No longer did I need to work so hard to think, pray, or trust, because the Holy Spirit's "gentle whisper" in my heart was God's prayer in the secret places of my soul. It was His answer to all my questions, and His life and strength for my soul and body. His voice became the essence of all knowledge, prayer, and blessings, for it was the living God Himself as my life and my all.

This is precisely how our spirit drinks in the life of our risen Lord. And then we are enabled to face life's conflicts and responsibilities, like a flower that has absorbed the cool and refreshing drops of dew through the darkness of the night. Yet just as *dew never falls on a stormy night*, the dew of His grace never covers a restless soul. A. B. Simpson

JULY 1

My words . . . will come true at their appointed time.

Luke 1:20

Blessed is she who has believed that the Lord
would fulfill his promise to her!

Luke 1:45

The Lord is sure to accomplish those things
A loving heart has waited long to see;

Those words will be fulfilled to which she clings,
Because her God has promised faithfully;
And, knowing Him, she ne'er can doubt His Word;
He speaks and it is done. The mighty Lord!

The Lord is sure to accomplish those things,
O burdened heart, rest ever in His care;
In quietness beneath His shadowing wings
Await the answer to your longing prayer.
When you have "cast your cares," the heart then sings,
The Lord is sure to accomplish those things.

The Lord is sure to accomplish those things,
O tired heart, believe and wait and pray;
Peacefully, the evening chime still rings,
Though cloud and rain and storm have filled the day.
Faith pierces through the mist of doubt that bars
The coming night sometimes, and finds the stars.

The Lord is sure to accomplish those things,
O trusting heart, the Lord to you has told;
Let Faith and Hope arise, and lift their wings,
To soar toward the sunrise clouds of gold;
The doorways of the rosy dawn swing wide,
Revealing joys the darkness of night did hide.

BESSIE PORTER

Matthew Henry said, "We can depend on God to fulfill His promise, even when all the roads leading to it are closed. 'For no matter how many promises God has made, they are "Yes" in Christ. And so through him the "Amen" [so be it] is spoken by us to the glory of God' [2 Corinthians 1:20]."

JULY 2

When you walk, your steps will not be hampered;
when you run, you will not stumble.
PROVERBS 4:12

THE LORD ONLY BUILDS A BRIDGE OF FAITH DIRECTLY UNDER THE feet of a faithful traveler. He never builds the bridge a few steps ahead, for then it would not be one of faith. "We live by faith, not by sight" (2 Corinthians 5:7).

Years ago automatic gates were sometimes used on country roads. They would securely block the road as a vehicle approached, and if the traveler stopped before coming to the gate, it would not open. But if the traveler drove straight toward it, the weight of the vehicle would compress the springs below the roadway, and the gate would swing back to let him pass. The vehicle had to keep moving forward, or the gate would remain closed.

This illustrates the way to pass through every barrier that blocks the road of service for God. Whether the barrier is a river, a mountain, or a gate, all a child of Jesus must do is head directly toward it. If it is a river, it will dry up as he comes near it, as long as he still forges ahead. If it is a mountain, it will be removed and "cast into the sea" (Mark 11:23 KJV), providing he approaches it with unflinching confidence.

Is some great barrier blocking your path of service right now? Then head straight for it, in the name of the Lord, and it will no longer be there.
HENRY CLAY TRUMBULL

We sit and weep in vain, while the voice of the Almighty tells us to never stop moving upward and onward. Let us advance boldly, whether it is dark and we can barely see the forest in front of us, or our road leads us through the mountain pass, where from any vantage point we can only see a few steps ahead.

Press on! And if necessary, like the ancient Israelites we will find a pillar of clouds and fire to lead the way on our journey through the wilderness. God will provide guides and inns along the road, and we will discover food, clothing, and friends at every stage of our journey. And as Samuel Rutherford, the great Scottish minister, once stated so simply, "Whatever happens, the worst will only be a weary traveler receiving a joyful and heavenly welcome home."

I'm going by the upper road, for that
still holds the sun,
I'm climbing through night's pastures where
the starry rivers run:
If you should think to seek me in my
old dark abode,
You'll find this writing on the door,
"He's on the Upper Road."

SELECTED

JULY 3

When a farmer plows for planting, does he plow continually?

ISAIAH 28:24

ONE DAY IN EARLY SUMMER I WALKED PAST A LOVELY MEADOW. THE grass was as soft, thick, and beautiful as an immense green Oriental rug. At one end of the meadow stood a fine old tree that served as a sanctuary for countless wild birds, whose happy songs seemed to fill the crisp, sweet air. I saw two cows who lay in the shade as the very picture of contentment. And down by the road, eye-catching dandelions mingled their gold with the royal purple of the wild violets. I leaned against the fence for a long time, feasting my hungry eyes and thinking in my soul that God never made a more beautiful place than this lovely meadow.

The next day I passed that way again, and to my great dismay, the hand of the destroyer had been there. A farmer with a large tractor, which was now sitting idle in the meadow, had in one day inflicted terrible devastation. Instead of seeing the soft, green grass, I now saw the ugly, bare, and brown earth. Gone were the dandelions and the pretty violets. And instead of the multitude of singing birds, there were now only a few, who were industriously scratching the ground for worms. In my grief I said, "How could anyone spoil something so beautiful?"

Then suddenly my eyes were opened, as if by some unseen hand, and I saw a vision. The vision was that of a field of ripe corn ready for harvest. I could see the giant, heavily laden stalks in the autumn sun, and I could almost hear the music of the wind as it swept across the golden tassels. And before I realized it, the bare earth took on a splendor it did not have the day before.

Oh, if only we would always catch the vision of the abundant harvest when the great Master Farmer comes, as He often does, to plow through our very souls—uprooting and turning under that which we thought most beautiful and leaving only the bare and the unlovely before our agonizing eyes. SELECTED

Why should I be frightened and surprised by the plow of the Lord, which makes deep furrows in my soul? I know He is not some arbitrary or irrational farmer—His purpose is to yield a harvest. SAMUEL RUTHERFORD

JULY 4

The revelation awaits an appointed time. . . . Though it linger, wait for it; it will certainly come and will not delay.

HABAKKUK 2:3

IN THE CAPTIVATING BOOKLET *Expectation Corner*, ONE OF THE characters, Adam Slowman, was led into the Lord's treasurehouse. Among the many wonders revealed to him there was the "Delayed Blessing Office," where God stored the answers to certain prayers until it was wise to send them.

For some who pray expecting an answer, it takes a long time to learn that *delays of answers are not denials.* In fact, in the "Delayed Blessing

Office," there are deep secrets of love and wisdom that we have never imagined! We tend to want to pick our blessings from the tree while they are still green, yet God wants us to wait until they are fully ripe.

"The LORD longs to be gracious to you. . . . *Blessed are all who wait for him!*" (Isaiah 30:18). The Lord watches over us in all the difficult places, and He will not allow even one trial that is too much for us. He will use His refining fire to burn away our impurities and will then gloriously come to our rescue.

Do not grieve Him by doubting His love. Instead, lift up your eyes and begin praising Him *right now* for the deliverance that is on its way to you. Then you will be abundantly rewarded for the delay that has tried your faith.

O you of little faith,
God has not failed you yet!
When all looks dark and gloomy,
You do so soon forget—

Forget that He has led you,
And gently cleared your way;
On clouds has poured His sunshine,
And turned your night to day.

And if He's helped you to this point,
He will not fail you now;
How it must wound His loving heart
To see your anxious brow!

Oh! doubt not any longer,
To Him commit your way,
Whom in the past you trusted,
And is just the same today.

SELECTED

JULY 5

I am now going to allure her; I will lead her into the wilderness. . . . There I will give her back her vineyards.

HOSEA 2:14–15

THE WILDERNESS IS CERTAINLY A STRANGE PLACE TO FIND VINEYARDS! Can it be true that the riches of life that we need can be found in the wilderness—a place that symbolizes loneliness, and through which we can seldom find our way? Not only is this true but verse 15 goes on to say, "I . . . will make the Valley of Achor a door of hope. *There she will respond as in the days of her youth.*" "Achor" means "troubled," yet the Valley of Achor is called "a door of hope."

Yes, God knows our need for a wilderness experience. He knows exactly where and how to produce enduring qualities in us. The person who has been idolatrous, has been rebellious, has forgotten God, and has said with total self-will, "I will go after my lovers" (Hosea 2:5), will find her path blocked by God. "She will chase after her lovers but not catch them; she will look for them but not find them" (Hosea 2:7). And once she feels totally hopeless and abandoned, God will say, "I am now going to allure her; I will lead her into the wilderness and speak tenderly to her."

What a loving God we have! CRUMBS

We never know where God has hidden His streams. We see a large stone and have no idea that it covers the source of a spring. We see a rocky area and never imagine that it is hiding a fountain. God leads me into hard and difficult places, and it is there I realize I am where eternal streams abide. SELECTED

JULY 6

We do not know what to do, but our eyes are on you.

2 CHRONICLES 20:12

An Israelite named Uzzah lost his life because he "reached out and took hold of the ark of God" (2 Samuel 6:6). He placed his hands on it with the best of intentions—to steady it, "because the oxen stumbled" (2 Samuel 6:6)—but nevertheless, he had overstepped his bounds by touching the Lord's work, and "therefore God struck him down" (2 Samuel 6:7). *Living a life of faith often requires us to leave things alone.*

If we have completely entrusted something to God, we must keep our hands off it. He can guard it better than we can, and He does not need our help. "Be still before the Lord and wait patiently for him; do not fret when people succeed in their ways, when they carry out their wicked schemes" (Psalm 37:7).

Things in our lives may seem to be going all wrong, but God knows our circumstances better than we do. And He will work at the perfect moment, if we will completely trust Him to work in His own way and in His own time. Often there is nothing as godly as inactivity on our part, or nothing as harmful as restless working, for God has promised to work His sovereign will. A. B. Simpson

Being perplexed, I say,
"Lord, make it right!
Night is as day to You,
Darkness as light.
I am afraid to touch
Things that involve so much;
My trembling hand may shake,
My skilless hand may break;
Yours can make no mistake."

Being in doubt I say,
"Lord, make it plain;
Which is the true, safe way?
Which would be gain?

I am not wise to know,
Nor sure of foot to go;
What is so clear to Thee,
Lord, make it clear to me!"

It is such a comfort to drop the entanglements and perplexities of life into God's hands and leave them there.

JULY 7

He made me into a polished arrow.

Isaiah 49:2

Pebble Beach, on the California coast, has become quite famous for the beautiful pebbles found there. The raging white surf continually roars, thundering and pounding against the rocks on the shore. These stones are trapped in the arms of the merciless waves. They are tossed, rolled, rubbed together, and ground against the sharp edges of the cliffs. Both day and night, this process of grinding continues relentlessly. And what is the result?

Tourists from around the world flock there to collect the beautiful round stones. They display them in cabinets and use them to decorate their homes. Yet a little farther up the coast, just around the point of the cliff, is a quiet cove. Protected from the face of the ocean, sheltered from the storms, and always in the sun, the sands are covered with an abundance of pebbles never sought by the travelers.

So why have these stones been left untouched through all the years? Simply because they have escaped all the turmoil and the grinding of the waves. The quietness and peace have left them as they have always been—rough, unpolished, and devoid of beauty—*for polish is the result of difficulties.*

Since God knows what niche we are to fill, let us trust Him to shape us to it. And since He knows what work we are to do, let us trust Him to grind us so we will be properly prepared.

O blows that strike! O hurts that pierce
This fainting heart of mine!
What are you but the Master's tools
Forming a work Divine?
Nearly all of God's jewels are crystallized tears.

JULY 8

They will soar on wings like eagles.
ISAIAH 40:31

THERE IS A FABLE ABOUT THE WAY BIRDS FIRST GOT THEIR WINGS. THE story goes that initially they were made without them. Then God made the wings, set them down before the wingless birds, and said to them, "Take up these burdens and carry them."

The birds had sweet voices for singing, and lovely feathers that glistened in the sunshine, but they could not soar in the air. When asked to pick up the burdens that lay at their feet, they hesitated at first. Yet soon they obeyed, picked up the wings with their beaks, and set them on their shoulders to carry them.

For a short time the load seemed heavy and difficult to bear, but soon, as they continued to carry the burden and to fold the wings over their hearts, the wings grew attached to their little bodies. They quickly discovered how to use them and were lifted by the wings high into the air. *The weights had become wings.*

This is a parable for us. We are the wingless birds, and our duties and tasks are the wings God uses to lift us up and carry us heavenward. We look at our burdens and heavy loads, and try to run from them, but if we will carry them and tie them to our hearts, they will become wings. And on them we can then rise and soar toward God.

There is no burden so heavy that when lifted cheerfully with love in our hearts will not become a blessing to us. God intends for our tasks to be our helpers; to refuse to bend our shoulders to carry a load is to miss a new opportunity for growth. J. R. Miller

No matter how overwhelming, any burden God has lovingly placed with His own hands on our shoulders is a blessing. Frederick William Faber

JULY 9

I have chosen thee in the furnace of affliction.

Isaiah 48:10 KJV

Doesn't God's Word come to us like a soft rain shower, dispelling the fury of the flames? Isn't it like fireproof armor, against which the heat is powerless? Then let afflictions come, for God has *chosen* me. Poverty, you may walk through my door, but God is already in my house, and He has *chosen* me. Sickness, you may intrude into my life, but I have a cure standing ready—God has *chosen* me. Whatever occurs in the valley of tears, I know He has *chosen* me.

Dear Christian, do not be afraid, for Jesus is with you. Through all your fiery trials, His presence is both your comfort and safety. He will never forsake those He has chosen for His own. "Do not be afraid, for I am with you" (Genesis 26:24) is His unfailing word of promise to His chosen ones who are experiencing "the furnace of affliction." Charles H. Spurgeon

Pain's furnace heat within me quivers,
God's breath upon the flame does blow;
And all my heart in anguish shivers

And trembles at the fiery glow; And yet I whisper,
"As God will!" And in the hottest fire hold still.
He comes and lays my heart, all heated,

On the hard anvil, minded so
Into His own fair shape to beat it
With His great hammer, blow on blow;
And yet I whisper, "As God will!"
And at His heaviest blows hold still.
He takes my softened heart and beats it;

The sparks fly off at every blow;
He turns it o'er and o'er and heats it,
And lets it cool, and makes it glow;
And yet I whisper, "As God will!"
And in His mighty hand hold still.
Why should I complain? for the sorrow

Then only longer-lived would be;
The end may come, and will tomorrow,
When God has done His work in me;
So I say trusting, "As God will!"
And, trusting to the end, hold still.

JULIUS STURM

The burden of suffering seems to be a tombstone hung around our necks. Yet in reality it is simply the weight necessary to hold the diver down while he is searching for pearls. JULIUS RICHTER

JULY 10

I called him but he did not answer.

SONG OF SONGS 5:6

Once the Lord has given us great faith, He has been known to test it with long delays. He has allowed His servants' voices to echo in their ears, as if their prayers were rebounding from a contemptuous sky. Believers have knocked at the heavenly gate, but it has remained immovable, as though its hinges had rusted. And like Jeremiah, they have cried, "*You have covered yourself with a cloud so that no prayer can get through*" (Lamentations 3:44).

True saints of God have endured lengthy times of patient waiting with no reply, not because their prayers were prayed without intensity, nor because God did not accept their pleas. They were required to wait because it pleased Him who is sovereign and who gives according to "his good purpose" (Philippians 2:13). And if it pleases Him to cause our patience to be exercised, should He not do as He desires with His own?

No prayer is ever lost, or any prayer ever breathed in vain. There is no such thing as prayer unanswered or unnoticed by God, and some things we see as refusals or denials are simply delays. Horatius Bonar

Christ sometimes delays His help so He may test our faith and energize our prayers. Our boat may be tossed by the waves while He continues to sleep, but He will awake before it sinks. He sleeps but He never oversleeps, for He is never too late. Alexander Maclaren

Be still, sad soul! lift up no passionate cry,
But spread the desert of your being bare
To the full searching of the All-seeing eye;
Wait! and through dark misgiving, deep despair,
God will come down in pity, and fill the dry
Dead place with light, and life, and springlike air.
John Campbell Shairp

JULY 11

Some time later the brook dried up because there had been no rain in the land.

1 Kings 17:7

Week after week, with an unwavering and steadfast spirit, Elijah watched the brook dwindle and finally dry up. Often tempted to stumble in unbelief, he nevertheless refused to allow his circumstances to come between himself and God. Unbelief looks at God through the circumstances, just as we often see the sun dimmed by clouds or smoke. But faith puts God between itself and its circumstances, and looks at them through Him.

Elijah's brook dwindled to only a silver thread, which formed pools at the base of the largest rocks. Then the pools evaporated, the birds flew away, and the wild animals of the fields and forests no longer came to drink, for the brook became completely dry. And only then, to Elijah's patient and faithful spirit, did the word of the Lord come and say, "Go at once to Zarephath" (v. 9).

Most of us would have become anxious and tired, and would have made other plans long before God spoke. Our singing would have stopped as soon as the stream flowed less musically over its rocky bed. We would have hung our harps on the willows nearby and begun pacing back and forth on the withering grass, worrying about our predicament. And probably, long before the brook actually dried up, we would have devised some plan, asked God to bless it, and headed elsewhere.

God will often extricate us from the mess we have made, because "his love endures forever" (1 Chronicles 16:34). Yet if we had only been patient and waited to see the unfolding of His plan, we would never have found ourselves in such an impossible maze, seeing no way out. We would also never have had to turn back and retrace our way, with wasted steps and so many tears of shame.

"*Wait* for the Lord" (Psalm 27:14). *Patiently wait!* F. B. Meyer

JULY 12

He knows the way that I take; when he has tested me, I will come forth as gold.

Job 23:10

Faith grows during storms. These are just four little words, but what significance they have to someone who has endured life-threatening storms!

Faith is that God-given ability that, when exercised, brings the unseen into plain view. It deals with the supernatural and makes impossible things possible. And yes, *it grows during storms*—that is, it grows through disturbances in the spiritual atmosphere. Storms are caused by conflicts between the physical elements, and the storms of the spiritual world are conflicts with supernatural, hostile elements. And it is in this atmosphere of conflict that faith finds its most fertile soil and grows most rapidly to maturity.

The strongest trees are found not in the thick shelter of the forest but out in the open, where winds from every direction bear down upon them. The fierce winds bend and twist them until they become giant in stature. These are the trees that toolmakers seek for handles for their tools, because of the wood's great strength.

It is the same in the spiritual world. Remember, when you see a person of great spiritual stature, the road you must travel to walk with him is not one where the sun always shines and wildflowers always bloom. Instead, the way is a steep, rocky, and narrow path, where the winds of hell will try to knock you off your feet, and where sharp rocks will cut you, prickly thorns will scratch your face, and poisonous snakes will slither and hiss all around you.

The path of faith is one of sorrow and joy, suffering and healing comfort, tears and smiles, trials and victories, conflicts and triumphs, and also hardships, dangers, beatings, persecutions, misunderstanding, trouble, and distress. Yet "in all these things we are more than conquerors through him who loved us" (Romans 8:37).

Yes, "in all these"—even *during storms*, when the winds are the most intense—"we are more than conquerors." You may be tempted to run from the ordeal of a fierce storm of testing, but head straight for it! God is there to meet you in the center of each trial. And He will whisper to you His secrets, which will bring you out with a radiant face and such an invincible faith that all the demons of hell will never be able to shake it. E. A. Kilbourne

JULY 13

God . . . calls into being things that were not.

Romans 4:17

What does this verse mean? It is the very reason why "Abraham in hope believed" (v. 18). That Abraham would become the father of a child at his advanced age seemed absurd and an utter impossibility, yet God called him "the father of many nations" (Genesis 17:4) long before there was any indication of fulfillment. And Abraham thought of himself as a father, because God had said so. That is genuine faith—believing and declaring what God has said, stepping out on what appears to be thin air and finding solid rock beneath your feet.

Therefore boldly declare what God says you have, and He will accomplish what you believe. You must, however, exhibit genuine faith and trust Him with your entire being. Crumbs

We must be willing to live by faith, not hoping or desiring to live any other way. We must be willing to have every light around us extinguished, to have every star in the heavens blotted out, and to live with nothing encircling us but darkness and danger. Yes, we must be willing to do all this, if God will only leave within our soul an inner radiance from the pure, bright light that faith has kindled. Thomas C. Upham

The moment has come when you must jump from your perch of distrust, leaving the nest of supposed safety behind and trusting the wings of faith. You must be like a young bird beginning to test the air with its untried wings. At first you may feel as though you will fall to the earth. The fledgling may feel the same way, but it does not fall, for its wings provide support. Yet even if its wings do fail, one of its parents will sweep under it, rescuing it on strong wings.

God will rescue you in the same way. Simply trust Him, for His "right hand sustains" (Psalm 18:35). Do you find yourself asking, "But am I to step out onto nothing?" That is exactly what the bird is seemingly asked to do, yet we know that the *air is there* and that the air is not nearly as insubstantial as it seems. And *you* know that the *promises of God are there*, and they certainly are not insubstantial at all. Do you still respond, "But it seems so unlikely that my poor, helpless soul would be sustained by such strength." Has God said it will? "Do you mean that my tempted, yielding nature will be victorious in the fight?" Has God said it will? "Do you mean that my timid, trembling heart will find peace?" Has God said it will?

If God has said so, surely you do not want to suggest He has lied! If He has spoken, will He not fulfill it? If He has given you His word—His sure word of promise—do not question it but trust it absolutely. You have His promise, and in fact you have even more—you have Him who confidently speaks the words.

"Yes, I tell you" (Luke 12:5). Trust Him! J. B. Figgis

JULY 14

Bind the festival sacrifice with cords to the horns of the altar.

Psalm 118:27 NASB

Is the altar of sacrifice calling you? Why not ask God to *bind* you to it, so you will never be tempted to turn away from a life of consecration, or dedication, to Him? There are times when life is full of promise and light, and we choose the cross; yet at other times, when the sky is gray, we run from it. Therefore it is wise to be *bound* to the altar.

Dear blessed Holy Spirit, will You bind us to the cross and fill us with such love for it that we will never abandon it? Please bind us with Your scarlet cord of redemption, Your gold cord of love, and the silver cord of hope in Christ's second coming. We ask this so we will not turn from the cross of sacrifice, or desire becoming anything but humble partners with our Lord in His pain and sorrow!

"The horns of the altar" are inviting you. Will you come? Are you willing to continually live a life of total surrender, giving yourself completely to the Lord? SELECTED

I once heard a story of a man who attended a tent revival meeting and tried to give himself to God. Every night at the altar, he would dedicate himself to the Lord. Yet as he left each evening, the Devil would come to him and convince him that since he did not *feel* changed, he was not truly redeemed.

Again and again he was defeated by the Adversary. Finally one evening he came to the meeting carrying an ax and a large wooden stake. After dedicating himself once more, he drove the stake into the ground where he had knelt to pray. As he was leaving the tent, the Devil came to him as usual, trying to make him believe that his commitment to God was not genuine. He quickly returned to the stake, pointed to it, and said, "Devil, do you see this stake? This is my witness that God has forever accepted me."

Immediately the Devil left him, and he never experienced doubts again. THE STILL SMALL VOICE

Beloved, if you are tempted to doubt the finality of your salvation experience, drive a stake into the ground and then let it be your witness before God, and even the Devil, that you have settled the question forever.

Are you groping for a blessing,
Never getting there?
Listen to a word of wisdom,
Get somewhere.

Are you struggling for salvation
By your anxious prayer?
Stop your struggling, simply trust, and—
Get somewhere.

Does the answer seem to linger
To your earnest prayer?
Turn your praying into praise, and—
Get somewhere.

You will never know His fullness
Till you boldly dare
To commit your all to Him, and—
Get somewhere.

Songs of the Spirit

JULY 15

This is the victory that has overcome the world, even our faith.

1 John 5:4

It is easy to love Him when the blue is in the sky,
When the summer winds are blowing, and we smell the roses nigh;
There is little effort needed to obey His precious will
When it leads through flower-decked valley, or over sun-kissed hill.

It is when the rain is falling, or the mist hangs in the air,
When the road is dark and rugged, and the wind no longer fair,
When the rosy dawn has settled in a shadowland of gray,
That we find it hard to trust Him, and are slower to obey.

It is easy to trust Him when the singing birds have come,
And their songs of praise are echoed in our heart and in our home;

But it's when we miss the music, and the days are dull and drear,
That we need a faith triumphant over every doubt and fear.

And our blessed Lord will give it; what we lack He will supply;
Let us ask in faith believing—on His promises rely;
He will ever be our Leader, whether smooth or rough the way,
And will prove Himself sufficient for the needs of every day.

Trusting even when it appears you have been forsaken; praying when it seems your words are simply entering a vast expanse where no one hears and no voice answers; believing that God's love is complete and that He is aware of your circumstances, even when your world seems to grind on as if setting its own direction and not caring for life or moving one inch in response to your petitions; desiring only what God's hands have planned for you; waiting patiently while seemingly starving to death, with your only fear being that your faith might fail—"this is the victory that has overcome the world"; this is genuine faith indeed. George MacDonald

JULY 16

"Because you have done this and have not withheld your son, your only son, I will . . . make your descendants as numerous as the stars in the sky . . . because you have obeyed me."

Genesis 22:16–18

From the time of Abraham, people have been learning that when they obey God's voice and surrender to Him whatever they hold most precious, He multiplies it thousands of times. Abraham gave up his one and only son at the Lord's command, and in doing so, all his desires and dreams for Isaac's life, as well as his own hope for a notable heritage, disappeared. Yet God restored Isaac to his father, and Abraham's family became "as numerous as the stars in the sky and as the sand on the seashore" (v. 17). And through his descendants, "when the set time had fully come, God sent his Son" (Galatians 4:4).

This is exactly how God deals with every child of His when we truly sacrifice. We surrender everything we own and accept poverty—then He sends wealth. We leave a growing area of ministry at His command—then He provides one better than we had ever dreamed. We surrender all our cherished hopes and die to self—then He sends overflowing joy and His "life . . . that [we] might have it more abundantly" (John 10:10 KJV).

The greatest gift of all was Jesus Christ Himself, and we can never fully comprehend the enormity of His sacrifice. Abraham, as the earthly father of the family of Christ, had to begin by surrendering himself and his only son, just as our heavenly Father sacrificed His only Son, Jesus. We could never have come to enjoy the privileges and joys as members of God's family *through any other way.* CHARLES GALLAUDET TRUMBULL

We sometimes seem to forget that *what God takes from us, He takes with fire,* and that the only road to a life of resurrection and ascension power leads us first to Gethsemane, the cross, and the tomb.

Dear soul, do you believe that Abraham's experience was unique and isolated? It is only an example and a pattern of how God deals with those who are prepared to obey Him whatever the cost. "After waiting patiently, Abraham received what was promised" (Hebrews 6:15), and so will you. The moment of your greatest sacrifice will also be the precise moment of your greatest and most miraculous blessing. God's river, which never runs dry, will overflow its banks, bringing you a flood of wealth and grace.

Indeed, there is nothing God will not do for those who will dare to step out in faith onto what appears to be only a mist. As they take their first step, they will find a rock beneath their feet. F. B. MEYER

JULY 17

"I will remain quiet and will look on from my dwelling place."

ISAIAH 18:4

In this passage, Assyria is marching against Ethiopia, whose people are described as "tall and smooth-skinned" (v. 2). As the army advances, God makes no effort to stop them, and it appears as though they will be allowed to do as they wish. The Lord is watching from His "dwelling place" while the sun continues to shine on them, yet "before the harvest" (v. 5) the entire proud army is defeated as easily as new growth is pruned from a vine.

Isn't this a beautiful picture of God—remaining quiet and watching? Yet His silence is not to be confused with passive agreement or consent. He is simply biding His time and will arise at the most opportune moment, just when the plans of the wicked are on the verge of success, in order to overwhelm the enemy with disaster. And as we see the evil of this world, as we watch the apparent success of wrongdoers, and as we suffer the oppression of those who hate us, let us remember those miraculous words of God—"I will remain quiet and will look on."

Yes, God does have another point of view, and there is wisdom behind His words. Why did Jesus watch His disciples straining at the oars through the stormy night? Why did He, though unseen by others, watch the sequence of anguishing events unfold in Bethany as Lazarus slowly passed through the stages of his terminal illness, succumbed to death, and was finally buried in a rocky tomb? Jesus was simply waiting for the perfect moment when He could intercede most effectively.

Is the Lord being *quiet* with you? Nevertheless, He is attentive and still sees everything. He has His finger on your pulse and is extremely sensitive to even the slightest change. And He will come to save you when the perfect moment has arrived. Daily Devotional Commentary

Whatever the Lord may ask of us or however slow He may seem to work, we can be absolutely sure He is never a confused or fearful Savior.

O troubled soul, beneath the rod,
Your Father speaks, be still, be still;
Learn to be silent unto God,
And let Him mold you to His will.

O praying soul, be still, be still,
He cannot break His promised Word;
Sink down into His blessed will,
And wait in patience on the Lord.

O waiting soul, be still, be strong,
And though He tarry, trust and wait;
Doubt not, He will not wait too long,
Fear not, He will not come too late.

JULY 18

The eyes of the Lord *range throughout the earth to strengthen those whose hearts are fully committed to him.*
2 Chronicles 16:9

God is looking for men and women whose hearts are firmly fixed on Him and who will continually trust Him for all He desires to do with their lives. God is ready and eager to work more powerfully than ever through His people, and the clock of the centuries is striking the eleventh hour.

The world is watching and waiting to see what God can do through a life committed to Him. And not only is the world waiting but God Himself awaits to see who will be the most completely devoted person who has ever lived: willing to be nothing so Christ may be everything; fully accepting God's purposes as his own; receiving Christ's humility, faith, love, and power yet never hindering God's plan but always allowing Him to continue His miraculous work. C. H. P.

There is no limit to what God can do through you, provided you do not seek your own glory.

George Mueller, at more than ninety years of age, in an address to ministers and other Christian workers, said, "*I was converted* in November 1825, but I didn't come to the point *of total surrender of my heart* until four years later, in July 1829. It was then I realized my love for money, prominence, position, power, and worldly pleasure was gone. God, and He alone, became my all in all. In Him I found everything I needed, and I desired nothing else. By God's grace, my understanding of His sufficiency has remained to this day, making me an exceedingly happy man. It has led me to care only about the things of God.

"And so, dear believers, I kindly ask if you have totally surrendered your heart to God, or is there something in your life you refuse to release, in spite of God's call?

"Before the point at which I surrendered my life, I read a little of the Scriptures but preferred other books. Yet since that time, the truth He has revealed to me of Himself has become an inexpressible blessing. Now I can honestly say from the depth of my heart that God is an infinitely wonderful Being.

"Please, never be satisfied until you too can express from your innermost soul, 'God is an infinitely wonderful Being!'" SELECTED

My prayer today is that God would make me an extraordinary Christian. GEORGE WHITEFIELD

JULY 19

"Shall I not drink the cup the Father has given me?"

JOHN 18:11

TO "DRINK THE CUP" WAS A GREATER THING THAN CALMING THE SEAS or raising the dead. The prophets and apostles could do amazing miracles, but they did not always do the will of God and thereby suffered as a result. Doing God's will and thus experiencing suffering is still the highest form of faith, and the most glorious Christian achievement.

Having your brightest aspirations as a young person forever crushed; bearing burdens daily that are always difficult, and never seeing relief; finding yourself worn down by poverty while simply desiring to do good for others and provide a comfortable living for those you love; being shackled by an incurable physical disability; being completely alone, separated from all those you love, to face the trauma of life alone; yet in all these, still being able to say through such a difficult school of discipline, "Shall I not drink the cup the Father has given me?"—this is faith at its highest, and spiritual success at its crowning point.

Great faith is exhibited not so much in doing as in suffering. CHARLES PARKHURST

In order to have a sympathetic God, we must have a suffering Savior, for true sympathy comes from understanding another person's hurt by suffering the same affliction. Therefore we cannot help others who suffer without paying a price ourselves, because afflictions are the cost we pay for our ability to sympathize. Those who wish to help others must first suffer. If we wish to rescue others, we must be willing to face the cross; experiencing the greatest happiness in life through ministering to others is impossible without drinking the cup Jesus drank and without submitting to the baptism He endured.

The most comforting of David's psalms were squeezed from his life by suffering, and if Paul had not been given "a thorn in the flesh" (2 Corinthians 12:7 KJV), we would have missed much of the heartbeat of tenderness that resonates through so many of his letters.

If you have surrendered yourself to Christ, your present circumstances that seem to be pressing so hard against you are the perfect tool in the Father's hand to chisel you into shape for eternity. So trust Him and never push away the instrument He is using, or you will miss the result of His work in your life.

Strange and difficult indeed
We may find it,
But the blessing that we need
Is behind it.

The school of suffering graduates exceptional scholars.

JULY 20

Since we have a great high priest . . . , Jesus the Son of God, let us hold firmly to the faith we profess. . . . Let us then approach God's throne of grace with confidence, so that we may receive mercy and find grace to help us in our time of need.

HEBREWS 4:14, 16

OUR GREAT HELPER IN PRAYER IS THE LORD JESUS CHRIST. HE IS OUR Advocate, ever pleading our case before the Father. He is our "great high priest," whose primary ministry has for centuries been intercession and prayer on our behalf. It is He who receives our imperfect petitions from our hands, cleanses them of their defects, corrects their error, and then claims their answer from His Father. And He does so strictly on the basis of His worth and righteousness through the sufficiency of His atonement.

Believer, are you lacking power in prayer? Look to Christ, for your blessed Advocate has already claimed your answer. And if you give up the fight just as the moment of victory approaches, you will grieve and disappoint Him. He has already entered "the Most Holy Place" (Exodus 26:33) on your behalf, holding up your name on the palms of His hands. The messenger is now on his way to bring you your blessing, and the Holy Spirit simply awaits your act of trust, so He may whisper in your heart the echo of the answer from the throne of God, "*It is done*" (Revelation 21:6). A. B. SIMPSON

The Holy Spirit is the one who works to make our prayers acceptable, yet we often forget this truth. He enlightens our mind so we may clearly see our desires, then softens our heart so we may feel them, and finally He awakens and focuses those desires toward godly things. He gives us a clear view of God's power and wisdom, provides grace "in our time of need," and strengthens our confidence in His truth so we will never waver.

Prayer is a wonderful thing, and each person of the Trinity is involved in every acceptable prayer. J. ANGELL JAMES

JULY 21

Let me make just one more request. Allow me one more test with the fleece.

JUDGES 6:39

THERE ARE THREE LEVELS OF FAITH IN THE CHRISTIAN EXPERIENCE. The first is being able to believe only when we see some sign or have some strong emotion. Like Gideon, we feel the fleece and are willing to trust God if it is wet. This may be genuine faith but it is imperfect. It is continually looking to feelings or some other sign instead of the Word of God. We have taken a great step toward maturity when we trust God without relying on our feelings. It is more of a blessing when we believe without experiencing any emotion.

While the first level of faith believes when our emotions are favorable, the second believes when all feelings are absent. And the third level transcends the other two, for it is faith that believes God and His Word when circumstances, emotions, appearances, people, and human reason all seem to urge something to the contrary. Paul exercised this level of faith when he said, "When neither sun nor stars appeared for many days and the storm continued raging, we finally gave up all hope of being saved" (Acts 27:20), then nevertheless went on to say, "Keep up your courage, men, *for I have faith in God* that it will happen just as he told me" (Acts 27:25).

May God grant us faith to completely trust His Word, even when every other sign points the other way. C. H. P.

When is the time to trust?
Is it when all is calm,
When waves the victor's palm,
And life is one glad psalm
Of joy and praise?

No! For the time to trust
Is when the waves beat high,
When storm clouds fill the sky,
And prayer is one long cry,
"Oh, help and save!"

When is the time to trust?
Is it when friends are true?
Is it when comforts woo,
And in all we say and do
We meet but praise?

No! For the time to trust
Is when we stand alone,
And summer birds have flown,
And every prop is gone,
All else but God.

When is the time to trust?
Is it some future day,
When you have tried your way,
And learned to trust and pray
By bitter woe?

No! For the time to trust
Is in this moment's need,
Poor, broken, bruised reed!
Poor, troubled soul, make speed
To trust your God.

When is the time to trust?
Is it when hopes beat high,

When sunshine gilds the sky,
And joy and ecstasy
Fill all the heart?

No! For the time to trust
Is when our joy has fled,
When sorrow bows the head,
And all is cold and dead,
All else but God.

Selected

JULY 22

Therefore will the Lord *wait, that he may be gracious unto you . . . blessed are all they that wait for him.*

Isaiah 30:18 KJV

We should not only understand the importance of our waiting on God but also realize something even more wonderful—the Lord waits on us. And the very thought of His waiting on us will give us renewed motivation and inspiration to "wait for him." It will also provide inexpressible confidence that our waiting will never be in vain. Therefore, in the spirit of waiting on God, let us seek to discover exactly what it means right now.

The Lord has an inconceivably glorious purpose for each of His children. "If this is true," you ask, "why is it that He continues to wait longer and longer to offer His grace and to provide the help I seek, even after I have come and waited on Him?" He does so because He is a wise gardener who "waits for the land to yield its valuable crop" and is [patient] . . . for the autumn and spring rains" (James 5:7). God knows He cannot gather the fruit until it is ripe, and He knows precisely when we are spiritually ready to receive blessings for our gain and His glory. And waiting in the sunshine of His love is what will ripen our soul for His blessings. Also, waiting under the clouds of trials is as important, for they will ultimately produce showers of blessings.

Rest assured that if God waits longer than we desire, it is simply to make the blessings doubly precious. Remember, He waited four thousand years, "but when the set time had fully come, God sent his Son" (Galatians 4:4). Our time is in His hands, and He will quickly avenge those He has chosen, swiftly coming to our support without ever delaying even one hour too long. ANDREW MURRAY

JULY 23

Sing . . . to the Lord, always giving thanks
to God the Father for everything.
EPHESIANS 5:19–20

NO MATTER THE SOURCE OF THE EVIL CONFRONTING YOU, IF YOU ARE in God and thereby completely surrounded by Him, you must realize that it has first passed through Him before coming to you. Because of this, you can thank Him for everything that comes your way. This does not mean thanking Him for the sin that accompanies evil, but offering thanks for what He will bring out of it and through it. May God make our life one of continual thanksgiving and praise, so He will then make everything a blessing.

I once saw a man draw some black dots on a piece of paper. Several of us looked at it yet saw nothing but an irregular arrangement of dots. Then he also drew a few lines, put in a few rests, and added a treble clef at the beginning. Suddenly we realized that the dots were musical notes, and as we began to sound them out, we were singing,

Praise God from whom all blessings flow,
Praise Him all creatures here below.

Each of us has many black dots or spots in our life, and we cannot understand *why* they are there or *why* God permitted them. But when we allow Him into our life to adjust the dots in the proper way, to draw the lines He desires, and to put rests at the proper places to separate us from certain things, then from the black dots and spots He will compose a glorious harmony.

So let us not hinder Him in His glorious work! C. H. P.

Would we know that the major chords were sweet,
If there were no minor key?
Would the painter's work be fair to our eyes,
Without shade on land or sea?
Would we know the meaning of happiness,
Would we feel that the day was bright,
If we'd never known what it was to grieve,
Nor gazed on the dark of night?

Many people owe the grandeur of their lives to their tremendous difficulties. CHARLES H. SPURGEON

When an organist presses the black keys of a great organ, the notes are just as beautiful as when he presses the white ones. Yet to fully demonstrate the capabilities of the instrument, he must press them all. SELECTED

JULY 24

Then they believed his promises and sang his praise. But they soon forgot what he had done and did not wait for his plan to unfold. In the desert they gave in to their craving; in the wilderness they put God to the test. So he gave them what they asked for, but sent a wasting disease among them.

PSALM 106:12–15

In Hebrews 11:27, we read that Moses "persevered because he saw him who is invisible." Yet in the above passage, exactly the opposite was true of the children of Israel. They persevered only when their circumstances were favorable, because they were primarily influenced by whatever appealed to their senses, instead of trusting in the invisible and eternal God.

Even today we have people who live an inconsistent Christian life because they have become preoccupied with things that are external. Therefore they focus on their circumstances rather than focusing on God. And God desires that we grow in our ability to see Him in everything and to realize the importance of seemingly insignificant circumstances if they are used to deliver a message from Him.

We read of the children of Israel, "*Then* they believed his promises." They did not believe until *after* they saw—once they saw Him work, "*then* they believed." They unabashedly doubted God when they came to the Red Sea, but when He opened the way and led them across and they *saw* Pharaoh and his army drowned—"*then* they believed." The Israelites continued to live this kind of up-and-down existence, because their faith was dependent on their circumstances. And this is certainly not the kind of faith God wants us to have.

The world says that "seeing is believing," but God wants us to believe in order to see. The psalmist said, "I would have despaired unless I had *believed that I would see* the goodness of the Lord in the land of the living" (Psalm 27:13 NASB).

Do you believe God only when your circumstances are favorable, or do you believe no matter what your circumstances may be? C. H. P.

Faith is believing what we do not see, and the reward for this kind of faith is to see what we believe. Saint Augustine

JULY 25

"You do not realize now what I am doing,
but later you will understand."

John 13:7

In this life, we have an incomplete view of God's dealings, seeing His plan only half finished and underdeveloped. Yet once we stand in the magnificent temple of eternity, we will have the proper perspective and will see everything fitting gracefully together!

Imagine going to the mountains of Lebanon during the reign of Israel's great king Solomon. Can you see the majestic cedar? It is the pride of all the other trees and has wrestled many years with the cold north winds! The summer sun has loved to smile upon it, while the night has caused its soft leaves to glisten with drops of dew. Birds have built their nests in its branches, and weary travelers and wandering shepherds have rested in its shade from the midday heat or taken shelter from the raging storms. And suddenly we realize that this old inhabitant of the forest has been doomed to fall victim to the woodsman's ax!

We watch as the ax makes its first gash on the cedar's gnarled trunk. Then we see its noble limbs stripped of their branches as the tree comes crashing to the ground. We cry out against the wanton destruction of this "Tree of God," as it is distinctively known, and express our anger over the demolition of this proud pillar in the forest temple of nature. We are tempted to exclaim with the prophet Zechariah, "*Wail, you juniper for the cedar has fallen . . . !*" (Zechariah 11:2), as if inviting the sympathy of every less-majestic plant and invoking inanimate things to also resent the offense.

We should not be so quick to complain but should follow the gigantic tree as the workmen of "Hiram king of Tyre" (2 Chronicles 2:3) take it down the mountainside. From there we should watch it being sailed on rafts along the blue water of the Mediterranean. And finally, we should behold it being placed as a glorious and polished beam in the temple of God. As you contemplate its final destination, seeing it in the Holy of Holies as a jewel in the diadem of the almighty King, can you honestly complain that this crown jewel of Lebanon was cut down, removed from the forest, and placed in such a noble setting? The cedar had once stood majestically in nature's sanctuary, but "the glory of this present house will be greater than the glory of the former house" (Haggai 2:9).

So many people are like these cedars of old! God's axes of trials have stripped them bare, and yet we can see no reason for such harsh and difficult circumstances. But God has a noble goal and purpose in mind: to place them as everlasting pillars and rafters in His heavenly Zion. And He says to them, "You will be a crown of splendor in the LORD's hand, a royal diadem in the hand of your God" (Isaiah 62:3). J. R. MACDUFF

I do not ask my cross to understand,
My way to see—
Better in darkness just to feel Your hand,
And follow Thee.

JULY 26

Through the Spirit we eagerly await by faith
the righteousness for which we hope.
GALATIANS 5:5

THERE ARE TIMES WHEN EVERYTHING LOOKS VERY DARK TO ME—SO dark that I have to wait before I have hope. Waiting *with* hope is very difficult, but true patience is expressed when we must even wait *for* hope. When we see no hint of success yet refuse to despair, when we see nothing but the darkness of night through our window yet keep the shutters open because stars may appear in the sky, and when we have an empty place in our heart yet will not allow it to be filled with anything less than God's best—that is the greatest kind of patience in the universe. It is the story of Job in the midst of the storm, Abraham on the road to Moriah, Moses in the desert of Midian, and the Son of Man in the Garden of Gethsemane. And there is no patience as strong as that which endures because we see "him who is invisible" (Hebrews 11:27). It is the kind of patience that waits for hope.

Dear Lord, You have made waiting beautiful and patience divine. You have taught us that Your will should be accepted, simply because it *is* Your will. You have revealed to us that a person may see nothing but sorrow in his cup yet still be willing to drink it because of a conviction that Your eyes see further than his own.

Father, give me Your divine power—the power of Gethsemane. Give me the strength to wait for hope—to look through the window when there are no stars. Even when my joy is gone, give me the strength to stand victoriously in the darkest night and say, "To my heavenly Father, the sun still shines."

I will have reached the point of greatest strength once I have learned to wait for hope. George Matheson

Strive to be one of the few who walk this earth with the ever present realization—every morning, noon, and night—that the unknown that people call heaven is directly behind those things that are visible.

JULY 27

Test me in this . . . and see if I will not throw open the floodgates of heaven and pour out so much blessing that there will not be room enough to store it.

Malachi 3:10

Here is what God is saying in this verse: "My dear child, I still have floodgates in heaven, and they are still in service. The locks open as easily as before, and the hinges have not grown rusty. In fact, I would rather throw them open to pour out the blessings than hold them back. I opened them for Moses, and the sea parted. I opened them for Joshua, and the Jordan River was stopped. I opened them for Gideon, and the armies of the enemy fled. And I will open them for you—*if you will only let Me.*

"On My side of the floodgates, heaven is still the same rich storehouse as always. The fountains and streams still overflow, and the treasure-rooms are still bursting with gifts. The need is not on *My* side but on *yours.*

I am waiting for you to '*test me in this.*' But you must first meet the condition I have set to 'bring the whole tithe into the storehouse' [Malachi 3:10], and thereby *give Me the opportunity to act.*" SELECTED

I will never forget my mother's concise paraphrase of Malachi 3:10. The actual Bible text begins with the words "Bring the whole tithe into the storehouse" and ends with "I will . . . pour out so much blessing that," in effect, "you will be embarrassed over your lack of space to receive it." But my mother's paraphrase was this: "Give all He asks and take all He promises." SAMUEL DICKEY GORDON

God's ability to perform is far beyond our prayers—even our greatest prayers! I have recently been thinking of some of the requests I have made of Him innumerable times in my prayers. And what have I requested? I have asked for a cupful, while He owns the entire ocean! I have asked for one simple ray of light, while He holds the sun! My best asking falls immeasurably short of my Father's ability to give, which is far beyond what we could ever ask. JOHN HENRY JOWETT

All the rivers of Your grace I claim,
Over every promise write my name. [Ephesians 1:8–19]

JULY 28

His way is in the whirlwind and the storm.
NAHUM 1:3

I REMEMBER WHEN I WAS A YOUNG PERSON ATTENDING SCHOOL IN THE vicinity of Mount Pleasant. One day I sat on the side of the mountain and watched a storm as it moved through the valley. The skies were filled with darkness, and thunder began to shake the earth. It seemed as though the lush landscape were completely changed, and its beauty gone forever. But the storm passed quickly and soon moved out of the valley.

If I had sat in the same place the following day and said, "Where is that intense storm and all its terrible darkness?" the grass would have said, "Part of it is in me." The beautiful daisy would have said, "Part of it is in me." And all the other flowers, fruits, and everything that grows in the ground would have said, "Part of the storm has produced the radiance in me."

Have you ever asked the Lord to make you like Him? Have you ever desired the fruit of the Spirit and prayed for sweetness, gentleness, and love? If so, then never fear the fierce storms that even now may be blowing through your life. Storms bring blessings, and rich fruit will be harvested later. HENRY WARD BEECHER

The flowers live by the tears that fall
From the sad face of the skies;
And life would have no joys at all,
Were there no watery eyes.
Love the sorrow, for grief will bring
Its own reward in later years;
The rainbow! See how fair a thing
God has built up from tears.
HENRY S. SUTTON

JULY 29

Have you entered the storehouses . . . which
I reserve for times of trouble?
JOB 38:22–23

OUR TRIALS ARE GREAT OPPORTUNITIES, BUT ALL TOO OFTEN WE SIMPLY see them as large obstacles. If only we would recognize every difficult situation as something God has chosen to prove His love to us, each obstacle would then become a place of shelter and rest, and a demonstration to others of His inexpressible power. If we would look for the signs of His glorious handiwork, then every cloud would indeed become a rainbow, and every difficult mountain path would become one of ascension, transformation, and glorification.

If we would look at our past, most of us would realize that the times we endured the greatest stress and felt that every path was blocked were the very times our heavenly Father chose to do the kindest things for us and bestow His richest blessings.

God's most beautiful jewels are often delivered in rough packages by very difficult people, but within the package we will find the very treasures of the King's palace and the Bridegroom's love. A. B. Simpson

We must trust the Lord through the darkness, and honor Him with unwavering confidence even in the midst of difficult situations. The reward of this kind of faith will be like that of an eagle shedding its feathers is said to receive—a renewed sense of youth and strength. J. R. Macduff

If we could see beyond today
As God can see;
If all the clouds should roll away,
The shadows flee;
O'er present griefs we would not fret.
Each sorrow we would soon forget,
For many joys are waiting yet
For you and me.

If we could know beyond today
As God does know,
Why dearest treasures pass away
And tears must flow;
And why the darkness leads to light,
Why dreary paths will soon grow bright;
Some day life's wrongs will be made right,
Faith tells us so.

"If we could see, if we could know,"
We often say,
But God in love a veil does throw
Across our way;
We cannot see what lies before,
And so we cling to Him the more,
He leads us till this life is o'er;
Trust and obey.

JULY 30

"If anyone gives even a cup of cold water . . . that person will certainly not lose [his] reward."
MATTHEW 10:42

WHAT SHALL I DO? I EXPECT TO PASS THROUGH THIS WORLD BUT ONCE. Therefore any good work, kindness, or service I can render to any person or animal, let me do it now. Let me not neglect or delay to do it, for I will not pass this way again. QUAKER SAYING

It isn't the thing you do, dear,
It's the thing you leave undone,
That gives you the bitter heartache
At the setting of the sun;
The tender word unspoken,
The letter you did not write,
The flower you might have sent, dear,
Are your haunting ghosts at night.

The stone you might have lifted
Out of your brother's way,
The bit of heartfelt counsel

You were hurried too much to say;
The loving touch of the hand, dear,
The gentle and winsome tone,
That you had no time or thought for,
With troubles enough of your own.

These little acts of kindness,
So easily out of mind,
These chances to be angels,
Which even mortals find—
They come in nights of silence,
To take away the grief,
When hope is faint and feeble,
And a drought has stopped belief.

For life is all too short, dear.
And sorrow is all too great,
To allow our slow compassion
That tarries until too late.
And it's not the thing you do,
dear, It's the thing you leave undone,
That gives you the bitter heartache,
At the setting of the sun.
ADELAIDE PROCTOR

Give what you have, for you never know—to someone else it may be better than you can even dare to think. HENRY WADSWORTH LONGFELLOW

JULY 31

With skillful hands he led them.

PSALM 78:72

When you are unsure which course to take, totally submit your own judgment to that of the Spirit of God, asking Him to shut every door except the right one. But meanwhile keep moving ahead and consider the absence of a direct indication from God to be the evidence of His will that you are on His path. And as you continue down the long road, you will find that He has gone before you, locking doors you otherwise would have been inclined to enter. Yet you can be sure that somewhere beyond the locked doors is one He has left unlocked. And when you open it and walk through, you will find yourself face to face with a turn in the river of opportunity—one that is broader and deeper than anything you ever dared to imagine, even in your wildest dreams. So set sail on it, because it flows to the open sea.

God often guides us through our circumstances. One moment, our way may seem totally blocked, but then suddenly some seemingly trivial incident occurs, appearing as nothing to others but speaking volumes to the keen eye of faith. And sometimes these events are repeated in various ways in response to our prayers. They certainly are not haphazard results of chance but are God opening up the way we should walk, by directing our circumstances. *And they begin to multiply as we advance toward our goal*, just as the lights of a city seem to increase as we speed toward it while traveling at night. F. B. Meyer

If you go to God for guidance, He will guide you. But do not expect Him to console you by showing you His list of purposes concerning you, when you have displayed distrust or even half-trust in Him. What He will do, if you will trust Him and go cheerfully ahead when He shows you the way, is to guide you still farther. Horace Bushnell

As moves my fragile boat across the storm-swept sea,
Great waves beat o'er her side, as north wind blows;
Deep in the darkness hid lie threat'ning rocks and reefs;
But all of these, and more, my Pilot knows.

Sometimes when darkness falls, and every light's gone out,
I wonder to what port my frail ship goes;
Although the night be long, and restless all my hours,
My distant goal, I'm sure, my Pilot knows.

Thomas Curtis Clark

AUGUST 1

Offer yourselves to God as those who have
been brought from death to life.

Romans 6:13

One night I went to hear a sermon on consecration. Nothing special came to me from the message, but as the preacher knelt to pray, he said, "O Lord, You know we can trust the Man who died for us." That was my message. As I rose from my knees and walked down the street to catch the train, I deeply pondered all that consecration would mean to my life. I was afraid as I considered the personal cost, and suddenly, above the noise of the street traffic, came this message: "You can trust the Man who died for you." I boarded the train, and as I traveled toward home, I thought of the changes, sacrifices, and disappointments that consecration might mean in my life—and I was still afraid.

Upon arriving home, I went straight to my room, fell on my knees, and saw my life pass before my eyes. I was a Christian, an officer in the church, and a Sunday school superintendent, but I had never yielded my life to God with a definite act of my will. Yet as I thought of my own "precious" plans that might be thwarted, my beloved hopes to be surrendered, and my chosen profession that I might have to abandon—*I was afraid.*

I completely failed to see the better things God had for me, so my soul was running from Him. And then for the last time, with a swift force of convicting power to my inmost heart, came that searching message: "*My child, you can trust the Man who died for you. If you cannot trust Him, then whom can you trust?*" Finally that settled it for me, for in a flash of light I realized that the Man who loved me enough to die for me could be absolutely trusted with the total concerns of the life He had saved.

Dear friend, you can trust the Man who died for you. You can trust Him to thwart each plan that should be stopped and to complete each one that results in His greatest glory and your highest good. You can trust Him to lead you down the path that is the very best in this world for you. J. H. M.

Just as I am, Thy love unknown,
Has broken every barrier down,
Now to be Thine, yea, Thine alone,
O Lamb of God, I come!

Life is not wreckage to be saved out of the world but an investment to be used in the world.

AUGUST 2

"I will turn all my mountains into roads."

ISAIAH 49:11

GOD WILL MAKE OUR OBSTACLES SERVE HIS PURPOSES. WE ALL HAVE mountains in our lives, and often they are people and things that threaten to block the progress of our spiritual life. The obstacles may be untruths told about us; a difficult occupation; "a thorn in [the] flesh" (2 Corinthians 12:7); or our daily cross. And often we pray for their removal, for we tend to think that if only these were removed, we would live a more tender, pure, and holy life.

"How foolish you are, and how slow to believe . . . !" (Luke 24:25). These are the very conditions we need for achievement, and they have been put in our lives as the means of producing the gifts and qualities for which we have been praying so long. We pray for patience for many years, and when something begins to test us beyond our endurance, we run from it. We try to avoid it, we see it as some insurmountable obstacle to our desired goal, and we believe that if it was removed, we would experience immediate deliverance and victory.

This is not true! We would simply see the temptations to be impatient end. This would not be patience. The only way genuine patience can be acquired is by enduring the very trials that seem so unbearable today.

Turn from your running and submit. Claim by faith to be a partaker in the patience of Jesus and face your trials in Him. There is nothing in your life that distresses or concerns you that cannot become submissive to the highest purpose. Remember, they are *God's* mountains. He puts them there for a reason, and we know He will never fail to keep His promise.

"God understands the way to it and he alone knows where it dwells, for he views the ends of the earth and sees everything under the heavens" (Job 28:23–24). So when we come to the foot of the mountains, we will find our way. F. B. MEYER

The purpose of our trials is not only to test our worthiness but also to increase it, just as the mighty oak is tested by the storms as well as strengthened by them.

AUGUST 3

Be courageous; be strong.

1 CORINTHIANS 16:13

NEVER PRAY FOR AN EASIER LIFE—PRAY TO BE A STRONGER PERSON! Never pray for tasks equal to your power—pray for power equal to your tasks. Then doing your work will be no miracle—*you* will be the miracle. PHILLIPS BROOKS

We must remember that Christ will not lead us to greatness through an easy or self-indulgent life. An easy life does not lift us up but only takes us down. Heaven is always above us, and we must continually be looking toward it.

Some people always avoid things that are costly, or things that require self-denial, self-restraint, and self-sacrifice. Yet it is hard work and difficulties that ultimately lead us to greatness, for greatness is not found by walking the moss-covered path laid out for us through the meadow. It is found by being sent to carve out our own path with our own hands.

Are you willing to sacrifice to reach the glorious mountain peaks of God's purpose for you? SELECTED

Be strong!
We are not here to play, to dream, to drift;
We have hard work to do, and loads to lift.
Shun not the struggle; face it.
It's God's gift.
Be strong!
Say not the days are evil—Who's to blame?
Or fold your hands, as in defeat—O shame!
Stand up, speak out, and bravely,
In God's name.
Be strong!
It matters not how deep entrenched the wrong,
How hard the battle goes, the day how long,
Faint not, fight on!
Tomorrow comes the song.

MALTBIE D. BABCOCK

AUGUST 4

Jesus looked up and said, "Father, I thank you that you have heard me."

JOHN 11:41

The sequence of events in this passage seems strange and unusual. Lazarus was still in his tomb, yet Jesus' thanksgiving *preceded* the miracle of raising him from the dead. It seems that thanks would only have been lifted up once the great miracle had been accomplished and Lazarus had been restored to life. But Jesus gave thanks for what He was about to receive. His gratitude sprang forth *before* the blessing had arrived, in an expression of assurance that it was certainly on its way. The song of victory was sung *before* the battle had been fought. It was the Sower singing the song of harvest—it was thanksgiving before the miracle!

Who ever thinks of announcing a victory song as the army is just heading out to the battlefield? And where do we ever hear a song of gratitude and thanksgiving for an answer that has not yet been received?

Yet in this Scripture passage, there is nothing strange, forced, or unreasonable to the Master's sequence of praise before the miracle. *Praise* is actually the most vital preparation to the working of miracles. Miracles are performed through spiritual power, and our spiritual power is always in proportion to our *faith*. John Henry Jowett

Praise Changes Things

Nothing pleases God more than praise as part of our prayer life, and nothing blesses someone who prays as much as the praise that is offered. I once received a great blessing from this while in China. I had recently received bad news from home, and deep shadows of darkness seemed to cover my soul. I prayed but the darkness remained. I forced myself to endure but the shadows only deepened. Then suddenly one day, as I entered a missionary's home at an inland station, I saw these words on the wall: "Try giving thanks." So I did, and in a moment every shadow was gone, never to return. Yes, the psalmist was right: "It is good to praise the Lord" (Psalm 92:1). Henry W. Frost

AUGUST 5

"My grace is sufficient for you."

2 CORINTHIANS 12:9

"GOD WAS PLEASED" (1 CORINTHIANS 1:21) TO TAKE MY YOUNGEST child from this world, under circumstances that caused me severe trials and pain. And as I returned home from the church cemetery, having just laid my little one's body in the grave, I felt a compulsion to preach to my people on the meaning of trials.

I found that the verse "My grace is sufficient for you" was the text of next week's Sunday school lesson, so I chose it as my Master's message to the congregation, as well as His message to me. Yet while trying to write the sermon, I found that in all honesty, I could not say that the words were true in my life. Therefore I knelt down and asked the Lord to make His grace sufficient for me. While I was pleading in this way, I opened my eyes and saw this exact verse framed and hanging on the wall. My mother had given it to me a few days before, when I was still at the vacation resort where our little child had been taken from us. I had asked someone to hang it on the wall at home during my absence but had not yet noticed its words. Now as I looked up and wiped my eyes, the words met my gaze: "My grace *is* sufficient for you."

The word "is" was highlighted in bright green, while the words "my" and "you" were painted in yet another color. In a moment, a message flashed straight to my soul, coming as a rebuke for having prayed such a prayer as, "Lord, make Your grace sufficient for me." His answer was almost an audible voice that said, "How dare you ask for something that *is*? I cannot make My grace any more sufficient than I have already made it. Get up and believe it, and you will find it to be true in your life."

The Lord says it in the simplest way: "My grace *is* [not will be or may be] sufficient for you." The words "my," "is," and "you" were from that moment indelibly written upon my heart. And thankfully, I have been trying to live in the reality of that truth from that day to the present time.

The underlying lesson that came to me through this experience, and that I seek to convey to others, is this: *Never change God's facts into hopes or prayers but simply accept them as realities, and you will find them to be powerful as you believe them.* H. W. Webb Peploe

He giveth more grace when the burdens grow greater,
He sendeth more strength when the labors increase;
To added affliction He addeth His mercies,
To multiplied trials His multiplied peace.

When we have exhausted our store of endurance,
When our strength has failed ere the day is half done,
When we reach the end of our hoarded resources
Our Father's full giving is only begun.

His love has no limit, His grace has no measure,
His power no boundary known unto men;
For out of His infinite riches in Jesus
He giveth and giveth and giveth again.

Annie Johnson Flint

AUGUST 6

Awake, north wind, and come, south wind! Blow on my garden, that its fragrance may spread everywhere.

Song of Songs 4:16

Let us examine the meaning of this prayer for a moment. It is rooted in the fact that in the same way beautiful fragrances may lie *hidden* in a spice plant, certain *gifts* may lie unused or undeveloped in a Christian's heart. Many seeds of a profession of faith may be planted, but from some the air is never filled with the aroma of holy desires or godly deeds. The same winds blow on the thistle and the spice plant, but only *one* of them emits a rich fragrance.

Sometimes God causes severe winds of trial to blow upon His children to develop their gifts. Just as a torch burns more brightly when waved back and forth, and just as a juniper plant smells sweetest when thrown into the flames, so the richest qualities of a Christian often arise under the strong winds of suffering and adversity. Bruised hearts often emit the fragrance that God loves to smell.

I had a tiny box, a precious box
Of human love—my perfume of great price;
I kept it close within my heart of hearts
And scarce would lift the lid lest it should waste
Its fragrance on the air. One day a strange
Deep sorrow came with crushing weight, and fell
Upon my costly treasure, sweet and rare,
And broke the box to pieces. All my heart
Rose in dismay and sorrow at this waste,
But as I mourned, behold a miracle
Of grace Divine. My human love was changed
To Heaven's own, and poured in healing streams
On other broken hearts, while soft and clear
A voice above me whispered, "Child of Mine,
With comfort wherewith you are comforted,
From this time forth, go comfort others,
And you will know blest fellowship with Me,
Whose broken heart of love has healed the world."

AUGUST 7

After they prayed, the place where they were meeting was shaken. And they were all filled with the Holy Spirit and spoke the word of God boldly. . . . With great power the apostles continued to testify to the resurrection of the Lord Jesus.

ACTS 4:31, 33

Christmas Evans, a Welsh preacher of the late-eighteenth and early-nineteenth centuries, once wrote the following account in his diary.

"One Sunday afternoon I was traveling by horseback to an appointment. Suddenly as I went along a very lonely road, I was convicted of having a cold heart. I dismounted, tethered my horse to a tree, and found a secluded spot. Then, walking back and forth in agony, I reviewed my life. I waited before God in brokenness and sorrow for three hours. Finally a sweet sense of His forgiving love broke over me, and I received a fresh filling of His Holy Spirit.

"As the sun was setting, I walked back to the road, found my horse, and rode on to my appointment. The following day I preached with so much new power, to a vast gathering of people on a hillside, that revival broke out and ultimately spread through all of Wales."

This explains the great question of the born-again—the password of the early church—"*Did you receive the Holy Spirit when you believed?*" (Acts 19:2).

Oh, the Spirit-filled life; is it thine, is it thine?
Is your soul wholly filled with the Spirit Divine?
As a child of the King, has He fallen on thee?
Does He reign in your soul, so that all men may see
The dear Savior's blest image reflected in thee?

Has He swept through your soul like the waves of the sea?
Does the Spirit of God daily rest upon thee?
Does He sweeten your life, does He keep you from care?
Does He guide you and bless you in answer to prayer?
Is your joy to be led of the Lord ev'rywhere?

Is He near you each hour, does He stand at your side?
Does He clothe you with strength, has He come to abide?
Does He teach you to know that all things may be done

Through the grace and the power of the Crucified One?
Does He witness to you of the glorified Son?

Has He purified you with the fire from above?
Is He first in your thoughts, does He have all your love?
Is His service your choice, and your sacrifice sweet?
Is your doing His will both your drink and your meat?
Do you run at His calling with glad eager feet?

Has He freed you from self and from all of your greed?
Do you hasten to comfort your brother in need?
As a soldier of Christ does your power endure?
Is your hope in the Lord everlasting and sure?
Are you patient and meek, are you tender and pure?

Oh, the Spirit-filled life may be thine, may be thine,
Ever in your soul Shechinah glory may shine;
It is yours to live with the tempests all stilled,
It is yours with God's blest Holy Spirit to be filled;
It is yours, even yours, for your Lord has so willed.

AUGUST 8

You are my King and my God, who decrees victories for Jacob.

PSALM 44:4

THERE ARE NO ENEMIES TO YOUR GROWTH IN GRACE, OR TO YOUR Christian work, that were not included in your Savior's victory. Remember, "The LORD said to Joshua, 'Do not be afraid of them, because . . . I will hand all of them . . . over to [you]'" (Joshua 11:6). Also recall the fact that when you resist your enemies, they "will flee from you" (James 4:7). And remember what Joshua said to the people: "Do not be afraid; do not be discouraged. Be strong and courageous" (Joshua 10:25). The Lord is with you, "mighty men of valour" (Joshua 1:14 KJV), and you are mighty because you are one with the Mightiest. So claim victory!

Whenever your enemies are closing in on you, *claim victory*! Whenever your heart and your flesh fail you, look up and claim VICTORY! Be sure you claim your share in the triumph that Jesus won, for He won it not for Himself alone but for us all. Remember that you were in Him when He won it—so *claim victory*!

Count Christ's victory as yours and gather the spoils of the war. Neither the giant "descendants of Anak" (Numbers 13:33) nor fortified cities need intimidate or defeat you. You are a part of the conquering army. *Claim your share in the Savior's victory.* F. B. MEYER

We are children of the King. Therefore which of these most honors our divine Sovereign: failing to claim our rights and even doubting they belong to us, or asserting our privilege as children of the Royal Family and demanding the rights that accompany our inheritance?

AUGUST 9

Blessed are those whose strength is in you . . . As they pass through the Valley of Baca, they make it a place of springs.

PSALM 84:5–6

COMFORT IS NOT GIVEN TO US WHEN WE ARE LIGHTHEARTED AND cheerful. We must travel the depths of emotion in order to experience comfort—one of God's most precious gifts. And then we must be prepared to become coworkers with Him.

When the shadows of night—needed night—gather over the garden of our souls, when leaves close up and flowers no longer reflect any sunlight within their folded petals, and when we experience even the thickest darkness, we must remember that we will never be found wanting and that the comforting drops of heavenly dew fall only after the sun has set.

I have been through the valley of weeping,
The valley of sorrow and pain;
But the "God of all comfort" was with me,
At hand to uphold and sustain.

As the earth needs the clouds and sunshine,
Our souls need both sorrow and joy;
So He places us oft in the furnace,
The dross from the gold to destroy.

When he leads through some valley of trouble,
His omnipotent hand we trace;
For the trials and sorrows He sends us,
Are part of His lessons in grace.

Oft we run from the purging and pruning,
Forgetting the Gardener knows
That the deeper the cutting and trimming,
The richer the cluster that grows.

Well He knows that affliction is needed;
He has a wise purpose in view,
And in the dark valley He whispers,
"Soon you'll understand what I do."

As we travel through life's shadowed valley,
Fresh springs of His love ever rise;
And we learn that our sorrows and losses,
Are blessings just sent in disguise.

So we'll follow wherever He leads us,
Let the path be dreary or bright;

For we've proved that our God can give comfort;
Our God can give songs in the night.

AUGUST 10

[Yet] when he heard that Lazarus was sick, he
stayed where he was two more days.

JOHN 11:6

THIS MIRACULOUS STORY BEGINS WITH THE FOLLOWING DECLARATION: "Jesus loved Martha and her sister and Lazarus" (v. 5). It is as if God were teaching us that at the very heart and foundation of all His dealings with us, no matter how dark and mysterious they may be, we must dare to believe in and affirm His infinite, unmerited, and unchanging love. Yet love permits pain to occur.

Mary and Martha never doubted that Jesus would quickly avert every obstacle to keep their brother from death, "yet when he heard that Lazarus was sick, he stayed where he was two more days."

What a startling word: "*Yet*"! Jesus refrained from going not because He did not love them but because He *did* love them. It was His love alone that kept Him from hurrying at once to their beloved yet grief-stricken home. Anything less than infinite love would have rushed instantly to the relief of those beloved and troubled hearts, in an effort to end their grief, to have the blessing of wiping and stopping the flow of their tears, and to cause their sorrow and pain to flee. Only the power of divine love could have held back the spontaneity of the Savior's tenderheartedness until the angel of pain had finished his work.

Who can estimate the great debt we owe to suffering and pain? If not for them, we would have little capacity for many of the great virtues of the Christian life. Where would our faith be if not for the trials that test it; or patience, without anything to endure or experience and without tribulations to develop it? SELECTED

Loved! then the way will not be drear;
For One we know is ever near,
Proving it to our hearts so clear
That we are loved.

Loved when our sky is clouded o'er,
And days of sorrow press us sore;
Still we will trust Him evermore,
For we are loved.

Time, that affects all things below,
Can never change the love He'll show;
The heart of Christ with love will flow,
And we are loved.

AUGUST 11

Though the fig tree does not bud and there are no grapes on the vines, though the olive crop fails and the fields produce no food, though there are no sheep in the pen and no cattle in the stalls, yet I will rejoice in the LORD, *I will be joyful in God my Savior.*

HABAKKUK 3:17–18

I ASK YOU TO OBSERVE WHAT A DISASTROUS SITUATION IS BEING described in this passage and to notice how courageous is the faith that is expressed. It is as if the writer were actually saying, "Even if I am forced to undergo the extreme condition of not knowing where to find my next meal, and although my house is empty and my fields yield no crops and I see the evidence of divine pestilence where I once saw the fruits of God's plentiful provision, '*yet I will rejoice in the* LORD.'"

I believe that these words are worthy of being *written forever in stone with a diamond tool.* Oh, by God's grace, may they be deeply etched on the tablets of each of our hearts! Although the above verse is very concise, it nevertheless implies or expresses the following thoughts of the writer: that in his time of distress he would flee to God; that he would maintain his spiritual composure under the darkest of circumstances; and that in the midst of everything, he would delight himself with a sacred joy in God and have cheerful expectations of Him.

Heroic confidence! Glorious faith! Unconquerable love! PHILIP DODDRIDGE

Last night I heard a robin singing in the rain,
And the raindrop's patter made a sweet refrain,
Making all the sweeter the music of the strain.

So, I thought, when trouble comes, as trouble will,
Why should I stop singing? Just beyond the hill
It may be that sunshine floods the green world still.

He who faces the trouble with a heart of cheer
Makes the burden lighter. If there falls a tear,
Sweeter is the cadence in the song we hear.

I have learned your lesson, bird with spotted wing,
Listening to your music with its tune of spring—
When the storm cloud darkens, it's the time to sing.

EBEN EUGENE REXFORD

AUGUST 12

He has given us his very great and precious promises.

2 PETER 1:4

When a shipbuilder erects a boat, does he do so only to keep it on the scaffolding? No, he builds it to sail the seas and to weather the storms. In fact, if he does not think of strong winds and hurricanes as he builds it, he is a poor shipbuilder.

In the same way, when God made you a believer, He meant to test you. And when He gave you promises and asked you to trust them, He made His promises suitable for times of storms and high seas. Do you believe that some of His promises are counterfeit, similar to a life vest that looks good in the store but is of no use in the sea?

We have all seen swords that are beautiful but are useless in war, or shoes made for decoration but not for walking. Yet God's shoes are made of iron and brass, and we can walk all the way to heaven in them, without ever wearing them out. And we could swim the Atlantic a thousand times in His life vest, with no fear of ever sinking. His Word of promise is meant to be tried and tested.

There is nothing Christ dislikes more than for His people to publicly profess Him and then not use Him. He loves for us to make use of Him, for His covenant blessings are not simply meant to be looked at but should be appropriated. Our Lord Jesus has been given to us for our present use. Are you making use of Him as you should?

O beloved, I plead with you not to treat God's promises as something to be displayed in a museum but to use them as everyday sources of comfort. And whenever you have a time of need, trust the Lord. Charles H. Spurgeon

Go to the depths of God's promise,
And claim whatsoever you will;
The blessing of God will not fail you,
His Word He will surely fulfill.

How can God say no to something He has promised?

AUGUST 13

If clouds are full of water, they pour rain upon the earth.

ECCLESIASTES 11:3

IF WE BELIEVE THE MESSAGE OF THIS VERSE, THEN WHY DO WE DREAD the clouds that darken our sky? It is true that for a while the dark clouds hide the sun, but it is not extinguished and it will soon shine again. Meanwhile those clouds are filled with rain, and the darker they are, the more likely they are to bring plentiful showers.

How can we have rain without clouds? Our troubles have always brought us blessings, and they always will, for they are the dark chariots of God's bright and glorious grace. Before long the clouds will be emptied, and every tender plant will be happier due to the showers. Our God may drench us with grief, but He will refresh us with His mercy. Our Lord's love letters often come to us in dark envelopes. His wagons may rumble noisily across the sky, but they are loaded with benefits. And His rod blossoms with sweet flowers and nourishing fruits. So let us not worry about the clouds. Instead, let us sing because May flowers are brought to us through April clouds and showers.

O Lord, "clouds are the dust of [your] feet" (Nahum 1:3)! Help us remember how near You are during the dark and cloudy days! Love beholds You and is glad. Faith sees the clouds emptying themselves and thereby making the hills on every side rejoice. CHARLES H. SPURGEON

What seems so dark to your dim sight
May be a shadow, seen aright
Making some brightness doubly bright.

The flash that struck your tree—no more
To shelter thee—lets heaven's blue floor
Shine where it never shone before.

The cry wrung from your spirit's pain
May echo on some far-off plain,
And guide a wanderer home again.

The blue sky of heaven is much larger than the dark clouds.

AUGUST 14

"You would have no power over me if it were not given to you from above."
JOHN 19:11

NOTHING THAT IS NOT PART OF GOD'S WILL IS ALLOWED TO COME INTO the life of someone who trusts and obeys Him. This truth should be enough to make our life one of ceaseless thanksgiving and joy, because God's will is the most hopeful, pleasant, and glorious thing in the world. It is the continuous working of His omnipotent power for our benefit, with nothing to prevent it, *if* we remain surrendered and believing.

Someone who was passing through the deep water of affliction wrote a friend:

> Isn't it glorious to know that no matter how unjust something may be, even when it seems to have come from Satan himself, *by the time it reaches us it is God's will for us* and will ultimately work to our good?

"And we know that in all things God works for the good of those who love him" (Romans 8:28). Think of what Christ said even as He was betrayed: "*Shall I not drink the cup the Father has given me?*" (John 18:11).

We live fascinating lives if we are living in the center of God's will. All the attacks that Satan hurls at us through the sins of others are not only powerless to harm us but are transformed into blessings along the way.
HANNAH WHITALL SMITH

In the center of the circle
Of the will of God I stand:
There can come no second causes,
All must come from His dear hand.
All is well! for it's my Father
Who my life has planned.

Shall I pass through waves of sorrow?
Then I know it will be best;
Though I cannot tell the reason,
I can trust, and so am blest.
God is Love, and God is faithful.
So in perfect Peace I rest.

With the shade and with the sunshine,
With the joy and with the pain,
Lord, I trust You! both are needed,
Each Your wayward child to train,
Earthly loss, if we will know it,
Often means our heavenly gain.

I. G. W.

AUGUST 15

We must go through many hardships to enter the kingdom of God.

Acts 14:22

The best things in life are the result of being wounded. Wheat must be crushed before becoming bread, and incense must be burned by fire before its fragrance is set free. The earth must be broken with a sharp plow before being ready to receive the seed. And it is a broken heart that pleases God.

Yes, the sweetest joys of life are the fruits of sorrow. Human nature seems to need suffering to make it fit to be a blessing to the world.

Beside my cottage door it grows,
The loveliest, daintiest flower that blows,
A sweetbrier rose.

At dewy morn or twilight's close,
The rarest perfume from it flows,
This strange wild rose.

But when the raindrops on it beat,
Ah, then, its odors grow more sweet,
About my feet.

Often with loving tenderness,
Its soft green leaves I gently press,
In sweet caress.

A still more wondrous fragrance flows
The more my fingers close
And crush the rose.

Dear Lord, oh, let my life be so
Its perfume when strong winds blow,
The sweeter flow.

And should it be Your blessed will,
With crushing grief my soul to fill,
Press harder still.

And while its dying fragrance flows
I'll whisper low, "He loves and knows
His crushed brier rose."

If you aspire to be a person of consolation, if you want to share the priestly gift of sympathy, if you desire to go beyond giving commonplace comfort to a heart that is tempted, and if you long to go through the daily exchanges of life with the kind of tact that never inflicts pain, then you must be prepared to pay the price for a costly education—for like Christ, you must suffer. Frederick William Robertson

AUGUST 16

I waited patiently for the Lord.

Psalm 40:1

Waiting is much more difficult than walking, for waiting requires patience, and patience is a rare virtue. We enjoy knowing that God builds hedges around His people, when we look at the hedge from the aspect of protection. But when we see it growing higher and higher until we can no longer see over it, we wonder if we will ever get out of our little sphere of influence and service, where we feel trapped. Sometimes it is hard for us to understand why we do not have a larger area of service, and it becomes difficult for us to "brighten the corner" where we are. But God has a purpose in all of *His* delays. "The steps of a good man are ordered by the Lord" (Psalm 37:23 KJV).

Next to this verse, in the margin of his Bible, George Mueller made this note: "And the *stops* too." It is a sad mistake for someone to break through God's hedges. It is a vital principle of the Lord's guidance for a Christian never to move from the spot where he is sure God has placed him, until the "pillar of cloud" (Exodus 13:21) moves. Sunday School Times

Once we learn to wait for the Lord's leading in everything, we will know the strength that finds *its highest point in an even and steady walk.* Many of us are lacking the strength we so desire, but God gives complete power for every task He calls us to perform. Waiting—keeping yourself faithful to His leading—this is the secret of strength. And anything that does not align with obedience to Him is a waste of time and energy. Watch and wait for His leading. Samuel Dickey Gordon

Must life be considered a failure for someone compelled to stand still, forced into inaction and required to watch the great, roaring tides of life from shore? No—victory is then to be won by standing still and quietly waiting. Yet this is a thousand times harder to do than in the past, when you rushed headlong into the busyness of life. It requires much more courage to stand and wait and still not lose heart or lose hope, to submit to the will of God, to give up opportunities for work and leave honors to others, and to be quiet, confident, and rejoicing while the busy multitude goes happily along their way.

The greatest life is: "after you have done everything, to stand" (Ephesians 6:13). J. R. Miller

AUGUST 17

I have faith in God that it will happen just as he told me.

Acts 27:25

A number of years ago I went to America with a steamship captain who was a very devoted Christian. When we were off the coast of Newfoundland, he said to me, "The last time I sailed here, which was five weeks ago, something happened that revolutionized my entire Christian life. I had been on the bridge for twenty-four straight hours when George Mueller of Bristol, England, who was a passenger on board, came to me and said, 'Captain, I need to tell you that I must be in Quebec on Saturday afternoon.' 'That is impossible,' I replied. 'Very well,' Mueller responded, 'if your ship cannot take me, God will find some other way, for I have never missed an engagement in fifty-seven years. Let's go down to the chartroom to pray.'

"I looked at this man of God and thought to myself, 'What lunatic asylum did he escape from?' I had never encountered someone like this.

'Mr. Mueller,' I said, 'do you realize how dense the fog is?' 'No,' he replied. *'My eye is not on the dense fog but on the living God, who controls every circumstance of my life.'*

"He then knelt down and prayed one of the most simple prayers I've ever heard. When he had finished, I started to pray, but he put his hand on my shoulder and told me *not* to pray. He said, 'First, you do not believe God will answer, and second, I BELIEVE HE HAS. Consequently, there is no need whatsoever for you to pray about it.'

"As I looked at him, he said, 'Captain, I have known my Lord for fifty-seven years, and there has never been even a single day that I have failed to get an audience with the King. Get up, Captain, and open the door, and you will see that the fog is gone.' I got up, and indeed the fog was gone. And on Saturday afternoon George Mueller was in Quebec for his meeting." SELECTED

If our love were just more simple,
We would take Him at His word;
And our lives would be all sunshine,
In the sweetness of our Lord.

AUGUST 18

The LORD alone led him.

DEUTERONOMY 32:12

The hill was steep, but cheered along the way
By conversation sweet, climbing with the thought
That it might be so till the height was reached;
But suddenly a narrow winding path
Appeared, and then the Master said, "My child,
Here you will walk safest with Me alone."

I trembled, yet my heart's deep trust replied,
"So be it, Lord." He took my feeble hand
In His, accepting thus my will to yield Him
All, and to find all in Him. One long, dark moment,
And no friend I saw, save Jesus only.
But oh! so tenderly He led me on
And up, and spoke to me such words of cheer,
Such secret whisperings of His wondrous love,
That soon I told Him all my grief and fear,
And leaned on His strong arm confidingly.
And then I found my footsteps quickened,
And light unspeakable, the rugged way
Illumined, such light as only can be seen
In close companionship with God.
A little while, and we will meet again
The loved and lost; but in the rapturous joy
Of greetings, such as here we cannot know,
And happy song, and heavenly embraces,
And tender recollections rushing back
Of life now passed, I think one memory
More dear and sacred than the rest, will rise,
And we who gather in the golden streets,
Will oft be stirred to speak with grateful love
Of that dark day Jesus called us to climb
Some narrow steep, leaning on Him alone.

There is never a majestic mountain without a deep valley, and there is no birth without pain. DANIEL CRAWFORD

AUGUST 19

Sorrowful, yet always rejoicing.

2 Corinthians 6:10

Sorrow was beautiful, but his beauty was the beauty of the moonlight shining through the leafy branches of the trees in the woods. His gentle light made little pools of silver here and there on the soft green moss of the forest floor. And when he sang, his song was like the low, sweet calls of the nightingale, and in his eyes was the unexpectant gaze of someone who has ceased to look for coming gladness. He could weep in tender sympathy with those who weep, but to rejoice with those who rejoice was unknown to him.

Joy was beautiful, too, but hers was the radiant beauty of a summer morning. Her eyes still held the happy laughter of childhood, and her hair glistened with the sunshine's kiss. When she sang, her voice soared upward like a skylark's, and her steps were the march of a conqueror who has never known defeat. She could rejoice with anyone who rejoices, but to weep with those who weep was unknown to her.

Sorrow longingly said, "We can never be united as one." "No, never," responded Joy, with eyes misting as she spoke, "for *my* path lies through the sunlit meadows, the sweetest roses bloom when I arrive, and songbirds await my coming to sing their most joyous melodies."

"Yes, and *my* path," said Sorrow, turning slowly away, "leads through the dark forest, and moonflowers, which open only at night, will fill my hands. Yet the sweetest of all earthly songs—the love song of the night—will be mine. So farewell, dear Joy, farewell."

Yet even as Sorrow spoke, he and Joy became aware of someone standing beside them. In spite of the dim light, they sensed a kingly Presence, and suddenly a great and holy awe overwhelmed them. They then sank to their knees before Him.

"I see Him as the King of Joy," whispered Sorrow, "for on His head are many crowns, and the nailprints in His hands and feet are the scars of a great victory. And before Him all my sorrow is melting away into deathless love and gladness. I now give myself to Him forever."

"No, Sorrow," said Joy softly, "for I see Him as the King of Sorrow, and the crown on His head is a crown of thorns, and the nailprints in His hands and feet are the scars of terrible agony. I also give myself to Him forever, for sorrow with Him must be sweeter than any joy I have ever known."

"Then we are *one* in Him," they cried in gladness, "for no one but He could unite Joy and Sorrow." Therefore they walked hand in hand into the world, to follow Him through storms and sunshine, through winter's severe cold and the warmth of summer's gladness, and to be "sorrowful, yet always rejoicing."

Does Sorrow lay his hand upon your shoulder,
And walk with you in silence on life's way,
While Joy, your bright companion once, grown colder,
Becomes to you more distant day by day?
Run not from the companionship of Sorrow,
He is the messenger of God to thee;
And you will thank Him in His great tomorrow—
For what you do not know now, you then will see;
He is God's angel, clothed in veils of night,
With whom "we walk by faith" and "not by sight." (2 Corinthians 5:7 KJV*)*

AUGUST 20

Jacob was left alone, and a man wrestled with him till daybreak.

Genesis 32:24

In this passage, God is wrestling with Jacob more than Jacob is wrestling with God. The "man" referred to here is the Son of Man—the Angel of the Covenant. It was God in human form, pressing down on Jacob to press his old life from him. And by daybreak God had prevailed, for Jacob's "hip was wrenched" (v. 25). As Jacob "fell" from his old life, he fell into the arms of God, clinging to Him but also wrestling until his blessing came. His blessing was that of a new life, so he rose from the earthly to the heavenly, the human to the divine, and the natural to the supernatural. From that morning forward, he was a weak and broken man from a human perspective, but God was there. And the Lord's heavenly voice proclaimed, "*Your name will no longer be Jacob, but Israel, because you have struggled with God and with humans and have overcome*" (v. 28).

Beloved, this should be a typical scene in the life of everyone who has been transformed. If God has called us to His highest and best, each of us will have a time of crisis, when all our resources will fail and when we face either ruin or something better than we have ever dreamed. But before we can receive the blessing, we must rely on God's infinite help. We must be willing to let go, surrendering completely to Him, and cease from our own wisdom, strength, and righteousness. We must be "crucified with Christ" (Galatians 2:20) and yet alive in Him. God knows how to lead us to the point of crisis, and He knows how to lead us through it.

Is God leading you in this way? Is this the meaning of your mysterious trial, your difficult circumstances, your impossible situation, or that trying place you cannot seem to move past without Him? But do you have enough of Him to win the victory?

Then turn to Jacob's God! Throw yourself helplessly at His feet. Die in His loving arms to your own strength and wisdom, and rise like Jacob into His strength and sufficiency. There is no way out of your difficult and narrow situation except at the top. You must win deliverance by rising higher, coming into a new experience with God. And may it bring you into all that is meant by the revelation of "the Mighty One of Jacob" (Isaiah 60:16)! There is no way out *but God*.

At Your feet I fall, Yield
You up my all,
To suffer, live, or die
For my Lord crucified.

AUGUST 21

He brought me out into a spacious place; he
rescued me because he delighted in me.

Psalm 18:19

What is this "spacious place"? What can it be but God Himself—the infinite Being through whom all other beings find their source and their end of life? God is indeed a "spacious place." And it was through humiliation, degradation, and a sense of worthlessness that David was taken to it. Madame Guyon

"I carried you on eagles' wings and brought you to myself" (Exodus 19:4).

Fearing to launch on "full surrender's" tide,
I asked the Lord where would its waters glide
My little boat, "To troubled seas I dread?"
"Unto Myself," He said.

Weeping beside an open grave I stood,
In bitterness of soul I cried to God:
"Where leads this path of sorrow that I tread?"
"Unto Myself," He said.

Striving for souls, I loved the work too well;
Then disappointments came; I could not tell
The reason, till He said, "I am your all;
Unto Myself I call."

Watching my heroes—those I love the best—
I saw them fail; they could not stand the test,
Even by this the Lord, through tears not few,
Unto Himself me drew.

Unto Himself! No earthly tongue can tell
The bliss I find, since in His heart I dwell;
The things that charmed me once seem all as naught;
Unto Himself I'm brought.

SELECTED

AUGUST 22

The rest were to get there on planks or on pieces of the ship. In this way everyone reached land in safety.

ACTS 27:44

THE MIRACULOUS STORY OF PAUL'S VOYAGE TO ROME, WITH ITS TRIALS and triumphs, is a wonderful example of the light and the darkness through the journey of faith of human life. And the most remarkable part of the journey is the difficult and narrow places that are interspersed with God's extraordinary providence and intervention.

It is a common misconception that the Christian's walk of faith is strewn with flowers and that when God intervenes in the lives of His people, He does so in such a wonderful way as to always lift us out of our difficult surroundings. In actual fact, however, the real experience is quite the opposite. And the message of the Bible is one of alternating trials and triumphs in the lives of "a great cloud of witnesses" (Hebrews 12:1), everyone from Abel to the last martyr.

Paul, more than anyone else, is an example of how much a child of God can suffer without being defeated or broken in spirit. Because of his testimony given in Damascus, he was hunted down by persecutors and forced to flee for his life. Yet we see no heavenly chariot, amid lightning bolts of fire, coming to rescue the holy apostle from the hands of his enemies. God instead worked a simple way of escape for Paul: "His followers took him by night and lowered him in a basket through an opening in the wall" (Acts 9:25). Yes, he was in an old clothes basket, like a bundle of laundry or groceries. The servant of the Lord Jesus Christ was lowered from a window over the wall of Damascus, and in a humble way escaped the hatred of his foes.

Later we find him languishing for months in lonely dungeons, telling of his "sleepless nights and hunger" (2 Corinthians 6:5), of being deserted by friends, and of his brutal, humiliating beatings. And even after God promised to deliver him, we see him left for days to toss upon a stormy sea and compelled to protect a treacherous sailor. And finally, once his deliverance comes, it is not by way of some heavenly ship sailing from the skies to rescue this illustrious prisoner. Nor is there an angel who comes walking on the water to still the raging sea. There is no supernatural sign at all of surpassing greatness being carried out, for one man is required to grab a piece of the mast to survive, another a floating timber, another a small fragment of the shipwreck, and yet another is forced to swim for his life.

In this account, we also find God's pattern for our own lives. It is meant to be good news to those who live in this everyday world in ordinary surroundings and who face thousands of ordinary situations, which must be met in completely ordinary ways.

God's promises and His providence do not lift us from the world of common sense and everyday trials, for it is through these very things that our faith is perfected. And it is in this world that God loves to interweave the golden threads of His love with the twists and turns of our common, everyday experiences. HARD PLACES IN THE WAY OF FAITH

AUGUST 23

By faith Abraham . . . obeyed and went, even though he did not know where he was going.

HEBREWS 11:8

THIS IS FAITH WITHOUT SIGHT. *Seeing* IS NOT FAITH BUT REASONING. When crossing the Atlantic by ship, I once observed this very principle of faith. I *saw* no path marked out on the sea, nor could I even see the shore.

Yet each day, we marked our progress on a chart as if we had been following a giant chalk line across the water. And when we came within sight of land on the other side of the Atlantic, we knew exactly where we were, as if we had been able to see it from three thousand miles away.

How had our course been so precisely plotted? Every day, our captain had taken his instruments, looked to the sky, and determined his course by the sun. He was sailing using heavenly lights, not earthly ones.

Genuine faith also looks up and sails, by using God's great Son. It never travels by *seeing* the shoreline, earthly lighthouses, or paths along the way. And the steps of faith often lead to total uncertainty or even darkness and disaster, but the Lord will open the way and often makes the darkest of midnight hours as bright as the dawning of the day.

Let us move forth today, not knowing or seeing, but trusting. DAYS OF HEAVEN UPON EARTH

Too many of us want to see our way through a new endeavor before we will even start. Imagine if we could see our way from beginning to end. How would we ever develop our Christian gifts? *Faith, hope, and love cannot be picked from trees, like ripe apples.* Remember, after the words "In the beginning" (Genesis 1:1) comes the word "God." It is our first step of faith that turns the key in the lock of His powerhouse. It is true that God helps those who help themselves, but *He also helps those who are helpless.* So no matter your circumstance, you can depend on Him every time.

Waiting on God brings us to the end of our journey much faster than our feet.

Many an opportunity is lost while we deliberate after He has said, "Move!"

AUGUST 24

I have received full payment have more than enough.

PHILIPPIANS 4:18

In one of my garden books there is a chapter with a very interesting title: "Flowers That Grow in the Shade." It deals with those areas of a garden that never catch direct sunlight, and it lists the kinds of flowers that not only grow in the dark corners but actually seem to like them and to flourish in them.

There are similarities here to the spiritual world. There are Christians who seem to blossom when their material circumstances become the most harsh and severe. They grow in the darkness and shade. If this were not true, how could we otherwise explain some of the experiences of the apostle Paul?

When he wrote the above verse, he was a prisoner in Rome. The primary mission of his life appeared to have been broken. But it was in this persistent darkness that flowers began to show their faces in bright and fascinating glory. Paul may have seen them before, growing along the open road, but certainly never in the incomparable strength and beauty in which they now appeared. And words of promise opened their treasures to him in ways he had never before experienced.

Among those treasures were such wonderful things as Christ's grace, love, joy, and peace, and it seemed as though they had needed the circumstance of darkness to draw out their secret and inner glory. The dark and dingy prison had become the home of the revealed truth of God, and Paul began to realize as never before the width and the wealth of his spiritual inheritance.

Haven't we all known men and women who begin to wear strength and hopefulness like a regal robe as soon as they must endure a season of darkness and solitude? People like that may be put in prison by the world, but their treasure will be locked away with them, for true treasure cannot be locked out of their lives. Their material condition may look like a desert, but "the desert and the parched land will be glad; the wilderness will rejoice and blossom" (Isaiah 35:1). John Henry Jowett

Every flower, even the most beautiful, has its own shadow beneath it as it basks in the sunlight.

Where there is much light, there is also much shade.

AUGUST 25

Before the coming of this faith we were held in custody . . . locked up until the faith that was to come would be revealed.

GALATIANS 3:23

GOD, IN TIMES PAST, CAUSED PEOPLE TO BE KEPT SUBJECT TO HIS LAW so they would learn the more excellent way of faith. For it was through the law that they would see God's holy standard and thereby realize their own utter helplessness. Then they would gladly learn His way of faith.

God still causes us to be "locked up until faith" is learned. Our own nature, circumstances, trials, and disappointments all serve to keep us submissive and "locked up" until we see that the only way out is His way of faith. Moses attempted the deliverance of his people by using self-effort, his personal influence, and even violence. So God "locked [him] up" for forty years in the wilderness before he was prepared for His work.

Paul and Silas were called of God to preach the gospel in Europe. In Philippi they were "severely flogged, they were thrown into prison, and the jailer . . . fastened their feet in the stocks" (Acts 16:23–24). They were "locked up" to faith. They trusted God and sang praises to Him in their darkest hour, and God brought deliverance and salvation.

The apostle John was also "locked up" to faith, when he was banished to the Isle of Patmos. And if he had never been sent there, he would never have seen such glorious visions of God.

Dear reader, are you in some terrible trouble? Have you experienced some distressing disappointment, sorrow, or inexpressible loss? Are you in a difficult situation? Cheer up! You have been "locked up" to faith. Accept your troubles in the proper way and commit them to God. Praise Him "that in all things God works for the good of those who love him" (Romans 8:28) and that He "acts on behalf of those who wait for him" (Isaiah 64:4). God will send you blessings and help, and will reveal truths to you that otherwise would never have come your way. And many others will also receive great insights and blessings because you were "locked up" to learn the way of faith. C. H. P.

Great things are done when man and mountains meet,
These are not done by walking down the street.

AUGUST 26

It is not in me.
Job 28:14

I remember saying one summer, "What I really need is a trip to the ocean." So I went to the beach, but the ocean seemed to say, "*It is not in me!*" The ocean did not do for me what I thought it would. Then I said, "Perhaps the mountains will provide the rest I need." I went to the mountains, and when I awoke the first morning, I gazed at the magnificent mountain I had so longed to see. But the sight did not satisfy, and the mountain said, "*It is not in me!*"

What I really needed was the deep ocean of God's love, and the high mountains of His truth within me. His wisdom had depths and heights that neither the ocean nor the mountains could contain and that could not be compared with jewels, gold, or precious stones. *Christ is wisdom and He is our deepest need.* Our inner restlessness can only be pacified by the revelation of His eternal friendship and love for us. Margaret Bottome

My heart is there!
Where, on eternal hills, my loved one dwells
Among the lilies and asphodels;
Clad in the brightness of the Great White Throne,
Glad in the smile of Him who sits thereon,
The glory gilding all His wealth of hair
And making His immortal face more fair—

there is my treasure and my heart is there.
My heart is there!
With Him who made all earthly life so grand,
So fit to live, and yet to die His plan;
So mild, so great, so gentle and so brave,
So ready to forgive, so strong to save.
His fair, pure Spirit makes the Heavens more fair,
And that is where rises my longing prayer—
there is my treasure and my heart is there.

FAVORITE POEM OF THE LATE CHARLES E. COWMAN

You can never expect to keep an eagle in the forest. You might be able to gather a group of the most beautiful birds around him, provide a perch for him on the tallest pine, or enlist other birds to bring him the choicest of delicacies, but he will reject them all. He will spread his proud wings and, with his eye on an Alpine cliff, soar away to his own ancestral halls of rock, where storms and waterfalls make their natural music.

Our soul longs to soar as an eagle and will find rest with nothing short of the Rock of Ages. Its ancestral halls are the halls of heaven, made with the rock of the attributes of God. And the span of its majestic flight is eternity! "Lord, YOU have been our dwelling place throughout all generations" (Psalm 90:1). J. R. MACDUFF

"My Home is God Himself"; Christ brought me there.
I placed myself within His mighty arms;
He took me up, and safe from all alarms
He bore me "where no foot but His has trod,"
Within the holiest at Home with God,
And had me dwell in Him, rejoicing there.
O Holy Place! O Home divinely fair!
And we, God's little ones, abiding there.

"My Home is God Himself"; it was not so!
A long, long road I traveled night and day,
And sought to find within myself some way.
Nothing I did or felt could bring me near.
Self-effort failed, and I was filled with fear,
And then I found Christ was the only way,
That I must come to Him and in Him stay,
And God had told me so.
And now "my Home is God," and sheltered there,
God meets the trials of my earthly life,
God compasses me round from storm and strife,
God takes the burden of my daily care.
O Wondrous Place! O Home divinely fair!
And I, God's little one, safe hidden there.
Lord, as I dwell in You and You in me,
So make me dead to everything but Thee;
That as I rest within my Home most fair,
My soul may evermore and only see
My God in everything and everywhere;
My Home is God.

Author Unknown

AUGUST 27

He took him aside, away from the crowd.

Mark 7:33

Paul withstood not only the tests that came while he was active in his service to Christ but also the tests of solitude during captivity. We may be able to withstand the strain of the most intense labor, even if coupled with severe suffering, and yet completely break down if set aside from all Christian activity and work.

This would be especially true if we were forced to endure solitary confinement in a prison cell.

Even the most majestic bird, which soars higher than all others and endures the longest flights, will sink into despair when placed in a cage, where it is forced to helplessly beat its wings against its prison bars. Have you ever seen a magnificent eagle forced to languish in a small cage? With bowed head and drooping wings, it is a sad picture of the sorrow of inactivity.

To see Paul in prison is to see another side of life. Have you noticed how he handled it? He seemed to be looking over the top of his prison wall and over the heads of his enemies. Notice how he even signed his name to his letters—not as the prisoner of Festus, nor of Caesar, and not as a victim of the Sanhedrin, but as "*a prisoner for the Lord*" (Ephesians 4:1). Through it all, he saw only the hand of God at work. To him, the prison became a palace, with its corridors resounding with shouts of triumphant praise and joy.

Forced from the missionary work he loved so well, Paul built a new pulpit—a new witness stand. And from his place of bondage arose some of the most encouraging and helpful ministries of Christian liberty. What precious messages of light came from the dark shadows of his captivity.

Also think of the long list of saints who have followed in the footsteps of Paul and were imprisoned for their faith. For twelve long years, John Bunyan's voice was silenced in an English jail in Bedford. Yet it was there he wrote the greatest work of his life, *Pilgrim's Progress*—read by more people than any other book except the Bible. He once said, "I was at home in prison, and my great joy led me to sit and write and write." And the darkness of his long captivity became a wonderful dream to light the path of millions of weary pilgrims.

Madame Guyon, the sweet-spirited French saint, endured a lengthy time behind prison walls. And like the sounds of some caged birds whose songs are more beautiful as a result of their confinement, the music of her soul has traveled far beyond her dungeon walls to remove the sadness of many discouraged hearts.

Oh, the heavenly consolation that God has caused to flow out of places of solitude! S. C. Rees

Taken aside by Jesus,
To feel the touch of His hand;
To rest for a while in the shadow
Of the Rock in a weary land.

Taken aside by Jesus,
In the loneliness dark and drear,
Where no other comfort may reach me,
Than His voice to my heart so dear.

Taken aside by Jesus,
To be quite alone with Him,
To hear His wonderful tones of love
'Mid the silence and shadows dim.

Taken aside by Jesus,
Shall I resist the desert place,
When I hear as I never heard before,
And see Him "face to face"?

AUGUST 28

There He tested them.

Exodus 15:25 NASB

I ONCE VISITED THE TESTING ROOM OF A LARGE STEEL MILL. I WAS SURrounded by instruments and equipment that tested pieces of steel to their limits and measured their breaking point. Some pieces had been twisted until they broke, and then were labeled with the level of pressure they could withstand. Some had been stretched to their breaking point, with their level of strength also noted. Others had been compressed to their crushing point and measured. Because of the testing, the manager of the mill knew exactly how much stress and strain each piece of steel could endure if it was used to build a ship, building, or bridge.

It is often much the same with God's children. He does not want us to be like fragile vases of glass or porcelain. He wants us to be like these toughened pieces of steel, able to endure twisting and crushing pressure to the utmost without collapse.

God does not want us to be like greenhouse plants, which are sheltered from rough weather, but like storm-beaten oaks; not like sand dunes that are driven back and forth by every gust of wind but like granite mountains that withstand the fiercest storms. Yet to accomplish this, He must take us into His testing room of suffering. And many of us need no other argument than our own experiences to prove that suffering is indeed God's testing room of faith. J. H. M.

It is quite easy for us to talk and to theorize about faith, but God often puts us into His crucible of affliction to test the purity of our gold and to separate the dross from the metal. How happy we are if the hurricanes that blow across life's raging sea have the effect of making Jesus more precious to us! It is better to weather the storm with Christ than to sail smooth waters without Him. J. R. MACDUFF

What if God could not manage to mature your life without suffering?

AUGUST 29

Carrying his own cross.

JOHN 19:17

"The Changed Cross" is a poem that tells of a weary woman who thought that the cross she must bear surely was heavier than those of other people, so she wished she could choose another person's instead. When she went to sleep, she dreamed she was taken to a place where there were many different crosses from which to choose. There were various shapes and sizes, but the most beautiful one was covered with jewels and gold. "This I could wear with comfort," she said. So she picked it up, but her weak body staggered beneath its weight. The jewels and gold were beautiful, yet they were much too heavy for her to carry.

The next cross she noticed was quite lovely, with beautiful flowers entwined around its sculptured form. Surely this was the one for her. She lifted it, but beneath the flowers were large thorns that pierced and tore her skin.

Finally she came to a plain cross without jewels or any carvings and with only a few words of love inscribed on it. When she picked it up, it proved to be better than all the rest, and the easiest to carry. And as she looked at it, she noticed it was bathed in a radiance that fell from heaven. Then she recognized it as her own old cross. She had found it once again, and it was the best of all, and the lightest for her.

You see, God knows best what cross we need to bear, and we never know how heavy someone else's cross may be. We envy someone who is rich, with a cross of gold adorned with jewels, but we do not know how heavy it is. We look at someone whose life seems so easy and who carries a cross covered with flowers. Yet if we could actually test all the crosses we think are lighter than ours, we would never find one better suited for us than our own. Glimpses Through Life's Windows

If you, with impatience, give up your cross,
You will not find it in this world again;
Nor in another, but here and here alone
Is given for you to suffer for God's sake.
In the next world we may more perfectly

Love Him and serve Him, praise Him,
Grow nearer and nearer to Him with delight.
But then we will not anymore
Be called to suffer, which is our assignment here.
Can you not suffer, then, one hour or two?
If He should call you from your cross today,
Saying, "It is finished—that hard cross of yours
From which you pray for deliverance,"
Do you not think that some emotion of regret
Would overcome you? You would say,
"So soon? Let me go back and suffer yet awhile
More patiently. I have not yet praised God."
So whenever it comes, that summons we all look for,
It will seem soon, too soon. Let us take heed in life
That God may now be glorified in us.

"Sermon in a Hospital" by Ugo Bassi

AUGUST 30

Some went out on the sea in ships; they were merchants on the mighty waters. They saw the works of the Lord, his wonderful deeds in the deep.

Psalm 107:23–24

The person who has not learned that every wind that blows can be used to guide us toward heaven has certainly not mastered the art of sailing and is nothing but an apprentice. In fact, the only thing that helps no one is a dead calm. Every wind, whether from the north, south, east, or west, may help us toward that blessed port. So seek only this: *to stay well out to sea*—and then have no fear of stormy winds. May our prayer be that of an old Englishman: "O Lord, send us into the deep water of the sea, for we are so close to shore that even a small breeze from the Devil could break

our ship to pieces on the rocks. Again, Lord, send us into the deep water of the sea, where there will be plenty of room to win a glorious victory."
MARK GUY PEARSE

Remember, our faith is always at its greatest point when we are in the middle of the trial, and confidence in the flesh will never endure testing. Fair-weather faith is not faith at all. CHARLES H. SPURGEON

AUGUST 31

"Blessed are those who have not seen and yet have believed."
JOHN 20:29

HOW IMPORTANT IT IS FOR GOD TO KEEP US FOCUSED ON THINGS THAT are unseen, for we are so easily snared by the things we can see! If Peter was ever going to walk on the water, he had to walk, but if he was going to swim to Jesus, he had to swim. He could not do both. If a bird is going to fly, it must stay away from fences and trees, trusting the buoyancy of its wings. And if it tries to stay within easy reach of the ground, it will never fly very well.

God had to bring Abraham to the end of his own strength and let him see that with his own body he could do nothing. He had to consider his own body "as good as dead" (Hebrews 11:12) and then trust God to do all the work. When he looked away from himself and trusted only God, he became "fully persuaded that God had power to do what he had promised" (Romans 4:21).

This is what God is teaching us, and He has to keep results that are encouraging away from us until we learn to trust Him without them. Then He loves to make His Word as real to us in actuality as it is in our faith.
A. B. SIMPSON

I do not ask that He must prove
His Word is true to me,

And that before I can believe
He first must let me see.
It is enough for me to know
It's true because He says it's so;
On His unchanging Word I'll stand
And trust till I can understand.
E. M. Winter

SEPTEMBER 1

"I will rebuild you with stones of turquoise."
Isaiah 54:11

The stones in the wall said, "We have come from mountains far away—from the sides of rugged cliffs. Fire and water have worked on us for ages but have only produced crevices. Yet human hands like yours have made us into homes where children of your immortal race are born, suffer, rejoice, find rest and shelter, and learn the lessons that our Maker and yours is teaching. But to come to the point of being used for this purpose, we have endured much. Dynamite has torn at our very heart, and pickaxes have broken and split us into pieces. Often as we lay disfigured and broken in the quarry, everything seemed to be without design or meaning. But gradually we were cut into blocks, and some of us were chiseled with sharper instruments until we had a fine edge. Now we are complete, are in our proper places, and are of service.

"You, however, are still in your quarry. You are not complete, and because of that, as once was the case with us, there is much you do not understand. But you are destined for a higher building, and someday you will be placed in it by angelic hands, becoming a living stone in a heavenly temple."

In the still air the music lies unheard;
In the rough marble beauty hides unseen;

To make the music and the beauty needs
The master's touch, the sculptor's chisel keen.
Great Master, touch us with Your skillful hands;
Let not the music that is in us die!
Great Sculptor, hew and polish us; nor let,
Hidden and lost, Your form within us lie!

SEPTEMBER 2

It has been granted to you . . . to suffer for him.
PHILIPPIANS 1:29

GOD RUNS A COSTLY SCHOOL, FOR MANY OF HIS LESSONS ARE LEARNED through tears. Richard Baxter, the seventeenth-century Puritan preacher, once said, "O God, I thank You for the discipline I have endured in this body for fifty-eight years." And he certainly is not the only person who has turned trouble into triumph.

Soon the school of our heavenly Father will close for us, for the end of the school term is closer every day. May we never run from a difficult lesson or flinch from the rod of discipline. Richer will be our crown, and sweeter will heaven be, if we cheerfully endure to the end. Then we will graduate in glory. THEODORE L. CUYLER

The world's finest china is fired in ovens at least three times, and some many more. Dresden china is always fired three times. *Why* is it forced to endure such intense heat? Shouldn't once or twice be enough? No, it is necessary to fire the china three times so the gold, crimson, and other colors are brighter, more beautiful, and permanently attached.

We are fashioned after the same principle. The human trials of life are burned into us numerous times, and through God's grace, beautiful colors are formed in us and made to shine forever. CORTLAND MYERS

Earth's fairest flowers grow not on sunny plain,
But where some vast upheaval tore in twain

The smiling land.
After the whirlwind's devastating blast,
And molten lava, fire, and ashes fall,
God's still small voice breathes healing over all.
From broken rocks and fern-clad chasms deep,
Flow living waters as from hearts that weep,
There in the afterglow soft dews distill
And angels tend God's plants when night falls still,
And the Beloved passing by the way
Will gather lilies at the break of day.

J. H. D.

SEPTEMBER 3

He saw the disciples straining at the oars.

Mark 6:48

Straining and striving does not accomplish the work God gives us to do. Only God Himself, who always works without stress and strain and who never overworks, can do the work He assigns to His children. When we restfully trust Him to do it, the work will be completed and will be done well. And the way to let Him do His work through us is to so fully abide in Christ by faith that He fills us to overflowing.

A man who learned this secret once said, "I came to Jesus and drank, and I believe I will never be thirsty again. My life's motto has become '*Not overwork but overflow,*' and it has already made all the difference in my life."

There is no straining effort in an overflowing life, and it is quietly irresistible. It is the normal life of omnipotent and ceaseless accomplishment into which Christ invites each of us to enter—today and always.

Sunday School Times

Be all at rest, my soul, O blessed secret,
Of the true life that glorifies the Lord:
Not always does the busiest soul best serve Him,
But he that rests upon His faithful Word.
Be all at rest, let not your heart be rippled,
For tiny wavelets mar the image fair,
Which the still pool reflects of heaven's glory—
And thus the image He would have you bear.

Be all at rest, my soul, for rest is service,
To the still heart God does His secrets tell;
Thus will you learn to wait, and watch, and labor,
Strengthened to bear, since Christ in you does dwell.
For what is service but the life of Jesus,
Lived through a vessel of earth's fragile clay,
Loving and giving and poured forth for others,
A living sacrifice from day to day.

Be all at rest, so then you'll be an answer
To those who question, "Who is God and where?"
For God is rest, and where He dwells is stillness,
And they who dwell in Him, His rest will share.
And what will meet the deep unrest around you,
But the calm peace of God that filled His breast?
For still a living Voice calls to the weary,
From Him who said, "Come unto Me and rest."

FREDA HANBURY ALLEN

In Resurrection stillness there is Resurrection power.

SEPTEMBER 4

When you hear them sound a long blast on the trumpets, have the whole army give a loud shout; then the wall of the city will collapse and the army will go up, everyone straight in.

JOSHUA 6:5

THE "LOUD SHOUT" OF STEADFAST FAITH IS THE EXACT OPPOSITE OF the groans of wavering faith and the complaints of discouraged hearts. Of all "the secret[s] of the LORD" (Psalm 25:14 KJV), I do not believe there are any more valuable than the secret of this *"loud shout" of faith.* "The LORD said to Joshua, 'See, I have delivered Jericho into your hands, along with its king and its fighting men'" (Joshua 6:2). He did not say, "I *will* deliver" but "I *have* delivered." The victory already belonged to the children of Israel, and now they were called to take possession of it. But the big question still remaining was *how.* It looked impossible, but the Lord had a plan.

No one would normally believe that a shout could cause city walls to fall. Yet the *secret* of their victory lay precisely in just that shout, for it was the shout of faith. And it was a faith that dared to claim a promised victory solely on the basis of the authority of God's Word, even though there were no physical signs of fulfillment. God answered His promise in response to their faith, for when they shouted, He caused the walls to fall.

God had declared, "I *have delivered* Jericho into your hands," and faith believed this to be true. And many centuries later the Holy Spirit recorded this triumph of faith in the book of Hebrews as follows: "By faith the walls of Jericho fell, after the army had marched around them for seven days" (Hebrews 11:30). HANNAH WHITALL SMITH

Faith can never reach its consummation,
Till the victor's thankful song we raise:
In the glorious city of salvation,
God has told us all the gates are praise.

SEPTEMBER 5

Blessed are all who wait for him!

ISAIAH 30:18

WE OFTEN HEAR ABOUT WAITING *on* GOD, WHICH ACTUALLY MEANS that He is waiting until we are ready. There is another side, however. When we wait *for* God, we are waiting until He is ready.

Some people say, and many more believe, that as soon as we meet all His conditions, God will answer our prayer. They teach that He lives in an eternal *now*, that with Him there is no past or future, and that if we can fulfill all He requires to be obedient to His will, *immediately* our needs will be met, our desires satisfied, and our prayers answered.

While there is much truth in this belief, it expresses only one side of the truth. God *does* live in an eternal *now*, yet He works out His purposes over *time*. A petition presented to God is like a seed dropped into the ground. Forces above and beyond our control must work on it until the actual accomplishment of the answer. THE STILL SMALL VOICE

I longed to walk along an easy road,
And leave behind the dull routine of home,
Thinking in other fields to serve my God;
But Jesus said, "My time has not yet come."

I longed to sow the seed in other soil,
To be unshackled in the work, and free,
To join with other laborers in their toil;
But Jesus said, "It's not My choice for thee."

I longed to leave the desert, and be led
To work where souls were sunk in sin and shame,
That I might win them; but the Master said,
"I have not called you, publish here My name."

I longed to fight the battles of my King,
Lift high His standards in the thickest strife;
But my great Captain had me wait and sing
Songs of His conquests in my quiet life.

I longed to leave the hard and difficult sphere,
Where all alone I seemed to stand and wait,
To feel I had some human helper near,
But Jesus had me guard one lonely gate.

I longed to leave the common daily toil,
Where no one seemed to understand or care;
But Jesus said, "I choose for you this soil,
That you might raise for Me some blossoms rare."

And now I have no longing but to do
At home, or far away, His blessed will,
To work amid the many or the few;
Thus, "choosing not to choose," my heart is still.

SELECTED

And Patience was willing to wait. PILGRIM'S PROGRESS

SEPTEMBER 6

You remain.

HEBREWS 1:11

THERE ARE SO MANY PEOPLE WHO SIT BY THEIR FIREPLACE ALL ALONE! They sit by another chair, once filled, and cannot restrain the tears that flow. They sit alone so much, but there *is* someone who is unseen and just within their reach. But for some reason, they don't *realize* His presence.

Realizing it is blessed yet quite rare. It is dependent upon their mood, their feelings, their physical condition, and the weather. The rain or thick fog outside, the lack of sleep and the intense pain, seem to affect their mood and blur their vision so they do not realize His presence.

There is, however, something even better than *realizing*, and even more blessed. It is completely independent of these other conditions and is something that will abide with you. It is this: *recognizing* that unseen presence, which is so wonderful, quieting, soothing, calming, and warming. So *recognize* the presence of the Master. He is here, close to you, and His presence is real. Recognizing will also help your ability to realize but is never dependent upon it.

Yes, there is immeasurably more—the truth is a presence, not a thing, a fact, or a statement. Some *One* is present, and He is a warmhearted Friend and the all-powerful Lord. This is a joyful truth for weeping hearts everywhere, no matter the reason for the tears, or whatever stream their weeping willow is planted beside. SAMUEL DICKEY GORDON

When from my life the old-time joys have vanished,
Treasures once mine, I may no longer claim,
This truth may feed my hungry heart, and famished:
Lord, You remain here! You are still the same!

When streams have dried, those streams of glad refreshing—
Friendships so blest, so rich, so free;
When sun-kissed skies give place to clouds depressing,
Lord, You remain here! Still my heart has Thee.

When strength has failed, and feet, now worn and weary,
On happy errands may no longer go,
Why should I sigh, or let the days be dreary?
Lord, You remain here! Could You more bestow?

Thus through life's days—whoe'er or what may fail me,
Friends, friendships, joys, in small or great degree,
Songs may be mine, no sadness need assault me,
Lord, You remain here! Still my heart has Thee.
J. Danson Smith

SEPTEMBER 7

God is our refuge and strength, an ever-present help in trouble.
Psalm 46:1

"Why didn't God help me sooner?" This is a question that is often asked, but it is not His will to act on *your* schedule. He desires to change you through the trouble and cause you to learn a lesson from it. He has promised, "I will be with him *in* trouble, I will deliver him and honor him" (Psalm 91:15). He will be with you *in* trouble all day and through the night. Afterward he will take you out of it, but not until you have stopped being restless and worried over it and have become calm and quiet. Then He will say, "It is enough."

God uses trouble to teach His children precious lessons. Difficulties are intended to educate us, and when their good work is done, a glorious reward will become ours through them. There is a sweet joy and a real value in difficulties, for He regards them not as difficulties but as opportunities. Selected

Not always out of our troubled times,
And the struggles fierce and grim,
But in—deeper in—to our sure rest,
The place of our peace, in Him.
Annie Johnson Flint

I once heard the following statement from a simple old man, and I have never forgotten it: "When God tests you, it is a good time to test Him by putting His promises to the test and then claiming from Him exactly what your trials have made necessary." There are two ways of getting out of a trial. One is simply to try to get rid of the trial, and then to be thankful when it is over. The other is to recognize the trial as a challenge from God to claim a larger blessing than we have ever before experienced, and to accept it with delight as an opportunity of receiving a greater measure of God's divine grace.

In this way, even the Adversary becomes a help to us, and all the things that seem to be against us turn out to assist us along our way. Surely this is what is meant by the words "In all these things we are more than conquerors through him who loved us" (Romans 8:37). A. B. Simpson

SEPTEMBER 8

Thou hast enlarged me when I was in distress.

Psalm 4:1 KJV

This verse is one of the greatest testimonies ever written regarding the effectiveness of God's work on our behalf during times of crisis. It is a statement of thanksgiving for having been set free not *from* suffering but rather *through* suffering. In stating, "Thou hast enlarged me when I was in distress," the psalmist is declaring that the sorrows of life have themselves been the source of life's enlargement.

Haven't each of us experienced this a thousand times and found it to be true? Someone once said of Joseph that when he was in the dungeon, "iron entered his soul." And the strength of iron is exactly what he needed, for earlier he had only experienced the glitter of gold. He had been rejoicing in youthful dreams, and dreaming actually hardens the heart. Someone who sheds great tears over a simple romance will not be of much help in a real crisis, for true sorrow will be too deep for him. We all need the iron in life to enlarge our character. The gold is simply a passing vision, whereas the iron is the true experience of life. The chain that is the common bond uniting us to others must be one of iron. The common touch of humanity that gives the world true kinship is not joy but sorrow—gold is partial to only a few, but iron is universal.

Dear soul, if you want your sympathy for others to be enlarged, you must be willing to have your life narrowed to certain degrees of suffering. Joseph's dungeon was the very road to his throne, and he would have been unable to lift the iron load of his brothers had he not experienced the iron in his own life. Your life will be enlarged in proportion to the amount of iron you have endured, for it is in the shadows of your life that you will find the actual fulfillment of your dreams of glory. So do not complain about the shadows of darkness—in reality, they are better than your dreams could ever be. Do not say that the darkness of the prison has shackled you, for your shackles are wings—wings of flight into the heart and soul of humanity. And the gate of your prison is the gate into the heart of the universe. God has enlarged you through the suffering of sorrow's chain. George Matheson

If Joseph had never been Egypt's prisoner, he would have never been Egypt's governor. The iron chain that bound his feet brought about the golden chain around his neck. Selected

SEPTEMBER 9

"Some [seed] fell on rocky places, where it did not have much soil. It sprang up quickly, because the soil was shallow."

Matthew 13:5

Shallow! From the context of the teaching of this parable, it seems that we must have something to do with the depth of the soil. The fruitful seed fell on "good soil" (v. 8), or good and honest hearts. I suppose the shallow people are those who "*did not have much soil*"—those who have no real purpose in life and are easily swayed by a tender appeal, a good sermon, or a simple melody. And at first it seems as if they will amount to something for God, but because they "*[do] not have much soil,*" they have no depth or genuine purpose, and no earnest desire to know His will in order to do it. Therefore we should be careful to maintain the soil of our hearts.

When a Roman soldier was told by his guide that if he insisted on taking a certain journey, it would probably be fatal, he answered, "It is necessary for me to go—it is not necessary for me to live." That was true depth of conviction, and only when we are likewise convicted will our lives amount to something. But a shallow life lives on its impulses, impressions, intuitions, instincts, and largely on its circumstances. Those with profound character, however, look beyond all these and move steadily ahead, seeing the future, where sorrow, seeming defeat, and failure will be reversed. They sail right through storm clouds into the bright sunshine, which always awaits them on the other side.

Once God has deepened us, He can give us His deepest truths, His most profound secrets, and will trust us with greater power. Lord, lead us into the depths of Your life and save us from a shallow existence!

On to broader fields of holy vision;
On to loftier heights of faith and love;
Onward, upward, apprehending wholly,
All for which He calls you from above.

A. B. Simpson

SEPTEMBER 10

The Lord will vindicate me.

Psalm 138:8

There is a divine mystery in suffering, one that has a strange and supernatural power and has never been completely understood by human reason. No one has ever developed a deep level of spirituality or holiness without experiencing a great deal of suffering. When a person who suffers reaches a point where he can be calm and carefree, inwardly smiling at his own suffering, and no longer asking God to be delivered from it, then the suffering has accomplished its blessed ministry, perseverance has "finish[ed] its work" (James 1:4), and the pain of the Crucifixion has begun to weave itself into a crown.

It is in this experience of complete suffering that the Holy Spirit works many miraculous things deep within our soul. In this condition, our entire being lies perfectly still under the hand of God; every power and ability of the mind, will, and heart are at last submissive; a quietness of eternity settles into the entire soul; and finally, the mouth becomes quiet, having only a few words to say, and stops crying out the words Christ quoted on the cross: "My God, my God, why have you forsaken me?" (Psalm 22:1).

At this point the person stops imagining castles in the sky, and pursuing foolish ideas, and his reasoning becomes calm and relaxed, with all choices removed, because the only choice has now become the purpose of God. Also, his emotions are weaned away from other people and things, becoming deadened so that nothing can hurt, offend, hinder, or get in his way. He can now let the circumstances be what they may, and continue to seek only God and His will, with the calm assurance that He is causing everything in the universe, whether good or bad, past or present, to work "for the good of those who love him" (Romans 8:28).

Oh, the blessings of absolute submission to Christ! What a blessing to lose our own strength, wisdom, plans, and desires and to be where every ounce of our being becomes like a peaceful Sea of Galilee under the omnipotent feet of Jesus! Soul Food

The main thing is to suffer without becoming discouraged. François Fénelon

The heart that serves, and loves, and clings,
Hears everywhere the rush of angel wings.

SEPTEMBER 11

After waiting patiently, Abraham received what was promised.
HEBREWS 6:15

ABRAHAM WAS TESTED FOR A VERY LONG TIME, BUT HE WAS RICHLY rewarded. The Lord tested him by delaying the fulfillment of His promise. Satan tested him through temptation, and people tested him through their jealousy, distrust, and opposition to him. Sarah tested him through her worrisome temperament. Yet he patiently endured, not questioning God's truthfulness and power or doubting God's faithfulness and love. Instead, Abraham submitted to God's divine sovereignty and infinite wisdom. And he was silent through many delays, willing to wait for the Lord's timing. Having patiently endured, he then obtained the fulfillment of the promise.

Beloved, God's promises can never fail to be accomplished, and those who patiently wait can never be disappointed, for believing faith leads to realization. Abraham's life condemns a spirit of hastiness, admonishes those who complain, commends those who are patient, and encourages quiet submission to God's will and way.

Remember, Abraham was tested but he patiently waited, ultimately received what was promised, and was satisfied. If you will imitate his example, you will share the same blessing. SELECTED

SEPTEMBER 12

Who is this coming up from the wilderness leaning on her beloved?
SONG OF SONGS 8:5

I once learned a great lesson at a prayer meeting at a southern church. As one man prayed, he asked the Lord for various blessings, just as you or I would, and he thanked the Lord for many blessings already received, just as you or I would. But he closed his prayer with this unusual petition: "And, O Lord, support us! Yes, support us on every leaning side!"

Do you have any "leaning sides"? This humble man's prayer pictured them in a new way and illustrated the Great Supporter in a new light as well. He saw God as always walking alongside the Christian, ready to extend His mighty arm to steady the weak on "every *leaning* side."

Child of My love, lean hard,
And let Me feel the pressure of your care;
I know your burden, child. I shaped it;
Balanced it in Mine Own hand; made no proportion
In its weight to your unaided strength,
For even as I laid it on, I said,
"I will be near, and while she leans on Me,
This burden will be Mine, not hers;
So will I keep My child within the circling arms
Of My Own love." Here lay it down, nor fear
To impose it on a shoulder that upholds
The government of worlds. Yet closer come:
You are not near enough. I would embrace your care;
So I might feel My child reclining on My breast.
You love Me, I know. So then do not doubt;
But loving Me, lean hard.

SEPTEMBER 13

"In the morning . . . come up. . . . Present yourself
to me there on top of the mountain."
Exodus 34:2

THE "MORNING" IS THE TIME I HAVE SET TO MEET WITH THE LORD. "*Morning*"—the very word itself is like a cluster of luscious grapes to crush into sacred wine for me to drink. In the morning! This is when God wants me at my best in strength and hope so that I may begin my daily climb, not in weakness but in strength. Last night I buried yesterday's fatigue, and this morning I took on a new supply of energy. Blessed is the day when the morning is sanctified—set apart to God! Successful is the day when the first victory is won in prayer! Holy is the day when the dawn finds me on the mountaintop with God!

Dear Father, I am coming to meet with You. Nothing on the common, everyday plain of life will keep me away from Your holy heights. At Your calling I come, so I have the assurance that You will meet with me. Each morning begun so well on the mountain will make me strong and glad the rest of the day! JOSEPH PARKER

Still, still with You, when the purple morning breaks,
When the birds awake, and the shadows flee;
Fairer than morning, lovelier than daylight,
Dawns the sweet consciousness, I am with Thee.

Alone with You, amid the misty shadows,
The solemn hush of nature newly born;
Alone with You in breathless adoration,
In the calm dew and freshness of the morn.

As in a sunrise o'er a waveless ocean,
The image of the morning star does rest,
So in this stillness, You discerning only
Your image in the waters of my breast.

When sinks the soul, subdued by toil, to slumber,
Its closing eyes look up to You in prayer;

Sweet the repose, beneath Your wings o'ershadowing,
But sweeter still to wake and find You there.
Harriet Beecher Stowe

My mother made it a habit every day, immediately after breakfast, to spend an hour in her room, reading the Bible, meditating over it, and praying to the Lord. That hour was like a blessed fountain from which she drew the strength and sweetness that prepared her to complete all her tasks. It also enabled her to maintain a genuine peacefulness in spite of the normal trying worries and pettiness that so often accompany life in a crowded neighborhood.

As I think of her life and all that she had to endure, I see the absolute triumph of the grace of God in the ideal Christian lady. She was such a lovely person that I never saw her lose her temper or speak even one word in anger. I never heard her participate in idle gossip or make a disparaging remark about another person. In fact, I never saw in her even the hint of an emotion unbecoming to someone who had drunk from "the river of the water of life" (Revelation 22:1) and who had eaten of "the living bread that came down from heaven" (John 6:51). Frederick William Farrar

Give God the fresh blossom of the day. Never make Him wait until the petals have faded.

SEPTEMBER 14

"Whoever wants to be my disciple must deny themselves and take up their cross and follow me."
Mark 8:34

The cross that my Lord calls me to carry may assume many different shapes. I may have to be content with mundane tasks in a limited area of service, when I may believe my abilities are suited for much greater work. I may be required to continually cultivate the same field year after year, even though it yields no harvest whatsoever. I may be asked of God to nurture kind and loving thoughts about the very person who has wronged me and to speak gently to him, take his side when others oppose him, and bestow sympathy and comfort to him. I may have to openly testify of my Master before those who do not want to be reminded of Him or His claims. And I may be called to walk through this world with a bright, smiling face while my heart is breaking.

Yes, there are many crosses, and every one of them is heavy and painful. And it is unlikely that I would seek out even one of them on my own. Yet Jesus is never as near to me as when I lift my cross, lay it submissively on my shoulder, and welcome it with a patient and uncomplaining spirit.

He draws close to me in order to mature my wisdom, deepen my peace, increase my courage, and supplement my power. All this He does so that through the very experience that is so painful and distressing to me, I will be of greater use to others.

And then I will echo these words of one of the Scottish Covenantors of the seventeenth century, imprisoned for his faith by John Graham of Claverhouse—"*I grow under the load.*" Alexander Smellie

Use the cross you bear as a crutch to help you on your way, not as a stumbling block that causes you to fall.

You may others from sadness to gladness beguile,
If you carry your cross with a smile.

SEPTEMBER 15

Awake, north wind, and come, south wind! Blow on my garden, that its fragrance may spread everywhere.
Song of Songs 4:16

Some of the spices and plants mentioned in verse 14 of the above chapter are very descriptive and symbolic. The juice of the aloe plant has a bitter taste but is soothing when applied to the skin, so it tells us of the sweetness of bitter things, the bittersweet, having an important application that only those who have used it will understand. Myrrh is symbolic of death, having been used to embalm the dead. It represents the sweetness that comes to the heart after it has died to self-will, pride, and sin.

What inexpressible charm seems to encircle some Christians, simply because they carry upon their pure countenance and gentle spirit the imprint of the cross! It is the holy evidence of having died to something that was once proud and strong but is now forever surrendered at the feet of Jesus. And it is also the heavenly charm of a broken spirit and a contrite heart, the beautiful music that rises from a minor key, and the sweetness brought about by the touch of frost on ripened fruit.

Finally, frankincense was a fragrance that arose only after being touched with fire. The burning incense became clouds of sweetness arising from the heart of the flames. It symbolizes a person's heart whose sweetness has been brought forth by the flames of affliction until the holy, innermost part of the soul is filled with clouds of praise and prayer.

Beloved, are our lives yielding spices and perfumes—sweet fragrances of the heart? The Love-Life of Our Lord

A Persian fable says: One day
A wanderer found a lump of clay
So savory of sweet perfume
Its odors scented all the room.
"What are you?" was his quick demand,
"Are you some gem from Samarkand,
Or pure nard in this plain disguise,
Or other costly merchandise?"
"No, I am but a lump of clay."

"Then whence this wondrous perfume—say!"
"Friend, if the secret I disclose,
I have been dwelling with the rose."
Sweet parable! and will not those
Who love to dwell with Sharon's rose,
Distill sweet odors all around,
Though low and poor themselves are found?
Dear Lord, abide with us that we
May draw our perfume fresh from Thee.

SEPTEMBER 16

Hide in the Kerith Ravine.

1 Kings 17:3

God's servants must be taught the value of the hidden side of life. The person who is to serve in a lofty place before others must also assume a lowly place before his God. We should not be surprised if God occasionally says to us, "Dear child, you have had enough of this hurried pace, excitement, and publicity. Now I want you to go and hide yourself—'hide in the Kerith Ravine' of sickness, the 'Kerith Ravine' of sorrow, or some place of total solitude, from which the crowds have turned away." And happy is the person who can reply to the Lord, "Your will is also mine. Therefore I run to hide myself in You. 'I long to dwell in your tent forever and take refuge in the shelter of your wings' [Psalm 61:4]."

Every saintly soul that desires to wield great influence over others must first win the power in some hidden "Kerith Ravine." Acquiring spiritual power is impossible unless we hide from others and ourselves in some deep ravine where we may absorb the power of the eternal God. May our lives be like the vegetation centuries ago that absorbed the power of the sunshine and now gives the energy back after having become coal.

Lancelot Andrews, a bishop of the Church of England and one of the translators of the King James Bible of 1611, experienced his "Kerith

Ravine," in which he spent five hours of every day in prayer and devotion to God. John Welsh, a contemporary of Andrews, and a Presbyterian who was imprisoned for his faith by James VI of Scotland, also had his "ravine." He believed his day to be wasted if he did not spend eight to ten hours of isolated communion with God. David Brainerd's "ravine" was the forests of North America while he served as a pioneer missionary to the American Indians during the eighteenth century. And Christmas Evans, a preacher of the late-eighteenth and early-nineteenth centuries, had his long and lonely journeys through the hills of Wales.

Looking back to the blessed age from which we date the centuries, there are many notable "ravines." The Isle of Patmos, the solitude of the Roman prisons, the Arabian Desert, and the hills and valleys of Palestine are all as enduringly memorable as those experienced by the people who have shaped our modern world.

Our Lord Himself lived through His "Kerith Ravine" in Nazareth, in the wilderness of Judea, amid the olive trees of Bethany, and in the solitude of the city of Gadara. So none of us is exempt from a "ravine" experience, where the sounds of human voices are exchanged for the waters of quietness that flow from the throne of God, and where we taste the sweetness and soak up the power of a life "hidden with Christ" (Colossians 3:3). F. B. Meyer

SEPTEMBER 17

He is the Lord; let him do what is good in his eyes.

1 Samuel 3:18

If I see God in everything, He will calm and color everything I see! Perhaps the circumstances causing my sorrows will not be removed and my situation will remain the same, but if Christ is brought into my grief and gloom as my Lord and Master, He will "surround me with songs of deliverance" (Psalm 32:7). To see *Him* and to be sure that His wisdom and power never fail and His love never changes, to know that even His most distressing dealings with me are for my deepest spiritual gain, is to be able to say in the midst of bereavement, sorrow, pain, and loss, "The LORD gave and the LORD has taken away; may the name of the LORD be praised" (Job 1:21).

Seeing God in everything is the only thing that will make me loving and patient with people who annoy and trouble me. Then I will see others as the instruments God uses to accomplish His tender and wise purpose for me, and I will even find myself inwardly thanking them for the blessing they have become to me. Nothing but seeing God will completely put an end to all complaining and thoughts of rebellion. HANNAH WHITALL SMITH

"Give me a new idea," I said,
While thinking on a sleepless bed;
"A new idea that'll bring to earth
A balm for souls of priceless worth;
That'll give men thoughts of things above,
And teach them how to serve and love,
That'll banish every selfish thought,
And rid men of the sins they've fought."

The new thought came, just how, I'll tell:
'Twas when on bended knee I fell,
And sought from Him who knows full well
The way our sorrow to expel.
See God in all things, great and small,
And give Him praise whate'er befall,
In life or death, in pain or woe,
See God, and overcome your foe.

I saw Him in the morning light,
He made the day shine clear and bright;
I saw Him in the noontide hour,

And gained from Him refreshing shower.
At evening, when worn and sad,
He gave me help, and made me glad.
At midnight, when on tossing bed
My weary soul to sleep He led.

I saw Him when great losses came,
And found He loved me just the same.
When heavy loads I had to bear,
I found He lightened every care.
By sickness, sorrow, sore distress,
He calmed my mind and gave me rest.
He's filled my heart with joyous praise
Since I gave Him the upward gaze.

'Twas new to me, yet old to some,
This thought that to me has become
A revelation of the way
We all should live throughout the day;
For as each day unfolds its light,
We'll walk by faith and not by sight.
Life will, indeed, a blessing bring,
If we see God in everything.

A. E. Finn

SEPTEMBER 18

Where there is no vision, the people perish.

Proverbs 29:18 kjv

Waiting upon God is vital in order to see Him and receive a vision from Him. And the amount of time spent before Him is also critical, for our hearts are like a photographer's film—the longer exposed, the deeper the impression. For God's vision to be impressed on our hearts, we must sit in *stillness* at His feet for quite a long time. Remember, the *troubled* surface of a lake will not reflect an image.

Yes, our lives must be quiet and peaceful if we expect to see God. And the vision we see from Him has the power to affect our lives in the same way a lovely sunset brings peace to a troubled heart. Seeing God always transforms human life.

Jacob "crossed the ford of the Jabbok" (Genesis 32:22), saw God, and became Israel. Seeing a vision of God transformed Gideon from a coward into a courageous soldier. And Thomas, after seeing Christ, was changed from a doubting follower into a loyal, devoted disciple.

People since Bible times have also had visions of God. William Carey, English pioneer missionary of the eighteenth century who is considered by some to be the Father of Modern Missions, saw God and left his shoemaker's bench to go to India. David Livingstone saw God and left everything in Britain behind to become a missionary and explorer, following the Lord's leading through the thickest jungles of Africa during the nineteenth century. And literally thousands more have since had visions of God and today are serving Him in the uttermost parts of the earth, seeking the timely evangelization of the lost. DR. PARDINGTON

It is very unusual for there to be complete quiet in the soul, for God almost continually whispers to us. And whenever the sounds of the world subside in our soul, we hear the whispering of God. Yes, He continues to whisper to us, but we often do not hear Him because of the noise and distractions caused by the hurried pace of our lives. FREDERICK WILLIAM FABER

Speak, Lord, in the stillness,
While I wait on Thee;
Hushing my heart to listen
In expectancy.

Speak, O blessed Master,
In this quiet hour;
Let me see Your face, Lord,
Feel Your touch of power.

For the words that You speak,
"They are life," indeed;
Living bread from Heaven,
Now my spirit feed!

Speak, Your servant hears You!
Be not silent, Lord;
My soul on You does wait
For Your life-giving word!

SEPTEMBER 19

"My Father is the gardener."
JOHN 15:1

IT IS A COMFORTING THOUGHT THAT TROUBLE, IN WHATEVER FORM IT comes to us, is a heavenly messenger that brings us something from God. Outwardly it may appear painful or even destructive, but inwardly its spiritual work produces blessings. Many of the richest blessings we have inherited are the fruit of sorrow or pain. We should never forget that redemption, the world's greatest blessing, is the fruit of the world's greatest sorrow. And whenever a time of deep pruning comes and the knife cuts deeply and the pain is severe, what an inexpressible comfort it is to know: "My Father is the gardener."

John Vincent, a Methodist Episcopal bishop of the late-nineteenth and early-twentieth centuries and a leader of the Sunday school movement in America, once told of being in a large greenhouse where clusters of luscious grapes were hanging on each side. The owner of the greenhouse told him, "When the new gardener came here, he said he would not work with the vines unless he could cut them completely down to the stalk. I allowed him to do so, and we had no grapes for two years, but this is now the result."

There is rich symbolism in this account of the pruning process when applied to the Christian life. Pruning *seems* to be destroying the vine, and the gardener *appears* to be cutting everything away. Yet he sees the future and knows that the final result will be the enrichment of the life of the vine, and a greater abundance of fruit.

There are many blessings we will never receive until we are ready to pay the price of pain, for the path of suffering is the only way to reach them. J. R. MILLER

I walked a mile with Pleasure,
She chattered all the way;
But left me none the wiser
For all she had to say.

I walked a mile with Sorrow,
And ne'er a word said she;
But oh, the things I learned from her
When Sorrow walked with me.

SEPTEMBER 20

"Did I not tell you that if you believe,
you will see the glory of God?"
JOHN 11:40

MARY AND MARTHA COULD NOT UNDERSTAND WHAT THEIR LORD WAS doing. Each of them had said to Him, "*Lord, if you had been here, my brother would not have died*" (vv. 21, 32). And behind their words we seem to read their true thoughts: "Lord, we do not understand *why* You waited so long to come or *how* You could allow the man You love so much to die. We do not understand *how You could allow such sorrow and suffering to devastate* our lives, when Your presence might have stopped it all. *Why* didn't You come? Now it's too late, because Lazarus has been dead four days!" But Jesus simply had one great truth in answer to all of this. He said, in essence, "You may not understand, but I am telling you that if you *believe*, you will *see*."

Abraham could not understand *why* God would ask him to sacrifice his son, but he trusted Him. Then he *saw* the Lord's glory when the son he loved was restored to him. Moses could not understand *why* God would require him to stay forty years in the wilderness, but he also trusted Him. Then he *saw* when God called him to lead Israel from Egyptian bondage.

Joseph could not understand his brothers' cruelty toward him, the false testimony of a treacherous woman, or the long years of unjust imprisonment, but he trusted God and finally he *saw* His glory in it all. And Joseph's father, Jacob, could not understand *how* God's strange providence could allow Joseph to be taken from him. Yet later he *saw* the Lord's glory when he looked into the face of his son, who had become the governor for a great king and the person used to preserve his own life and the lives of an entire nation.

Perhaps there is also something in your life causing you to question God. Do you find yourself saying, "I do not understand *why* God allowed my loved one to be taken. I do not understand *why* affliction has been permitted to strike me. I do not understand *why* the Lord has led me down these twisting paths. I do not understand *why* my own plans, which seemed so good, have been so disappointing. I do not understand *why* the blessings I so desperately need are so long in coming."

Dear friend, you do not *have* to understand all God's ways of dealing with you. He does not expect you to understand them. You do not expect *your* children to understand everything you do—you simply want them to trust you. And someday you too will *see* the glory of God in the things you do not understand. J. H. M.

If we could push ajar the gates of life,
And stand within, and all God's working see,
We might interpret all this doubt and strife,
And for each mystery could find a key.

But not today. Then be content, dear heart;
God's plans, like lilies pure and white, unfold.
We must not tear the close-shut leaves apart—
Time will someday reveal the blooms of gold.

And if, through patient toil, we reach the land
Where tired feet, with sandals loosed, may rest,
When we shall clearly know and understand,
I think that we will say, "God knew best."

SEPTEMBER 21

I consider everything a loss because of the surpassing worth of knowing Christ Jesus my Lord.
PHILIPPIANS 3:8

THE AUTUMN SEASON WE ARE NOW ENTERING IS ONE OF CORNFIELDS ripe for harvest, of the cheerful song of those who reap the crops, and of gathered and securely stored grain. So allow me to draw your attention to the sermon of the fields. This is its solemn message: "You must die in order to live. You must refuse to consider your own comfort and well-being. You must be crucified, not only to your desires and habits that are obviously sinful, but also to many others that may appear to be innocent and right. If you desire to save others, you cannot save yourself, and if you desire to bear much fruit, you must be buried in darkness and solitude."

My heart fails me as I listen. But when the words are from Jesus, may I remind myself that it is my great privilege to enter into "the fellowship of his sufferings" (Philippians 3:10 KJV) and I am therefore in great company. May I also remind myself that all the suffering is designed to make me a vessel suitable for His use. And may I remember that His Calvary blossomed into abundant fruitfulness, and so will mine.

Pain leads to plenty, and death to life—it is the law of the kingdom! IN THE HOUR OF SILENCE

Do we call it dying when a bud blossoms into a flower? SELECTED

Finding, following, keeping, struggling,
Is He sure to bless?
Saints, apostles, prophets, martyrs,
Answer, "Yes."

SEPTEMBER 22

"Satan has asked to sift you as wheat. But I have prayed for you, Simon, that your faith may not fail."
LUKE 22:31–32

OUR FAITH IS THE CENTER OF THE TARGET GOD AIMS AT WHEN HE tests us, and if any gift escapes untested, it certainly will not be our faith. There is nothing that pierces faith to its very marrow—to find whether or not it is the faith of those who are immortal—like shooting the arrow of the feeling of being deserted into it. And only genuine faith will escape unharmed from the midst of the battle after having been stripped of its armor of earthly enjoyment and after having endured the circumstances coming against it that the powerful hand of God has allowed.

Faith must be tested, and the sense of feeling deserted is "the furnace heated seven times hotter than usual" (Daniel 3:19) into which it may be thrown. Blessed is the person who endures such an ordeal! CHARLES H. SPURGEON

Paul said, "I have kept the faith" (2 Timothy 4:7), but his head was removed! They cut it off, but they could not touch his faith. This great apostle to the Gentiles rejoiced in three things: he had "fought the good fight," he had "finished the race," and he had "kept the faith." So what was the value of everything else? The apostle Paul had won the race and gained the ultimate prize—he had won not only the admiration of those on earth today but also the admiration of heaven. So why do we not live as if it pays to lose "all things . . . that [we] may gain Christ" (Philippians 3:8)? Why are we not as loyal to the truth as Paul was? It is because our math is different—he counted in a different way than we do. What we count as *gain*, he counted as *loss*. If we desire to ultimately wear the same crown, we must have his faith and live it.

SEPTEMBER 23

"Whoever believes in me, as the Scripture has said, rivers of living water will flow from within them."

John 7:38

Some of us are troubled, wondering why the Holy Spirit doesn't fill us. The problem is that we have plenty coming in but we are not giving out to others. If you will give the blessing you have received, planning your life around greater service and being a blessing to those around you, then you will quickly find that the Holy Spirit is with you. He will bestow blessings to you for service, giving you all He can trust you to give away to others.

No music is as heavenly as that made by an aeolian harp. It is a beautiful occurrence of nature, but it has a spiritual parallel. The harp is nothing but a wooden box with strings arranged in harmony, waiting to be touched by the unseen fingers of the wandering wind. As the breath of heaven floats over the strings, notes that are nearly divine float upon the air, as if a choir of angels were wandering about and touching the strings.

In the same way, it is possible to keep our hearts so open to the touch of the Holy Spirit that He may play them as He chooses, while we quietly wait on the pathway of His service. Days of Heaven upon Earth

When the apostles "were filled with the Holy Spirit" (Acts 2:4), they did not lease the Upper Room and stay there to hold holiness meetings. They went everywhere, preaching the gospel. Will Huff

"If I have eaten my morsel alone,"
The patriarch spoke with scorn;
What would he think of the Church were he shown
Heathendom—huge, forlorn, Godless,
Christless, with soul unfed,
While the Church's ailment is fullness of bread,
Eating her morsel alone?

"Freely you have received, so give,"
He says, who has given us all.
How will the soul in us longer live
Deaf to their starving call,
For whom the blood of the Lord was shed,
And His body broken to give them bread,
If we eat our morsel alone!
Archbishop William Alexander

"Where is your brother Abel?" (Genesis 4:9).

SEPTEMBER 24

When they came to the border of Mysia, they tried to enter Bithynia, but the Spirit of Jesus would not allow them to.
Acts 16:7

WHAT A STRANGE THING FOR THE LORD TO PROHIBIT, FOR THEY WERE going into Bithynia to do Christ's work! And the door was shut before them by Christ's own Spirit.

There have been times when I have experienced the same thing. Sometimes I have been interrupted in what seemed to be quite productive work. And at times, opposition came and forced me to go back, or sickness came and forced me to rest in some isolated place.

During such times, it was difficult for me to leave my work unfinished when I believed it was service done in the power of His Spirit. But I finally remembered that *the Spirit requires not only a service of work but also a service of waiting.* I came to see that in the kingdom of Christ, there are not only times for action but times to refrain from action. And I also came to learn that a place of isolation is often the most useful place of all in this diverse world. Its harvest is more rich than the seasons when the corn and wine were the most abundant. So I have learned to thank the blessed Holy Spirit that many a beautiful Bithynia had to be left without a visit from me.

Dear Holy Spirit, my desire is still to be led by You. Nevertheless, my opportunities for usefulness seem to be disappointed, for today the door appears open into a life of service for You but tomorrow it closes before me just as I am about to enter. Teach me to see another door even in the midst of the inaction of this time. Help me to find, even in the area of service where You have closed a door, a new entrance into Your service. Inspire me with the knowledge that a person may sometimes be called to serve by doing nothing, by staying still, or by waiting. And when I remember the power of Your "gentle whisper" (1 Kings 19:12), I will not complain that sometimes the Spirit allows me *not* to go. GEORGE MATHESON

When I cannot understand my Father's leading,
And it seems to be but hard and cruel fate,
Still I hear that gentle whisper ever pleading,
God is working, God is faithful, only wait.

SEPTEMBER 25

Why must I go about mourning?
PSALM 42:9

DEAR BELIEVER, CAN YOU ANSWER THE ABOVE QUESTION? CAN YOU find any reason why you are so often mourning instead of rejoicing? Why do you allow your mind to dwell on gloomy thoughts? Who told you that night will never end in day? Who told you that the winter of your discontent would continue from frost to frost and from snow, ice, and hail to even deeper snow and stronger storms of despair?

Don't you know that day dawns after night, showers displace drought, and spring and summer follow winter? Then, have hope! Hope forever, for God will not fail you! CHARLES H. SPURGEON

He was better to me than all my hopes;
He was better than all my fears;
He made a bridge of my broken works,
And a rainbow of my tears.

The stormy waves that marked my ocean path,
Did carry my Lord on their crest;
When I dwell on the days of my wilderness march
I can lean on His love for the rest.

He emptied my hands of my treasured store,
And His covenant love revealed,
There was not a wound in my aching heart,
The balm of His breath has not healed.

Oh, tender and true was His discipline sore,
In wisdom, that taught and tried,
Till the soul that He sought was trusting in Him,
And nothing on earth beside.

He guided my paths that I could not see,
By ways that I have not known;
The crooked was straight, and the rough was plain
As I followed the Lord alone.

I praise Him still for the pleasant palms,
And the desert streams by the way,
For the glowing pillar of flame by night,
And the sheltering cloud by day.

Never a time on the dreariest day,
But some promise of love endears;
I read from the past, that my future will be
Far better than all my fears.

Like the golden jar, of the wilderness bread,
Stored up with the blossoming rod,
All safe in the ark, with the law of the Lord,
Is the covenant care of my God.

SEPTEMBER 26

We live by faith, not by sight.
2 CORINTHIANS 5:7

AS BELIEVERS, "WE LIVE BY FAITH, NOT BY SIGHT"—GOD NEVER wants us to live by our feelings. Our inner self may want to live by feelings, and Satan may want us to, but God wants us to face the facts, not feelings. He wants us to face the facts of Christ and His finished and perfect work for us. And once we face these precious facts, and believe them simply because God says they are facts, He will take care of our feelings.

Yet God never gives us feelings to enable or encourage us to trust

Him, and He never gives them to show us that we have already completely trusted Him. God only gives us feelings when He sees that we trust Him apart from our feelings, resting solely on His Word and His faithfulness to His promise. And these feelings that can only come from Him will be given at such a time and to such a degree as His love sees best for each individual circumstance.

Therefore we must choose between facing our feelings or facing the facts of God. Our feelings may be as uncertain and changing as the sea or shifting sand. God's facts, however, are as certain as the Rock of Ages Himself—"Jesus Christ . . . the same yesterday and today and forever" (Hebrews 13:8).

When darkness veils His lovely face
I rest on His unchanging grace;
In every strong and stormy gale,
My anchor holds within the veil.

SEPTEMBER 27

I have found a ransom for them.

Job 33:24

Divine healing is actually divine life. It is the lordship of Christ over the body—or the life of Christ in the framework of the human body. It is the union of the parts of our bodies with His very body, exhibiting His life flowing throughout our bodies.

It is as real as His risen and glorified body. And it is as reasonable as the fact that He was raised from the dead, is a living person with an actual body, and sits today as an understanding soul at God's right hand.

That same Christ, with all His attributes and mighty power, belongs to us. We are members of His body, His flesh, and His bones, and if we will only believe this and receive it, we may actually draw our life from the very life of the Son of God.

Dear God, help me to know and to live this verse: "The body, however is . . . for the Lord, and the Lord for the body" (1 Corinthians 6:13). A. B. Simpson

"*The* Lord *your God is with you, the Mighty Warrior who saves*" (Zephaniah 3:17). This was the verse that initially brought the truth of divine healing to my mind and my worn-out body more than twenty years ago. It is now a door more wide open than ever and is the gate through which the living Christ enters moment by moment into my redeemed body. He enters to fill, energize, and vitalize me with the presence and power of His own personality, transforming my entire being into "a new heaven and a new earth" (Revelation 21:1).

Another verse reads, "*The Lord your God*" (Luke 10:27). If the Lord is *my* God, then all that is in almighty God is mine. It all resides within me to the extent that I am willing and able to appropriate Him and all that belongs to Him. "God, whose name is the Lord Almighty" (Jeremiah 32:18), is indeed the *all* mighty God and is my *inside* God. Just as the sun is the center of our solar system, He is centered within me, living as the Father, Son, and Holy Spirit. He is the great generator of the power plant at the center of my threefold being, working in the midst of my physical being, including my brain and other parts of my nervous system.

For twenty-one years this truth not only has been a living reality to me but has grown deeper and richer. Now, at the age of seventy, I am in every way a much younger and stronger person than I was at thirty. Today I live using God's strength, accomplishing fully twice as much mentally and physically as I ever did in the past, yet with only half the effort. My physical, mental, and spiritual life is like an artesian well—always full and overflowing. Speaking, teaching, and traveling by day or by night through sudden and violent changes in weather or climate is of no more effort to me than it is for the wheels of an engine to turn when the pressure of the steam is at full force or than it is for a pipe to let water run through it.

My body, soul, and spirit thus redeemed,
Sanctified and healed I give, O Lord, to Thee,
A consecrated offering Yours evermore to be.
That all my powers with all their might
In Your sole glory may unite—Hallelujah!

Henry Wilson

SEPTEMBER 28

"In me . . . peace."

John 16:33

There is a vast difference between pleasure and blessedness. Paul experienced imprisonment, pain, sacrifice, and suffering to their very limits, yet through it all he was blessed. All the beatitudes became real in his heart and life, *in the midst* of his difficult circumstances.

Paganini, the great Italian violinist, once stepped onstage only to discover there was something wrong with his violin, just as the audience was ending their applause. He looked at the instrument for a moment and suddenly realized it was not his best and most valuable one. In fact, the violin was not his at all. Momentarily he felt paralyzed, but he quickly turned to his audience, telling them there had been some mistake and he did not have his own violin. He stepped back behind the curtain, thinking he must have left it backstage, but discovered that someone had stolen his and left the inferior one in its place.

After remaining behind the curtain for a moment, Paganini stepped onstage again to speak to the audience. He said, "Ladies and Gentlemen, I will now demonstrate to you that the music is not in the instrument but in the soul." Then he played as never before, and beautiful music flowed from that inferior instrument until the audience was so enraptured that their enthusiastic applause nearly lifted the ceiling of the concert hall. He had indeed revealed to them that the music was not in his instrument but in his own soul!

Dear tested and tried believer, it is your mission to walk onto the stage of this world in order to reveal to all of heaven and earth that the music of life lies not in your circumstances or external things but in your own soul.

If peace be in your heart,
The wildest winter storm is full of solemn beauty,
The midnight flash but shows your path of duty,
Each living creature tells some new and joyous story,
The very trees and stones all catch a ray of glory,
If peace be in your heart.

Charles Francis Richardson

SEPTEMBER 29

I am a man of prayer.

Psalm 109:4

All too often we are in a "holy" hurry in our devotional time. How much actual time do we spend in quiet devotion on a daily basis? Can it be easily measured in minutes? Can you think of even one person of great spiritual stature who did not spend much of his time in prayer? Has anyone ever exhibited much of the spirit of prayer who did not devote a great deal of time to prayer?

George Whitefield, the English preacher who was one of the leading figures in the eighteenth-century American revival known as the Great Awakening, once said, "I have spent entire days and weeks lying prostrate on the ground, engaged in silent or spoken prayer." And the words of another person, whose life confirmed his own assertion, were these: "Fall to your knees and *grow* there."

It has been said that no great work of literature or science has ever been produced by someone who did not love solitude. It is also a fundamental principle of faith that no tremendous growth in holiness has ever been achieved by anyone who has not taken the time frequently, and for long periods, to be *alone with God.* THE STILL HOUR

"Come, come," He calls you, "O soul oppressed and weary,
Come to the shadows of My desert rest;
Come walk with Me far from life's noisy discords,
And peace will breathe like music in your breast."

SEPTEMBER 30

He guarded him . . . like an eagle that stirs up its nest and hovers over its young, that spreads its wings to catch them and carries them aloft. The LORD alone led him; no foreign god was with him.

DEUTERONOMY 32:10–12

OUR ALMIGHTY GOD IS LIKE A PARENT WHO DELIGHTS IN LEADING the tender children in His care to the very edge of a precipice and then shoving them off the cliff into nothing but air. He does this so they may learn that they already possess an as-yet-unrealized power of flight that can forever add to the pleasure and comfort of their lives. Yet if, in their attempt to fly, they are exposed to some extraordinary peril, He is prepared to swoop beneath them and carry them skyward on His mighty wings. When God brings any of His children into a position of unparalleled difficulty, they may always count on Him to deliver them. THE SONG OF VICTORY

When God places a burden upon you, He places His arms underneath you.

There once was a little plant that was small and whose growth was stunted, for it lived under the shade of a giant oak tree. The little plant valued the shade that covered it and highly regarded the quiet rest that its noble friend provided. Yet there was a greater blessing prepared for this little plant.

One day a woodsman entered the forest with a sharp ax and felled the giant oak. The little plant began to weep, crying out, "My shelter has been taken away. Now every fierce wind will blow on me, and every storm will seek to uproot me!"

The guardian angel of the little plant responded, "No! Now the sun will shine and showers will fall on you more abundantly than ever before. Now your stunted form will spring up into loveliness, and your flowers, which could never have grown to full perfection in the shade, will laugh in the sunshine. And people in amazement will say, 'Look how that plant has grown! How gloriously beautiful it has become by removing that which was its shade and its delight!'"

Dear believer, do you understand that God may take away your comforts and privileges in order to make you a stronger Christian? Do you see why the Lord always trains His soldiers not by allowing them to lie on beds of ease but by calling them to difficult marches and service? He makes them wade through streams, swim across rivers, climb steep mountains, and walk many long marches carrying heavy backpacks of sorrow. This is how He develops soldiers—not by dressing them up in fine uniforms to strut at the gates of the barracks or to appear as handsome gentlemen to those who are strolling through the park. No, God knows that soldiers can only be made in battle and are not developed in times of peace. We may be able to grow the raw materials of which soldiers are made, but turning them into true warriors requires the education brought about by the smell of gunpowder and by fighting in the midst of flying bullets and exploding bombs, not by living through pleasant and peaceful times.

So, dear Christian, could this account for your situation? Is the Lord uncovering your gifts and causing them to grow? Is He developing in you the qualities of a soldier by shoving you into the heat of the battle? Should you not then use every gift and weapon He has given you to become a conqueror? CHARLES H. SPURGEON

OCTOBER 1

It was good for me to be afflicted.

Psalm 119:71

It is a remarkable occurrence of nature that the most brilliant colors of plants are found on the highest mountains, in places that are the most exposed to the fiercest weather. The brightest lichens and mosses, as well as the most beautiful wildflowers, abound high upon the windswept, storm-ravaged peaks.

One of the finest arrays of living color I have ever seen was just above the great Saint Bernard Hospice near the ten-thousand-foot summit of Mont Cenis in the French Alps. The entire face of one expansive rock was covered with a strikingly vivid yellow lichen, which shone in the sunshine like a golden wall protecting an enchanted castle. Amid the loneliness and barrenness of that high altitude and exposed to the fiercest winds of the sky, this lichen exhibited glorious color it has never displayed in the shelter of the valley.

As I write these words, I have two specimens of the same type of lichen before me. One is from this Saint Bernard area, and the other is from the wall of a Scottish castle, which is surrounded by sycamore trees. The difference in their form and coloring is quite striking. The one grown amid the fierce storms of the mountain peak has a lovely yellow color of a primrose, a smooth texture, and a definite form and shape. But the one cultivated amid the warm air and the soft showers of the lowland valley has a dull, rusty color, a rough texture, and an indistinct and broken shape.

Isn't it the same with a Christian who is afflicted, storm-tossed, and without comfort? Until the storms and difficulties allowed by God's providence beat upon a believer again and again, his character appears flawed and blurred. Yet the trials actually clear away the clouds and shadows, perfect the form of his character, and bestow brightness and blessing to his life.

Amidst my list of blessings infinite
Stands this the foremost, that my heart has bled;
For all I bless You, most for the severe.
Hugh Macmillan

OCTOBER 2

He took them with him and they withdrew by themselves.
Luke 9:10

In order to grow in grace, we must spend a great deal of time in quiet solitude. Contact with others in society is not what causes the soul to grow most vigorously. In fact, one quiet hour of prayer will often yield greater results than many days spent in the company of others. It is in the desert that the dew is freshest and the air is the most pure.
Andrew Bonar

Come with Me by yourselves and rest awhile,
I know you're weary of the stress and throng,
Wipe from your brow the sweat and dust of toil,
And in My quiet strength again be strong.

Come now aside from all the world holds dear,
For fellowship the world has never known,
Alone with Me, and with My Father here,
With Me and with My Father, not alone.

Come, tell Me all that you have said and done,
Your victories and failures, hopes and fears.
I know how hardened hearts are wooed and won;
My choicest wreaths are always wet with tears.

Come now and rest; the journey is too great,
And you will faint beside the way and sink;
The bread of life is here for you to eat,
And here for you the wine of love to drink.

Then from fellowship with your Lord return,
And work till daylight softens into even:
Those brief hours are not lost in which you learn
More of your Master and His rest in Heaven.

OCTOBER 3

After the earthquake came a fire. . . . And
after the fire came a gentle whisper.
1 KINGS 19:12

A WOMAN WHO HAD MADE RAPID PROGRESS IN HER UNDERSTANDING of the Lord was once asked the secret of her seemingly easy growth. Her brief response was, "*Mind the checks.*"

The reason many of us do not know and understand God better is that we do not heed His gentle "checks"—His delicate restraints and constraints. His voice is "a gentle whisper." A whisper can hardly be heard, so it must be felt as a faint and steady pressure upon the heart and mind, like the touch of a morning breeze calmly moving across the soul. And when it is heeded, it quietly grows clearer in the inner ear of the heart.

God's voice is directed to the ear of love, and true love is intent upon hearing even the faintest whisper. Yet there comes a time when His love ceases to speak, when we do not respond to or believe His message. "God is love" (1 John 4:8), and if you want to know Him and His voice, you must continually listen to His gentle touches.

So when you are about to say something in conversation with others, and you sense a gentle restraint from His quiet whisper, heed the restraint and refrain from speaking. And when you are about to pursue some course of action that seems perfectly clear and right, yet you sense in your spirit another path being suggested with the force of quiet conviction, heed that conviction. Follow the alternate course, even if the change of plans appears to be absolute folly from the perspective of human wisdom.

Also learn to wait on God until He unfolds His will before you. Allow Him to develop all the plans of your heart and mind, and then let Him accomplish them. Do not possess any wisdom of your own, for often His performance will appear to contradict the plan He gave you. God will seem to work against Himself, so simply listen, obey, and trust Him, even when it appears to be the greatest absurdity to do so. Ultimately, "we know that in all things God works for the good of those who love him" (Romans 8:28), but many times, in the initial stages of the performance of His plans:

In His own world He is content
To play a losing game.

Therefore if you desire to know God's voice, never consider the final outcome or the possible results. Obey Him even when He asks you to move while you still see only darkness, for He Himself will be a glorious light within you. Then there will quickly spring up within your heart a knowledge of God and a fellowship with Him, which will be overpowering enough in themselves to hold you and Him together, even in the most severe tests and under the strongest pressures of life. WAY OF FAITH

OCTOBER 4

The LORD blessed the latter part of Job's life more than the first.

JOB 42:12

Job found his legacy through the grief he experienced. He was tried that his godliness might be confirmed and validated. In the same way, my troubles are intended to deepen my character and to clothe me in gifts I had little of prior to my difficulties, for my ripest fruit grows against the roughest wall. I come to a place of glory only through my own humility, tears, and death, just as Job's afflictions left him with a higher view of God and more humble thoughts of himself. At last he cried, "*Now my eyes have seen you*" (v. 5).

If I experience the presence of God in His majesty through my pain and loss, so that I bow before Him and pray, "*Your will be done*" (Matthew 6:10), then I have gained much indeed. God gave Job glimpses of his future glory, for in those weary and difficult days and nights, he was allowed to penetrate God's veil and could honestly say, "*I know that my redeemer lives*" (Job 19:25). So truly: "The Lord blessed the latter part of Job's life more than the first." In the Hour of Silence

Trouble never comes to someone unless it brings a nugget of gold in its hand.

Apparent adversity will ultimately become an advantage for those of us doing what is right, if we are willing to keep serving and to wait patiently. Think of the great victorious souls of the past who worked with steadfast faith and who were invincible and courageous! There are many blessings we will never obtain if we are unwilling to accept and endure suffering. There are certain joys that can come to us only through sorrow. There are revelations of God's divine truth that we will receive only when the lights of earth have been extinguished. And there are harvests that will grow only once the plow has done its work. Selected

It is from suffering that the strongest souls ever known have emerged; the world's greatest display of character is seen in those who exhibit the scars of sorrow; the martyrs of the ages have worn their coronation robes that have glistened with fire, yet through their tears and sorrow have seen the gates of heaven. Chapin

I will know by the gleam and glitter
Of the golden chain you wear,
By your heart's calm strength in loving,
Of the fire you have had to bear.
Beat on, true heart, forever;
Shine bright, strong golden chain;
And bless the cleansing fire
And the furnace of living pain!

Adelaide Proctor

OCTOBER 5

Some time later the brook dried up.

1 Kings 17:7

The education of our faith is incomplete if we have yet to learn that God's providence works through loss, that there is a ministry to us through failure and the fading of things, and that He gives the gift of emptiness. It is, in fact, the material insecurities of life that cause our lives to be spiritually established. The dwindling brook at the Kerith Ravine, where Elijah sat deep in thought, is a true picture of each of our lives. "*Some time later the brook dried up*"—this is the history of our yesterdays, and a prophecy of our tomorrows.

One way or the other, we must all learn the difference between trusting in the gift and trusting in the Giver. The gift may last for a season, but the Giver is the only eternal love.

The Kerith Ravine was a difficult problem for Elijah until he arrived at Zarephath, and suddenly everything became as clear as daylight to him. God's hard instructions are never His last words to us, for the woe, the waste, and the tears of life belong to its interlude, not its finale.

If the Lord had led Elijah directly to Zarephath, he would have missed something that helped to make him a wiser prophet and a better man—living by faith at Kerith. And whenever our earthly stream or any other outer resource has dried up, it has been allowed so we may learn that our hope and help are in God, who made heaven and earth. F. B. Meyer

Perhaps you, too, have camped by such sweet waters,
And quenched with joy your weary, parched soul's thirst;
To find, as time goes on, your streamlet alters
From what it was at first.

Hearts that have cheered, or soothed, or blest, or strengthened;
Loves that have lavished unreservedly;
Joys, treasured joys—have passed, as time has lengthened,
Into obscurity.

If then, O soul, the brook your heart has cherished
Does fail you now—no more your thirst assuage—
If its once glad refreshing streams have perished,
Let Him your heart engage.

He will not fail, nor mock, nor disappoint you;
His comfort and care change not with the years;
With oil of joy He surely will anoint you,
And wipe away your tears.

J. Danson Smith

OCTOBER 6

He did not open his mouth.

Isaiah 53:7

What grace it requires when we are misunderstood yet handle it correctly, or when we are judged unkindly yet receive it in holy sweetness! Nothing tests our character as a Christian more than having something evil said about us. This kind of grinding test is what exposes whether we are solid gold or simply gold-plated metal. If we could only see the blessings that lie hidden in our trials, we would say like David, when Shimei cursed him, "Let him curse, for the LORD will return good to me instead of his cursing this day" (2 Samuel 16:11–12 NASB).

Some Christians are easily turned away from the greatness of their life's calling by pursuing instead their own grievances and enemies. They ultimately turn their lives into one petty whirlwind of warfare. It reminds me of trying to deal with a hornet's nest. You may be able to disperse the hornets, but you will probably be terribly stung and receive nothing for your pain, for even their honey has no value.

May God grant us more of the Spirit of Christ, who, "when they hurled their insults at him, . . . did not retaliate. . . . Instead, he entrusted himself to him who judges justly" (1 Peter 2:23). "Consider him who endured such opposition from sinners, so that you will not grow weary and lose heart" (Hebrews 12:3). A. B. SIMPSON

For you He walked along the path of woe,
He was sharply struck with His head bent low.
He knew the deepest sorrow, pain, and grief,
He knew long endurance with no relief,
He took all the bitter from death's deep cup,
He kept no blood drops but gave them all up.
Yes, for you, and for me, He won the fight
To take us to glory and realms of light.

L. S. P.

OCTOBER 7

Who among you fears the LORD and obeys the word of his servant? Let him who walks in the dark, who has no light, trust in the name of the LORD and rely on [his] God.

ISAIAH 50:10

What is a believer to do in times of darkness—a darkness of perplexities and confusion—a darkness not of the heart but of the mind? These times of darkness come to a faithful and believing disciple who is walking obediently in the will of God. They come as seasons when he does not know what to do or which way to turn. His sky becomes overcast with clouds, and the clear light of heaven does not shine on his path, so that he feels as if he were groping his way through complete darkness.

Dear believer, does this describe you? What should you do in times of darkness? Listen to God's Word: "Let [him] . . . trust in the name of the Lord and rely on his God." Actually, the first thing to do is nothing. This is a difficult thing for our lowly human nature to do. There is a saying, "When you're rattled, don't rush." In other words, "When you are confused and do not know what to do, do nothing." When you find yourself in a spiritual fog, do not run ahead, but slow the pace of your life. And if necessary, keep your life's ship anchored or tied to the dock.

The right thing is simply to trust God, for while we trust, He can work. Worrying, however, prevents Him from doing anything for us. If the darkness covering us strikes terror in our hearts and we run back and forth, seeking in vain to find a way of escape from the dark trial where God's providence has placed us, then the Lord cannot work on our behalf.

Only the peace of God will quiet our minds and put our hearts at rest. We must place our hand in His as a little child and allow Him to lead us into the bright sunshine of His love. He knows the way out of the dense, dark forest, so may we climb into His arms, trusting Him to rescue us by showing us the shortest and most reliable road. Dr. Pardington

Remember, we are never without a pilot—even when we do not know which way to steer.

Hold on, my heart, in your believing—
Only the steadfast wins the crown;
He who, when stormy winds are heaving,
Parts with his anchor, will go down;
But he who Jesus holds through all,

Will stand, though Heaven and earth should fall.
Hold on! An end will come to sorrow;
Hope from the dust will conquering rise;
The storm foretells a summer's morrow;
The Cross points on to Paradise;
The Father reigns! So cease all doubt;
Hold on, my heart. Hold on, hold out.

OCTOBER 8

Do not be anxious about anything.
PHILIPPIANS 4:6

QUITE A FEW CHRISTIANS LIVE IN A TERRIBLE STATE OF ANXIETY, constantly fretting over the concerns of life. The secret of living in perfect peace amid the hectic pace of daily life is one well worth knowing. What good has worrying ever accomplished? It has never made anyone stronger, helped anyone do God's will, or provided for anyone a way of escape out of their anxiety or confusion. Worry only destroys the effectiveness of lives that would otherwise be useful and beautiful. Being restless and having worries and cares are absolutely forbidden by our Lord, who said, "So do not worry, saying, 'What shall we eat?' or 'What shall we drink?' or 'What shall we wear?'" (Matthew 6:31). He does not mean that we are not to think ahead or that our life should never have a plan or pattern to it. He simply means that we are not to worry about these things.

People will know that you live in a constant state of anxiety by the lines on your face, the tone of your voice, your negative attitude, and the lack of joy in your spirit. So scale the heights of a life abandoned to God, and your perspective will change to the point that you will look down on the clouds beneath your feet. DARLOW SARGEANT

It is a sign of weakness to always worry and fret, question everything, and mistrust everyone. Can anything be gained by it? Don't we only make ourselves unfit for action, and separate our minds from the ability to make wise decisions? We simply sink in our struggles when we could float by faith.

Oh, for the grace to be silent! Oh, to "be still, and know that [Jehovah is] God" (Psalm 46:10)! "The Holy One of Israel" (Psalm 89:18) will defend and deliver His own. We can be sure that His every word will stand forever, even though the mountains may fall into the sea. He deserves our total confidence. So come, my soul, return to your place of peace, and rest within the sweet embrace of the Lord Jesus. SELECTED

Peace your inmost soul will fill
When you're still!

OCTOBER 9

The LORD longs to be gracious to you; therefore
he will rise up to show you compassion.
ISAIAH 30:18

THE GREENEST GRASS IS FOUND WHEREVER THE MOST RAIN FALLS. So I suppose it is the fog and mist of Ireland that makes it "the Emerald Isle." And wherever you find the widespread fog of trouble and the mist of sorrow, you always find emerald green hearts that are full of the beautiful foliage of the comfort and love of God.

Dear Christian, do not say, "Where are all the swallows? They are all gone—they are dead." No, they are not dead. They have simply skimmed across the deep, blue sea, flying to a faraway land; but they will be back again soon.

Child of God, do not say, "All the flowers are dead—the winter has killed them, so they are gone." No! Although the winter has covered them with a white coat of snow, they will push up their heads again and will be alive very soon.

O believer, do not say that the sun has burned out, just because a cloud has hidden it. No, it is still there, planning a summer for you; for when it shines again, it will have caused those clouds to have dropped their April showers, each of them a mother to a sweet May flower.

Above all, remember—when God hides His face from you, do not say that He has forgotten you. He is simply waiting for a little while to make you love Him more. And once He comes, you will rejoice with the inexpressible "joy of the LORD" (Nehemiah 8:10). Waiting on Him exercises your gift of grace and tests your faith. Therefore continue to wait in hope, for although the promise may linger, it will never come too late. CHARLES H. SPURGEON

Oh, every year has its winter,
And every year has its rain—
But a day is always coming
When the birds go north again.

When new leaves sprout in the forest,
And grass springs green on the plain,
And tulips boast their blossoms—
And the birds go north again.

Oh, every heart has its sorrow,
And every heart has its pain—
But a day is always coming
When the birds go north again.

It's the sweetest thing to remember,
If your courage starts to wane,
When the cold, dark days are over—
That the birds go north again.

OCTOBER 10

Do not fret.

PSALM 37:1

I BELIEVE THAT THIS VERSE IS AS MUCH A DIVINE COMMAND AS "*You shall not steal*" (Exodus 20:15). But what does it mean to fret? One person once defined it as that which makes a person rough on the surface, causing him to rub and wear himself and others away. Isn't it true that an irritable, irrational, and critical person not only wears himself out but is also very draining and tiring to others? When we worry and fret, we are a constant annoyance. This psalm not only says, "Do not fret because of those who are evil" but leaves no room for fretting whatsoever. It is very harmful, and God does not want us to hurt ourselves or others.

Any physician can tell you that a fit of anger is more harmful to your system than a fever and that a disposition of continual fretting is not conducive to a healthy body. The next step down from fretting is being quick-tempered, and that amounts to anger. May we set it aside once and for all and simply be obedient to the command "*Do not fret.*" MARGARET BOTTOME

OVERHEARD IN AN ORCHARD

Said the Robin to the Sparrow:
"I should really like to know
Why these anxious human beings
Rush about and worry so."

Said the Sparrow to the Robin:
"Friend, I think that it must be
That they have no Heavenly Father
Such as cares for you and me."

ELIZABETH CHENEY

OCTOBER 11

Dying, and yet we live on.
2 Corinthians 6:9

Last summer I had a flower bed of asters that nearly covered my garden in the country. They were planted late in the season, but how beautiful they were! While the outer portion of the plants were still producing fresh flowers, the tops had gone to seed, and when an early frost came, I found that the radiant beauty of the blossoms had withered. All I could say at this point was, "Oh well, I guess the season has been too much for them, and they have died." So I wished them a fond farewell.

After this I no longer enjoyed looking at the flower bed, for it seemed to be only a graveyard of flowers. Yet several weeks ago one of the gardeners called my attention to the fact that across the entire garden, asters were now sprouting up in great abundance. It appeared that every plant I thought the winter had destroyed had replanted fifty to take its place. What had the frost and the fierce winter wind done?

They had taken my flowers and destroyed them, casting them to the ground. They had walked across them with their snowy feet and, once finished with their work, said, "*This is the end of you.*" And yet in the spring, for every one destroyed, fifty witnesses arose and said, "*It is through 'dying . . . we live on.'*"

As it is in the plant world, so it is in God's kingdom. Through death came everlasting life. Through crucifixion and the tomb came the throne and the palace of the eternal God. Through apparent defeat came victory.

So do not be afraid of suffering or defeat. It is through being "struck down, but not destroyed" (2 Corinthians 4:9) and through being broken to pieces, and those pieces being torn to shreds, that we become people of strength. And it is the endurance of one believer that produces a multitude.

Others may yield to the appearance of things and follow the world. They may blossom quickly and find momentary prosperity, but their end will be one of eternal death. Henry Ward Beecher

Measure your life by loss and not by gain,
Not by the wine drunk but by the wine poured forth.
For love's strength is found in love's sacrifice,
And he who suffers most has most to give.

OCTOBER 12

Joseph's master took him and put him in prison. . . . But . . . the Lord was with him . . . and gave him success in whatever he did.

Genesis 39:20–21, 23

When God allows us to go to prison because of our service to Him, it is nearly the most blessed place in the world that we could be, because He goes with us. Joseph seems to have known this truth. He did not sulk, become discouraged and rebellious, or engage in self-pity by thinking "everything was against him." If he had done so, the prison warden would never have trusted him.

May we remember that if self-pity is allowed to set in, we will never be used by God again until it is totally removed. Joseph simply placed everything in joyful trust upon the Lord, and as a result, the prison warden placed everything into Joseph's care.

Lord Jesus, when the prison door closes behind me, keep me trusting in You with complete and overflowing joy. Give Your work through me great success, and even in prison make me "free indeed" (John 8:36).
Selected

A little bird I am,
Shut from the fields of air,
And in my cage I sit and sing
To Him who placed me there;
Well pleased a prisoner to be,
Because, My God, it pleases Thee.

My cage confines me round,
Freely I cannot fly,
But though my wings are closely bound,
My soul is at liberty;
For prison walls cannot control
The flight or freedom of the soul.

I have learned to love the darkness of sorrow, for it is there I see the brightness of God's face. MADAME GUYON

OCTOBER 13

Do not be anxious about anything.

PHILIPPIANS 4:6

ANXIETY SHOULD NEVER BE FOUND IN A BELIEVER. IN SPITE OF THE magnitude, quantity, and diversity of our trials, afflictions, and difficulties, anxiety should not exist under any circumstances. This is because we have a Father in heaven who is almighty, who loves His children as He loves His "one and only Son" (John 3:16), and whose complete joy and delight it is to continually assist them under all circumstances. We should heed His Word, which says, "Do not be anxious about anything, but in every situation, by prayer and petition, with thanksgiving, present your requests to God."

"*In every situation*"—not simply when our house is on fire or when our beloved spouse and children are gravely ill, but even in the smallest matters of life. We are to take everything to God—little things, very little things, even what the world calls trivial things. Yes, we are to take *everything*, living all day long in holy fellowship with our heavenly Father and our precious Lord Jesus. We should develop something of a spiritual instinct, causing us to immediately turn to God when a concern keeps us awake at night. During those sleepless nights, we should speak to Him, bringing our various concerns before Him, no matter how small they may be. Also speak to the Lord about any trial you are facing or any difficulties you may have in your family or professional life.

"*By prayer and petition*"—earnestly pleading, persevering and enduring, and waiting, waiting, waiting on God.

"*With thanksgiving*"—always laying a good foundation. Even if we have no possessions, there is one thing for which we can always be thankful—that He has saved us from hell. We can also give thanks that He has given us His Holy Word, His Holy Spirit, and the most precious gift of all—His Son. Therefore when we consider all this, we have abundant reasons for thanksgiving. May this be our goal!

"*And the peace of God, which transcends all understanding, will guard your hearts and your minds in Christ Jesus*" (Philippians 4:7). This is such a wonderful, genuine, and precious blessing that to truly know it, you must experience it, for it "transcends all understanding."

May we take these truths to heart, instinctively walking in them, so the result will be lives that glorify God more abundantly than ever before.
George Mueller, Life of Trust

Search your heart several times a day, and if you find something that is disturbing your peace, remember to take the proper steps to restore the calm. Francis de Sales

OCTOBER 14

Suddenly an angel of the Lord appeared and a light shone in the cell. He struck Peter on the side and woke him up. "Quick, get up!" he said, and the chains fell off Peter's wrists.

Acts 12:7

About midnight Paul and Silas were praying and singing hymns to God. . . . Suddenly there was such a violent earthquake that the foundations of the prison were shaken. At once all the prison doors flew open, and everyone's chains came loose.

Acts 16:25–26

THIS IS THE WAY GOD WORKS. IN OUR DARKEST HOUR, HE WALKS TO US across the waves, just as an angel came to Peter's cell when the day of Peter's execution dawned. And when the scaffold was completed for Mordecai's execution, the king's sleeplessness ultimately led to his action favoring God's favored race (Esther 6).

Dear soul, you may have to experience the very worst before you are delivered, but you will be delivered! God may keep you waiting, but He will always remember His promise and will appear in time to fulfill His sacred Word that cannot be broken. F. B. MEYER

God has a simplicity about Him in working out His plans, and yet He possesses a resourcefulness equal to any difficulty. His faithfulness to His trusting children is unwavering, and He is steadfast in holding to His purpose. In Joseph's life, we see God work through a fellow prisoner, later through a dream, and finally through lifting Joseph from a prison to the position of governor. And the length of Joseph's prison stay gave him the strength and steadiness he needed as governor.

It is always safe to trust God's methods and to live by His clock. SAMUEL DICKEY GORDON

God in His providence has a thousand keys to open a thousand different doors in order to deliver His own, no matter how desperate the situation may have become. May we be faithful to do our part, which is simply to suffer for Him, and to place Christ's part on Him and then leave it there. GEORGE MACDONALD

Difficulty is actually the atmosphere surrounding a miracle, or a miracle in its initial stage. Yet if it is to be a great miracle, the surrounding condition will be not simply a difficulty but an utter impossibility. And it is the clinging hand of His child that makes a desperate situation a delight to God.

OCTOBER 15

The sacrifices of God are a broken spirit; A broken and contrite heart, O God, You will not despise.

PSALM 51:17

Those people God uses most to bring glory to Himself are those who are completely broken, for the sacrifice He accepts is a "broken and contrite heart." It was not until Jacob's natural strength was broken, when "his hip was wrenched" (Genesis 32:25) at Peniel, that he came to the point where God could clothe him with spiritual power. And it was not until Moses struck the rock at Horeb, breaking its surface, that cool "water [came] out of it for the people to drink" (Exodus 17:6).

It was not until Gideon's three hundred specially chosen soldiers "broke the jars that were in their hands" (Judges 7:19), which symbolized brokenness in their lives, that the hidden light of the torches shone forth, bringing terror to their enemies. It was once the poor widow broke the seal on her only remaining jar of oil and began to pour it that God miraculously multiplied it to pay her debts and thereby supplied her means of support (2 Kings 4:1–7).

It was not until Esther risked her life and broke through the strict laws of a heathen king's court that she obtained favor to rescue her people from death (Esther 4:16).

It was once Jesus took "the five loaves . . . and broke them" (Luke 9:16) that the bread was multiplied to feed the five thousand. Through the very process of the loaves being broken, the miracle occurred. It was when Mary broke her beautiful "alabaster jar of very expensive perfume" (Matthew 26:7), destroying its future usefulness and value, that the wonderful fragrance filled the house. And it was when Jesus allowed His precious body to be broken by thorns, nails, and a spear that His inner life was poured out like an ocean of crystal-clear water, for thirsty sinners to drink and then live.

It is not until a beautiful kernel of corn is buried and broken in the earth by death that its inner heart sprouts, producing hundreds of other seeds or kernels. And so it has always been, down through the history of plants, people, and all of spiritual life—God uses broken things.

Those who have been gripped by the power of the Holy Spirit and are used for God's glory are those who have been broken in their finances, broken in their self-will, broken in their ambitions, broken in their lofty ideals, broken in their worldly reputation, broken in their desires, and often broken in their health. Yes, He uses those who are despised by the world and who seem totally hopeless and helpless, just as Isaiah said: "The lame will carry off plunder" (Isaiah 33:23).

Oh, break my heart; but break it as a field
Is plowed and broken for the seeds of corn;
Oh, break it as the buds, by green leaf sealed,
Are, to unloose the golden blossom, torn;
Love would I offer unto Love's great Master,
Set free the fragrance, break the alabaster.

Oh, break my heart; break it, victorious God,
That life's eternal well may flow abroad;
Oh, let it break as when the captive trees,
Breaking cold bonds, regain their liberties;
And as thought's sacred grove to life is springing,
Be joys, like birds, their hope, Your victory singing.

Thomas Toke Bunch

OCTOBER 16

Let us throw off everything that hinders and the sin that so easily entangles. And let us run with perseverance the race marked out for us.

Hebrews 12:1

There are certain things that are not sins themselves but that tend to weigh us down or become distractions and stumbling blocks to our Christian growth. One of the worst of these is the feeling of despair or hopelessness. A heavy heart is indeed a weight that will surely drag us down in our holiness and usefulness.

The failure of the children of Israel to enter the Promised Land began with their complaining, or as the Word says it, *"All the Israelites grumbled"* (Numbers 14:2). It may have started with a faint desire to complain and be discontent, but they allowed it to continue until it blossomed and ripened into total rebellion and ruin.

We should never give ourselves the freedom to doubt God or His eternal love and faithfulness toward us in everything. We can be determined to set our own will against doubt just as we do against any other sin. Then as we stand firm, refusing to doubt, the Holy Spirit will come to our aid, giving us the faith of God and crowning us with victory.

It is very easy to fall into the habit of doubting, worrying, wondering if God has forsaken us, and thinking that after all we have been through, our hopes are going to end in failure. But let us refuse to be discouraged and unhappy! Let us "consider it pure joy" (James 1:2), even when we do not feel any happiness. Let us rejoice by faith, by firm determination, and by simply regarding it as true, and we will find that God will make it real to us. SELECTED

The Devil has two very masterful tricks. The first is to tempt us to become *discouraged*, for then we are defeated and of no service to others, at least for a while. The other is to tempt us to *doubt*, thereby breaking the bond of faith that unites us with the Father. So watch out! Do not be tricked either way. G. E. M.

I like to cultivate the spirit of *happiness*! It retunes my soul and keeps it so perfectly in tune that Satan is afraid to touch it. The chords of my soul become so vibrant and full of heavenly electricity that he takes his fiendish fingers from me and goes somewhere else! Satan is always wary of interfering with me when my heart is full of the happiness and joy of the Holy Spirit.

My plan is simply to shun the spirit of *sadness* as I would normally shun Satan, but unfortunately I am not always successful. Like the Devil himself, sadness confronts me while I am on the highway of *usefulness*. And it stays face-to-face with me until my poor soul turns blue and sad!

In fact, sadness discolors everything around me and produces a mental paralysis. Nothing has any appeal to me, future prospects seem clouded in darkness, and my soul loses all its aspirations and power!

An elderly believer once said, "*Cheerfulness* in our faith causes any act of service to be performed with *delight*, and we are never moved ahead as swiftly in our spiritual calling as when we are carried on the wings of happiness. *Sadness*, however, clips those wings or, using another analogy, causes the wheels to fall off our chariot of service. Our chariot then becomes like those of the Egyptians at the Red Sea, dragging heavily on its axle and slowing our progress."

OCTOBER 17

May I never boast except in the cross of our Lord
Jesus Christ, through which the world has been
crucified to me, and I to the world.
GALATIANS 6:14

THEY WERE PEOPLE WHO WERE LIVING TO THEMSELVES. THEIR HOPES, promises, and dreams still controlled them, but the Lord began to fulfill their prayers. They had asked for a repentant heart and had surrendered themselves with a willingness to pay any price for it, and He sent them sorrow. They had asked for purity, and He sent them sudden anguish. They had asked for meekness, and He had broken their hearts. They had asked to be dead to the world, and He killed all their living hopes. They had asked to be made like Him, so He placed them in the fire "as a refiner and purifier of silver" (Malachi 3:3), until they could reflect His image. They had asked to help carry His cross, yet when He held it out to them, it cut and tore their hands.

They had not fully understood what they asked, but He had taken them at their word and granted them all their requests. They had been unsure whether to follow Him such a long distance or whether to come so close to Him. An awe and a fear was upon them, as Jacob at Bethel when he dreamed of "a stairway . . . reaching to heaven" (Genesis 28:12), or Eliphaz "amid disquieting dreams in the night" (Job 4:13), or as the disciples when "they were startled and frightened, thinking they saw a ghost" (Luke 24:37), not realizing it was Jesus. The disciples were so filled with awe, they felt like asking Him either to depart from them or to hide His glory.

They found it easier to obey than to suffer, to work than to give up, and to carry the cross than to hang upon it. But now they could not turn back, for they had come too close to the unseen cross of the spiritual life, and its virtues had pierced them too deeply. And the Lord was fulfilling this promise of His to them: "I, when I am lifted up from the earth, will draw all people to myself" (John 12:32).

Now at last their opportunity had come. Earlier they had only heard of the mystery, but now they felt it. He had fastened His eyes of love on them, as He had on Mary and Peter, so they could only choose to follow Him. And little by little, from time to time, with quick glimmers of light, the mystery of His cross shone upon them. They saw Him "lifted up from the earth," and gazed on the glory that radiated from the wounds of His holy suffering. As they looked upon Him, they approached Him and were changed into His likeness. His name then shone out through them, for He lived within them. Their life from that moment on was one of inexpressible fellowship solely with Him above. They were willing to live without possessions that others owned and that they could have had, in order to be unlike others so they would be more like Him.

This is the description of all those throughout the ages who "follow the Lamb wherever he goes" (Revelation 14:4). If they had chosen selfishly for themselves or if their friends had chosen for them, they would have made other choices. Their lives would have shone more brightly here on earth but less gloriously in His kingdom. Their legacy would have been that of Lot instead of Abraham. And if they had stopped along the way or if God had removed His hand from them, allowing them to stray, what would they have lost? What would they have forfeited at their resurrection?

Yet God strengthened them and protected them, even from themselves. Often, in His mercy He held them up when they otherwise would have slipped and fallen. And even in this life, they knew that all He did was done well. They knew it was good to suffer in this life so they would reign in the one to come; to bear the cross below, to wear a crown above; and to know that not their will but His was done in them and through them.

OCTOBER 18

"Know for certain that for four hundred years your descendants will be strangers in a country not their own and that they will be . . . mistreated there. But . . . afterward they will come out with great possessions."

GENESIS 15:13–14

I CAN BE SURE THAT PART OF GOD'S PROMISED BLESSING TO ME IS delay and suffering. The delay in Abraham's lifetime that seemed to put God's promise well beyond fulfillment was then followed by the seemingly unending delay experienced by Abraham's descendants. But it was indeed only a delay—the promise was fulfilled, for ultimately they did "*come out with great possessions.*"

God is going to test me with delays, and along with the delays will come suffering. Yet through it all God's promise stands. I have His new covenant in Christ, and His sacred promise of every smaller blessing that I need. The delays and the suffering are actually part of the promised blessings, so may I praise Him for them today. May I "be strong and take heart and wait for the LORD" (Psalm 27:14). CHARLES GALLAUDET TRUMBULL

Unanswered yet the prayer your lips have pleaded
In agony of heart these many years?

Does faith begin to fail? Is hope departing?
And think you all in vain your falling tears?
Say not the Father has not heard your prayer;
You will have your desire sometime, somewhere.

Unanswered yet? No, do not say ungranted;
Perhaps your work is not yet wholly done.
The work began when first your prayer was uttered,
And God will finish what He has begun.
If you will keep the incense burning there,
His glory you will see sometime, somewhere.

Unanswered yet? Faith cannot be unanswered,
Its feet are firmly planted on the Rock;
Amid the wildest storms it stands undaunted,
Nor shakes before the loudest thunder shock.
It knows Omnipotence has heard its prayer,
And cries, "It will be done"—sometime, somewhere.

Ophelia G. Browning

OCTOBER 19

The ark of the covenant of the Lord went before them.

Numbers 10:33

God sometimes does influence us with a simple touch or feeling, but not so we would act on the feeling. If the touch is from Him, He will then provide sufficient evidence to confirm it beyond the slightest doubt.

Consider the beautiful story of Jeremiah, when he felt God leading him to purchase the field at Anathoth. He did not act on his initial feeling but waited for God to completely fulfill His words to him before taking action. Then once his cousin came to him, bringing the external evidence of God's direction by making a proposal for the purchase, he responded and said, "*I knew that this was the word of the* LORD" (Jeremiah 32:8).

Jeremiah waited until God confirmed his feeling through a providential act, and then he worked with a clear view of the facts, which God could also use to bring conviction to others. God wants us to act only once we have His mind on a certain situation. We are not to ignore the Shepherd's personal voice to us, but like "Paul and his companions" (Acts 16:6) at Troas, we are to listen and also examine His providential work in our circumstances, in order to glean the full mind of the Lord. A. B. SIMPSON

Wherever God's finger points, His hand will clear a way.

Never say in your heart what you will or will not do but wait until God reveals His way to you. As long as that way is hidden, it is clear that there is no need of action and that *He holds Himself accountable for all the results of keeping you exactly where you are.* SELECTED

For God through ways we have not known,
Will lead His own.

OCTOBER 20

The peace of God, which transcends all understanding, will guard your hearts and your minds in Christ Jesus.

PHILIPPIANS 4:7

THERE IS A PART OF THE SEA KNOWN AS "THE CUSHION OF THE SEA." IT lies beneath the surface that is agitated by storms and churned by the wind. It is so deep that it is a part of the sea that is never stirred. When the ocean floor in these deep places is dredged of the remains of plant or animal life, it reveals evidence of having remained completely undisturbed for hundreds, if not thousands, of years.

The peace of God is an eternal calm like the cushion of the sea. It lies so deeply within the human heart that no external difficulty or disturbance can reach it. And anyone who enters the presence of God becomes a partaker of that undisturbed and undisturbable calm. ARTHUR TAPPAN PIERSON

When winds are raging o'er the upper ocean,
And waves are tossed wild with an angry roar,
It's said, far down beneath the wild commotion,
That peaceful stillness reigns forevermore.

Far, far beneath, noise of tempests falls silent,
And silver waves lie ever peacefully,
And no storm, however fierce or violent,
Disturbs the Sabbath of that deeper sea.

So to the heart that knows Your love, O Father,
There is a temple sacred evermore,
And all life's angry voices causing bother
Die in hushed silence at its peaceful door.

Far, far away, the roars of strife fall silent,
And loving thoughts rise ever peacefully,
And no storm, however fierce or violent,
Disturbs the soul that dwells, O Lord, in Thee.

HARRIET BEECHER STOWE

Pilgrim was taken to a large upper room that faced the sunrise. And the name of the room was Peace. PILGRIM'S PROGRESS

OCTOBER 21

For we know that if the earthly tent we live in is destroyed, we have a building from God, an eternal house in heaven, not built by human hands.

2 CORINTHIANS 5:1

THE OWNER OF THE HOUSE I HAVE LIVED IN FOR MANY YEARS HAS notified me that he will do little or nothing to keep it in repair. He also advised me to be ready to move.

At first this was not very welcome news. In many respects the surrounding area is quite pleasant, and if not for the evidence of a somewhat declining condition, the house seems rather nice. Yet a closer look reveals that even a light wind causes it to shake and sway, and its foundation is not sufficient to make it secure. Therefore I am getting ready to move.

As I consider the move, it is strange how quickly my interest is transferred to my prospective new home in another country. I have been consulting maps and studying accounts of its inhabitants. And someone who has come from there to visit has told me that it is beautiful beyond description and that language is inadequate to fully describe what he heard while there. He said that in order to make an investment there, he has suffered the loss of everything he owned here, yet rejoices in what others would call a sacrifice. Another person, whose love for me has been proved by the greatest possible test, now lives there. He has sent me several clusters of the most delicious grapes I have ever eaten, and after tasting them everything here tastes very bland.

Several times I have gone to the edge of the river that forms the boundary between here and there and have longed to be with those singing praises to the King on the other side. Many of my friends have moved across that river, but before leaving here they spoke of my following them later. I have seen the smile on their faces as they passed from my sight. So each time I am asked to make some new investment here, I now respond, "I am getting ready to move." SELECTED

The words of Jesus during His last days on earth vividly express His desire to go "back to the Father" (John 16:28). We, as His people, also have a vision of something far beyond the difficulties and disappointments of this life and are traveling toward fulfillment, completion, and an enriched life. We too are going "to the Father." Much of our new home is still unclear to us, but two things are certain. Our "Father's house" (John 14:2) is our home. And it is in the presence of the Lord. As believers, we know and understand that we are all travelers and not permanent residents of this world. R. C. Gillie

The little birds trust God, for they go singing
From northern woods where autumn winds have blown,
With joyous faith their unmarked pathway winging
To summer lands of song, afar, unknown.

Let us go singing, then, and not go crying:
Since we are sure our times are in His hand,
Why should we weep, and fear, and call it dying?
It's merely flying to a Summer Land.

OCTOBER 22

Now Moses was tending the flock of Jethro his father-in-law, the priest of Midian, and he led the flock to the far side of the wilderness and came to Horeb, the mountain of God. There the angel of the Lord appeared to him in flames of fire from within a bush.
Exodus 3:1–2

The vision of the Angel of the Lord came to Moses while he was involved in his everyday work. That is exactly where the Lord delights in giving His revelations. He seeks a man traveling an ordinary road, and "suddenly a light from heaven" (Acts 9:3) shines on him. And a "stairway resting on the earth" (Genesis 28:12) can reach from the marketplace to heaven, transforming a life from one of drudgery to one of grace.

Beloved Father, help me to expect you as I travel the ordinary road of life. I am not asking for sensational experiences. Fellowship with me through my everyday work and service, and be my companion when I take an ordinary journey. And let my humble life be transformed by Your presence.

Some Christians think they must always be on the mountaintop of extraordinary joy and revelation, but this is not God's way. Those high spiritual times and wonderful communication with the unseen world are *not* promised to us, but a daily life of communion with Him *is*. And it is enough for us, for He will give us those times of exceptional revelation if it is the right thing for us.

There were only three disciples allowed to see the Transfiguration, and the same three also experienced the darkness of Gethsemane. No one can stay on the mountaintop of favor forever, for there are responsibilities in the valley. Christ fulfilled His life's work not in the glory but in the valley, and it was there He was truly and completely the Messiah.

The value of the vision and the accompanying glory is its gift of equipping us for service and endurance. SELECTED

OCTOBER 23

Not one word has failed of all the good promises he gave.

1 KINGS 8:56

SOMEDAY WE WILL UNDERSTAND THAT GOD HAS A REASON BEHIND every no He gives us through the course of our lives. Yet even in this life, He always makes it up to us. When God's people are worried and concerned that their prayers are not being answered, how often we have seen Him working to answer them in a far greater way! Occasionally we catch a glimpse of this, but the complete revelation of it will not be seen until later.

If God says yes to our prayer, dear heart,
And the sunlight is golden, the sky is blue,
While the smooth road beckons to me and you,
And songbirds are singing as on we go,
Pausing to pick the flowers at our feet,
Stopping to drink of the streams that we meet,
Happy, more happy, our journey will grow,
If God says yes to our prayer, dear heart.

If God says no to our prayer, dear heart,
And the clouds hang heavy and dull and gray;
If the rough rocks hinder and block the way,
While the sharp winds pierce us and sting with cold;
Yet, dear, there is home at the journey's end,
And these are the trials the Father does send
To draw us as sheep to His Heavenly fold,
If God says no to our prayer, dear heart.

If only we had the faith not to rush into things but to "be still before the LORD and wait patiently for him" (Psalm 37:7)—waiting for His full explanation that will not be revealed until Jesus Christ comes again! When has God ever taken anything from a person without restoring it many times over? Yet what are we to think if He does not immediately restore what has been taken? Is today His only day to work? Does He have any concerns beyond this little world of ours? Can He still work beyond our death, or does the door of the grave open on nothing but infinite darkness and eternal silence?

Even if we confine our thinking to this life, it is true that God never touches the heart with a trial without intending to bestow a greater gift or compassionate blessing. *The person who knows how to wait has grown to an exceptional degree in God's grace.* SELECTED

When the frosts are in the valley,
And the mountaintops are gray,
And the choicest blooms are blighted,
And the blossoms die away,
A loving Father whispers,
"This all comes from my hand";
Blessed are you if you trust
When you cannot understand.

If, after years of toiling,
Your wealth should fly away
And leave your hands all empty,
And your hair is turning gray,
Remember then your Father
Owns all the sea and land;
Blessed are you if you trust
When you cannot understand.

SELECTED

OCTOBER 24

"I will make you into a threshing sledge, new and sharp."

ISAIAH 41:15

AROUND THE TURN OF THE TWENTIETH CENTURY, A BAR OF STEEL was worth about $5. Yet when forged into horseshoes, it was worth $10; when made into needles, its value was $350; when used to make small pocketknife blades, its worth was $32,000; when made into springs for watches, its value increased to $250,000. What a pounding the steel bar had to endure to be worth this much! But the more it was shaped, hammered, put through fire, beaten, pounded, and polished, the greater its value.

May we use this analogy as a reminder to be still, silent, and long-suffering, for it is those who suffer the most who yield the most. And it is through pain that God gets the most out of us, for His glory and for the blessing of others. SELECTED

Oh, give Your servant patience to be still,
And bear Your will;
Courage to venture wholly on Your arm
That will not harm;
The wisdom that will never let me stray
Out of my way;
The love that, now afflicting, yet knows best
When I should rest.

Our life is very mysterious. In fact, it would be totally unexplainable unless we believed that God was preparing us for events and ministries that lie unseen beyond the veil of the eternal world—where spirits like tempered steel will be required for special service.

The sharper the Craftsman's knives, the finer and more beautiful His work.

OCTOBER 25

"Until now you have not asked for anything in my name.
Ask and you will receive, and your joy will be complete."
JOHN 16:24

DURING THE AMERICAN CIVIL WAR, A CERTAIN MAN HAD A SON WHO enlisted in the Union army. The father was a banker, and although he gave his consent to his son, it seemed as if it would break his heart to let him go.

Once his son had left, he became deeply interested in the plight of soldiers, and whenever he saw one in uniform, his heart went out to him as he thought of his own dear boy. Often to the neglect of his business, he began spending his time and money to care for the soldiers who came home disabled. His friends pleaded with him not to neglect his business in this way, by spending so much time and energy on the soldiers. So he decided to give it all up, taking his friends' advice.

After he had made this decision, however, a young private in a faded, worn uniform stepped into the bank. It was easy to discern from the wounds on his face and hands that he had been in the army field hospital. The poor young man was fumbling in his pocket to find something, when the banker saw him. Perceiving his purpose for coming into the bank, he said to the soldier, "My dear man, I cannot help you today. I am extremely busy. You will have to go to the army headquarters, where the officers will take care of you."

The poor wounded soldier still stood there, not seeming to fully understand what was being said to him. He continued to fumble in his pockets and finally pulled out a scrap of dirty paper. He laid the filthy page before the banker, who read the following words written in pencil:

> Dear Father,
>
> This is one of my friends, who was wounded in the last battle and is coming to you directly from the hospital. Please receive him as you would me.
>
> Charlie

All the banker's previous resolve to focus solely on his business instead of soldiers quickly flew away. He took the young man to his own magnificent home and gave him Charlie's room and seat at the dinner table. He cared for him until the food, rest, and love had returned him to health, and then sent him back to his place of service to again risk his life for his country's flag. SELECTED

"Now you will see what I will do" (Exodus 6:1).

OCTOBER 26

He went up on a mountainside by himself to pray. Later that night, he was there alone.

MATTHEW 14:23

CHRIST JESUS, IN HIS HUMANITY, FELT THE NEED OF COMPLETE SOLITUDE—to be entirely by Himself, alone with Himself. Each of us knows how draining constant interchange with others can be and how it exhausts our energy. As part of humankind, Jesus knew this and felt the need to be by Himself in order to regain His strength. Solitude was also important to Him in order to fully realize His high calling, His human weakness, and His total dependence on His Father.

As a child of God, how much more do we need times of complete solitude—times to deal with the spiritual realities of life and to be alone with God the Father. If there was ever anyone who could dispense with special times of solitude and fellowship, it was our Lord. Yet even He could not maintain His full strength and power for His work and His fellowship with the Father without His quiet time. God desires that every servant of His would understand and perform this blessed practice, that His church would know how to train its children to recognize this high and holy privilege, and that every believer would realize the importance of making time for God alone.

Oh, the thought of having God all alone to myself and knowing that God has me all alone to Himself! ANDREW MURRAY

Lamartine, the first of the French Romantic poets and a writer of the nineteenth century, in one of his books wrote of how his mother had a secluded spot in the garden where she spent the same hour of each day. He related that nobody ever dreamed of intruding upon her for even a moment of that hour. It was the holy garden of the Lord to her.

Pity those people who have no such Beulah land! (Isaiah 62:4.) Jesus said, "Go into your room, close the door and pray" (Matthew 6:6), for it is in quiet solitude that we catch the deep and mysterious truths that flow from the soul of the things God allows to enter our lives.

A Meditation

My soul, practice being alone with Christ! The Scripture says, "*When he was alone with his own disciples, he explained everything*" (Mark 4:34). Do not wonder about the truth of this verse, for it can be true of your life as well. If you desire to have understanding, then dismiss the crowd, just as Jesus did. (Matthew 14:22.) Let them "go away one at a time . . . until only Jesus [is] left" (John 8:9) with you. Have you ever pictured yourself as the last remaining person on earth, or the only person left in the entire universe?

If you were the only person remaining in the universe, your every thought would be, "God and I . . . ! God and I . . . !" And yet He is already as close to you as that. He is as near as if no heart but His and yours ever beat throughout the boundlessness of space.

O my soul, practice that solitude! Practice dismissing the crowd! Practice the stillness of your heart! Practice the majestic song "God and I! God and I!" Let no one come between you and your wrestling angel! You will receive conviction yet pardon, when you meet Jesus alone! George Matheson

OCTOBER 27

All your waves and breakers have swept over me.

Psalm 42:7

They are His waves, whether they break over us,
Hiding His face in smothering spray and foam;
Or smooth and sparkling, spread a path before us,
And to our haven bear us safely home.

They are His waves, whether for our sure comfort
He walks across them, stilling all our fear;
Or to our cry there comes no aid nor answer,
And in the lonely silence none is near.

They are His waves, whether we are hard-striving
Through tempest-driven waves that never cease,
While deep to deep with turmoil loud is calling;
Or at His word they hush themselves in peace.

They are HIS waves, whether He separates them,
Making us walk dry ground where seas had flowed;
Or lets tumultuous breakers surge about us,
Rushing unchecked across our only road.

They are His waves, and He directs us through them;
So He has promised, so His love will do.
Keeping and leading, guiding and upholding,
To His sure harbor, He will bring us through.

Annie Johnson Flint

Stand firmly in the place where your dear Lord has put you, and do your best there. God sends us trials or tests, and places life before us as a face-to-face opponent. It is through the pounding of a serious conflict that He expects us to grow strong. The tree planted where the fierce winds twist its branches and bend its trunk, often nearly to the point of breaking, is commonly more firmly rooted than a tree growing in a secluded valley where storms never bring any stress or strain.

The same is true of human life. The strongest and greatest character is grown through hardship. Selected

OCTOBER 28

Because of his great love for us, God, who is rich in mercy, made us alive with Christ even when we were dead in transgressions. . . . And God raised us up with Christ and seated us with him in the heavenly realms in Christ Jesus.

Ephesians 2:4–6

This is our rightful place—"seated . . . with him in the heavenly realms in Christ Jesus," yet seated and *still.* But how few of us actually experience this! In fact, most of us believe it is impossible to sit still "in the heavenly realms" while living our everyday life in a world so full of turmoil.

Oh, we believe it may be possible to visit these "heavenly realms" on Sundays or now and then during times of great spiritual emphasis and praise, but to actually be "seated" there *all day, every day,* is a completely different matter. Yet it is clear from the Scriptures that it is meant not only for Sundays but for weekdays as well.

A quiet spirit is of priceless value when performing outward activities. Nothing so greatly hinders the work of God's unseen spiritual forces, upon which our success in everything truly depends, as the spirit of unrest and anxiety.

There is tremendous power in stillness. A great believer once said, "All things come to him who knows how to trust and to be silent." This fact is rich with meaning, and a true understanding of it would greatly change our ways of working. Instead of continuing our restless striving, we would "sit down" inwardly before the Lord, allowing the divine forces of His Spirit to silently work out the means to accomplish our goals and aspirations.

You may not see or feel the inner workings of His silent power, but rest assured it is always mightily at work. And it will work for you, if you will only quiet your spirit enough to be carried along by the current of its power. Hannah Whitall Smith

There is a point of rest
At the great center of the cyclone's force,
A silence at its secret source;
A little child might slumber undisturbed,
Without the ruffle of one fair curl,
In that strange, central calm, amid the mighty whirl.

Make it your business to learn to be peaceful and safe in God through every situation.

OCTOBER 29

He will sit as a refiner and purifier of silver.
MALACHI 3:3

OUR FATHER, WHO SEEKS TO PERFECT HIS SAINTS IN HOLINESS, KNOWS the value of the refiner's fire. It is with the most precious metals that a metallurgist will take the greatest care. He subjects the metal to a hot fire, for only the refiner's fire will melt the metal, release the dross, and allow the remaining, pure metal to take a new and perfect shape in the mold.

A good refiner never leaves the crucible but, as the above verse indicates, *"will sit" down by it* so the fire will not become even one degree too hot and possibly harm the metal. And as soon as he skims the last bit of dross from the surface and sees his face reflected in the pure metal, he extinguishes the fire. ARTHUR TAPPAN PIERSON

He sat by a fire of sevenfold heat,
As He looked at the precious ore,
And closer He bent with a searching gaze
As He heated it more and more.
He knew He had ore that could stand the test,
And He wanted the finest gold

To mold as a crown for the King to wear,
Set with gems with a price untold.
So He laid our gold in the burning fire,
Though we would have asked for delay,
And He watched the dross that we had not seen,
And it melted and passed away.
And the gold grew brighter and yet more bright,
But our eyes were so dim with tears,
We saw but the fire—not the Master's hand,
And questioned with anxious fears.
Yet our gold shone out with a richer glow,
As it mirrored a Form above,
That bent o'er the fire, though unseen by us,
With a look of unspeakable love.
Should we think that it pleases His loving heart
To cause us a moment's pain?
Not so! for He saw through the present cross
The joy of eternal gain.
So He waited there with a watchful eye,
With a love that is strong and sure,
And His gold did not suffer a bit more heat,
Than was needed to make it pure.

OCTOBER 30

Let us run with patience.
HEBREWS 12:1 KJV

RUNNING "WITH PATIENCE" IS A VERY DIFFICULT THING TO DO. THE word "running" itself suggests the *absence* of patience, or an eagerness to reach the goal. Yet we often associate patience with lying down or standing still. We think of it as an angel who guards the bed of the disabled. Yet I do not believe that the kind of patience a disabled person may have is the hardest to achieve.

There is another kind of patience that I believe is harder to obtain—the patience that runs. Lying down during a time of grief, or being quiet after a financial setback, certainly implies great strength, but I know of something that suggests even greater strength—the power to continue working after a setback, the power to still run with a heavy heart, and the power to perform your daily tasks with deep sorrow in your spirit. This is a Christlike thing!

Many of us could tearlessly deal with our grief if only we were allowed to do so in private. Yet what is so difficult is that most of us are called to exercise our patience not in bed but in the open street, for all to see. We are called upon to bury our sorrows not in restful inactivity but in active service—in our workplace, while shopping, and during social events—contributing to other people's joy. No other way of burying our sorrow is as difficult as this, for it is truly what is meant by running "with patience."

Dear Son of Man, this was *Your* kind of patience. It was both waiting and running at one time—waiting for the ultimate goal while in the meantime doing lesser work. I see You at Cana of Galilee, turning water into wine so the marriage feast would not be ruined. I see You in the desert, feeding the multitude with bread, simply to relieve a temporary need. Yet all the time, You were bearing a mighty grief—not shared or spoken. Others may ask for a "rainbow in the clouds" (Genesis 9:13), but I would ask for even more from You. Make me, in my cloud, a rainbow bringing the ministry of joy to others. My patience will only be perfect when it works in Your vineyard. George Matheson

When all our hopes are gone,
It is best our hands keep toiling on
For others' sake:
For strength to bear is found in duty done;

And he is best indeed who learns to make
The joy of others cure his own heartache.

OCTOBER 31

In the same way, the Spirit helps us in our weakness. We do not know what we ought to pray for, but the Spirit himself intercedes for us through wordless groans. And he who searches our hearts knows the mind of the Spirit, because the Spirit intercedes for God's people in accordance with the will of God.

ROMANS 8:26–27

THIS IS A DEEP MYSTERY OF PRAYER. IT IS A DELICATE, DIVINE TOOL that words cannot express and theology cannot explain, but the humblest believer knows, even when he does not understand.

Oh, the burdens we lovingly bear but cannot understand! Oh, the inexpressible longings of our hearts for things we cannot comprehend! Yet we know they are an echo from the throne of God, and a whisper from His heart. They are often a groan rather than a song, and a burden rather than a floating feather. But they are a blessed burden, and a groan whose undertone is praise and unspeakable joy. They are groans that words cannot express. We cannot always express them ourselves, and often all we understand is that God is praying in us for something that only He understands and that needs His touch.

So we can simply pour from the fullness of our heart the burden of our spirit and the sorrow that seems to crush us. We can know that He hears, loves, understands, receives, and separates from our prayer everything that is in error, imperfect, or wrong. And then He presents the remainder, along with the incense of the great High Priest, before His throne on high. We may be assured that our prayer is heard, accepted, and answered in His name. A. B. SIMPSON

It is not necessary to be continually speaking to God, or always hearing from God, in order to have communion or fellowship with Him, for there is an unspeakable fellowship that is sweeter than words. A little child can sit all day long beside his mother, totally engrossed in his playing, while his mother is consumed by her work, and although both are busy and few words are spoken by either, they are in perfect fellowship. The child knows his mother is there, and she knows that he is all right.

In the same way, a believer and his Savior can continue many hours in the silent fellowship of love. And although the believer may be busy with the ordinary things of life, he can be mindful that every detail of his life is touched by the character of God's presence, and can have the awareness of His approval and blessing.

Then when troubled with burdens and difficulties too complicated to put into words and too puzzling to express or fully understand, how sweet it is to fall into the embrace of His blessed arms and to simply sob out the sorrow that we cannot speak! SELECTED

NOVEMBER 1

When the cloud remained . . . the Israelites . . . did not set out.

NUMBERS 9:19

THIS WAS THE ULTIMATE TEST OF OBEDIENCE. IT WAS RELATIVELY EASY to fold up their tents when the fleecy cloud slowly gathered over the tabernacle and began to majestically float ahead of the multitude of the Israelites. Change normally seems pleasant, and the people were excited and interested in the route, the scenery, and the habitat of the next stopping place.

Yet having to wait was another story altogether. "When the cloud remained," however uninviting and sweltering the location, however trying to flesh and blood, however boring and wearisome to those who were impatient, however perilously close their exposure to danger—there was no option but to remain encamped.

The psalmist said, "*I waited patiently for the* LORD; *he turned to me and heard my cry*" (Psalm 40:1). And what God did for the Old Testament saints, He will do for believers down through the ages, yet He will often keep us waiting. Must we wait when we are face to face with a threatening enemy, surrounded by danger and fear, or below an unstable rock? Would this not be the time to fold our tents and leave? Have we not already suffered to the point of total collapse? Can we not exchange the sweltering heat for "green pastures . . . [and] quiet waters" (Psalm 23:2)?

When God sends no answer and "the cloud remain[s]," we must wait. Yet we can do so with the full assurance of God's provision of manna, water from the rock, shelter, and protection from our enemies. He never keeps us at our post without assuring us of His presence or sending us daily supplies.

Young person, wait—do not be in such a hurry to make a change! Minister, stay at your post! You must wait where you are until the cloud clearly begins to move. Wait for the Lord to give you His good pleasure! He will not be late! DAILY DEVOTIONAL COMMENTARY

An hour of waiting!
Yet there seems such need
To reach that spot sublime!
I long to reach them—but I long far more
To trust His time!
"Sit still, My children"—
Yet the heathen die,
They perish while I stay!
I long to reach them—but I long far more
To trust His way!
It's good to get,
It's good indeed to give!
Yet it is better still—
O'er breadth, through length, down depth, up height,
To trust His will!

F. M. N.

NOVEMBER 2

Peter was kept in prison, but the church was earnestly praying to God for him.

ACTS 12:5

PRAYER IS THE LINK THAT CONNECTS US WITH GOD. IT IS THE BRIDGE that spans every gulf and carries us safely over every chasm of danger or need.

Think of the significance of this story of the first-century church: Everything seemed to be coming against it, for Peter was in prison, the Jews appeared triumphant, Herod still reigned supreme, and the arena of martyrdom was eagerly awaiting the next morning so it could drink the apostle's blood. *"But the church was earnestly praying to God for him."* So what was the outcome? The prison was miraculously opened, the apostle freed, the Jews bewildered, and as a display of God's punishment, wicked King Herod "was eaten by worms and died." And rolling on to even greater victory, "the word of God continued to spread and flourish" (vv. 23–24).

Do we truly know the power of our supernatural weapon of prayer? Do we dare to use it with the authority of a faith that not only asks but also commands? God baptizes us with holy boldness and divine confidence, for He is looking not for great people but for people who will dare to prove the greatness of their God! *"But the church was earnestly praying."* A. B. SIMPSON

In your prayers, above everything else, beware of limiting God, not only through unbelief but also by thinking you know exactly what He can do. Learn to expect the unexpected, *beyond all* that you ask or think.

So each time you intercede through prayer, first be quiet and worship God in His glory. Think of what He can do, how He delights in Christ His Son, and of your place in Him—then expect great things. ANDREW MURRAY

Our prayers are God's opportunities.

Are you experiencing sorrow? Prayer can make your time of

affliction one of strength and sweetness. Are you experiencing happiness? Prayer can add a heavenly fragrance to your time of joy. Are you in grave danger from some outward or inward enemy? Prayer can place an angel by your side whose very touch could shatter a millstone into smaller grains of dust than the flour it grinds, and whose glance could destroy an entire army.

What will prayer do for you? My answer is this: Everything that God can do for you. "Ask for whatever you want me to give you" (2 Chronicles 1:7). FREDERICK WILLIAM FARRAR

Wrestling prayer can wonders do,
Bring relief in dire straits;
Prayer can force a passage through
Iron bars and heavy gates.

NOVEMBER 3

"You who bring good news to Zion, go up on a high mountain."
ISAIAH 40:9

TOYS AND TRINKETS ARE EASILY EARNED, BUT THE MOST VALUABLE things carry a heavy price. The highest places of power are always bought with blood, and you can attain those pinnacles if you have enough blood to pay. That is the condition of conquering holy heights everywhere. The story of true heroics is always the story of sacrificial blood. The greatest values and character in life are not blown randomly across our path by wayward winds, for great souls experience great sorrows.

Great truths are dearly bought, the common truths,
Such as we give and take from day to day,
Come in the common walk of easy life,
Blown by the careless wind across our way.

Great truths are greatly won, not found by chance,
Nor wafted on the breath of summer dream;
But grasped in the great struggle of our soul,
Hard buffeting with adverse wind and stream.

But in the day of conflict, fear, and grief,
When the strong hand of God, put forth in might,
Plows up the subsoil of our stagnant heart,
And brings the imprisoned truth seed to the light.

Wrung from the troubled spirit, in hard hours
Of weakness, solitude, and times of pain,
Truth springs like harvest from the well-plowed field,
And our soul feels it has not wept in vain.

Our capacity for knowing God is enlarged when we are brought by Him into circumstances that cause us to exercise our faith. So when difficulties block our paths, may we thank God that He is taking time to deal with us, and then may we lean heavily on Him.

NOVEMBER 4

I was among the exiles by the Kebar River, the
heavens were opened and I saw visions of God. . . .
There the hand of the LORD was on [me].
EZEKIEL 1:1, 3

THERE IS NOTHING THAT MAKES THE SCRIPTURES MORE PRECIOUS TO us than a time of "captivity." The old psalms of God's Word have sung for us with compassion by our stream at Babel and have resounded with new joy as we have seen the Lord deliver us from captivity and "restore our fortunes, . . . like streams in the Negev" (Psalm 126:4).

A person who has experienced great difficulties will not be easily parted from his Bible. Another book may appear to others to be identical, but to him it is not the same. Over the old and tear-stained pages of his Bible, he has written a journal of his experiences in words that are only visible to his eyes. Through those pages, he has time and again come to the pillars of the house of God and "to Elim, where there were . . . palm trees" (Exodus 15:27). And each of those pillars and trees have become a remembrance for him of some critical time in his life.

In order to receive any benefit from our captivity, we must accept the situation and be determined to make the best of it. Worrying over what we have lost or what has been taken from us will not make things better but will only prevent us from improving what remains. We will only serve to make the rope around us tighter if we rebel against it.

In the same way, an excitable horse that will not calmly submit to its bridle only strangles itself. And a high-spirited animal that is restless in its yoke only bruises its own shoulders. Everyone will also understand the analogy that Laurence Sterne, a minister and author of the eighteenth century, penned regarding a starling and a canary. He told of the difference between a restless starling that broke its wings struggling against the bars of its cage and continually cried, "I can't get out! I can't get out!" and a submissive canary that sat on its perch and sang songs that surpassed even the beauty of those of a lark that soared freely to the very gates of heaven.

No calamity will ever bring only evil to us, if we will immediately take it in fervent prayer to God. Even as we take shelter beneath a tree during a downpour of rain, we may unexpectedly find fruit on its branches. And when we flee to God, taking refuge beneath the shadow of His wing, we will always find more in Him than we have ever before seen or known.

Consequently, it is through our trials and afflictions that God gives us fresh revelations of Himself. Like Jacob, we must cross "the ford of the Jabbok" (Genesis 32:22) if we are ever to arrive at Peniel, where he wrestled with the Lord, was blessed by Him, and could say, "I saw God face to face, and yet my life was spared" (Genesis 32:30).

Make this story your own, dear captive, and God will give you "songs in the night" (Job 35:10) and will turn your "midnight into dawn" (Amos 5:8). Nathaniel William Taylor

Submission to God's divine will is the softest pillow on which to rest.

It filled the room, and it filled my life,
With a glory of source unseen;
It made me calm in the midst of strife,
And in winter my heart was green.
And the birds of promise sang on the tree
When the storm was breaking on land and sea.

NOVEMBER 5

Is anything too hard for the Lord?
Genesis 18:14

This is God's loving challenge to you and me each day. He wants us to think of the deepest, highest, and worthiest desires and longings of our hearts. He wants us to think of those things that perhaps were desires for ourselves or someone dear to us, yet have gone unfulfilled for so long that we now see them as simply lost desires. And God urges us to think of even the one thing that we once saw as possible but have given up all hope of seeing fulfilled in this life.

That very thing, as long as it aligns with what we know to be His expressed will—as a son was to Abraham and Sarah—God intends to do for us. Yes, if we will let Him, God will do that very thing, even if we know it is such an utter impossibility that we would simply laugh at the absurdity of anyone ever suggesting it could come to pass.

"*Is anything too hard for the Lord?*" No, nothing is too difficult when we believe in Him enough to go forward, doing His will and letting Him do the impossible for us. Even Abraham and Sarah could have blocked God's plan if they had continued to disbelieve.

The only thing "too hard for the LORD" is our deliberate and continual disbelief in His love and power, and our ultimate rejection of His plans for us. Nothing is impossible for Jehovah to do for those who trust Him. MESSAGES FOR THE MORNING WATCH

NOVEMBER 6

Those whom I love I rebuke and discipline.
REVELATION 3:19

GOD SELECTS THE BEST AND MOST NOTABLE OF HIS SERVANTS FOR THE best and most notable afflictions, for those who have received the most grace from Him are able to endure the most afflictions. In fact, an affliction hits a believer never by chance but by God's divine direction. He does not haphazardly aim His arrows, for each one is on a special mission and touches only the heart for whom it is intended. It is not only the grace of God but also His glory that is revealed when a believer can stand and quietly endure an affliction. JOSEPH CARYL

If all my days were sunny, could I say,
"In His fair land He wipes all tears away"?

If I were never weary, could I keep
This blessed truth, "He gives His loved ones sleep"?

If no grave were mine, I might come to deem
The Life Eternal but a baseless dream.

My winter, and my tears, and weariness,
Even my grave, may be His way to bless.

I call them ills; yet that can surely be
Nothing but love that shows my Lord to me!

SELECTED

Christians with the most spiritual depth are generally those who have been taken through the most intense and deeply anguishing fires of the soul. If you have been praying to know more of Christ, do not be surprised if He leads you through the desert or through a furnace of pain.

Dear Lord, do not punish me by removing my cross from me. Instead, comfort me by leading me into submission to Your will and by causing me to love the cross. Give me only what will serve You best, and may it be used to reveal the greatest of all Your mercies: bringing glory to Your name through me, according to Your will. A CAPTIVE'S PRAYER

NOVEMBER 7

Whatever was to my profit I now consider
loss for the sake of Christ.
PHILIPPIANS 3:7

WHEN GEORGE MATHESON, THE BLIND SCOTTISH PREACHER, WAS buried, they lined his grave with red roses commemorating his life of love and sacrifice. And it was Matheson, this man who was so beautifully and significantly honored, who wrote the following hymn in 1882. It was written in five minutes, during a period he later called "the most severe mental suffering," and it has since become known around the world.

O Love that wilt not let me go,
I rest my weary soul in Thee,
I give Thee back the life I owe,
That in thine ocean depths its flow
May richer, fuller be.

O Light that followest all my way,
I yield my flickering torch to Thee,
My heart restores its borrowed ray,

That in Thy sunshine's glow its day
May brighter, fairer be.

O Joy that seekest me through pain,
I cannot close my heart to Thee,
I trace the rainbow through the rain,
And feel the promise is not vain,
That morn shall tearless be.

O Cross that liftest up my head,
I dare not ask to hide from Thee,
I lay in dust life's glory dead,
And from the ground there blossoms red,
Life that shall endless be.

There is a legend of an artist who had found the secret of a wonderful red that no other artist could imitate. He never told the secret of the color, but after his death an old wound was discovered over his heart. It revealed the source of the matchless hue in his pictures.

The moral of the legend is that no great achievement can be made, no lofty goal attained, nor anything of great value to the world accomplished, except at the cost of the heart's blood.

NOVEMBER 8

He took Peter, John and James with him and went up onto a mountain to pray. As he was praying, the appearance of his face changed, and his clothes became as bright as a flash of lightning. . . . Peter and his companions . . . saw his glory.

LUKE 9:28–29, 32

If you are pleased with me, teach me your ways.

EXODUS 33:13

When Jesus took these three disciples up onto the mountain alone, He brought them into close communion with Himself. They "saw his glory" and said, "It is good for us to be here" (Luke 9:32–33). Heaven is never far from those who linger on a mountain with their Lord.

Who of us in certain moments of meditation and prayer has not caught a glimpse of the heavenly gates? Who has not in the secret place of holy communion felt a surging wave of emotion—a taste of the blessed joy yet to come?

The Master had special times and places for quiet conversation with His disciples. He met with them once on Mount Hermon but more often on the sacred slopes of the Mount of Olives. Every Christian should have his own Mount of Olives. Most of us today, especially those of us in cities, live under great stress. From early morning until bedtime we are exposed to the whirlwind of life. Amid all the turmoil, there is little opportunity for quiet thought, God's Word, prayer, and fellowship of the heart!

Even Daniel needed to have his Mount of Olives in his room amid the roar of idolatrous Babylon. Peter found a rooftop in Joppa, and Martin Luther found an "upper room" in Wittenberg, a place that is still considered sacred.

Joseph Parker, an English Congregationalist preacher of the nineteenth century, once said, "If we, as the church, do not get back to spiritual visions, glimpses of heaven, and an awareness of a greater glory and life, we will lose our faith. Our altar will become nothing but cold, empty stone, never blessed with a visit from heaven." And this is the world's need today—*people who have seen their Lord.* The Lost Art of Meditation

Come close to Him! Perhaps He will take you today to the mountaintop—the same place He took Peter with his blundering, and James and John, the "Sons of Thunder" (Mark 3:17), who time and again totally misunderstood their Master and His mission. There is no reason why He will not take you, so do not shut yourself out by saying, "Oh, these wonderful visions and revelations of the Lord are only for certain people!" They may be for you! John Thomas McNeill

NOVEMBER 9

People will dwell again in his shade; they will flourish like the grain, they will blossom like the vine.

Hosea 14:7

The day ended with heavy showers, and the plants in my garden were beaten down by the pelting storm. I looked at one plant I had previously admired for its beauty and had loved for its delicate fragrance. After being exposed to the merciless storm, its flowers had drooped, all its petals were closed, and it appeared that its glory was gone. I thought to myself, *I suppose I will have to wait till next year to see those beautiful flowers again.*

Yet the night passed, the sun shone again, and the morning brought strength to my favorite plant. The light looked at its flowers and the flowers looked at the light. There was contact and communion, and power passed into the flowers. They lifted their heads, opened their petals, regained their glory, and seemed more beautiful than before. I wondered how this took place—these feeble flowers coming into contact with something much stronger, and gaining strength!

I cannot explain exactly how we are able to receive the power to serve and to endure through communion with God, but I know it is a fact. Are you in danger of being crushed by a heavy and difficult trial? Then seek communion with Christ and you will receive strength and the power to be victorious, for God has promised, "I will strengthen you" (Isaiah 41:10).

Yesterday's Grief

The falling rain of yesterday is ruby on the roses,
Silver on the poplar leaf, and gold on willow stem;
The grief that fell just yesterday is silence that encloses
God's great gifts of grace, and time will never trouble them.

The falling rain of yesterday makes all the hillsides glisten,
Coral on the laurel and beryl on the grass;
The grief that fell just yesterday has taught the soul to listen
For whispers of eternity in all the winds that pass.

O faint of heart, storm-beaten, this rain will shine tomorrow,
Flame within the columbine and jewels on the thorn,
Heaven in the forget-me-not; though sorrow now is sorrow,
Yet sorrow will be beauty in the magic of the morn.

KATHERINE LEE BATES

NOVEMBER 10

Against all hope, Abraham in hope believed.

ROMANS 4:18

ABRAHAM'S FAITH SEEMED TO BE IN COMPLETE AGREEMENT WITH THE power and constant faithfulness of Jehovah. By looking at the outer circumstances in which he was placed, he had no reason to expect the fulfillment of God's promise. Yet he believed the Word of the Lord and looked forward to the time when his descendants would be "as numerous as the stars in the sky" (Genesis 26:4).

Dear soul, you have not been given only one promise, like Abraham, *but a thousand promises.* And you have been given the example of many faithful believers as a pattern for your life. Therefore it is simply to your advantage to rely with confidence upon the Word of God. And although He may delay in sending His help, and the evil you are experiencing may seem to become worse and worse, do not be weak. Instead, be strong and rejoice, for God usually steps forward to save us when we least expect it, fulfilling His most glorious promises in a miraculous way.

He generally waits to send His help until the time of our greatest need, so that His hand will be plainly seen in our deliverance. He chooses this method so we will not trust anything that we may see or feel, as we are so prone to do, but will place our trust solely on His Word—which we may always depend upon, no matter our circumstance. C. H. von Bogatzky

Remember, the very time for faith to work is when our sight begins to fail. And the greater the difficulties, the easier it is for faith to work, for as long as we can see certain natural solutions to our problems, we will not have faith. Faith never works as easily as when our natural prospects fail. George Mueller

NOVEMBER 11

May he be like rain falling on a mown field.
Psalm 72:6

Amos tells of "the king's mowings" (Amos 7:1 kjv). Our King also has many scythes and is constantly using them to mow His lawns. The bell-like sound of the whetstone against the scythe foretells of the cutting down of countless blades of grass, daisies, and other flowers. And as beautiful as they were in the morning, within a few hours they will lie in long, faded rows.

In human life, we try to take a brave stand before the scythe of pain, the shears of disappointment, or the sickle of death. And just as there is no way to cultivate a lawn like velvet without repeated mowings, there is no way to develop a life of balance, tenderness, and sympathy for others without enduring the work of God's scythes.

Think how often the Word of God compares people to grass, and God's glory to its flower. But when the grass is cut, when all the tender blades are bleeding, and when desolation seems to reign where flowers once were blooming, the perfect time has come for God's rain to fall as delicate showers so soft and warm.

Dear soul, God has been mowing you! Time and again the King has come to you with His sharp scythe. But do not dread His scythe—for it is sure to be followed by His shower. F. B. Meyer

When across the heart deep waves of sorrow
Break, as on a dry and barren shore;
When hope glistens with no bright tomorrow,
And the storm seems sweeping evermore;

When the cup of every earthly gladness
Bears no taste of the life-giving stream;
And high hopes, as though to mock our sadness,
Fade and die as in some restless dream,

Who will hush the weary spirit's chiding?
Who the aching void within will fill?
Who will whisper of a peace abiding,
And each surging wave will calmly still?

Only He whose wounded heart was broken
With the bitter cross and thorny crown;
Whose dear love glad words of joy had spoken,
Who His life for us laid meekly down.

Blessed Healer, all our burdens lighten;
Give us peace. Your own sweet peace, we pray!
Keep us near You till the morn does brighten,
And all the mists and shadows flee away!

NOVEMBER 12

These were the potters, and those that dwelt among plants and hedges: there they dwelt with the king for his work.

1 Chronicles 4:23 KJV

We may dwell "with the King for his work" anywhere and everywhere. We may be called to serve Him in the most unlikely places and under the most adverse conditions. It may be out in the countryside, far away from the King's many activities in the city. Or it may be "among plants and hedges" of all kinds—hindrances that surround us, blocking our way. Perhaps we will be one of "the potters," with our hands full of all types of pottery, accomplishing our daily tasks.

It makes no difference! The King who placed us "*there*" will come and dwell with us. The hedges, or hindrances, are right for us, or He will quickly remove them. And doesn't it stand to reason that whatever seems to block our way may also provide for our protection? As for the pottery—it is exactly what He has seen fit to place in our hands and is for now "*his work.*" Frances Ridley Havergal

Go back to your garden plot, sweetheart!
Go back till the evening falls,
And tie your lilies and train your vines,
Till for you the Master calls.

Go make your garden fair as you can,
You will never work alone;
Perhaps he whose plot is next to yours
Will see it and mend his own.

Brightly colored sunsets and starry heavens, majestic mountains and shining seas, and fragrant fields and fresh-cut flowers are not even half as beautiful as a soul who is serving Jesus out of love, through the wear and tear of an ordinary, unpoetic life. Frederick William Faber

The most saintly souls are often those who have never distinguished themselves as authors or allowed any major accomplishment of theirs to become the topic of the world's conversation. No, they are usually those who have led a quiet inner life of holiness, having carried their sweet bouquets unseen, like a fresh lily in a secluded valley on the edge of a crystal stream. Kenelm Digby

NOVEMBER 13

"I have chosen him, so that he will direct his children."

Genesis 18:19

God chooses people He can depend upon. He knew what to expect from Abraham and said of him, "I have chosen him, so that he will direct his children . . . that the Lord will bring about for Abraham what he has promised him." God knew Abraham *would* "direct his children." The Lord can be depended upon, and He desires for us to be just as reliable, determined, and stable. This is simply the meaning of faith.

God is looking for people on whom He can place the weight of His entire love, power, and faithful promises. And His engines are strong enough to pull any weight we may attach to them. Unfortunately, the cable we fasten to the engine is often too weak to handle the weight of our prayers. Therefore God continues to train and discipline us in His school of stability and certainty in the life of faith. May we learn our lessons well and then stand firm. A. B. Simpson

God knows that you can withstand your trial, or else He would not have given it to you. His trust in you explains the trials of your life, no matter how severe they may be. God knows your strength, and He measures it to the last inch. Remember, no trial has ever been given to anyone that was greater than that person's strength, through God, to endure it.

NOVEMBER 14

Unless a kernel of wheat falls to the ground and dies, it remains only a single seed. But if it dies, it produces many seeds.

John 12:24

In Northampton, Massachusetts, stands the old cemetery where David Brainerd is buried. Brainerd, a pioneer American missionary, died in 1747 at the age of twenty-nine after suffering from tuberculosis. His grave is beside that of Jerusha Edwards, the daughter of Jonathan Edwards, a Puritan theologian of that day. Brainerd loved Jerusha and they were engaged to be married, but he did not live until the wedding.

Imagine what hopes, dreams, and expectations for the cause of Christ were buried in the grave with the withered body of that young missionary. At that point, nothing remained but memories and several dozen Indian converts! Yet Jonathan Edwards, that majestic old Puritan saint, who had hoped to call Brainerd his son, began to write the story of that short life in a little book. The book took wings, flew across the sea, and landed on the desk of a Cambridge student by the name of Henry Martyn.

Poor Henry Martyn! In spite of his education, brilliance, and great opportunities, he—after reading that little book on the life of Brainerd—threw his own life away! Afterward, what had he accomplished once he set his course toward home from India in 1812? With his health then broken, he dragged himself as far north as the town of Tokat, Turkey, near the Black Sea. There he lay in the shade of a pile of saddles, to cool his burning fever, and died alone at the age of thirty-one.

What was the purpose behind these "wasted lives"? From the grave of a young David Brainerd, and the lonely grave of Henry Martyn near the shores of the Black Sea, have arisen a mighty army of modern missionaries. Leonard Woolsey Bacon

Is there some desert, or some boundless sea,
Where You, great God of angels, will send me?
Some oak for me to rend,
Some sod for me to break,
Some handful of Your corn to take
And scatter far afield,
Till it in turn will yield

Its hundredfold
Of grains of gold
To feed the happy children of my God?
Show me the desert, Father, or the sea;
Is it Your enterprise? Great God, send me!
And though this body lies where ocean rolls,
Father, count me among all faithful souls.

NOVEMBER 15

We were under great pressure.
2 CORINTHIANS 1:8

So that Christ's power may rest on me.
2 CORINTHIANS 12:9

GOD ALLOWED THE CRISIS IN JACOB'S LIFE AT PENIEL TO TOTALLY surround him until he ultimately came to the point of making an earnest and humble appeal to God Himself. That night, he wrestled with God and literally came to the place where he could take hold of Him as never before. And through his narrow brush with danger, Jacob's faith and knowledge of God was expanded, and his power to live a new and victorious life was born.

The Lord had to force David, through the discipline of many long and painful years, to learn of the almighty power and faithfulness of his God. Through those difficult years, he also grew in his knowledge of faith and godliness, which were indispensable principles for his glorious career as the king of Israel.

Nothing but the most dangerous circumstances in which Paul was constantly placed could ever have taught him, and thus the church through him, the full meaning of the great promise of God he learned to claim: "My grace is sufficient for you" (2 Corinthians 12:9). And nothing but the great trials and dangers we have experienced would ever have led some of us to know Him as we do, to trust Him as we have, and to draw from Him the great measure of His grace so indispensable during our times of greatest need.

Difficulties and obstacles are God's challenges to our faith. When we are confronted with hindrances that block our path of service, we are to recognize them as vessels for faith and then to fill them with the fullness and complete sufficiency of Jesus.

As we move forward in faith, simply and fully trusting Him, we may be tested. Sometimes we may have to wait and realize that "perseverance [must] finish its work" (James 1:4). But ultimately we will surely find "the stone rolled away" (Luke 24:2) and the Lord Himself waiting to bestow a double blessing on us for our time of testing. A. B. Simpson

NOVEMBER 16

They triumphed over him by the blood of the Lamb . . . they did not love their lives so much as to shrink from death.

Revelation 12:11

When James and John came to Christ with their mother, asking Him to give them the best place in His kingdom, He did not refuse their request. He told them that the place would be given to them if they could do His work, drink His cup, and be baptized with His baptism (Mark 10:38).

Are we willing to compete for God's best, with the knowledge that the best things are always achieved by the most difficult paths? We must endure steep mountains, dense forests, and the Enemy's chariots of iron, since hardship is the price of the victor's coronation. Arches of triumph are made not of rose blossoms and strands of silk but of hard blows and bloody scars. The very hardships you are enduring in your life today have been given to you by the Master, for the express purpose of enabling you to win your crown.

Therefore do not always look ahead to your tomorrows for some ideal situation, exotic difficulty, or faraway emergency in which to shine. Rise today to face the circumstances in which the providence of God has placed you. Your crown of glory is hidden in the heart of these things—the hardships and trials pressing in on you this very hour, week, and month of your life. Yet the most difficult things are not those seen and known by the world but those deep within your soul, unseen and unknown by anyone except Jesus. It is in this secret place that you experience a little trial that you would never dare to mention to anyone else and that is more difficult for you to bear than martyrdom.

Beloved, your crown lies there. May God help you to overcome and to wear it. Selected

It matters not how the battle goes,
The day how long;
Faint not! Fight on!
Tomorrow comes the song.

NOVEMBER 17

"Listen to what the unjust judge says. And will not God bring about justice for his chosen ones, who cry out to him day and night? Will he keep putting them off? I tell you, he will see that they get justice, and quickly."

Luke 18:6–8

God's timing is not ours to command. If we do not start the fire with the first strike of our match, we must try again. God does hear our prayer, but He may not answer it at the precise time we have appointed in our own minds. Instead, He will reveal Himself to our seeking hearts, though not necessarily when and where we may expect. Therefore we have a need for perseverance and steadfast determination in our life of prayer.

In the old days of flint, steel, and brimstone matches, people had to strike the match again and again, perhaps even dozens of times, before they could get a spark to light their fire, and they were very thankful if they finally succeeded. Should we not exercise the same kind of perseverance and hope regarding heavenly things? When it comes to faith, we have more certainty of success than we could ever have had with flint and steel, for we have God's promises as a foundation.

May we, therefore, never despair. God's time for mercy will come—in fact, it has already come, if our time for believing has arrived. Ask in faith without wavering, but never cease to petition the King simply because He has delayed His reply.

Strike the match again and make the sparks fly. Yet be sure to have your tinder ready, for you will get a fire before long. CHARLES H. SPURGEON

I do not believe there is such a thing in the history of God's eternal kingdom as a right prayer, offered in the right spirit, that remains forever unanswered. THEODORE L. CUYLER

NOVEMBER 18

Blessed is he, whosoever shall not be offended in me.

LUKE 7:23 KJV

IT IS SOMETIMES VERY DIFFICULT NOT TO BE OFFENDED IN JESUS Christ, for the offense may be the result of my circumstances. I may find myself confined to narrow areas of service, or isolated from others through sickness or by taking an unpopular stance, when I had hoped for much wider opportunities. Yet the Lord knows what is best for me, and my surroundings are determined by Him. Wherever He places me, He does so to strengthen my faith and power and to draw me into closer communion with Himself. And even if confined to a dungeon, my soul will prosper.

The offense that causes me to turn from Christ may be emotional. I may be continually confused and troubled over questions I cannot solve.

When I gave myself to Him, I had hoped that my skies would always be fair, but often they are overcast with clouds and rain. But I must believe that when difficulties remain, it is that I may learn to trust Him completely—to trust and not be afraid. And it is through my mental and emotional struggles that I am being trained to tutor others who are being tossed by the storm.

The offense causing me to turn away may be spiritual. I had imagined that once within His fold, I would never again suffer from the stinging winds of temptation. Yet it is best for me the way it is, for when I endure temptation His grace is magnified, my own character matures, and heaven seems sweeter at the end of the day.

Once I arrive at my heavenly home, I will look back across the turns and trials along my path and will sing the praises of my Guide. So whatever comes my way, I will welcome His will and refuse to be offended in my loving Lord. Alexander Smellie

Blessed is he whose faith is not offended,
When all around his way
The power of God is working out deliverance
For others day by day;

Though in some prison dark his own soul does fail,
Till life itself be spent,
Yet still can trust his Father's love and purpose,
And rest therein content.

Blessed is he, who through long years of suffering,
Not now from active toil,
Still shares by prayer and praise the work of others,
And thus "divides the spoil."

Blessed are you, O child of God, who does suffer,
And cannot understand

The reason for your pain, yet will gladly leave
Your life in His blest Hand.

Yes, blessed are you whose faith is "not offended"
By trials unexplained,
By mysteries unsolved, past understanding,
Until the goal is gained.
FREDA HANBURY ALLEN

NOVEMBER 19

Though you have made me see troubles, many
and bitter, you will restore my life again.
PSALM 71:20

GOD *makes* YOU "SEE TROUBLES." SOMETIMES, AS PART OF YOUR EDUcation being carried out, you must "go down to the depths of the earth" (Psalm 63:9), travel subterranean passages, and lie buried among the dead. But not for even one moment is the bond of fellowship and oneness between God and you strained to the point of breaking. And ultimately, from the depths, He "will restore [your] life again."

Never doubt God! Never say that He has forsaken or forgotten you or think that He is unsympathetic. He "*will* restore [your] life again." No matter how many twists and turns the road may have, there is always one smooth, straight portion. Even the longest day has a sunset, and the winter snow may stay quite some time, but it will finally melt.

Be steadfast, "because you know that your labor in the Lord is not in vain" (1 Corinthians 15:58). He will turn to you again and comfort you. And when He does, your heart that has forgotten how to sing will break forth in thankful and jubilant song, just like the psalmist who sang, "My tongue will sing of your righteousness" (Psalm 51:14). SELECTED

Though the rain may fall and the wind be blowing,
And chilled and cold is the wintry blast;
Though the cloudy sky is still cloudier growing,
And the dead leaves tell that the summer has passed;
My face is fixed on the stormy heaven,
My heart is as calm as the summer sea,
Glad to receive what my God has given,
Whate'er it be.
When I feel the cold, I can say, "He sends it,"
And His winds blow blessing, I surely know;
For I've never a need but that He will meet it;
And my heart beats warm, though the winds may blow.

NOVEMBER 20

Blessed is the one who waits.

DANIEL 12:12

WAITING MAY SEEM LIKE AN EASY THING TO DO, BUT IT IS A DISCIPLINE that a Christian soldier does not learn without years of training. Marching and drills are much easier for God's warriors than standing still.

There are times of indecision and confusion, when even the most willing person, who eagerly desires to serve the Lord, does not know what direction to take. So what should you do when you find yourself in this situation? Should you allow yourself to be overcome with despair? Should you turn back in cowardice or in fear or rush ahead in ignorance?

No, you should simply wait—but *wait in prayer.* Call upon God and plead your case before Him, telling Him of your difficulty and reminding Him of His promise to help.

Wait in faith. Express your unwavering confidence in Him. And believe that even if He keeps you waiting until midnight, He will come at the right time to fulfill His vision for you.

Wait in quiet patience. Never complain about what you believe to be the cause of your problems, as the children of Israel did against Moses. Accept your situation exactly as it is and then simply place it with your whole heart into the hand of your covenant God. And while removing any self-will, say to Him, "Lord, 'Not my will, but yours be done' [Luke 22:42]. I do not know what to do, and I am in great need. But I will wait until You divide the flood before me or drive back my enemies. I will wait even if You keep me here many days, for my heart is fixed on You alone, dear Lord. And my spirit will wait for You with full confidence that You will still be my joy and my salvation, 'for you have been my refuge, [and] a strong tower against the foe' [Psalm 61:3]." MORNING BY MORNING

Wait, patiently wait,
God never is late;
Your budding plans are in Your Father's holding,
And only wait His grand divine unfolding.
Then wait, wait,
Patiently wait.
Trust, hopefully trust,
That God will adjust
Your tangled life; and from its dark concealings,
Will bring His will, in all its bright revealings.
Then trust, trust,
Hopefully trust.
Rest, peacefully rest
On your Savior's breast;
Breathe in His ear your sacred high ambition,
And He will bring it forth in blest fruition.
Then rest, rest,
Peacefully rest!

MERCY A. GLADWIN

NOVEMBER 21

Commit your way to the L*ORD.*

PSALM 37:5

TALK TO GOD ABOUT WHATEVER MAY BE PRESSURING YOU AND THEN commit the entire matter into His hands. Do this so that you will be free from the confusion, conflicts, and cares that fill the world today. In fact, anytime you are preparing to do something, undergoing some trial, or simply pursuing your normal business, tell the Father about it. Acquaint Him with it; yes, even *burden Him with it*, and you will have put the concerns and cares of the matter behind you. From that point forward, exercise quiet, sweet diligence in your work, recognizing your dependence on Him to carry the matter for you. Commit your cares and yourself with them, as one burden, to your God. R. LEIGHTON

Build a little fence of trust
Around today;
Fill the space with loving work
And therein stay.
Look not through the protective rails
Upon tomorrow;
God will help you bear what comes
Of joy or sorrow.
MARY BUTTS

You will find it impossible to "commit your way to the LORD," unless your way has met with His approval. It can only be done through faith, for if there is even the slightest doubt in your heart that your way is not a good one, faith will refuse to have anything to do with it. Also, this committing of your way to Him must be continuous, not just one isolated action. And no matter how unexpected or extraordinary His guidance may seem and no matter how close to the edge of the cliff He may lead you, never snatch the guiding reins from His hands.

Are you willing to submit all your ways to God, allowing Him to pass judgment on them? There is nothing a Christian needs to more closely examine than his own confirmed views and habits, for we are so prone to taking God's divine approval of them for granted. And that is why some Christians are so anxious and fearful. They have obviously not truly committed their way to the Lord and *left it with Him*. They took it to Him but walked away with it again. SELECTED

NOVEMBER 22

"Do you believe that I am able to do this?"
MATTHEW 9:28

GOD DEALS WITH IMPOSSIBILITIES. IT IS NEVER TOO LATE FOR HIM TO do so, as long as that which is impossible is brought to Him in complete faith by the person whose life and circumstances would be impacted if God is to be glorified. If we have experienced rebellion, unbelief, sin, and ruin in our life, it is never too late for God to deal triumphantly with these tragic things, if they are brought to Him in complete surrender and trust.

It has often been said, and truthfully so, that Christianity is the only religion that can deal with a person's past. God "will repay you for the years the locusts have eaten" (Joel 2:25), and He is trustworthy to do it unreservedly. He does so not because of *what* we are but because of *who* He is. God forgives and heals and restores, for He is "the God of all grace" (1 Peter 5:10). May we praise Him and trust Him. SUNDAY SCHOOL TIMES

Nothing is too hard for Jesus
No man can work like Him.

We have a God who delights in impossibilities and who asks, "Is anything too hard for me?" (Jeremiah 32:27). ANDREW MURRAY

NOVEMBER 23

You have shown your people desperate times.

Psalm 60:3

I have always been glad that the psalmist said to God that certain times of life are desperate or difficult. Make no mistake about it, there are difficult things in life.

This summer someone gave me some beautiful pink flowers, and as I took them, I asked, "What kind are they?" My friend answered, "They are rock flowers. They grow and bloom only on rocks where you can see no soil." Then I thought of God's flowers growing in desperate times and hard places, and I somehow feel that He may have a certain tenderness for His "rock flowers" that He may not have for His lilies and roses. Margaret Bottome

The trials of life are sent to make us, not to break us. Financial troubles may destroy a person's business but build up his character. And a direct blow to the outer person may be the greatest blessing possible to the inner person. So if God places or allows anything difficult in our lives, we can be sure that the real danger or trouble will be what we will lose if we run or rebel against it. Maltbie D. Babcock

Heroes are forged on anvils hot with pain,
And splendid courage comes but with the test.
Some natures ripen and some natures bloom
Only on blood-wet soil, some souls prove great
Only in moments dark with death or doom.

God finds His best soldiers on the mountain of affliction.

NOVEMBER 24

"Be still, and know that I am God."

Psalm 46:10

Is there any note in all the music of the world as mighty as the grand pause? Is there any word in the Psalms more eloquent than the word "Selah," meaning pause? Is there anything more thrilling and awe-inspiring than the calm before the crashing of the storm, or the strange quiet that seems to fall upon nature before some supernatural phenomenon or disastrous upheaval? And is there anything that can touch our hearts like the *power of stillness*?

For the hearts that will cease focusing on themselves, there is "the peace of God, which transcends all understanding" (Philippians 4:7); "quietness and trust" (Isaiah 30:15), which is the source of all strength; a "great peace" that will never "make them stumble" (Psalm 119:165); and a deep rest, which the world can never give nor take away. Deep within the center of the soul is a chamber of peace where God lives and where, if we will enter it and quiet all the other sounds, we can hear His "gentle whisper" (1 Kings 19:12).

Even in the fastest wheel that is turning, if you look at the center, where the axle is found, there is no movement at all. And even in the busiest life, there is a place where we may dwell alone with God in eternal stillness.

There is only one way to know God: "Be still, and know." "The Lord is in his holy temple; let all the earth be silent before him" (Habakkuk 2:20). Selected

All-loving Father, sometimes we have walked under starless skies that dripped darkness like drenching rain. We despaired from the lack of light from the sun, moon, and stars. The gloomy darkness loomed above us as if it would last forever. And from the dark, there spoke no soothing voice to mend our broken hearts. We would gladly have welcomed even a wild clap of thunder, if only to break the torturing stillness of that mournfully depressing night.

Yet Your soft whisper of eternal love spoke more sweetly to our bruised and bleeding souls than any winds that breathe across a wind harp. It was Your "gentle whisper" that spoke to us. We were listening and we heard You, and then we looked and saw Your face, which was radiant with the light of Your love. And when we heard Your voice and saw Your face, new life returned to us, just as life returns to withered blossoms that drink the summer rain.

NOVEMBER 25

"Take the arrows. . . . Strike the ground." He struck it three times and stopped. The man of God was angry with him and said, "You should have struck the ground five or six times."

2 KINGS 13:18–19

HOW STRIKING AND POWERFUL IS THE MESSAGE OF THESE WORDS! Jehoash, king of Israel, thought he had done quite well when he struck the ground "three times and stopped." To him, it seemed to be an extraordinary act of his faith, but the Lord and the prophet Elisha were deeply disappointed, *because he had stopped halfway.*

Yes, he did receive something; in fact, he received a great deal—exactly what he had believed God for, in the final analysis. Yet Jehoash did not receive everything that Elisha meant for him to have or that the Lord wanted to bestow on him. He missed much of the meaning of the promise, and the fullness of the blessing. He did receive more than any human could have offered, but he did not receive God's best.

Dear believer, how sobering is the truth of this story! How important it is for us to learn to pray through our circumstances and to fully examine our hearts with God's message to us!

Otherwise, we will never claim all the fullness of His promise or all the possibilities that believing prayer offers. A. B. SIMPSON

"To him who is able to do immeasurably more than all we ask or imagine, according to his power that is at work within us, to him be glory" (Ephesians 3:20–21).

In no other place does the apostle Paul use these seemingly redundant words: "immeasurably more than all." Each word is packed with God's infinite love and power "to do" for His praying believers. Yet there is the following limitation: "according to his power that is at work within us." He will only do as much *for* us as we will allow Him to do *in* us. The same power that saved us, washed us with His blood, filled us with the power of His Holy Spirit, and protected us through numerous temptations will work *for* us to meet every emergency, every crisis, every circumstance, and every adversary. THE ALLIANCE

NOVEMBER 26

Caleb asked her, "What can I do for you?" She replied, "Do me a special favor. Since you have given me land in the Negev, give me also springs of water." So Caleb gave her the upper and lower springs.

JOSHUA 15:18–19

THERE ARE BOTH "UPPER AND LOWER SPRINGS" IN LIFE, AND THEY ARE *springs*, not stagnant pools. They are the joys and blessings that flow from heaven above, through the hottest summer and through the most barren desert of sorrow and trials. The land belonging to Acsah was in the Negev under the scorching sun and was often parched from the burning heat. But from the hills came the inexhaustible springs that cooled, refreshed, and fertilized all the land.

These springs flow through the low places, the difficult places, the desert places, the lonely places, and even the ordinary places of life. And no matter what our situation may be, these springs can always be found. Abraham found them amid the hills of Canaan. Moses found them among the rocks of Midian. David found them among the ashes of Ziklag, when his property was gone and his family had been taken captive. And although his "men were talking of stoning him . . . David found strength in the LORD his God" (1 Samuel 30:6).

Isaiah found them in the terrible days when King Sennacherib of

Assyria invaded Judah, when the mountains themselves seemed to be thrown into the midst of the sea. Yet his faith could still sing: "There is a river whose streams make glad the city of God, the holy place where the Most High dwells. God is within her, she will not fall" (Psalm 46:4–5).

The Christian martyrs found them amid the flames, the church reformers amid their enemies and struggles, and we can find them each day of the year if we have the Comforter in our hearts and have learned to say with David, "*All my springs of joy are in you*" (Psalm 87:7 NASB).

How plentiful and how precious these springs are, and how much more there is to be possessed of God's own fullness! A. B. SIMPSON

I said, "The desert is so wide!"
I said, "The desert is so bare!
What springs to quench my thirst are there?
Where will I from the tempest hide?"

I said, "The desert is so lone!
No gentle voice, nor loving face
To brighten any smallest space."
I paused before my cry was done!

I heard the flow of hidden springs;
Before me palms rose green and fair;
The birds were singing; all the air
Was filled and stirred with angels' wings!

And One asked softly, "Why, indeed,
Take overanxious thought for what
Tomorrow brings you? See you not
The Father knows just what you need?"

SELECTED

NOVEMBER 27

Nothing will be impossible with God.

LUKE 1:37 NASB

HIGH IN THE SNOW-COVERED ALPINE VALLEYS, GOD WORKS ONE OF His miracles year after year. In spite of the extremes of sunny days and frozen nights, a flower blooms unblemished through the crust of ice near the edge of the snow. How does this little flower, known as the soldanelle plant, accomplish such a feat?

During the past summer the little plant spread its leaves wide and flat on the ground in order to soak up the sun's rays, and it kept that energy stored in its roots throughout the winter. When spring came, life stirred even beneath its shroud of snow, and as the plant sprouted, it amazingly produced enough warmth to thaw a small dome-shaped pocket of snow above its head.

It grew higher and higher, and as it did, the small dome of air continued to rise just above its head until its flower bud was safely formed. At last the icy covering of the air compartment gave way, and the blossom burst into the sunshine. The crystalline texture of its mauve-colored petals sparkled like the snow itself, as if it still bore the marks of the journey it had endured.

This fragile flower sounds an echo in our hearts that none of the lovely flowers nestled in the warm grass of the lower slopes could ever awaken. Oh, how we love to see impossible things accomplished! And so does God.

Therefore may we continue to persevere, for even if we took our circumstances and cast all the darkness of human doubt upon them and then hastily piled as many difficulties together as we could find against God's divine work, we could never move beyond the blessedness of His miracle-working power. May we place our faith completely in Him, for He is the God of the impossible. SELECTED

NOVEMBER 28

Where morning dawns, where evening
fades, you call forth songs of joy.
PSALM 65:8

HAVE YOU EVER RISEN EARLY, CLIMBED A HILL, AND WATCHED GOD make a morning? The dull gray gives way as He pushes the sun toward the horizon, and then the tints and hues of every color begin to blend into one perfect light as the full sun suddenly bursts into view. As king of the day, the sun moves majestically across the sky, flooding the earth and every deep valley with glorious light. At this point, you can hear the music of heaven's choir as it sings of the majesty of God Himself and of the glory of the morning.

In the holy hush of the early dawn
I hear a Voice—
"I am with you all the day,
Rejoice! Rejoice!"

The clear, pure light of the morning made me yearn for the truth in my heart, which alone could make me pure and clear as the morning itself and tune my life to the concert pitch of nature around me. And the breeze that blew from the sunrise made me hope in God, who had breathed into my nostrils the breath of life. He had so completely filled me with His breath, mind, and Spirit that I would only think His thoughts and live His life. Within His life I had found my own, but now it was eternally glorified.

What would we poor humans do without our God's nights and mornings! GEORGE MACDONALD

In the early morning hours,
'Twixt the night and day,

While from earth the darkness passes
Silently away;

Then it's sweet to talk with Jesus
In your bedroom still—
For the coming day and duties
Ask to know His will.

Then He'll lead the way before you,
Laying mountains low;
Making desert places blossom,
Sweet'ning sorrow's flow.

Do you want a life of triumph,
Victory all the way?
Then put God in the beginning
Of each coming day.

NOVEMBER 29

Later on, however . . .

HEBREWS 12:11

THERE IS A LEGEND THAT TELLS OF A GERMAN BARON WHO, AT HIS castle on the Rhine, stretched wires in the air from tower to tower so that the wind might treat them as a wind harp and thereby create music as it blew across them. Yet as the soft breezes swirled around the castle, no music was born.

One night, however, a fierce storm arose, and the hill where the castle sat was struck with the fury of the violent wind. The baron looked out his doorway on the terror of the wind, and the wind harp was filling the air with melodies that rang out even above the noise of the storm. It had taken a fierce storm to produce the music!

Haven't we all known people whose lives have never produced any pleasing music during their days of calm prosperity but who, when fierce winds have blown across their lives, have astonished us by the power and beauty of their music?

Rain, rain
Beating against the pane!
How endlessly it pours
Out of doors
From the darkened sky—
I wonder why!
Flowers, flowers,
Springing up after showers,
Blossoming fresh and fair,
Everywhere!
God has now explained
Why it rained!

You can always count on God to make the "later on" of difficulties a thousand times richer and better than the present, if we overcome them correctly. "No discipline seems pleasant at the time. . . . Later on, however, it produces a harvest of righteousness and peace" (Hebrews 12:11). What a yield!

NOVEMBER 30

"Should you then seek great things for yourself? Do not seek them. For I will bring disaster on all people, declares the Lord*, but wherever you go I will let you escape with your life."*

Jeremiah 45:5

This is a promise given to you for the difficult places in which you may find yourself—a promise of safety and life even in the midst of tremendous pressure. And it is a promise that adjusts itself to fit the times as they continue to grow more difficult, as we approach the end of this age and the tribulation period.

What does it mean when it says that you will "escape with your life"? It means your life will be snatched from the jaws of the Enemy, as David snatched the lamb from the lion. It does not mean you will be spared the heat of the battle and confrontation with your foes, but it means "a table before [you] in the presence of [your] enemies" (Psalm 23:5), a shelter from the storm, a fortress amid the foe, and a life preserved in the face of continual pressure. It means comfort and hope from God, such as Paul received when he and his friends "were under great pressure, far beyond [their] ability to endure, so that [they] despaired even of life" (2 Corinthians 1:8). And it means the Lord's divine help, such as when Paul's "thorn in the flesh" (2 Corinthians 12:7 KJV) remained, but the power of Christ came to rest upon him, and he learned that God's "grace is sufficient" (2 Corinthians 12:9).

May the Lord "wherever you go . . . let you escape with your life" and help you today to be victorious in your difficulties. DAYS OF HEAVEN UPON EARTH

We often pray to be delivered from afflictions, and even trust God that we will be. But we do not pray for Him to make us what we should be while in the midst of the afflictions. Nor do we pray that we would be able to live within them, for however long they may last, in the complete awareness that we are held and sheltered by the Lord and can therefore continue within them without suffering any harm.

The Savior endured an especially difficult test in the wilderness while in the presence of Satan for forty days and nights, His human nature weakened by the need for food and rest. The three Hebrew young men were kept for a time in the flames of "the furnace heated seven times hotter than usual" (Daniel 3:19). In spite of being forced to endure the tyrant's last method of torture, they remained calm and composed as they waited for their time of deliverance to come. And after surviving an entire night sitting among the lions, "when Daniel was lifted from the den, no wound was found on him, because he had trusted in his God" (Daniel 6:23).

They were able to endure in the presence of their enemies because they dwelt in the presence of their God.

DECEMBER 1

There remains, then, a Sabbath-rest for the people of God.
HEBREWS 4:9

[That rest includes victory:] "The LORD *gave them rest on every side. . . . The* LORD *gave all their enemies into their hands."*
JOSHUA 21:44

Thanks be to God! He gives us the victory through our Lord Jesus Christ.
1 CORINTHIANS 15:57

A PROMINENT BELIEVER ONCE TOLD OF HIS MOTHER, WHO WAS A VERY anxious and troubled Christian. He would often talk with her for hours, trying to convince her of the sinfulness of worrying, but to no avail. She was like the elderly woman who once said that she had suffered a great deal, especially from the troubles that never came.

Then one morning his mother came to breakfast with a smile adorning her face. He asked her what had happened, and she began describing a dream she had in the night. In her dream, she was walking along a highway with a large crowd of people, all of whom seemed very tired and burdened. The people were all carrying little black bundles, and she noticed that more bundles were being dropped along the way by numerous repulsive-looking creatures that seemed quite demonic in nature. As the bundles were dropped, the people stooped down to pick them up and carry them.

Like everyone else in her dream, she also carried her needless load, being weighted down with the Devil's bundles. After a while, she looked up and saw a Man whose face was loving and bright as He moved through the crowd, comforting the people. Finally He came to her, and she realized it was her Savior. She looked at Him, telling Him how tired she was, and He smiled sadly and said, "My dear child, these bundles you carry are not from me, and you have no need of them. They are the Devil's burdens, and they are wearing out your life. You need to drop them and simply refuse to touch them with even one of your fingers. Then you will find your path easy, and you will feel as if 'I carried you on eagles' wings' [Exodus 19:4]."

The Savior touched her hand, and peace and joy quickly filled her soul. As she saw herself in her dream casting her burdens to the ground and ready to throw herself at His feet in joyful thanksgiving, she suddenly awoke, finding that all her worries were gone.

From that day forward to the end of her life, she was the most cheerful and happy member of her family.

And the night will be filled with music,
And the cares that besiege the day,
Will fold their tents like the Arabs,
And will silently steal away.

Henry Wadsworth Longfellow

DECEMBER 2

Perfect through sufferings.

Hebrews 2:10 KJV

Steel is the product of iron *plus* fire. Soil is rock *plus* heat and the crushing of glaciers. Linen is flax *plus* the water that cleans it, the comb that separates it, the flail that pounds it, and the shuttle that weaves it. In the same way, the development of human character requires a *plus* attached to it, for great character is made not through luxurious living but through suffering. And the world does not forget people of great character.

I once heard the story of a mother who brought a crippled boy with a hunched back into her home as a companion for her own son. She warned her son to be very careful not to refer to the other boy's deformity, since this was a sensitive matter to him. And she encouraged him to play with his new friend as if he were a normal child. But after listening to her son play with him for a few minutes, she heard him ask his companion, "Do you know what that is on your back?" The crippled boy was embarrassed, hesitated a moment, but before he could respond, his friend answered the question for him by saying, "It is the box that holds your wings, and someday God is going to break it open, and you will fly away to be an angel."

Someday God is going to reveal this fact to every Christian: the very things they now rebel against are the instruments He has used to perfect their character and to mold them into perfection, so they may later be used as polished stones in His heaven yet to come. CORTLAND MYERS

Suffering is a wonderful fertilizer for the roots of character. The great objective of this life is character, for it is the only thing we can carry with us into eternity. And gaining as much of the highest character possible is the purpose of our trials. AUSTIN PHELPS

The mountain of vision is won by no other road than the one covered with thorns.

DECEMBER 3

"Is your husband all right? Is your child all right?" "Everything is all right," she said.

2 KINGS 4:26

Be strong, my soul!
Your loved ones go
Within the veil. God's yours, e'en so;
Be strong.

Be strong, my soul!
Death looms in view.
Lo, hear your God! He'll bear you through;
Be strong.

For sixty-two years and five months I had my beloved wife, and now, in my ninety-second year, I am left alone. But I turn to the ever present Jesus as I walk around my room, and say, "Lord Jesus, I am alone. Yet I am not alone, for You are with me and are my Friend. Now, Lord, please comfort me, strengthen me, and give to Your poor servant everything that You see I need."

We should never be satisfied until we have come to the place where we know the Lord Jesus in this way—until we have discovered He is our eternal Friend—continually, under all circumstances, and constantly ready to prove Himself as our Friend. GEORGE MUELLER

Afflictions cannot injure when we blend them with submission.

Ice on trees will bend many a branch to the point of breaking. Similarly, I see a great many people bowed down and crushed by their afflictions. Yet every now and then I meet someone who sings in affliction, and then I thank God for my own circumstance as well as his. There is never a song more beautiful than that which is sung in the night. You may remember the story of a woman who, when her only child died, looked toward heaven as with the face of an angel and said, "I give you joy, my sweet child." That solitary, simple sentence has stayed with me for many years, often energizing and comforting me. HENRY WARD BEECHER

E'en for the dead I will not bind my soul to grief;
Death cannot long divide.
For is it not as though the rose that climbed my garden wall
Has blossomed on the other side?
Death does hide,
But not divide;
You are but on Christ's other side!
You are with Christ, and Christ with me;
In Christ united still are we.

DECEMBER 4

He went up on a mountainside by himself.
MATTHEW 14:23

ONE OF THE BLESSINGS OF THE OLD-TIME SABBATH DAY WAS THE calmness, restfulness, and holy peace that came from having a time of quiet solitude away from the world. There is a special strength that is born in solitude. Crows travel in flocks, and wolves in packs, but the lion and the eagle are usually found alone.

Strength is found not in busyness and noise but in quietness. For a lake to reflect the heavens on its surface, it must be calm. Our Lord loved the people who flocked to Him, but there are numerous accounts in the Scriptures of His going away from them for a brief period of time. On occasion He would withdraw from the crowd and quite often would spend His evenings alone in the hills. Most of His ministry was performed in the towns and cities by the seashore, but He loved the hills more and at nightfall would frequently seclude Himself in their peaceful heights.

The one thing we need today more than anything else is to spend time alone with our Lord, sitting at His feet in the sacred privacy of His blessed presence. Oh, how we need to reclaim the lost art of meditation! Oh, how we need "the secret place" (Psalm 91:1 KJV) as part of our lifestyle! Oh, how we need the power that comes from waiting upon God! SELECTED

It is good to live in the valley sweet,
Where the work of the world is done,
Where the reapers sing in the fields of wheat,
And work till the setting of the sun.
But beyond the meadows, the hills I see
Where the noises of traffic cease,
And I follow a Voice who calls out to me
From the hilltop regions of peace.

Yes, to live is sweet in the valley fair,
And work till the setting of the sun;
But my spirit yearns for the hilltop's air
When the day and its work are done.
For a Presence breathes o'er the silent hills,
And its sweetness is living yet;
The same deep calm all the hillside fills,
As breathed over Olivet.

Every life that desires to be strong must have its "Most Holy Place" (Exodus 26:33) into which only God enters.

DECEMBER 5

Lord, I know that people's lives are not their own;
it is not for them to direct their steps.
Jeremiah 10:23

Lead me in a straight path.
Psalm 27:11

Many people want to direct God instead of surrendering themselves to be directed by Him. They want to show Him the way instead of submissively following where He leads. Madame Guyon

I said, "Let me walk in the field";
God said, "No, walk in the town";
I said, "There are no flowers there";
He said, "No flowers, but a crown."

I said, "But the sky is black,
There is nothing but noise and din";
But He wept as He sent me back,
"There is more," He said, "there is sin."

I said, "But the air is thick,
And smog is veiling the sun";
He answered, "Yet souls are sick,
And your work is yet undone."

I said, "I will miss the light,
And friends will miss me, they say";
He answered me, "Choose tonight,
If I am to miss you, or they."

I pleaded for time to be given;
He said, "Is it hard to decide?
It will not seem hard in Heaven
To have followed the steps of your Guide."

I cast one look at the field,
Then set my face to the town;
He said, "My child, do you yield?
Will you leave the flowers for the crown?"

Then into His hand went mine,
And into my heart came He;
And I walk in a light Divine,
The path I had feared to see.

GEORGE MACDONALD

DECEMBER 6

I am coming soon. Hold on to what you have,
so that no one will take your crown.
REVELATION 3:11

GEORGE MUELLER, A LEADER AMONG THE PLYMOUTH BRETHREN, ONCE shared this testimony: "In July 1829 it pleased God to reveal to my heart the truth regarding the return of the Lord Jesus and to show me that I had made a great mistake by sitting back and watching for the complete conversion of the world. It produced the following effect on me: Deep within my soul, I was moved to feel compassion for perishing sinners and for a world lulled to sleep by the wicked Enemy. And I began to think, 'Should I not do whatever I can for the Lord Jesus and try to awake His slumbering church before He returns?'"

There may still be many difficult years of hard work ahead of us before the fulfillment of His prophetic return, but the signs of His coming today are very encouraging. In fact, I would not be at all surprised if I saw the apocalyptic angel spread its wings for its last triumphal flight before today's sunset. Nor would I be surprised if tomorrow morning's news thrilled us with the proclamation that Christ the Lord had arrived atop the Mount of Olives or Mount Calvary to declare His worldwide dominion.

O dead churches, wake up! O Christ, descend! Scarred head, take Your crown! Bruised hands, take Your scepter! Wounded feet, take Your throne! "For thine is the kingdom" (Matthew 6:13 KJV). THOMAS DEWITT TALMAGE

It may be in the evening,
When the work of the day is done,
And you have time to sit in the twilight,
And watch the sinking sun,
While the long bright day dies slowly

Over the sea,
And the hours grow quiet and holy
With thoughts of Me;
While you hear the village children
Running along the street—
Among those passing footsteps
May come the sound of My Feet.
Therefore I tell you, Watch!
By the Light of the evening star
When the room is growing darker
As the clouds afar,
Let your door be closed and latched
In your home,
For it may be in the evening
I will come.

DECEMBER 7

You will see neither wind nor rain, yet this valley will be filled with water, and you, your cattle and your other animals will drink. This is an easy thing in the eyes of the LORD; he will also deliver Moab into your hands.

2 KINGS 3:17–18

TO HUMAN REASON, WHAT GOD WAS PROMISING SEEMED SIMPLY impossible, but nothing is too difficult for Him. Without any sound or sign and from sources invisible and seemingly impossible, the water flowed the entire night, and "the next morning . . . there it was . . . ! And the land was filled with water. . . . The sun was shining on the water. . . . [And it] looked red—like blood" (vv. 20, 22).

Our unbelief is always desiring some *outward sign*, and the faith of many people is largely based on sensationalism. They are not convinced of the genuineness of God's promises without some visible manifestation.

But the greatest triumph of a person's faith is to "be still, and know that [He is] God" (Psalm 46:10).

The greatest victory of faith is to stand at the shore of the impassable Red Sea and to hear the Master say, "*Stand firm and you will see the deliverance the* LORD *will bring you today*" (Exodus 14:13), and "*Move on*" (Exodus 14:15). As we step out in faith, without any sign or sound, taking our first steps into the water, we will see the water divide. Continuing to march ahead, we will see a pathway open through the very midst of the sea.

Whenever I have seen God's wondrous work in the case of some miraculous healing or some extraordinary deliverance by His providence, the thing that has always impressed me most was the absolute quietness in which it was done. I have also been impressed by the absence of anything sensational and dramatic, and the utter sense of my own uselessness as I stood in the presence of this mighty God, realizing how easy all this was for Him to do without even the faintest effort on His part, or the slightest help from me.

It is the role of faith not to *question* but to simply *obey*. In the above story from Scripture, the people were asked to "make this valley full of ditches" (2 Kings 3:16 KJV). The people obeyed, and then water came pouring in from some supernatural source to fill them. What a lesson for our faith!

Are you desiring some spiritual blessing? Then dig the ditches and God will fill them. But He will do this in the most unexpected *places* and in the most unexpected *ways*. May the Lord grant us the kind of faith that acts "by faith, not by sight" (2 Corinthians 5:7), and may we expect Him to work although we see no wind or rain. A. B. SIMPSON

DECEMBER 8

As God's chosen people . . . clothe yourselves with . . . kindness.

COLOSSIANS 3:12

THERE IS AN OLD STORY OF AN ELDERLY MAN WHO ALWAYS CARRIED A little can of oil with him everywhere he went, and when he would go through a door that squeaked, he would squirt a little oil on the hinges. If he encountered a gate that was hard to open, he would oil the latch. And so he went through life, lubricating all the difficult places, making it easier for all those who came after him. People called the man eccentric, strange, and crazy, but he went steadily on, often refilling his can of oil when it was nearly empty, and oiling all the difficult places he found.

In this world, there are many lives that painfully creak and grate as they go about their daily work. Often it seems that nothing goes right with them and that they need lubricating with "the oil of joy" (Psalm 45:7), gentleness, or thoughtfulness.

Do you carry your own can of oil with you? Are you ready with your oil of helpfulness each morning? If you offer your oil to the person nearest you, it may just lubricate the entire day for him. Your oil of cheerfulness will mean more than you know to someone who is downhearted. Or the oil may be a word of encouragement to a person who is full of despair. Never fail to speak it, for our lives may touch others only once on the road of life, and then our paths may diverge, never to meet again.

The oil of kindness has worn the sharp, hard edges off many a sin-hardened life and left it soft and pliable, ready to receive the redeeming grace of the Savior. A pleasant word is a bright ray of sunshine on a saddened heart. Therefore give others the sunshine and tell Jesus the rest.

We cannot know the grief
That men may borrow;
We cannot see the souls
Storm-swept by sorrow;
But love can shine upon the way
Today, tomorrow;
Let us be kind.
Upon the wheel of pain so many weary lives are broken,

So may our love with tender words be spoken.
Let us be kind.

"Be devoted to one another in love" (Romans 12:10).

DECEMBER 9

Our light and momentary troubles are achieving for us an eternal glory that far outweighs them all.
2 CORINTHIANS 4:17

THE QUESTION IS OFTEN ASKED, "WHY IS HUMAN LIFE DRENCHED IN so much blood and soaked with so many tears?" The answer is found in the word "achieving," for these "momentary troubles are *achieving* for us" something very precious. They are teaching us not only the way to victory but, better still, the law of victory—there is a reward for every sorrow, and the sorrow itself produces the reward. It is the very truth expressed in this dear old hymn, written by Sarah Adams in 1840:

Nearer my God to Thee, nearer to Thee,
E'en though it be a cross that raiseth me.

Joy sometimes needs pain to give it birth. Fanny Crosby was a wonderful American hymn writer who lived from 1820 to 1915 and who wrote more than two thousand hymns. Yet she could never have written the beautiful words "I shall see Him face to face" if not for the fact that she had never gazed upon green fields, evening sunsets, nor even the twinkle in her mother's eye. It was the loss of her own vision that helped her to gain her remarkable spiritual discernment and insight.

It is comforting to know that sorrow stays only for the night and then takes its leave in the morning. And a thunderstorm is very brief when compared to a long summer day. Remember, "Weeping may stay for the night, but rejoicing comes in the morning" (Psalm 30:5). SONGS IN THE NIGHT

There is a peace that springs soon after sorrow,
Of hope surrendered, not of hope fulfilled;
A peace that does not look upon tomorrow,
But calmly on the storm that it has stilled.

A peace that lives not now in joy's excesses,
Nor in the happy life of love secure;
But in the unerring strength the heart possesses,
Of conflicts won while learning to endure.

A peace there is, in sacrifice secluded,
A life subdued, from will and passion free;
It's not the peace that over Eden brooded,
But that which triumphed in Gethsemane.

DECEMBER 10

If we are distressed, it is for your comfort and salvation; if we are comforted, it is for your comfort, which produces in you patient endurance of the same sufferings we suffer. And our hope for you is firm, because we know that just as you share in our sufferings, so also you share in our comfort.

2 Corinthians 1:6–7

Are there some people in your circle of friends to whom you naturally go in times of trials and sorrow—people who always seem to say just the right words and who give you the very counsel you so desire? If so, you may not realize the high cost they have paid to become so skilled at binding up your gaping wounds and drying your tears. Yet if you were to investigate their past, you would find they have suffered more than most other people.

They have watched the silver cord on which the lamp of life hung slowly unravel. They have seen the golden bowl of joy smashed at their feet, and its contents spilled. They have experienced raging tides, withering crops, and darkness at high noon, but all this has been necessary to make them into the nurses, physicians, and ministers of others.

Cartons containing spices from the Orient may be cumbersome to ship and slow in coming, but once they arrive the beautiful fragrances fill the air. In the same way, suffering is trying and difficult to bear, but hiding just below its surface is discipline, knowledge, and limitless possibilities. Each of these not only strengthens and matures us but also equips us to help others. So do not worry or clench your teeth, simply waiting with stubborn determination for the suffering to pass. Instead, be determined to get everything you can from it, both for yourself and for the sake of those around you, according to the will of God. SELECTED

Once I heard a song of sweetness,
As it filled the morning air,
Sounding in its blest completeness,
Like a tender, pleading prayer;
And I sought to find the singer,
Where the wondrous song was borne;
And I found a bird, quite wounded,
Pinned down by a cruel thorn.

I have seen a soul in sadness,
While its wings with pain were furled,
Giving hope, and cheer and gladness
That should bless a weeping world
And I knew that life of sweetness,
Was of pain and sorrow borne,
And a stricken soul was singing,
With its heart against a thorn.

You are told of One who loved you,
Of a Savior crucified,

You are told of nails that held Him,
And a spear that pierced His side;
You are told of cruel scourging,
Of a Savior bearing scorn,
And He died for your salvation,
With His brow against a thorn.

You "are not above the Master."
Will you breathe a sweet refrain?
And His grace will be sufficient,
When your heart is pierced with pain.
Will you live to bless His loved ones,
Though your life be bruised and torn,
Like the bird that sang so sweetly,
With its heart against a thorn?

SELECTED

DECEMBER 11

Praise the LORD, all you servants of the LORD who minister by night in the house of the LORD. . . . May the LORD bless you from Zion, he who is the maker of heaven and earth.

PSALM 134:1, 3

YOU MAY SEE THIS AS A STRANGE TIME TO WORSHIP—"MINISTER[ING] by night in the house of the LORD." Indeed, worshiping at night, during the depth of our sorrows, is a difficult thing. Yet therein lies the blessing, for it is the test of perfect faith. If I desire to know the true depth of my friend's love, I must see how he responds during the winter seasons of my life. And it is the same with divine love.

It is easy for me to worship in the summer sunshine, when the beautiful melodies of life seem to fill the air, and the lush fruit of life is still on the trees. But when the songbirds cease and the fruit falls from the trees, will my heart continue to sing? Will I remain in God's house at night? Will I love Him simply for who He is? Am I willing to "keep watch for one hour" (Mark 14:37) with Him in His Gethsemane? Will I help Him carry His cross up the road of suffering to Calvary? Will I stand beside Him in His dying moments, with Mary, His mother, and John, the beloved disciple? Would I be able, with Joseph of Arimathea and Nicodemus, to take the dead Christ from His cross?

If I can do these things, then my worship is complete and my blessing glorious. Then I have indeed shown Him love during the time of His humiliation. My faith has seen Him in His lowest state, and yet my heart has recognized His majesty through His humble disguise. And at last I truly know that I desire not the gift but the Giver. Yes, when I can remain in His house through the darkness of night and worship Him, I have accepted Him for Himself alone. George Matheson

My goal is God Himself, not joy, nor peace,
Nor even blessing, but Himself, my God;
It's His to lead me there, not mine, but His—
"At any cost, dear Lord, by any road!"

So faith bounds forward to its goal in God,
And love can trust her Lord to lead her there;
Upheld by Him, my soul is following hard
Till the Lord has fulfilled my deepest prayer.

No matter if the way is sometimes dark,
No matter though the cost is often great,
He knows the way for me to reach the mark,
The road that leads to Him is sure and straight.

One thing is sure, I cannot tell Him no;
One thing I do, I press towards my Lord;

Giving God my glory here, as I go,
Knowing in heaven waits my Great Reward.

DECEMBER 12

I am already being poured out like a drink offering, and the time for my departure is near. I have fought the good fight, I have finished the race, I have kept the faith.
2 TIMOTHY 4:6–7

JUST AS OLD SOLDIERS COMPARE THEIR BATTLE SCARS AND STORIES OF war when they get together, when we arrive at our heavenly home, we will tell of the goodness and faithfulness of God, who brought us through every trial along the way. I would not like to stand with the multitude clothed in robes made "white in the blood of the Lamb" (Revelation 7:14) and hear these words: "'These are they who have come out of the great tribulation'—*all except you.*"

How would *you* like to stand there and be pointed out as the only saint who never experienced sorrow? Never! You would feel like a stranger in the midst of a sacred fellowship. Therefore may we be content to share in the battle, for we will soon wear a crown of reward and wave a palm branch of praise. CHARLES H. SPURGEON

During the American Civil War, at the battle of Lookout Mountain, Tennessee, a surgeon asked a soldier where he was hurt. The wounded soldier answered, "*Right near the top of the mountain.*" He was not thinking of his gaping wound but was only remembering that he had won the ground near the top of the mountain.

May we also go forth to higher endeavors for Christ, never resting until we can shout from the mountaintop, "I have fought the good fight, I have finished the race, I have kept the faith."

Finish your work, then rest,
Till then rest never;

Since rest for you with God
Is rest forever.

God will examine your life not for medals, diplomas, or degrees but for battle scars.

A medieval singer once sang of his hero:

With his trusty sword for aid;
Ornament it carried none,
But the notches on the blade.

What nobler medal of honor could any godly person seek than the scars of service, personal loss for the crown of reward, disgrace for the sake of Christ, and being worn out in the Master's service!

DECEMBER 13

I will give you the treasures of darkness.
ISAIAH 45:3 NASB

IN THE FAMOUS LACE SHOPS OF BRUSSELS, THERE ARE SPECIAL ROOMS devoted to the spinning of the world's finest lace, all with the most delicate patterns. The rooms are kept completely dark, except for the light that falls directly on the developing pattern, from one very small window. Only one person sits in each small room, where the narrow rays of light fall upon the threads he is weaving, for lace is always more beautifully and delicately woven when the weaver himself is in the dark, with only his work in the light.

Sometimes the darkness in our lives is worse, because we cannot even see the web we are weaving or understand what we are doing. Therefore we are unable to see any beauty or any possible good arising from our experience. Yet if we are faithful to forge ahead and "*if we do not give up*"

(Galatians 6:9), someday we will know that the most exquisite work of our lives was done during those days when it was the darkest.

If you seem to be living in deep darkness because God is working in strange and mysterious ways, do not be afraid. Simply go forward in faith and in love, never doubting Him. He is watching and will bring goodness and beauty from all of your pain and tears. J. R. Miller

The shuttles of His purpose move
To carry out His own design;
Seek not too soon to disapprove
His work, nor yet assign
Dark motives, when, with silent tread,
You view some somber fold;
For lo, within each darker thread
There twines a thread of gold.

Spin cheerfully,
Not tearfully,
He knows the way you plod;
Spin carefully,
Spin prayerfully,
But leave the thread with God.
Canadian Home Journal

DECEMBER 14

One of his disciples said to him, "Lord, teach us to pray. . . ." He said to them, "When you pray, say: 'Your kingdom come.'"
Luke 11:1–2

When one of the disciples said, "Teach us to pray," the Lord raised His eyes to the far horizon of His Father's world. He brought the ultimate goal of eternal life together with everything God desires to do in the life of humankind and packed it all into a powerful prayer that followed these words: "This, then, is how you should pray" (Matthew 6:9). And what a contrast between His prayer and what we often hear today!

How do we pray when we follow the desires of our own hearts? We say, "Lord, bless *me*, then my family, my church, my city, and my country." We start with those closest to us and gradually move outward, ultimately praying for the expansion of God's kingdom throughout the world.

Our Master's prayer, however, begins where we end. He taught us to pray for the world *first* and our personal needs second. Only after our prayer has covered every continent, every remote island of the sea, every person in the last hidden tribe, and every desire and purpose of God for the world are we taught to ask for a piece of bread for ourselves.

Jesus gave Himself for us and to us, paying a holy and precious price on the cross. After giving His all, is it too much for Him to ask us to do the same thing? No man or woman will ever amount to anything in God's kingdom or ever experience any of His power, until this lesson of prayer is learned—that Christ's business is the supreme concern of life and that all of our personal considerations, no matter how important or precious to us, are secondary. DR. FRANCIS

When Robert Moffat, the nineteenth-century Scottish explorer and missionary to South Africa, was once asked to write in a young lady's personal album, he wrote these words:

My album is a savage chest,
Where fierce storms brood and shadows rest,
Without one ray of light;
To write the name of Jesus there,
And see the savage bow in prayer,
And point to worlds more bright and fair,
This is my soul's delight.

"His kingdom will never end" (Luke 1:33), or as an old Moravian version says, "His Kingdom shall have no frontier."

Missionary work should never be an afterthought of the church, because it is Christ's forethought. HENRY JACKSON VAN DYKE

DECEMBER 15

Trust in him.

PSALM 37:5

THE WORD *trust* IS THE HEART OF FAITH AND IS THE OLD TESTAMENT word given to the infant, or early, stages of faith. The word *faith* conveys more an act of the will, while the word *belief* conveys an act of the mind or intellect, but trust is the language of the heart. The words *faith* and *belief* refer more to a truth believed or to something expected to happen.

Trust implies more than this, for it sees and feels and it leans on those who have a great, living, and genuine heart of love. Therefore let us "trust also in him" (Psalm 37:5 KJV), through all the delays, in spite of all the difficulties, and in the face of all the rejection we encounter in life. And in spite of our feelings and evidence to the contrary, and even when we cannot understand our way or our situation, may we still "trust also in him; [for] he shall bring it to pass." The way will open, our situation will be changed, and the end result will be peace. The cloud will finally be lifted, and the light of eternal noonday will shine at last.

Trust and rest when all around you
Puts your faith to stringent test;
Let no fear or foe confound you,
Wait for God and trust and rest.

Trust and rest with heart abiding,
Like a birdling in its nest,

Underneath His feathers hiding,
Fold your wings and trust and rest.

DECEMBER 16

There was also a prophet, Anna. . . . She never left the temple but worshiped night and day, fasting and praying.

LUKE 2:36–37

THERE IS NO DOUBT THAT IT IS BY PRAYING THAT WE LEARN TO PRAY, and that the more we pray, the better our prayers will be. People who pray in spurts are never likely to attain to the kind of prayer described in the Scriptures as "powerful and effective" (James 5:16).

Great power in prayer is within our reach, but we must work to obtain it. We should never even imagine that Abraham could have interceded so successfully for Sodom if he had not communed with God throughout the previous years of his life. Jacob's entire night of wrestling at Peniel was certainly not the first encounter he had with his God. And we can even look at our Lord's most beautiful and wonderful prayer in John 17, before His suffering and death, as the fruit of His many nights of devotion, and of His rising often before daybreak to pray.

If a person believes he can become powerful in prayer without making a commitment to it, he is living under a great delusion. The prayer of Elijah, which stopped the rain from heaven and later opened heaven's floodgates, was only one example of a long series of his mighty pleadings with God. Oh, if only we Christians would remember that perseverance in prayer is necessary for it to be effective and victorious!

The great intercessors, who are seldom mentioned in connection with the heroes and martyrs of the faith, were nevertheless the greatest benefactors of the church. Yet their becoming the channels of the blessings of mercy to others was only made possible by their abiding at the mercy seat of God.

Remember, we must pray to pray, and continue in prayer so our prayers may continue. CHARLES H. SPURGEON

DECEMBER 17

May God himself, the God of peace, sanctify you through and through. May your whole spirit, soul and body be kept blameless at the coming of our Lord Jesus Christ. The one who calls you is faithful, and he will do it.
1 THESSALONIANS 5:23–24

MANY YEARS AFTER I FIRST READ THAT "WITHOUT HOLINESS NO ONE will see the Lord" (Hebrews 12:14), I began following this truth and encouraging everyone with whom I spoke to do the same. Ten years later God gave me a clearer view than I had ever seen before of the way to obtain holiness—namely, by faith in the Son of God. Immediately I began sharing with everyone, "We are saved from sin *and* made holy by faith." I testified to this in private, in public, and in print, and God confirmed it through a thousand other witnesses. I have now declared this truth continuously for more than thirty years, and God has continued to confirm my work. JOHN WESLEY IN 1771

I knew Jesus, and He was very precious to me, but I found something deep within me that would not stay pleasant, patient, and kind. I did what I could to keep those traits suppressed, but they were still there. Finally I sought Jesus for help, and when I gave Him my will, He came to my heart and removed everything that would not stay pleasant, patient, and kind. And then *He* shut the door. GEORGE FOX

At this very moment, my entire heart does not have even a hint of thirst after my acceptance by God. I am alone with Him and He fills every void. I do not have one wish, one will, or one desire, except in Him. He has set my feet in His large room. And I am in awe, standing amazed that He has conquered everything within me, through His love. LADY HUNTINGTON

Suddenly I felt as if a hand—not weak but omnipotent, and not of wrath but of love—were laid on my forehead. Yet I did not feel it as much outwardly as inwardly. It seemed to be pressing in on my entire being and sending a holy, sin-consuming energy throughout me as it moved downward, my heart as well as my head was aware of the presence of this soul-cleansing energy. Under its power I fell to the floor, and in the joyful wonder of the moment, I cried out in a loud voice. This hand of power continued to work without and within me, and wherever it moved, it seemed to leave the glorious influence of the Savior's image. And for several minutes, the deep ocean of God's love swallowed me, as all its waves and billows rolled over me. BISHOP HAMLINE

Some of my views on holiness, as I once wrote them, are as follows: Holiness appears to me to have a sweet, calm, pleasant, charming, and serene nature, all of which brings an inexpressible purity, radiance, peacefulness, and overwhelming joy to the soul. In other words, holiness makes the soul like a field or garden of God, with every kind of pleasant fruit and flower, and each one delightful and undisturbed, enjoying a sweet calm and the gentle and refreshing rays of the sun. JONATHAN EDWARDS

Love's resistless current sweeping
All the regions deep within;
Thought and wish and senses keeping
Now, and every instant clean:
Full salvation! Full salvation!
From the guilt and power of sin.

DECEMBER 18

In all these things we are more than conquerors
through him who loved us.
ROMANS 8:37

The gospel and the gift of God are structured so wonderfully that the very enemies and forces that are marshaled to fight against us actually help pave our way to the very gates of heaven and into the presence of God. Those forces can be used in the same way an eagle uses the fierce winds of a storm to soar to the sky. At first he sits perfectly still, high on a cliff, watching the sky as it fills with darkness and as the lightning strikes all around him. Yet he never moves until he feels the burst of the storm, and then with a screech he dives toward the winds, using them to carry him ever higher.

This is also what God desires of each of His children. He wants us to be "more than conquerors," turning storm clouds into chariots of victory. It is obvious when an army becomes "more than conquerors," for it drives its enemies from the battlefield and confiscates their food and supplies. This is exactly what this Scripture passage means. There are spoils to be taken!

Dear believer, after experiencing the terrible valley of suffering, did you depart with the spoils? When you were struck with an injury and you thought you had lost everything, did you trust in God to the point that you came out richer than you were before? Being "more than [a] conqueror" means taking the spoils from the enemy and appropriating them for yourself. What your enemy had planned to use for your defeat, you can confiscate for your own use.

When Dr. Moon, of Brighton, England, was suddenly struck with blindness, he said, "Lord, I accept this 'talent' of blindness from You. Help me to use it for Your glory so that when You return, you may receive it 'back with interest' [Matthew 25:27]." Then God enabled him to invent the Moon Alphabet for the blind, through which thousands of blind people were enabled to read the Word of God and thereby come to the glorious saving knowledge of Christ. Selected

God did not remove Paul's "thorn in the flesh" (2 Corinthians 12:7 KJV). The Lord did something much better—He conquered it and made it Paul's servant. The ministry of *thorns* has often been a greater ministry to humankind than the ministry of *thrones*. Selected

DECEMBER 19

"And so you will bear testimony to me."

LUKE 21:13

LIFE IS A STEEP CLIMB, AND IT IS ALWAYS ENCOURAGING TO HAVE those ahead of us "call back" and cheerfully summon us to higher ground. We all climb together, so we should help one another. The mountain climbing of life is serious, but glorious, business; it takes strength and steadiness to reach the summit. And as our view becomes better as we gain altitude, and as we discover things of importance, we should "call back" our encouragement to others.

If you have gone a little way ahead of me, call back—
It will cheer my heart and help my feet along the stony track;
And if, perhaps, Faith's light is dim, because the oil is low,
Your call will guide my lagging course as wearily I go.

Call back, and tell me that He went with you into the storm;
Call back, and say He kept you when the forest's roots were torn;
That, when the heavens thunder and the earthquake shook the hill,
He bore you up and held you where the lofty air was still.

O friend, call back, and tell me for I cannot see your face;
They say it glows with triumph, and your feet sprint in the race;
But there are mists between us and my spirit eyes are dim,
And I cannot see the glory, though I long for word of Him.

But if you'll say He heard you when your prayer was but a cry,
And if you'll say He saw you through the night's sin-darkened sky—

If you have gone a little way ahead, O friend, call back—
It will cheer my heart and help my feet along the stony track.
SELECTED

DECEMBER 20

"I am not alone, for my Father is with me."
JOHN 16:32

IT IS CERTAINLY UNNECESSARY TO SAY THAT TURNING CONVICTION into action requires great sacrifice. It may mean renouncing or separating ourselves from specific people or things, leaving us with a strange sense of deprivation and loneliness. Therefore the person who will ultimately soar like an eagle to the heights of the cloudless day and live in the sunshine of God must be content to live a relatively lonely life.

There are no birds that live in as much solitude as eagles, for they never fly in flocks. Rarely can even two eagles be seen together. And a life that is dedicated to God *knows divine fellowship*, no matter how many human friendships have had to be forfeited along the way.

God seeks "eagle people," for no one ever comes into the full realization of the best things of God in his spiritual life without learning to walk alone with Him. We see Abraham alone "in the land of Canaan, while Lot lived among the cities . . . near Sodom" (Genesis 13:12). Moses, although educated in all the wisdom of Egypt, had to spend forty years alone with God in the desert. And Paul, who was filled with all the knowledge of the Greeks and who sat "at the feet of Gamaliel" (Acts 22:3 KJV), was required, after meeting Jesus, to go immediately "into Arabia" (Galatians 1:17) to learn of the desert life with God.

May we allow God to isolate us, but I do not mean the isolation of a monastery. It is in the experience of isolation that the Lord develops an independence of life and of faith so that the soul no longer depends on the continual help, prayers, faith, and care of others. The assistance and inspiration from others are necessary, and they have a place in a Christian's development, but at times they can actually become a hindrance to a person's faith and welfare.

God knows how to change our circumstances in order to isolate us. And once we yield to Him and He takes us through an experience of isolation, we are no longer dependent upon those around us, although we still love them as much as before. Then we realize that He has done a new work within us and that the wings of our soul have learned to soar in loftier air.

We must dare to be alone, in the way that Jacob had to be alone for the Angel of God to whisper in his ear, "Your name will no longer be Jacob, but Israel" (Genesis 32:28); in the way that Daniel had to be left alone to see heavenly visions; and in the way that John had to be banished to the Isle of Patmos to receive and record "the revelation of Jesus Christ, which God gave him" (Revelation 1:1).

He has "trodden the winepress alone" (Isaiah 63:3) for us. Therefore, are we prepared for a time of "glorious isolation" rather than to fail Him?

DECEMBER 21

"I will give him . . . the land he set his feet on, because he followed the Lord *wholeheartedly."*

Deuteronomy 1:36

Every difficult task that comes across your path—every one that you would rather not do, that will take the most effort, cause the most pain, and be the greatest struggle—brings a blessing with it. And refusing to do it regardless of the personal cost is to miss the blessing.

Every difficult stretch of road on which you see the Master's footprints and along which He calls you to follow Him leads unquestionably to blessings. And they are blessings you will never receive unless you travel the steep and thorny path.

Every battlefield you encounter, where you are required to draw your sword and fight the enemy, has the possibility of victory that will prove to be a rich blessing to your life. And every heavy burden you are called upon to lift hides within itself a miraculous secret of strength.
J. R. Miller

I cannot do it alone;
The waves surge fast and high,
And the fogs close all around,
The light goes out in the sky;
But I know that we two
Will win in the end,
Jesus and I.

Cowardly, wayward, and weak,
I change with the changing sky;
Today so eager and bright,
Tomorrow too weak to try;
But He never gives in,
So we two will win,
Jesus and I.

I could not guide it myself,
My boat on life's wild sea;
There's One who sits by my side,
Who pulls and steers with me.
And I know that we two
Will safe enter port,
Jesus and I.

DECEMBER 22

A thick and dreadful darkness came over him.

GENESIS 15:12

IN THIS SCRIPTURE PASSAGE, THE SUN HAD FINALLY GONE DOWN, AND the eastern night had swiftly cast its heavy veil over the entire scene. Worn out by the mental conflict, and the exertion and the cares of the day, Abraham "fell into a deep sleep" (v. 12). During his sleep, his soul was oppressed with "a thick and dreadful darkness," which seemed to smother him and felt like a nightmare in his heart.

Do you have an understanding of the horror of that kind of darkness? Have you ever experienced a terrible sorrow that seems difficult to reconcile with God's perfect love—a sorrow that comes crashing down upon you, wrings from your soul its peaceful rest in the grace of God, and casts it into a sea of darkness that is unlit by even one ray of hope? Have you experienced a sorrow caused by unkindness, when others cruelly mistreat your trusting heart, and you even begin to wonder if there is really a God above who sees what is happening yet continues to allow it? If you know this kind of sorrow, then you know something of this "thick and dreadful darkness."

Human life is made of brightness and gloom, shadows and sunshine, and dark clouds followed by brilliant rays of light. Yet through it all, God's divine justice is accomplishing His plan, affecting and disciplining each individual soul.

Dear friend, if you are filled with fear of the "thick and dreadful darkness" because of God's dealings with humankind, learn to trust His infallible wisdom, for it is equal to His unchanging justice. And know that He who endured the "dreadful darkness" of Calvary and the feeling of having been forsaken on the cross is ready to accompany you "through the valley of the shadow of death" (Psalm 23:4 KJV) until you can see the sun shining on the other side.

May we realize that "we have this hope as an anchor for the soul, firm and secure" and that "it enters the inner sanctuary behind the curtain" (Hebrews 6:19). And may we know that although it is unseen within His sanctuary, our anchor will be grounded and will never yield. It will hold firm until the day He returns, and then we too will follow it into the safe haven guaranteed to us in God's unchangeable Word. F. B. MEYER

The disciples thought that the angry sea separated them from Jesus. In fact, some of them thought something even worse—they thought that the trouble they were facing was a sign that He had forgotten them and did not care about them.

O dear friend, that is when your troubles can cause the most harm. The Devil comes and whispers to you, "God has forgotten you" or "God has forsaken you," and your unbelieving heart cries out, as Gideon once did, "If the LORD is with us, why has all this happened to us?" (Judges 6:13). God has allowed the difficulty to come upon you, in order to bring you closer to Himself. It has come not to separate you from Jesus but to cause you to cling to Him more faithfully, more firmly, and more simply. F. S. WEBSTER

We should abandon ourselves to God more fully at those times when He seems to have abandoned us. Let us enjoy His light and comfort when it is His pleasure to give it to us, but may we not attach ourselves to His gifts. May we instead attach ourselves to Him, and when He plunges us into the night, where *pure faith* is required, may we still press on through the agonizing darkness.

Oh, for faith that brings the triumph
When defeat seems very near!
Oh, for faith that brings the triumph
Into victory's ringing cheer—
Faith triumphant; knowing not defeat or fear.
HERBERT BOOTH

DECEMBER 23

The journey is too much for you.

1 Kings 19:7

What did God do with Elijah, His tired servant? He allowed him to sleep and then gave him something good to eat. Elijah had done tremendous work and in his excitement had run "ahead of Ahab['s chariot] all the way to Jezreel" (1 Kings 18:46). But the run had been too much for him and had sapped his physical strength, ultimately causing him to become *depressed*. Just as others in this condition need sleep and want their ailments treated, Elijah's physical requirements needed to be met.

There are many wonderful people who end up where Elijah did—"under a juniper tree" (1 Kings 19:4 KJV)! When this happens, the words of the Master are very soothing: "Get up and eat, for the journey is too much for you." In other words, "I am going to refresh you."

Therefore may we never confuse physical weariness with spiritual weakness.

I'm too tired to trust and too tired to pray,
Said I, as my overtaxed strength gave way.
The one conscious thought that my mind possessed,
Is, oh, could I just drop it all and rest.

Will God forgive me, do you suppose,
If I go right to sleep as a baby goes,
Without questioning if I may,
Without even trying to trust and pray?

Will God forgive you? Think back, dear heart,
When language to you was an unknown art,
Did your mother deny you needed rest,
Or refuse to pillow your head on her breast?

Did she let you want when you could not ask?
Did she give her child an unequal task?
Or did she cradle you in her arms,
And then guard your slumber against alarms?

Oh, how quickly a mother's love can see,
The unconscious yearnings of infancy.
When you've grown too tired to trust and pray,
When overworked nature has quite given way:

Then just drop it all, and give up to rest,
As you used to do on mother's breast,
He knows all about it—the dear Lord knows,
So just go to sleep as a baby goes;

Without even asking if you may,
God knows when His child is too tired to pray.
He judges not solely by uttered prayer,
He knows when the yearnings of love are there.

He knows you do pray, He knows you do trust,
And He knows, too, the limits of poor, weak dust.
Oh, the wonderful sympathy of Christ,
For His chosen ones in that midnight tryst,

When He told them, "Sleep and take your rest,"
While on Him the guilt of the whole world pressed—
You have trusted your life to Him to keep,
Then don't be afraid to go right to sleep.

Ella Conrad Cowherd

DECEMBER 24

He went out to the field one evening to meditate.

Genesis 24:63

We would be better Christians if we spent more time alone, and we would actually accomplish more if we attempted less and spent more time in isolation and quiet waiting upon God. The world has become too much a part of us, and we are afflicted with the idea that we are not accomplishing anything unless we are always busily running back and forth. We no longer believe in the importance of a calm retreat where we sit silently in the shade. As the people of God, we have become entirely too practical. We believe in having "all our irons in the fire" and that all the time we spend away from the anvil or fire is wasted time. Yet our time is never more profitably spent than when we set aside time for quiet meditation, talking with God, and looking up to heaven. We can never have too many of these open spaces in life—hours set aside when our soul is completely open and accessible to any heavenly thought or influence that God may be pleased to send our way.

Someone once said, "Meditation is the Sunday of the mind." In these hectic days, we should often give our mind a "Sunday," a time in which it will do no work but instead will simply be still, look heavenward, and spread itself before the Lord like Gideon's fleece, allowing itself to be soaked with the moisture of the dew of heaven. We should have intervals of time when we do nothing, think nothing, and plan nothing but simply lie on the green lap of nature and "rest a while" (Mark 6:31 KJV).

Time spent in this way is not lost time. A fisherman does not say he is losing time when he is mending his nets, nor does a gardener feel he has wasted his time by taking a few minutes to sharpen the blades on his mower. And people living in cities today would do well to follow the example of Isaac and as often as possible visit the fields of the countryside, away from the hustle and bustle of the city. After having grown weary from the heat and noise of the city, communion with nature is very refreshing and will bring a calming, healing influence. A walk through a field, a stroll by a seashore, or a hike across a meadow sprinkled with daisies will purge you of the impurities of life and will cause your heart to beat with new joy and hope.

The little cares that worried me,
I lost them yesterday,
Out in the fields with God.

A poem for Christmas Eve:

Bells Across the Snow

O Christmas, merry Christmas,
Has it really come again,
With its memories and greetings,
With its joy and with its pain!
Minor chords are in the carol
And a shadow in the light,
And a spray of cypress twining
With the holly wreath tonight.
And the hush is never broken
By laughter light and low,
As we listen in the starlight
To the "bells across the snow."

O Christmas, merry Christmas,
It's not so very long
Since other voices blended
With the carol and the song!
If we could but hear them singing,
As they are singing now,

If we could but see the radiance
Of the crown on each dear brow,
There would be no cry to cover,
No hidden tear to flow,
As we listen in the starlight
To the "bells across the snow."

O Christmas, merry Christmas,
This nevermore can be;
We cannot bring again the days
Of our unshadowed glee,
But Christmas, happy Christmas,
Sweet herald of goodwill,
With holy songs of glory
Brings holy gladness still.
For peace and hope may brighten,
And patient love may glow,
As we listen in the starlight
To the "bells across the snow."

Frances Ridley Havergal

DECEMBER 25

"They will call him Immanuel" (which means "God with us").

Matthew 1:23

Prince of Peace.

Isaiah 9:6

There's a song in the air!
There's a star in the sky!
There's a mother's deep prayer,

And a baby's low cry!
And the star rains its fire
While the beautiful sing,
For the manger of Bethlehem cradles a King.

A NUMBER OF YEARS AGO A REMARKABLE CHRISTMAS CARD WAS PUBlished by the title "If Christ Had Not Come." It was based on our Savior's own words, "If I had not come," in John 15:22. The card pictured a minister falling asleep in his study on Christmas morning and then dreaming of a world into which Jesus had never come.

In his dream, he saw himself walking through his house, but as he looked, he saw no stockings hung on the chimney, no Christmas tree, no wreaths of holly, and no Christ to comfort and gladden hearts or to save us. He then walked onto the street outside, but there was no church with its spire pointing toward heaven. And when he came back and sat down in his library, he realized that every book about our Savior had disappeared.

The minister dreamed that the doorbell rang and that a messenger asked him to visit a friend's poor dying mother. He reached her home, and as his friend sat and wept, he said, "I have something here that will comfort you." He opened his Bible to look for a familiar promise, but it ended with Malachi. There was no gospel and no promise of hope and salvation, and all he could do was bow his head and weep with his friend and his mother in bitter despair.

Two days later he stood beside her coffin and conducted her funeral service, but there was no message of comfort, no words of a glorious resurrection, and no thought of a mansion awaiting her in heaven. There was only "dust to dust, and ashes to ashes," and one long, eternal farewell. Finally he realized that *Christ had not come*, and burst into tears, weeping bitterly in his sorrowful dream.

Then suddenly he awoke with a start, and a great shout of joy and praise burst from his lips as he heard his choir singing these words in his church nearby:

O come, all ye faithful, joyful and triumphant,
O come ye, O come ye to Bethlehem!
Come and behold Him, born the King of angels,
O come let us adore Him, Christ the Lord!

Let us be glad and rejoice today, because He *has* come. And let us remember the proclamation of the angel: "I bring you good news that will cause great joy *for all the people.* Today in the town of David a Savior has been born to you; he is the Messiah, the Lord" (Luke 2:10–11).

He comes to make His blessing flow,
Far as the curse does go.

May our hearts go out to the unconverted people of foreign lands who have no blessed Christmas day. "Go and enjoy choice food and sweet drinks, and send some to those who have nothing prepared. This day is holy to our Lord" (Nehemiah 8:10).

DECEMBER 26

"Sit here while I go over there and pray."
MATTHEW 26:36

IT IS A VERY DIFFICULT THING TO BE KEPT IN THE BACKGROUND during a time of crisis. In the Garden of Gethsemane, eight of the eleven remaining disciples were left behind to do nothing. When Jesus went ahead to pray, Peter, James, and John went with Him to watch, but the rest sat down to wait. I believe that the ones left behind must have complained. They were *in* the garden, but that was all, for they had no part in the cultivation of its flowers. It was a stormy time of crisis and great stress, yet they were not allowed to participate.

You and I have certainly had that experience and felt the same disappointment. Perhaps you have seen a great opportunity for Christian service arise, and some people are sent immediately to the work, while still others are being trained to go. Yet *you* are forced to do nothing but sit and wait. Or perhaps sickness and poverty has come your way, or you have had to endure some terrible disgrace. Whatever your situation, you have been kept from service, and now you feel angry and do not understand why you should be excluded from this part of the Christian life. It seems unjust that you have been allowed to enter the garden but have found no path assigned to you once inside.

Be still, dear soul—things are not what they seem! You are *not* excluded from any part of the Christian life. Do you believe that the garden of the Lord only has places for those who walk or those who stand? No! It also has a place set apart for those who are compelled to *sit*. Just as there are three voices in a verb—active, passive, and neuter—there are three voices in Christ's verb "live." There are active people, who go straight to the battle, and struggle till the setting of the sun. There are passive people, who stand in the middle and simply report the progress of the fight. Yet there are also neuter people—those who can neither fight nor be spectators of the fight but must simply lie down and wait.

When this experience comes, do not think that you have been turned aside. Remember, it is *Christ himself* who says to you, "Sit here." *Your* place in the garden has *also* been set apart. God has selected it especially for you, and it is not simply a place of waiting. There are some lives He brings into this world neither to do great work nor to bear great burdens. Their job is simply to be—they are the neuter verbs, or the flowers in the garden that have no active mission. They have won no major victories and have never been honored with the best seats at a banquet—they have simply escaped the sight of people like Peter, James, and John.

However, *Jesus* is delighted by the sight of them, for through their mere fragrance and beauty, they have brought Him joy. And just their existence and the preservation of their loveliness in the valley has lifted the Master's heart. So you need not complain if you are one of these flowers! Selected

DECEMBER 27

His neck was put in irons.
PSALM 105:18

THE IRONS OF SORROW AND LOSS, THE BURDENS CARRIED AS A YOUTH, and the soul's struggle against sin all contribute to developing an iron tenacity and strength of purpose, as well as endurance and fortitude. And these traits make up the indispensable foundation and framework of noble character.

Never run from suffering, but bear it silently, patiently, and submissively, with the assurance that it is God's way of instilling iron into your spiritual life. The world is looking for iron leaders, iron armies, iron tendons, and muscles of steel. *But God is looking for iron saints*, and since there is no way to impart iron into His people's moral nature except by letting them suffer, He allows them to suffer.

Are the best years of your life slipping away while you suffer enforced monotony? Are you afflicted with opposition, misunderstandings, and the scorn of others? Do your afflictions seem as thick as the undergrowth confronting someone hiking through a jungle? Then take heart! Your time is not wasted, for God is simply putting you through His iron regimen. Your iron crown of suffering precedes your golden crown of glory, and iron is entering your soul to make it strong and brave. F. B. MEYER

But you will not mind the roughness, nor the steepness
of the way,
Nor the cold, unrested morning, nor the heat of the noonday;
And you will not take a turning to the left or the right,
But go straight ahead, nor tremble at the coming of the night,
For the road leads home.

DECEMBER 28

Rejoice in the Lord always. I will say it again: Rejoice!

PHILIPPIANS 4:4

Sing a little song of trust,
O my heart!
Sing it just because you must,
As leaves start;
As flowers push their way through dust;
Sing, my heart, because you must.

Wait not for an eager throng—
Bird on bird;
It's the solitary song
That is heard.
Every voice at dawn will start,
Be a nightingale, my heart!

Sing across the winter snow,
Pierce the cloud;
Sing when mists are drooping low—
Clear and loud;
But sing sweetest in the dark;
He who slumbers not will hark.

And when He hears you sing, He will bend down with a smile on His kind face. As He cheerfully listens, He will say, "Sing on, dear child. I hear you and I am coming to deliver you. I will carry that load for you. So just lean hard on Me, and the road will get smoother by and by."

DECEMBER 29

Come on . . . ! We have seen the land, and it is very good. Aren't you going to do something? Don't hesitate to go there and take it over. . . . God has put into your hands, a land that lacks nothing whatever.

JUDGES 18:9–10

"COME ON!" THIS COMMAND INDICATES THAT THERE IS SOMETHING definite for us to do and that nothing is ours unless we take it. "The children of Joseph, Manasseh and Ephraim, *took their inheritance*" (Joshua 16:4 KJV). The house of "Jacob will *possess its inheritance*" (Obadiah 17). "The upright shall have good things *in possession*" (Proverbs 28:10 KJV).

We need to have appropriating faith when it comes to God's promises and should make His Word our own personal possession. A child was once asked what appropriating faith was, and he answered, "It is taking a pencil and underlining every 'me,' 'my,' and 'mine' in the Bible."

Pick any word you want that He has spoken and say, "That word is my word." Put your finger on a promise and say, "It is mine." How much of God's Word have you received and endorsed, and how much have you been able to say, "This has been done in my life"? By how many of His promises have you signed your name and said, "This has been fulfilled to me"?

"My son, . . . you are always with me, and *everything* I have *is yours*" (Luke 15:31). Do not miss your inheritance through your own neglect.

When faith goes to the market, it always takes a basket.

DECEMBER 30

So Peter was kept in prison, but the church was earnestly praying to God for him.

ACTS 12:5

PETER WAS IN PRISON AWAITING HIS EXECUTION, AND THE CHURCH HAD no human power or influence that could save him. There was no earthly help available, but help could be obtained by way of heaven. So the church gave themselves to fervent and persistent prayer. And God sent an angel, who "struck Peter on the side and woke him up" (v. 7). Then the angel led him past "the first and second guards and [they] came to the iron gate leading to the city. It opened for them by itself" (v. 10), and Peter was free.

Perhaps there is some "iron gate" in your life, blocking your way. Like a caged bird, you have often beaten against the bars, but instead of helping your situation, you have become even more tired and exhausted and caused yourself more heartache. There is a secret for you to learn—the secret of *believing* prayer.

Then when you come to the iron gate, it will open as it did for Peter: "by itself."

How much wasted energy and painful disappointment will be saved once you learn to pray as the early church did in the "upper room" (Acts 1:13 KJV)! Insurmountable difficulties will disappear and adverse circumstances will turn favorable once you learn to pray—not with your own faith but with the faith of God. Many of your loved ones have been bound by Satan and imprisoned by him for years, and they are simply waiting for the gates to be opened. They will be set free in Christ when you pray fervently and persistently in faith to God. C. H. P.

Emergencies call for intense prayer. *When the person himself becomes the prayer* nothing can resist its touch. Elijah bowed to the ground on Mount Carmel with his face between his knees, and *he* became the prayer.

Spoken prayer is not always needed, for prayer can often be too intense for words. In the case of Elijah, his entire being was in touch with God and was aligned with Him against the powers of evil. And Elijah's evil enemies could not withstand this kind of prayer in human form—something that is greatly needed today. THE BENT-KNEE TIME

"Wordless groans" (Romans 8:26) are often prayers that God cannot refuse. CHARLES H. SPURGEON

DECEMBER 31

Thus far the L*ORD* *has helped us.*

1 SAMUEL 7:12

THE WORDS "THUS FAR" ARE LIKE A HAND POINTING IN THE DIRECTION of the *past.* It had been "a long time—twenty years in all" (v. 2), but even if it had been seventy years, "Thus far the LORD has helped"! Whether through poverty, wealth, sickness, or health; whether at home or abroad, or on land, sea, or air; and whether in honor, dishonor, difficulties, joy, trials, triumph, prayer, or temptation—"Thus far the LORD has helped"!

We always enjoy looking down a long road lined with beautiful trees. The trees are a delightful sight and seem to be forming a temple of plants, with strong wooden pillars and arches of leaves. In the same way you look down a beautiful road like this, why not look back on the road of the years of your life? Look at the large green limbs of God's mercy overhead and the strong pillars of His loving-kindness and faithfulness that have brought you much joy. Do you see any birds singing in the branches? If you look closely, surely you will see many, for they are singing of God's mercy received "thus far."

These words also point *forward.* Someone who comes to a certain point and writes the words "thus far" realizes he has not yet come to the end of the road and that he still has some distance to travel. There are still more trials, joys, temptations, battles, defeats, victories, prayers, answers, toils, and strength yet to come. These are then followed by sickness, old age, disease, and death.

Then is life over after death? No! These are still yet to come: arising in the likeness of Jesus; thrones, harps, and the singing of psalms; being "clothed in white garments" (Revelation 3:5 NASB), seeing the face of Jesus, and sharing fellowship with the saints; and experiencing the glory of God, the fullness of eternity, and infinite joy. So dear believer, "be strong and take heart" (Psalm 27:14), and with thanksgiving and confidence lift your voice in praise, for:

The Lord who "thus far" has helped you
Will help you all your journey through.

When the words "thus far" are read in heaven's light, what glorious and miraculous prospects they reveal to our grateful eyes! CHARLES H. SPURGEON

The shepherds of the Alps have a beautiful custom of ending the day by singing an evening farewell to one another. The air is so pure that the songs can be heard for very long distances. As the sun begins to set, they gather their flocks and begin to lead them down the mountain paths while they sing, "'Thus far has the Lord helped us.' Let us praise His name!"

Finally, as is their beautiful custom, they sing to one another the courteous and friendly farewell "Good night! Good night!" The words then begin to echo from mountainside to mountainside, reverberating sweetly and softly until the music fades into the distance.

Let us also call out to one another through the darkness until the night becomes alive with the sound of many voices, encouraging God's weary travelers. And may the echoes grow into a storm of hallelujahs that will break in thundering waves around His sapphire throne. Then as the morning dawns, we will find ourselves on the shore of the "sea of glass" (Revelation 4:6), crying out with the redeemed hosts of heaven, "To him who sits on the throne and to the Lamb be praise and honor and glory and power, for ever and ever!" (Revelation 5:13).

This my song through endless ages,
Jesus led me all the way.

"And again they shouted: 'Hallelujah!'" (Revelation 19:3).